McGraw-Hill Education

MCAT

CHEMICAL AND PHYSICAL
FOUNDATIONS OF BIOLOGICAL SYSTEMS

2016

McGraw-Hill Education

MCAT

Test Preparation Series

- Biomolecules
- Molecules, Cells, and Organs
- Systems of Tissues and Organs

- Physical Foundations of Biological Systems
- Chemical Foundations of Biological Systems

- Perception and Response
- Behavior
- Self and Others
- Social Structure
- Social Strata
- Critical Analysis and Reasoning Skills

- Practice Test 1
  - Answers and Explanations
- Practice Test 2
  - Answers and Explanations

McGraw-Hill Education

MCAT

CHEMICAL AND PHYSICAL
FOUNDATIONS OF BIOLOGICAL SYSTEMS
2016

George J. Hademenos, PhD

Candice McCloskey Campbell, PhD

Shaun Murphree, PhD

Amy B. Wachholtz, PhD

Jennifer M. Warner, PhD

Kathy A. Zahler, MS

Thomas A. Evangelist, MA   Contributor

1 2 3 4 5 6 7 8 9 10 CUS/CUS 1 2 1 0 9 8 7 6 5

ISBN   978-1-25-958837-2
MHID   1-25-958837-8

e-ISBN   978-1-25-958838-9
e-MHID   1-25-958838-6

MCAT is a registered trademark of the Association of American Medical Colleges, which was not involved in the production of, and does not endorse, this product.

McGraw-Hill Education products are available at special quantity discounts to use as premiums and sales promotions or for use in corporate training programs. To contact a representative, please visit the Contact Us pages at www.mhprofessional.com.

This book is printed on acid-free paper.

Contents

About the Authors vii

How to Use the McGraw-Hill Education
    MCAT Preparation Series ix

Introducing the MCAT xiii

MCAT Basics | The Computerized Test Format | Where and When to Take
the MCAT | How to Register for the MCAT | Taking the MCAT More Than
Once | Your MCAT Scores | How Medical Schools Use MCAT Scores |
Reporting Scores to Medical Schools | For Further Information | The
Format of the Test | What Is Tested in the Science Sections | What Is
Tested in Critical Analysis | General Test-Taking Strategies

Unit 1   Physical Foundations of Biological Systems

**Chapter 1   Translational Motion, Forces, Work, Energy, and Equilibrium
           in Living Systems** 3

Translational Motion | Forces and Equilibrium | Work, Energy, and Power

**Chapter 2   Importance of Fluids for the Circulation of Blood,
           Gas Movement, and Gas Exchange** 35

Fluids at Rest | Fluids in Motion | Circulatory System | Gases

**Chapter 3   Electrochemistry and Electrical Circuits and
           Their Elements** 53

Electrostatics | Electric Circuits | Magnetism | Electrochemistry |
Specialized Cells—Nerve Cells

Chapter 4   How Light and Sound Interact with Matter 85

Sound | Light | Molecular Structure and Spectra | Geometrical Optics

**Chapter 5   Atoms, Nuclear Decay, Electronic Structure,
and Atomic Chemical Behavior** **131**

Atomic Nucleus | Electronic Structure | The Periodic Table: Classification
of Elements into Groups by Electronic Structure | The Periodic Table:
Variations of Chemical Properties with Group and Row

Unit I MINITEST **153**

Unit II   Chemical Foundations of Biological Systems

Chapter 6   The Unique Nature of Water and Its Solutions **175**

Acid–Base Reactions | Ions in Solutions | Solubility | Acid–Base Titrations

Chapter 7   The Nature of Molecules and Intermolecular Interactions .. **203**

The Chemical Bond | Molecular Shape | Molecular Orbitals | Noncovalent
Bonds

Chapter 8   Separation and Purification Methods **247**

Principal Techniques | Special Applications for Biomolecules

**Chapter 9   Structure, Function, and Reactivity of Biologically
Relevant Molecules** **263**

Nomenclature of Organic Compounds | Fundamental Reaction Mechanisms
| Chemistry of Biologically Important Compound Classes

Chapter 10   Principles of Chemical Thermodynamics and Kinetics **337**

Enzymes | Principles of Bioenergetics | Thermodynamics: Energy Changes
in Chemical Reactions | Kinetics and Equilibrium: Rate Processes in
Chemical Reactions

Unit II MINITEST **367**

CUMULATIVE MINITEST **383**

EVALUATION CHART **401**

About the Authors

George J. Hademenos, PhD, is a former Visiting Assistant Professor of Physics at the University of Dallas. He received his BS from Angelo State University, received his MS and PhD from the University of Texas at Dallas, and completed postdoctoral fellowships in nuclear medicine at the University of Massachusetts Medical Center and in radiological sciences/biomedical physics at UCLA Medical Center. His research interests have involved potential applications of physics to the biological and medical sciences, particularly with cerebrovascular diseases and stroke. He has published his work in journals such as *American Scientist, Physics Today, Neurosurgery,* and *Stroke.* In addition, he has written several books including *The Physics of Cerebrovascular Diseases: Biophysical Mechanisms of Development, Diagnosis and Therapy,* and *Schaum's Outline of Biology.* He currently teaches general and advanced physics courses.

Candice McCloskey Campbell, PhD, received her doctorate in organic chemistry from Georgia Tech in 1985. She has been teaching at the undergraduate level since 1987. She currently teaches at Georgia Perimeter College in Dunwoody, Georgia. Her professional work has been in synthetic organic chemistry and mechanistic organic chemistry. She has been active with the Two-Year College Chemistry Consortium to enhance the chemistry curriculum at the two-year college level.

Shaun Murphree, PhD, is Professor and Chair of Chemistry at Allegheny College in Meadville, Pennsylvania. He received a BA in chemistry from Colgate University (Hamilton, New York) and a PhD in organic chemistry from Emory University (Atlanta, Georgia), and he conducted a postdoctoral study at Wesleyan University (Middletown, Connecticut). His current research interests include microwave-assisted organic synthesis (MAOS), synthetic methodology, and heterocyclic synthesis. In addition to the present work, he has coauthored a monograph on microwave chemistry, several chapters and reviews on heterocyclic synthesis, and numerous articles in both the synthetic chemistry and chemistry education literature.

Amy B. Wachholtz, PhD, MDiv, MS, is an Assistant Professor of Psychiatry at the University of Massachusetts Medical School and the Director of Health Psychology at UMass Memorial Medical Center. Dr. Wachholtz graduated with a Master of Divinity degree from Boston University, where she specialized in Bioethics. She then continued her education to earn a Master's and PhD in Clinical Psychology from Bowling Green State University, where she had a dual specialization in Behavioral Medicine and Psychology of Religion. She completed an internship through a fellowship at Duke University Medical Center, where she focused on medical psychology. She has also completed a postdoctoral Master's of Science degree in Psychopharmacology. Dr. Wachholtz has multiple funded research projects with her primary focus on (1) bio-psycho-social-spiritual model of chronic pain disorders and (2) the complexities of treating of comorbid pain and opioid addiction in both acute pain and chronic pain situations. She enjoys teaching students from a variety of health disciplines, both in the classroom and on the clinical floors of UMass Memorial Medical Center Hospitals.

Jennifer M. Warner, PhD, is the Director of the University Honors Program and a member of the faculty in the Department of Biological Sciences at the University of North Carolina at Charlotte. She received her BS in Biology from the University of North Carolina at Chapel Hill, her MS in Biology with a focus in microbiology from the University of North Carolina at Charlotte, and her PhD in Curriculum and Teaching from the University of North Carolina at Greensboro. Her current research interests revolve around variables that influence student success and retention in the sciences. She currently teaches a variety of courses including principles of biology, human biology, the nature of science, and pathogenic bacteriology.

Kathy A. Zahler, MS, is a widely published author and textbook writer. She has authored or coauthored numerous McGraw-Hill Education preparation guides for tests, including the GRE®, the Miller Analogies Test, the Test of Essential Academic Skills (TEAS®), and the Test Assessing Secondary Completion™ (TASC™).

How to Use the McGraw-Hill Education MCAT Preparation Series

Welcome to the McGraw-Hill Education MCAT Preparation series. You've made the decision to pursue a medical career, you've studied hard, you've taken and passed the most difficult science courses, and now you must succeed on this very tough exam. We're here to help you.

This series has been created by a dedicated team of scientists, teachers, and test-prep experts. Together, they have helped thousands of students to score high on all kinds of exams, from rigorous science tests to difficult essay-writing assignments. They have pooled their knowledge, experience, and test-taking expertise to make this the most effective self-study MCAT preparation program available.

The four books in this series contain a wealth of features to help you do your best. The four volumes are organized as follows:

MCAT Biological and Biochemical Foundations of Living Systems provides:

➤ **A general introduction to the MCAT,** including basic facts about the structure and format of the test and the kinds of questions you will encounter.

➤ **Important test-taking strategies** that can help you raise your score.

➤ **An in-depth review of all the topics tested in Part 1 of the exam: Biological and Biochemical Foundations of Living Systems.** This is the exam section that assesses your knowledge of foundational concepts in biology and biochemistry, and your understanding of how biological processes function both separately and together in living systems, including the human body.

➤ **Unit Minitests modeled on Part 1 of the exam.** These practice exams are designed to simulate the actual MCAT in format and degree of difficulty. The questions ask you to use your scientific research and reasoning skills to solve problems demonstrating your mastery of the skills required for success in medical school.

MCAT Chemical and Physical Foundations of Biological Systems provides:

➤ **A general introduction to the MCAT,** including basic facts about the structure and format of the test and the kinds of questions you will encounter.

➤ **Important test-taking strategies** that can help you raise your score.

➤ **An in-depth review of all the topics tested in Part 2 of the exam: Chemical and Physical Foundations of Biological Systems.** This is the exam section that assesses your knowledge of foundational concepts in organic chemistry and physics, and your understanding of how chemical and physical processes function both separately and together in living systems, including the human body.

➤ **Two Unit Minitests and a Cumulative Minitest modeled on Part 2 of the exam.** These practice exams are designed to simulate the actual MCAT in format and degree of difficulty. The questions ask you to use your scientific research and reasoning skills to solve problems demonstrating your mastery of the skills required for success in medical school.

MCAT Behavioral and Social Sciences & Critical Analysis provides:

➤ **A general introduction to the MCAT,** including basic facts about the structure and format of the test and the kinds of questions you will encounter.

➤ **An in-depth review of all the topics tested in Parts 3 and 4 of the exam: Psychological, Social, and Biological Foundations of Behavior and Critical Analysis and Reasoning Skills.** Part 3 of the exam tests your knowledge of basic concepts in psychology and sociology that are important to understanding how behavioral and socio-cultural factors affect health outcomes and the provision of healthcare. Part 4 of the exam tests your ability to analyze, evaluate, and apply information from reading passages in a wide range of social sciences and humanities areas.

➤ **Unit Minitests modeled on Parts 3 and 4 of the exam.** These practice exams are designed to simulate the actual MCAT in format and degree of difficulty. The questions ask you to use your scientific research and reasoning skills to solve problems that demonstrate your mastery of the skills required for success in medical school.

MCAT 2 Full-Length Practice Tests provides:

➤ **A general introduction to the MCAT,** including basic facts about the structure and format of the test and the kinds of questions you will encounter.

➤ **Important test-taking strategies** that can help you raise your score.

➤ **Two full-length practice MCAT tests** designed to simulate the real exam in structure, format, and degree of difficulty. Of course, these practice tests can provide only an approximation of how well you will do on the actual MCAT. However, if you approach them as you would the real test, they should give you a very good idea of how well you are prepared.

➤ **Explanations for every question.** After you take each test, read carefully through these explanations, paying special attention to those you answered incorrectly or had to guess on. If necessary, go back and reread the subject review sections in the corresponding chapters.

Different people have different ways of preparing for a test like the MCAT. You must find a preparation method that suits your schedule and your learning style. We have tried to make this series flexible enough for you to use in a way that works best for you, but to succeed on this extremely rigorous exam, there is no substitute for serious, intensive review and study. The more time and effort you devote to preparing, the better your chances of achieving your MCAT goals.

Introducing the MCAT

> **Read This Section to Learn About**
> - MCAT Basics
> - The Computerized Test Format
> - Where and When to Take the MCAT
> - How to Register for the MCAT
> - Taking the MCAT More Than Once
> - Your MCAT Scores
> - How Medical Schools Use MCAT Scores
> - Reporting Scores to Medical Schools
> - For Further Information
> - The Format of the Test
> - What Is Tested in the Science Sections
> - What Is Tested in Critical Analysis
> - General Test-Taking Strategies

MCAT BASICS

The Medical College Admission Test (MCAT) is a standardized exam that is used to assess applicants to medical schools. The test is sponsored by the Association of American Medical Colleges (AAMC) in cooperation with its member schools. It is required as part of the admissions process by most U.S. medical schools. The test is administered by Prometric, a private firm that is a leading provider of technology-based testing and assessment services.

The questions on the MCAT are basically designed to measure your problem-solving and critical-thinking skills. Two test sections assess your mastery of fundamental concepts in biology, biochemistry, general chemistry, organic chemistry, and physics. A third section tests your understanding of concepts in psychology, sociology, and biology that are important to understanding how behavioral and sociocultural factors affect health outcomes and the provision of health care. For most questions in these sections, choosing the correct answer requires more than just a rote response; you must calculate a solution, interpret and evaluate given data, or apply a particular scientific principle to a given situation. You will need to demonstrate that you can reason scientifically and employ the principles of research methodology and statistics. There is also a fourth section that tests your ability to analyze, evaluate, and apply information from reading passages on topics in ethics, philosophy, cross-cultural studies, and population health.

According to the AAMC, the skills tested on the MCAT are those identified by medical professionals and educators as essential for success in medical school and in a career as a physician. The importance of the biological, biochemical, and physical sciences is self-evident. Psychological and sociological concepts are included, according to the AAMC, because "knowledge of the behavioral and social determinants of health and wellness [is] becoming more important in medical education," and "tomorrow's doctors need to know [these concepts] in order to serve a more diverse population and to understand the impact of behavior on health and wellness."

THE COMPUTERIZED TEST FORMAT

You will take the MCAT on a computer. You will view the questions on the computer screen and indicate your answers by clicking on on-screen answer ovals. As you work through the on-screen questions, you will be able to highlight relevant portions of the reading passages for easy reference. You will also be able to strike out answer choices that you know are incorrect. This will help you use the process of elimination to pick the correct answer. You will also be allowed to make notes on scratch paper (although all of your notes will be collected at the end of the test). Within each test section, you will be able to go back, review questions that you have already answered, and change your answer if you decide to do so. However, once you have finished a test section, you cannot go back to it and make any changes.

Don't be concerned if you are not a whiz with computers; the skills required are minimal, and in any case, on test day you will have the opportunity to access a computer tutorial that will show you exactly what you need to do.

WHERE AND WHEN TO TAKE THE MCAT

The MCAT is offered at approximately 275 sites in the United States (including the U.S. territories of Puerto Rico and the Virgin Islands) and at 12 sites in Canada. All of these sites are testing labs operated by Prometric. The test is also offered at numerous locations outside North America, including sites in Europe, Great Britain, the Middle East, Africa, Asia, and Australia.

There are 22 test dates every year. Two of the dates are in January, and the rest are in the period from April through early September. Most test dates are weekdays, but a few are Saturdays. On some dates, the test is given only in the morning; on others, it is given only in the afternoon. On a few dates, the test is given in both morning and afternoon sessions.

It is a good idea to take the MCAT in the spring or summer of the year before the fall in which you plan to enroll in medical school. That way, you have enough time to submit your scores to meet the schools' application deadlines.

For up-to-date lists of testing sites and also for upcoming test dates, make sure to check the official MCAT website at www.aamc.org/mcat.

HOW TO REGISTER FOR THE MCAT

You can register for the MCAT online at www.aamc.org/mcat. Online registration for each test date begins six months prior to that date. Registration is available until two weeks before the test date. It's a good idea to register early, because seating at the testing centers may be limited and you want to make sure you get a seat at the center of your choice. When you register, you are charged a fee, which you can pay by credit card. If you wish to change your test date, you can do so online.

TAKING THE MCAT MORE THAN ONCE

If your MCAT score is lower than expected, you may want to take the test again. You can take the MCAT up to three times in the same year. However, the AAMC recommends retesting only if you have a good reason to think that you will do better the next time. For example, you might do better if, when you first took the test, you were ill, or you made mistakes in keying in your answers, or your academic background in one or more of the test subjects was inadequate.

If you are considering retesting, you should also find out how your chosen medical schools evaluate multiple scores. Some schools give equal weight to all MCAT scores; others average scores together, and still others look only at the highest scores. Check with admissions officers before making a decision.

YOUR MCAT SCORES

When you take the MCAT, your work on each of the four test sections first receives a "raw score." The raw score is calculated based on the number of questions you answer correctly. No points are deducted for questions answered incorrectly. Each raw score is then converted into a scaled score. Using scaled scores helps make test-takers' scores comparable from one version of the MCAT to another. For each of the four sections, scaled scores range from 118 (lowest) to 132 (highest). Scaled scores for the entire exam range from 472 (lowest) to 528 (highest).

Your score report will be mailed to you approximately 30 days after you take the MCAT. You will also be able to view your scores on the online MCAT Testing History

(THx) System as soon as they become available. (For details on the THx system, see the MCAT website.) MCAT score reports also include percentile rankings that show how well you did in comparison to others who took the same test.

HOW MEDICAL SCHOOLS USE MCAT SCORES

Medical college admission committees emphasize that MCAT scores are only one of several criteria that they consider when evaluating applicants. When making their decisions, they also consider students' college and university grades, recommendations, interviews, and involvement and participation in extracurricular or health care–related activities that, in the opinion of the admission committee, illustrate maturity, motivation, dedication, and other positive personality traits that are of value to a physician. If the committee is unfamiliar with the college you attend, they may pay more attention than usual to your MCAT scores.

There is no hard-and-fast rule about what schools consider to be an acceptable MCAT score. The AAMC recommends that admissions officers should not limit acceptance to students who score in the upper third of the range. Instead, they should focus on applicants who score "at the top of the curve," that is, those whose scores lie at the top of the curve on the graph of the percentage of applicants who achieved each score point total. Statistically speaking, those students are likely to graduate successfully from medical school and to pass later qualifying exams on their first try. The AAMC says that this focus is "consistent with wholistic review practices" and "is designed to draw attention to applicants who might otherwise be overlooked." The "top of the curve" scaled score for each MCAT test section is 125; for the entire exam it is 500.

Note that many medical schools do not accept MCAT scores that are more than three years old.

REPORTING SCORES TO MEDICAL SCHOOLS

Your MCAT scores are automatically reported to the American Medical College Application Service (AMCAS), the nonprofit application processing service used by nearly all U.S. medical schools. When you use this service, you complete and submit a single application, rather than separate applications to each of your chosen schools. Your scores are submitted to your designated schools along with your application. There is a fee for using AMCAS. If you wish to submit your scores to other application services or to programs that do not participate in AMCAS, you can do so through the online MCAT Testing History (THx) System.

FOR FURTHER INFORMATION

For further information about the MCAT, visit the official MCAT website at
www.aamc.org/mcat

For questions about registering for the test, reporting and interpreting scores, and similar issues, you may also contact:

Association of American Medical Colleges
Medical College Admission Test
655 K Street, NW, Suite 100
Washington, D.C. 20001-2399

THE FORMAT OF THE TEST

The MCAT consists of four separately timed sections as outlined in the following chart.

MCAT: Format of the Test		
Section	**Number of Questions**	**Time Allowed (minutes)**
1. Biological and Biochemical Foundations of Living Systems *Break: 10 minutes*	59	95
2. Chemical and Physical Foundations of Biological Systems *Break: 10 minutes*	59	95
3. Psychological, Social, and Biological Foundations of Behavior *Break: 10 minutes*	59	95
4. Critical Analysis and Reasoning Skills	53	90
Totals	**230**	**375 (= 6 hours, 15 minutes)**

WHAT IS TESTED IN THE SCIENCE SECTIONS

The natural sciences sections of the MCAT (sections 1 and 2) test your mastery of the concepts and principles of biology, biochemistry, general chemistry, organic chemistry, and physics as they apply to living systems, including the human body.

The behavioral and social sciences section of the MCAT (section 3) tests your understanding of the behavioral and sociocultural factors that play a role in health care.

These three sections have three main organizing principles:

1. **Foundational concepts:** what the AAMC calls the "big ideas" in the sciences that underlie the subjects taught in medical school
2. **Content categories:** the topics that support the foundational concepts
3. **Scientific inquiry and reasoning skills:** the skills needed to solve scientific problems

Foundational Concepts and Content Categories

According to the AAMS, the foundational concepts and categories for sections 1, 2, and 3 of the MCAT are as follows:

1. BIOLOGICAL AND BIOCHEMICAL FOUNDATIONS OF LIVING SYSTEMS

Foundational Concept 1: *Biomolecules have unique properties that determine how they contribute to the structure and function of cells and how they participate in the processes necessary to maintain life.*

Content categories:

➤ Structure and function of proteins and their constituent amino acids

➤ Transmission of genetic information from the gene to the protein

➤ Transmission of heritable information from generation to generation and the processes that increase genetic diversity

➤ Principles of bioenergetics and fuel molecule metabolism

Foundational Concept 2: *Highly organized assemblies of molecules, cells, and organs interact to carry out the functions of living organisms.*

Content categories:

➤ Assemblies of molecules, cells, and groups of cells within single cellular and multicellular organisms

➤ Structure, growth, physiology, and genetics of prokaryotes and viruses

➤ Processes of cell division, differentiation, and specialization

Foundational Concept 3: *Complex systems of tissues and organs sense the internal and external environments of multicellular organisms and, through integrated functioning, maintain a stable internal environment within an ever-changing external environment.*

Content categories:

➤ Structure and functions of the nervous and endocrine systems and ways in which these systems coordinate the organ systems

➤ Structure and integrative functions of the main organ systems

2. CHEMICAL AND PHYSICAL FOUNDATIONS OF BIOLOGICAL SYSTEMS

Foundational Concept 4: *Complex living organisms transport materials, sense their environment, process signals, and respond to changes using processes that can be understood in terms of physical principles.*

Content categories:

➤ Translational motion, forces, work, energy, and equilibrium in living systems

➤ Importance of fluids for the circulation of blood, gas movement, and gas exchange

➤ Electrochemistry and electrical circuits and their elements

➤ How light and sound interact with matter

➤ Atoms, nuclear decay, electronic structure, and atomic chemical behavior

Foundational Concept 5: *The principles that govern chemical interactions and reactions form the basis for a broader understanding of the molecular dynamics of living systems.*

Content categories:

➤ Unique nature of water and its solutions

➤ Nature of molecules and intermolecular interactions

➤ Separation and purification methods

➤ Structure, function, and reactivity of biologically relevant molecules

➤ Principles of chemical thermodynamics and kinetics

3. PSYCHOLOGICAL, SOCIAL, AND BIOLOGICAL FOUNDATIONS OF BEHAVIOR

Foundational Concept 6: *Biological, psychological, and sociocultural factors influence the ways that individuals perceive, think about, and react to the world.*

Content categories:

➤ Sensing the environment

➤ Making sense of the environment

➤ Responding to the world

Foundational Concept 7: *Biological, psychological, and sociocultural factors influence behavior and behavior change.*

Content categories:

➤ Individual influences on behavior

➤ Social processes that influence human behavior

➤ Attitude and behavior change

Foundational Concept 8: *Psychological, sociocultural, and biological factors influence the way we think about ourselves and others, as well as how we interact with others.*

Content categories:

➤ Self-identity

➤ Social thinking

➤ Social interactions

Foundational Concept 9: *Cultural and social differences influence well-being.*

   Content categories:

➤ Understanding social structure

➤ Demographic characteristics and processes

Foundational Concept 10: *Social stratification and access to resources influence well-being.*

   Content category:

➤ Social inequality

Scientific Inquiry and Reasoning Skills

The scientific inquiry and reasoning skills that are tested on Sections 1, 2, and 3 of the MCAT are as follows:

➤ **Skill 1:** Knowledge of Scientific Concepts and Principles

➤ **Skill 2:** Scientific Reasoning and Evidence-Based Problem Solving

➤ **Skill 3:** Reasoning About the Design and Execution of Research

➤ **Skill 4:** Data-Based and Statistical Reasoning

To demonstrate mastery of **Skill 1: Knowledge of Scientific Concepts and Principles,** you need to be able to recall and apply basic scientific concepts and principles to solve problems in science. In many cases, you will need to analyze and interpret information presented in diagrams, charts, graphs, and formulas.

To demonstrate mastery of **Skill 2: Scientific Reasoning and Evidence-Based Problem Solving,** you need to be able to understand and use scientific theories, to propose hypotheses, and to analyze scientific models or research studies in order to identify assumptions, make predictions, and draw conclusions.

To demonstrate mastery of **Skill 3: Reasoning About the Design and Execution of Research,** you need to be able to identify appropriate research designs for investigating specified research questions, to critique and evaluate those designs, to predict results, and to recognize ethical issues involved in research.

To demonstrate mastery of **Skill 4: Data-Based and Statistical Reasoning,** you need to be able to interpret data or to describe or evaluate the results of a research study using statistical concepts.

WHAT IS TESTED IN CRITICAL ANALYSIS

The Critical Analysis and Reasoning Skills section of the MCAT (Section 4) tests your ability to comprehend information in a reading passage, to analyze and evaluate arguments and supporting evidence, and to apply concepts and ideas to new situations. The passages in this section cover a wide range of topics in both the social sciences and the humanities. You may encounter readings in philosophy, ethics, cultural studies, and similar topics. All the information you need to answer the questions will be provided in the passage; no outside knowledge of the topics is required.

According to the AAMC, the questions in the Critical Analysis and Reasoning Skills section test the following four specific skills:

➤ **Comprehension:** the ability to understand new information or to view facts or ideas in a new light

➤ **Evaluation:** the ability to analyze ideas or arguments presented in a passage and to make judgments about their reasonableness, their credibility, and the soundness of supporting evidence

➤ **Application:** the ability to apply information in a passage to new conditions or situations and to predict possible outcomes

➤ **Incorporation of information:** the ability to consider how new information affects the ideas presented in a passage; for example, whether it strengthens or weakens an argument or a hypothesis

GENERAL TEST-TAKING STRATEGIES

The following sections present some general test-taking strategies that apply to the multiple-choice questions on the MCAT. These strategies can help you to gain valuable points when you take the actual test.

Take Advantage of the Multiple-Choice Format

All of the questions on the MCAT are in the multiple-choice format, which you have undoubtedly seen many times before. That means that for every question, the correct answer is right in front of you. All you have to do is pick it out from among three incorrect choices, called "distracters." Consequently, you can use the process of elimination to rule out incorrect answer choices. The more answers you rule out, the easier it is to make the right choice.

Answer Every Question

Recall that on the MCAT, there is no penalty for choosing a wrong answer. Therefore, if you do not know the answer to a question, you have nothing to lose by guessing. So make sure that you answer every question. If time is running out and you still have not answered some questions, make sure to enter an answer for the questions that you have not attempted. With luck, you may be able to pick up a few extra points, even if your guesses are totally random.

Make Educated Guesses

What differentiates great test takers from merely good ones is the ability to guess in such a way as to maximize the chance of guessing correctly. The way to do this is to use the process of elimination. Before you guess, try to eliminate one or more of the answer choices. That way, you can make an educated guess, and you have a better chance of picking the correct answer. Odds of one out of two or one out of three are better than one out of four!

Go with Your Gut

In those cases where you're not 100 percent sure of the answer you are choosing, it is often best to go with your gut feeling and stick with your first answer. If you decide to change that answer and pick another one, you may well pick the wrong answer because you have over-thought the problem. More often than not, if you know something about the subject, your first answer is likely to be the correct one.

Take Advantage of Helpful Computer Functions

On the MCAT, you have access to certain computer functions that can make your work easier. As you work through the on-screen questions, you are able to highlight relevant portions of the reading passages. This helps you save time when you need to find facts or details to support your answer choices. You are also able to cross out answer choices that you know are incorrect. This helps you use the process of elimination to pick the correct answer.

Use the Scratch Paper Provided

The MCAT is an all-computerized test, so there is no test booklet for you to write in. However, you are given scratch paper, so use it to your advantage. Jot down notes, make calculations, and write out an outline for each of your essays. Be aware, however, that you cannot remove the scratch paper from the test site. All papers are collected from you before you leave the room.

Because you cannot write on the actual MCAT, don't get into the habit of writing notes to yourself on the test pages of this book. Use separate scratch paper instead. Consider it an opportunity to learn to use scratch paper effectively.

Keep Track of the Time

Make sure that you're on track to answer all of the questions within the time allowed. With so many questions to answer in a short time period, you're not going to have a lot of time to spare. Keep an eye on your watch or on the computerized timer provided.

Do not spend too much time on any one question. If you find yourself stuck for more than a minute or two on a question, then you should make your best guess and move on. If you have time left over at the end of the section, you can return to the question and review your answer. However, if time runs out, don't give the question another thought. You need to save your focus for the rest of the test.

Don't Panic if Time Runs Out

If you pace yourself and keep track of your progress, you should not run out of time. If you do, however, run out of time, don't panic. Because there is no guessing penalty and you have nothing to lose by doing so, enter answers to all the remaining questions. If you are able to make educated guesses, you will probably be able to improve your score. However, even random guesses may help you pick up a few points. In order to know how to handle this situation if it happens to you on the test, make sure you observe the time limits when you take the practice tests. Guessing well is a skill that comes with practice, so incorporate it into your preparation program.

If Time Permits, Review Questions You Were Unsure Of

Within each test section, the computer allows you to return to questions you have already answered and change your answer if you decide to do so. (However, once you have completed an entire section, you cannot go back to it and make changes.) If time permits, you may want to take advantage of this function to review questions you were unsure of or to check for careless mistakes.

McGraw-Hill Education

MCAT

CHEMICAL AND PHYSICAL
FOUNDATIONS OF BIOLOGICAL SYSTEMS

2016

UNIT I

Physical Foundations of Biological Systems

Foundational Concept: Complex living organisms transport materials, sense their environment, process signals, and respond to changes using processes understood in terms of physical principles.

CHAPTER 1 Translational Motion, Forces, Work, Energy, and Equilibrium in Living Systems

CHAPTER 2 Importance of Fluids for the Circulation of Blood, Gas Movement, and Gas Exchange

CHAPTER 3 Electrochemistry and Electrical Circuits and Their Elements

CHAPTER 4 How Light and Sound Interact with Matter

CHAPTER 5 Atoms, Nuclear Decay, Electronic Structure, and Atomic Chemical Behavior

Unit I MINITEST

Translational Motion, Forces, Work, Energy, and Equilibrium in Living Systems

> ### Read This Chapter to Learn About
>
> ➤ Translational Motion
>
> ➤ Forces and Equilibrium
>
> ➤ Work, Energy, and Power

O n a scale as small as an atom or as large as a planet, motion is an important constant critical to all living things. It is easy to imagine that if all motion stopped, from the atom to the planets and everything in between, then life would cease to exist. The science of motion is referred to as **kinematics**. This chapter focuses on kinematics and the concepts and equations that describe the motion of objects.

TRANSLATIONAL MOTION

Translational motion describes the motion of an object that moves from one position to another without reference to a fixed point. This explanation of translational motion becomes clear when compared to **rotational motion**, which is the motion of an object that moves from one position to another with reference to a fixed point—an axis. Translational motion includes the motion of an object in a straight line (e.g., a car moving down the road or a ball thrown up in the air), and the curved, parabolic trajectory of a launched or thrown projectile. Kinematics, sometimes referred to as **translational**

kinematics, represents the set of equations that relate the important physical variables of motion.

Units and Dimensions

In physics, typical quantities that might be measured include the length of a lab table, the mass of a textbook, or the time required for an object to strike the ground when dropped from a known height. These quantities are described by **dimensions** or physical descriptions of a quantity. In physics, three basic dimensions are used, corresponding to the three examples of quantities noted previously: length (L), mass (M), and time (T). These are not the only basic dimensions in physics; in fact, in physics there are seven basic dimensions: **length, mass, time, temperature, amount of a substance, electric current**, and **luminous intensity**.

A quantity may also be described by some combination of these three dimensions. For example, consider the quantity of **force**, defined by Newton's Second Law of Motion as the product of mass and acceleration. The dimension of mass is M, and acceleration (defined as the change in velocity over the change in time) is L/T^2. So the dimension of force is $(M)(L/T^2)$, or ML/T^2.

UNITS OF MEASUREMENT

Although the dimension indicates the type of physical quantity expressed by a physical measurement, units indicate the amount of the physical quantity. Each of the dimensions described in the previous section (i.e., length, mass, and time) is measured in terms of a **unit**, which indicates the amount of a physical quantity. An appropriate unit for a specific quantity depends on the dimension of the quantity. For example, let's say you want to know the length of a pencil. Because the dimension of interest is length, the pencil can be measured in terms of various units, such as centimeters, meters, inches, or feet—all of which describe length. The choice of unit used to describe the length of the pencil depends on the size of the pencil; you probably would not measure the length of a pencil in terms of miles or kilometers.

Although there are several systems of units known in science, the system of units that has been adopted by the science community and that will be used throughout this review is the SI system of units (Système International d'Unités), also known as the **metric system**. In the **SI system of units**, the base unit of length is the **meter**, the base unit of mass is the **kilogram**, and the base unit of time is the **second**, as shown in the following table.

TABLE 1-1 Physical Quantities and SI Units of Measurement

Physical Quantity	Dimension	SI Base Unit
Length	L	meter, m
Mass	M	kilogram, kg
Time	T	second, s

5

CHAPTER 1:
Translational
Motion, Forces,
Work, Energy, and
Equilibrium in
Living Systems

UNIT CONVERSIONS

All physics equations must be equal in both dimensions and units. For example, consider the quantity speed. The units for speed must be consistent in terms of dimension $\left(\frac{L}{T}\right)$ and in units $\left(\frac{km}{h} \text{ or } \frac{m}{s}\right)$ in order for the final result to be physically logical. **Conversion factors** convert units through ratios of equivalent quantities from one system of measure to another. Following are some examples of the process of unit conversions:

1. Determine the number of grams (g) in 5 kilograms (kg).

$$5 \text{ kg} \times \frac{1000 \text{ g}}{1 \text{ kg}} = 5000 \text{ g}$$

In this problem, 5 kg is multiplied by the conversion factor $\frac{1000 \text{ g}}{1 \text{ kg}}$. The conversion factor is equal to 1 because 1 kg $=$ 1000 g, and any value (e.g., 5 kg) multiplied by 1 retains its value, even if expressed in different units. Although multiplication of a quantity by a conversion factor changes the numeric value of the quantity, it does not change the measurement of the physical quantity, because objects of mass 5 kg and 5000 g are identical. The arrangement of the conversion factor is important, because the final result must have units of grams. In order for this to happen, the conversion factor must have the kilogram unit on the bottom so that the unit cancels with the kilogram unit in 5 kg, yielding a quantity with a unit in grams.

2. Determine the number of seconds in 1 year. To find the number of seconds in 1 year, begin with the quantity of 1 year and multiply that quantity by appropriate conversion factors such that the last unit standing is seconds.

$$1 \text{ year} \times \frac{365 \text{ days}}{1 \text{ year}} \times \frac{24 \text{ hours}}{1 \text{ day}} \times \frac{60 \text{ minutes}}{1 \text{ hour}} \times \frac{60 \text{ seconds}}{1 \text{ minute}}$$

$$= \left(\frac{1 \times 365 \times 24 \times 60 \times 60}{1 \times 1 \times 1 \times 1}\right) \text{ seconds} = 3.15 \times 10^7 \text{ s}$$

ESTIMATING QUANTITIES USING UNIT CONVERSIONS

You may use this same conversion technique to estimate quantities. However, in making such estimations, you need to make several assumptions—and the more sound and robust your assumptions are, the more realistic your estimations will be.

EXAMPLE: Calculate the number of heartbeats that occur in an individual over a lifetime.

SOLUTION: Before you begin to solve this problem, you must make several assumptions including: (1) the average heartbeat rate of the individual over the course of a lifetime = 1.1 beats/s, and (2) the number of years in a lifetime = 80 years. The problem requires you to convert from 1.1 beats per second to the total number of beats occurring over 80 years.

$$\frac{\text{Number of beats}}{\text{Lifetime (80 years)}} = \frac{1.1 \text{ beats}}{1 \text{ second}} \times \frac{60 \text{ seconds}}{1 \text{ minute}} \times \frac{60 \text{ minutes}}{1 \text{ hour}} \times \frac{24 \text{ hours}}{1 \text{ day}}$$

$$\times \frac{365 \text{ days}}{1 \text{ year}} \times \frac{80 \text{ years}}{1 \text{ lifetime}}$$

$$= \left(\frac{1.1 \times 60 \times 60 \times 24 \times 365 \times 80}{1 \times 1 \times 1 \times 1 \times 1 \times 1} \right) \frac{\text{beats}}{\text{lifetime}}$$

$$= 2.78 \times 10^9 \frac{\text{beats}}{\text{lifetime}}$$

By this estimate, the number of heartbeats in a person's lifetime of 80 years is 2.78 billion beats. However, this calculation is an estimate of a quantity, and not an exact answer, primarily because of factors that were not addressed, such as: (1) the extra days not factored in during leap years; (2) the change in heart rate that occurs between night and day; (3) the effect of different emotions, medications, and illnesses; (4) family history, genetic disorders, and illnesses that affect the circulatory system; and (5) the moment that the heart begins to beat includes the time during fetal development in which the defined circulatory system begins circulating blood within the fetus (typically in the second trimester).

Vectors and Scalars

In physics, measurements of physical quantities, processes, and interactions can be classified according to two types. Some measurements, such as displacement, velocity, and acceleration, require both a magnitude (size) as well as a direction, while some measurements, such as distance and speed, are presented only as a magnitude or size. Those quantities that require both a magnitude and direction are known as **vector quantities**, whereas those quantities that require only magnitude are referred to as **scalar quantities**. Examples of scalar and vector quantities follow.

Scalar Quantities	Vector Quantities
Measurement	
Time	
Mass	
Area	
Volume	
Kinematics	
Distance	Displacement
Speed	Velocity
	Acceleration

7

CHAPTER 1:
Translational
Motion, Forces,
Work, Energy, and
Equilibrium in
Living Systems

Scalar Quantities	Vector Quantities
Dynamics	
Work	Force
Energy	Momentum
	Torque

A vector quantity is generally noted by a boldfaced letter, sometimes with an arrow drawn over the top of the letter. For example, a vector quantity S can be represented by the symbols, **S** or $\vec{\textbf{S}}$. The magnitude of the vector quantity S is typically indicated by the vector quantity symbol encased within the absolute value bars, |**S**| or |$\vec{\textbf{S}}$|. In addition, a vector quantity is represented graphically by an arrow, with the size of the arrow corresponding to the size or magnitude of the vector quantity and the orientation of the arrow corresponding to the direction of the vector quantity, as shown in Figure 1-1.

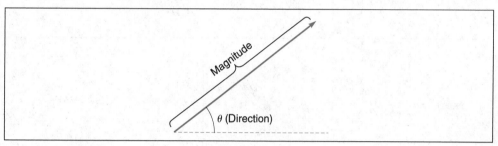

FIGURE 1-1 Representation of a vector quantity.

Vector Addition and Subtraction

Although scalar and vector quantities are similar in that they both can be added or subtracted, they are different in that scalar quantities can be added or subtracted arithmetically, but vector quantities must be added or subtracted in ways that take into account their direction as well as their magnitude. One method of vector addition is the **head-to-tail method**. A second method is called the **component method**.

HEAD-TO-TAIL METHOD OF VECTOR ADDITION

Let's say you have two vectors, **A** and **B**. In this method of vector addition, one of the vectors, **A**, is drawn to scale with its tail positioned at the origin. At the head of this vector, the tail of the second vector is drawn according to its scale. The **vector sum** or **resultant**, indicated by **R**, is the magnitude and direction of the arrow drawn from the tail of the first vector to the head of the second vector. This method can be extended to include more than two vectors.

If the two vectors **A** and **B** are one-dimensional (i.e., lie along the same dimension), then they may be added as shown in Figure 1-2.

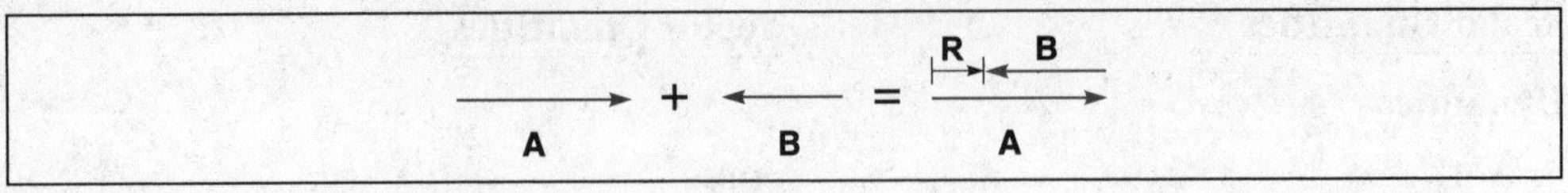

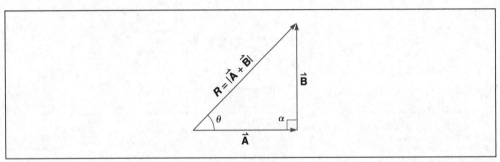

FIGURE 1-2 Adding one-dimensional vectors.

If the vectors are perpendicular to one another (i.e., vector **A** lies along the x-axis and vector **B** lies along the y-axis, as shown in Figure 1-3), then the resultant vector, **R**, represents the hypotenuse of the right triangle formed by the two perpendicular vectors, **A** and **B**. The magnitude of **R** can be found using the Pythagorean theorem:

$$c^2 = a^2 + b^2 \quad \text{or} \quad R^2 = A^2 + B^2$$

The following trigonometric function is used to determine the direction of the resultant vector:

$$\theta = \tan^{-1}\left(\frac{\text{opp}}{\text{adj}}\right) = \tan^{-1}\left(\frac{B}{A}\right)$$

FIGURE 1-3 Adding perpendicular vectors. *Source:* From George Hademenos, *Schaum's Outline of Physics for Pre-Med, Biology, and Allied Health Students*, McGraw-Hill, 1998; reproduced with permission of The McGraw-Hill Companies.

COMPONENT METHOD OF VECTOR ADDITION

The component method of vector addition requires that the x and y components of each vector be determined. In a two-dimensional coordinate system, a vector can be positioned solely along the x direction, solely along the y direction, or can have components both in the x and y directions. A vector quantity oriented at an angle implies that a component of the quantity is in the x direction and a component of the quantity is in the y direction, as shown in Figure 1-4. To determine exactly how much of a vector is in the x or the y directions, you use the following trigonometric functions to resolve the vector (**A**) in terms of its horizontal or x components (A_x) and its vertical or y components (A_y):

Horizontal component: $\quad \cos\theta = \dfrac{\text{adj}}{\text{hyp}} = \dfrac{A_x}{A}$

Vertical component: $\quad \sin\theta = \dfrac{\text{opp}}{\text{hyp}} = \dfrac{A_y}{A}$

9

CHAPTER 1:
Translational
Motion, Forces,
Work, Energy, and
Equilibrium in
Living Systems

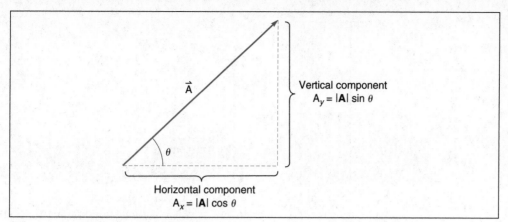

FIGURE 1-4 Component method of vector addition.

The angles $\theta = 90°$, $180°$, $270°$, and $360°$ are special cases. Assuming that $\theta = 0°$ corresponds to the $+x$ axis,

➤ A vector **A** at 90° has the components: $A_x = 0;\quad A_y = +|\mathbf{A}|$
➤ A vector **A** at 180° has the components: $A_x = -|\mathbf{A}|;\ A_y = 0$
➤ A vector **A** at 270° has the components: $A_x = 0;\quad A_y = -|\mathbf{A}|$
➤ A vector **A** at 360° has the components: $A_x = +|\mathbf{A}|;\ A_y = 0$

Nevertheless, each component of the vectors is added, with the sum of the x components now representing the x component of the resultant vector, R_x, and the sum of the y components representing the y component of the resultant vector, R_y. Once you know the x and y components of the resultant vector, you can determine the magnitude of the resultant vector by using the Pythagorean theorem:

$$R^2 = R_x^2 + R_y^2 \quad \text{or} \quad R = \sqrt{R_x^2 + R_y^2}$$

You can determine the direction by using the trigonometric function:

$$\theta = \tan^{-1}\left(\frac{\text{opp}}{\text{adj}}\right) = \tan^{-1}\left(\frac{R_y}{R_x}\right)$$

EXAMPLE: On a walk across a large parking lot, a shopper walks 25.0 m to the east and then turns and walks 40.0 m to the north. Find the resultant of the two displacement vectors representing the shopper's walk using: (1) the head-to-tail method of vector addition and (2) the component method of vector addition.

SOLUTION: The first leg of the shopper's walk, which we call vector **A**, is **A** = 25.0 m east. The second leg, which we call vector **B**, is **B** = 40.0 m north.

1. Using the head-to-tail method of vector addition, the two vectors are drawn as shown in Figure 1-5. You can calculate the magnitude of the resultant vector **R** drawn from the tail of vector **A** to the head of vector **B** by using the

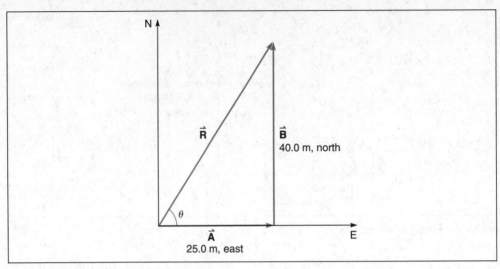

FIGURE 1-5 Diagram for shopper's walk.

Pythagorean theorem:

$$R^2 = A^2 + B^2 = (25.0 \text{ m})^2 + (40.0 \text{ m})^2 = 2225 \text{ m}^2$$

$$R = \sqrt{2225 \text{ m}^2} = 47.2 \text{ m}$$

You can determine the direction or angle of the resultant vector **R** from the trigonometric relationship:

$$\theta = \tan^{-1}\left(\frac{\text{opp}}{\text{adj}}\right) = \tan^{-1}\left(\frac{B}{A}\right) = \tan^{-1}\left(\frac{40.0 \text{ m}}{25.0 \text{ m}}\right)$$

$$= 57.9° \text{ (as measured from the positive } x\text{-axis)}$$

2. Use the component method of vector addition to resolve vectors **A** and **B** into their x and y components:

Vector **A**:	$A_x = 25.0 \text{ m}$	$A_y = 0 \text{ m}$
Vector **B**:	$B_x = 0 \text{ m}$	$B_y = 40.0 \text{ m}$
Vector **R**:	$R_x = A_x + B_x$	$R_y = A_y + B_y$
	$= 25.0 \text{ m} + 0 \text{ m}$	$= 0 \text{ m} + 40.0 \text{ m}$
	$= 25.0 \text{ m}$	$= 40.0 \text{ m}$

You can find the magnitude of the resultant vector **R** by using the Pythagorean theorem:

$$R^2 = R_x^2 + R_y^2 = (25.0 \text{ m})^2 + (40.0 \text{ m})^2 = 2225 \text{ m}^2$$

$$R = \sqrt{2225 \text{ m}^2} = 47.2 \text{ m}$$

The direction or angle of the resultant vector **R** can be determined from the trigonometric relationship:

$$\theta = \tan^{-1}\left(\frac{\text{opp}}{\text{adj}}\right) = \tan^{-1}\left(\frac{R_y}{R_x}\right) = \tan^{-1}\left(\frac{40.0 \text{ m}}{25.0 \text{ m}}\right)$$

$$= 57.9° \text{ (as measured from the positive } x\text{-axis)}$$

11

CHAPTER 1:
Translational
Motion, Forces,
Work, Energy, and
Equilibrium in
Living Systems

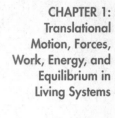

FIGURE 1-6 Vector subtraction.

VECTOR SUBTRACTION

Subtraction of a vector can be done by reversing the direction of the vector and adding it to the remaining vectors, as shown in Figure 1-6. Reversing the sign of the vector simply changes the direction of the vector without affecting its magnitude.

Displacement, Velocity, and Acceleration

Displacement (Δx) is defined as a distance in a given direction. Consider a typical trip to work in which you travel from point A (home, starting position) to point B (work, final position). Expressed in units of length (e.g., meters, kilometers, yards, or miles), displacement is a measure of the **length** [difference between the final position (x_f) and the initial position (x_i)] required to get from point A to point B, regardless of the path taken.

Displacement: $\Delta x = x_f - x_i$

Because displacement is a directed distance, it is possible that the displacement can be either positive or negative. A **negative displacement**, just as is the case for any negative quantity in physics, does not imply that the distance is a negative quantity; rather, it implies that the direction of displacement is opposite to that direction considered positive.

A similar quantity related to length is distance. Although displacement is the length between the final point and starting point, **distance** is the length required to get from the starting point to the ending point, dependent on the path taken. If you leave home, drop by the post office to mail some letters, take your children to school, and stop by the grocery store before reaching work, the path taken is much longer than the straight path between home and work. In this case, the distance (home → post office → school → grocery store → work) is much larger than the displacement (home → work).

Speed

Speed (s) is the rate of change of distance over a time interval and expressed in dimensions of length per unit time.

Velocity (v) is the rate of change of displacement over a time interval or the rate at which a directed distance between point A and point B is covered over an interval of time. Velocity, also expressed in dimensions of length per unit time, is the speed of an object in a given direction.

$$\text{Average velocity: } v = \frac{\Delta x}{\Delta t} = \frac{x_f - x_i}{t_f - t_i}$$

Average velocity represents velocity over a time interval. **Instantaneous velocity** represents velocity at a given instant of time, similar to the velocity of a car indicated by its speedometer.

Acceleration (a) is the rate at which velocity changes. Acceleration, expressed in dimensions of length per unit time squared, is the change of velocity in a given direction over a defined time interval.

$$\text{Average acceleration: } a = \frac{\Delta v}{\Delta t} = \frac{v_f - v_i}{t_f - t_i}$$

Average acceleration represents average velocity over a time interval. **Instantaneous acceleration** represents acceleration at a given instant of time.

Graphical Representation of Motion

In a typical motion graph, time [typically in seconds (s)] is always represented along the x-axis (horizontal), whereas the variable along the y-axis could be displacement [in meters (m), for example] or velocity [in meters per second (m/s), for example]. If there is an accompanying table with data points that are represented in a graph, the left column contains values representative of the **independent variable** (typically time) which are plotted along the horizontal or x-axis, whereas the right column contains values of the **dependent variable** (either displacement or velocity, respectively) which are plotted along the vertical or y-axis.

If you graph displacement versus time for an object, the velocity of the object is the slope of the line on the graph:

$$\text{Slope} = \frac{\text{rise}}{\text{run}} = \frac{y_2 - y_1}{x_2 - x_1} = \frac{\text{displacement (meters)}}{\text{time (seconds)}} = \text{velocity} \left(\frac{\text{meters}}{\text{second}} \right)$$

13

CHAPTER 1:
Translational
Motion, Forces,
Work, Energy, and
Equilibrium in
Living Systems

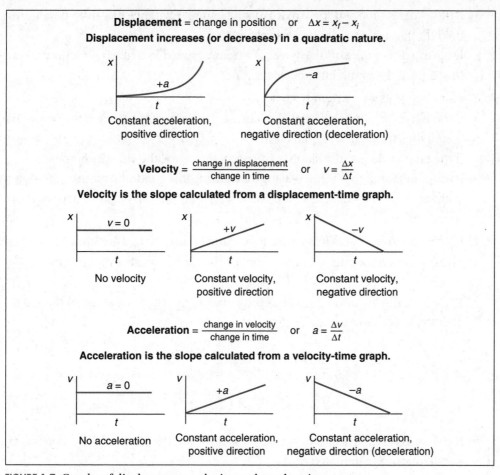

FIGURE 1-7 Graphs of displacement, velocity, and acceleration.

If you graph velocity versus time for an object, the acceleration of the object is represented by the slope of the line on the graph:

$$\text{Slope} = \frac{\text{rise}}{\text{run}} = \frac{y_2 - y_1}{x_2 - x_1} = \frac{\text{velocity (meters/second)}}{\text{time (seconds)}}$$
$$= \text{acceleration} \left(\frac{\text{meters}}{\text{second}^2} \right)$$

Velocity and acceleration represent a change in a variable (displacement or velocity, respectively) as a function of time. Figure 1-7 shows examples of graphs of displacement, velocity, and acceleration. Note that the slope and the y-intercept of each graphed quantity depend on the location of the object and the rate of change of motion of the object.

As you evaluate and interpret the graphs of motion data, you can obtain important information by considering the following questions:

➤ What is the physical significance of the data?
- What do the graphed data tell me about the nature and behavior of an object?
- What are the quantities presented in the columns of data found in a table and/or the quantities represented along the x- and y-axes of a graph?

- If the x-axis is time and the y-axis is displacement (distance in a given direction), then the slope of the graph gives velocity.
- If the x-axis is time and the y-axis is velocity (speed in a given direction), then the slope of the graph gives acceleration.

➤ Does y change as x is varied? If so, how?

- If there is a straight horizontal displacement—time graph, there is no change in y, and thus the velocity equals zero.
- If the graph is linear, the slope is constant; therefore, the velocity is constant.
- If the graph is nonlinear (increasing/decreasing in a quadratic nature), the slope is changing, indicating either a positive acceleration or a negative acceleration (deceleration).

➤ If there is motion, what is its quantitative value (in magnitude and units)?

- The quantitative value of motion implies the numeric value of the slope of the graph.
- If the x-axis is time and the y-axis is displacement, then the slope of the graph yields velocity, as calculated next.

$$\text{Slope} = \frac{\text{rise}}{\text{run}} = \frac{y_2 - y_1}{x_2 - x_1} = \frac{\text{displacement (meters)}}{\text{time (seconds)}}$$
$$= \text{velocity} \left(\frac{\text{meters}}{\text{second}} \right)$$

- If the x-axis is time and the y-axis is velocity, then the slope of the graph yields acceleration, as calculated next.

$$\text{Slope} = \frac{\text{rise}}{\text{run}} = \frac{y_2 - y_1}{x_2 - x_1} = \frac{\text{velocity (meters/second)}}{\text{time (seconds)}}$$
$$= \text{acceleration} \left(\frac{\text{meters}}{\text{second}^2} \right)$$

Uniformly Accelerated Motion

Up to this point, we have defined and discussed motion in terms of displacement, velocity, and acceleration. In order for you to be able to use these quantities and apply them to physics problems, you must be able to determine relations between them. For motion of an object with constant uniform acceleration along the x-axis, you can apply the following four equations:

1. Displacement with constant uniform acceleration:

$$\Delta x = \frac{1}{2} \left(v_i + v_f \right) \Delta t$$

$$\text{Displacement} = \frac{1}{2} \left(\text{initial velocity} + \text{final velocity} \right) \left(\text{time interval} \right)$$

15

CHAPTER 1:
Translational
Motion, Forces,
Work, Energy, and
Equilibrium in
Living Systems

2. Final velocity with constant uniform acceleration:

$$v_f = v_i + a\Delta t$$

Final velocity = initial velocity + (acceleration) (time interval)

3. Displacement with constant uniform acceleration:

$$\Delta x = v_i \Delta t + \frac{1}{2}a(\Delta t)^2$$

Displacement = (initial velocity) (time interval)

$$+ \frac{1}{2} \text{(acceleration) (time interval)}^2$$

4. Final velocity after any displacement:

$$v_f^2 = v_i^2 + 2a\Delta x$$

$$(\text{Final velocity})^2 = (\text{initial velocity})^2 + 2(\text{acceleration}) (\text{displacement})$$

You might ask why there are two equations used to calculate final velocity and two equations used to calculate displacement. Careful inspection of the equations indicates that each equation depends on four different variables. This gives you maximum flexibility to determine any related quantity of motion about an object given a specific scenario, depending on the given information.

EXAMPLE: A car initially moving at 20 m/s uniformly accelerates at 2.5 m/s^2. Find the final speed and displacement of the car after 8.0 s.

SOLUTION: The given information from this problem includes:

$$v_i = 20 \text{ m/s} \quad a = 2.5 \text{ m/s}^2 \quad \Delta t = 8.0 \text{ s}$$

To determine the final speed of the car, use the following equation:

$$v_f = v_i + a\Delta t = 20 \frac{m}{s} + \left(2.5 \frac{m}{s^2}\right)(8.0 \text{ s}) = 40 \frac{m}{s}$$

To determine the displacement of the car, use the following equation:

$$\Delta x = v_i \Delta t + \frac{1}{2}a(\Delta t)^2 = \left(20 \frac{m}{s}\right)(8.0 \text{ s}) + \frac{1}{2}\left(2.5 \frac{m}{s^2}\right)(8.0 \text{ s})^2 = 240 \text{ m}$$

Free-Fall Motion

The equations for uniformly accelerated motion presented previously dealt with motion primarily moving along the x-axis (from left to right, and vice versa). However, the same concepts, definitions, variables, and equations also apply to motion along the y-axis (from up to down, and vice versa). In the case of motion along the y-axis, a constant acceleration is caused by gravity. Any and all types of motion involving the y-axis, such as throwing a ball in the air or dropping a pencil, occur under the influence of gravity. But what is it about gravity that factors into the motion of such objects? **Gravity** is a force that pulls objects to Earth. That pull causes the objects to accelerate in a constant manner. The acceleration due to gravity, g, is given numerically by

$g = -9.8$ m/s^2 and always acts downward. Thus, the four equations of motion given previously that described motion of an object in the x-direction can also be applied to an object moving in the y-direction by making two minor changes: (1) displacement that was originally noted in the equations of motion as Δx now becomes Δy; and (2) the acceleration, a, now is replaced by g, the acceleration due to gravity.

1. Displacement with constant uniform acceleration:

$$\Delta y = \frac{1}{2}\left(v_i + v_f\right)\Delta t$$

2. Final velocity with constant uniform acceleration:

$$v_f = v_i + g\Delta t$$

3. Displacement with constant uniform acceleration:

$$\Delta y = v_i \Delta t + \frac{1}{2}g(\Delta t)^2$$

4. Final velocity after any displacement:

$$v_f^2 = v_i^2 + 2g\Delta y$$

A special case of motion along the y-axis is **free-fall motion**, which refers to motion of an object that is dropped from a certain height or y-direction and allowed to fall toward the ground. The first equation indicates how far an object has fallen per given time:

$$\Delta y = \frac{1}{2}g(\Delta t)^2$$

(Distance in the y-direction) $= \frac{1}{2}$ (acceleration due to gravity)(time in flight)^2

Note that this is the same equation as No. 3, displacement with constant uniform acceleration, with the initial velocity $v_i = 0$.

The other equation indicates how fast an object falls per given time:

$$v_f = g\Delta t$$

(Velocity in the y-direction) $=$ (acceleration due to gravity)(time in flight)

Note that this is the same equation as the second equation, final velocity with uniform acceleration, with the initial velocity $v_i = 0$.

EXAMPLE: A stone is dropped from a bridge that is 15 m in height. Determine the stone's velocity as it strikes the water below.

SOLUTION: The given information from this problem includes:

➤ $v_i = 0$ m/s, because it is dropped or released from rest

➤ $a = -9.8$ m/s^2, because it is accelerating downward as a result of gravity

➤ $\Delta y = -15.0$ m (This height is negative, because the origin is the object at the top of the bridge, and as it moves downward, it is moving in the negative direction.)

17

CHAPTER 1:
Translational
Motion, Forces,
Work, Energy, and
Equilibrium in
Living Systems

To determine the final speed of the stone, use the following equation:

$$v_f^2 = v_i^2 + 2g\Delta y = \left(0\ \frac{m}{s}\right)^2 + 2\left(-9.8\ \frac{m}{s^2}\right)(-15.0\ m) = 294\ \frac{m^2}{s^2}$$

$$v_f = \sqrt{294\ \frac{m^2}{s^2}} = 17.1\ \frac{m}{s}$$

Strategies for solving one-dimensional motion problems are described next.

STRATEGIES FOR SOLVING ONE-DIMENSIONAL MOTION PROBLEMS

1. Identify and list all given information (known and unknown variables).

   ➤ Do not assume that all information given in a problem is required to solve the problem.

   ➤ Look for key words that might be just as important as values: **rest**, **drop** implies $v_i = 0$, and **stop** implies $v_f = 0$. Also, words like **constant**, **speed up**, **increase**, **slow down**, and **decrease** are important in describing the acceleration of the object.

   ➤ Problems commonly involve the sign of g. Because gravity acts downward, g should be a negative quantity. However, care should be taken to ensure the proper sign convention of all other quantities as well. For example, an object dropped from a cliff will have fallen -5 m after 1 second. The negative value implies a distance in the $-y$ direction.

2. Make sure all units are consistent (in SI system of units), and if not, perform required conversions.

3. Choose an equation that can be solved with the known variables as noted in the following table.

TABLE 1-2

Involved Variables	Equation of Motion in x Direction	Equation of Motion in y Direction	Involved Variables
$\Delta x, v_i, v_f, \Delta t$	$\Delta x = \frac{1}{2}\left(v_i + v_f\right)\Delta t$	$\Delta y = \frac{1}{2}\left(v_i + v_f\right)\Delta t$	$\Delta y, v_i, v_f, \Delta t$
$v_i, v_f, \Delta t, a$	$v_f = v_i + a\Delta t$	$v_f = v_i + g\Delta t$	$v_i, v_f, \Delta t, g$
$\Delta x, v_i, \Delta t, a$	$\Delta x = v_i\Delta t + \frac{1}{2}a(\Delta t)^2$	$\Delta y = v_i\Delta t + \frac{1}{2}g(\Delta t)^2$	$\Delta y, v_i, \Delta t, g$
$v_i, v_f, \Delta x, a$	$v_f^2 = v_i^2 + 2a\Delta x$	$v_f^2 = v_i^2 + 2g\Delta y$	$v_i, v_f, \Delta y, g$

Each problem should include information about four variables. Match these four variables with the outer columns to find the correct equation.

4. Substitute all variables in proper units in the chosen equation, perform the necessary algebraic operations, arrive at the solution, and then ask yourself: Does the answer make sense?

FORCES AND EQUILIBRIUM

Up to now, this chapter has been discussing kinematics, or the concepts and equations that describe the motion of an object being uniformly accelerated. The variables and equations that describe an object's motion in one dimension (along the x- and y-axes) were defined and applied to specific problems and examples. This section explains the causes and the factors involved in motion.

Forces in Nature

Given any object, whether an electron, a person, or a planet, what causes the object to move? The answer is simple—a force. **Force** can be defined simply as a push or a pull. Forces cause objects to move. Forces occur everywhere in nature on every object—but the mere presence of a force does not mean that an object will necessarily move. It is electric forces that are responsible for the movement of current through an electric circuit, mechanical forces that can cause a person to move, and gravitational forces that cause planets to move. The reasons are discussed later as part of Newton's Laws of Motion.

A force is a vector quantity expressed in a unit called the **newton** (N):

$$1 \text{ newton} = 1 \, \frac{\text{kilogram} \cdot \text{meter}}{\text{second}^2} \quad \text{or} \quad 1 \, \frac{\text{kg} \cdot \text{m}}{\text{s}^2}$$

All forces, whether they are electric, mechanical, or gravitational, are expressed in units of newtons, regardless of their source. Gravitational forces are discussed later in this chapter and electric forces are discussed in Chapter 3. Weight, normal force, friction, and tension are four specific types of mechanical forces that exist in nature and are defined as follows:

1. **Weight** is the force exerted on an object by gravity. It is also referred to as the **force due to gravity**. Any object that has mass has weight. Weight can be calculated by the equation:

   Weight = (mass) (acceleration due to gravity)

   $$W = mg$$

2. **Normal force** is the force exerted on an object by a surface. It is also referred to as the **support force**. Normal force always acts perpendicular to the surface that is supporting the object.

3. **Friction** is a force generated by the properties of the interface between a moving object and a surface. Friction acts in a direction opposite to an object's motion. The force due to friction, $\mathbf{F}_f$, is defined as:

   Frictional force = (coefficient of friction) (normal force)

   $$\mathbf{F}_f = \mu \mathbf{N}$$

19

CHAPTER 1:
Translational
Motion, Forces,
Work, Energy, and
Equilibrium in
Living Systems

There are two types of frictional forces corresponding to the state of motion of the object. If the object is stationary, then a frictional force (static friction) is acting on the object to prevent motion, described by:

$$\mathbf{F}_{f,s} \leq \mu_s \mathbf{N}$$

where μ_s is the **coefficient of static friction**. If the object is set in motion (i.e., subject to an applied force that is greater in magnitude and opposite in direction than the static frictional force), then the object is subject to kinetic (sliding) friction, defined as:

$$\mathbf{F}_{f,k} = \mu_k \mathbf{N}$$

Static friction is generally greater in magnitude than kinetic friction because an object requires a larger force to start an object in motion than it does to be kept in motion.

4. **Tension** is the force exerted by a string, rope, or cable on a suspended object.

Newton's Three Laws of Motion

Before you can understand Newton's Laws of Motion, you must make a distinction between three physical terms that are often confused: mass, inertia, and weight.

➤ **Mass**, measured in SI units of kilograms, is the amount of substance that an object has.

➤ **Inertia** is an object's resistance to motion. What makes an object resistant to motion is not an object's size, but its mass. The more mass an object has, the more inertia it has, making the object more resistant to motion. Inertia does not have a physical unit, but is indicated by the object's mass.

➤ **Weight**, a force exerted on an object due to gravity, is often confused with mass. These are two very different quantities. Weight is a vector quantity expressed in units of newtons, whereas mass is a scalar quantity expressed in units of kilograms. The weight of an object is calculated by multiplying the mass of the object times the acceleration due to gravity, or

   Weight = (mass) (acceleration due to gravity)

The mass of an object does not change unless material is added or taken away. The weight of an object can change, for example, on a different planet, where the acceleration due to gravity is different. The mass of a person on Earth is the same as the mass of that person on Mars, as the mass always remains the same. However, the weight of the person differs because each planet has a different gravitational field and hence a different value of g (the acceleration due to gravity). Because the g on Mars is $g = -3.8 \text{ m/s}^2$, there is less of a pull on the person due to gravity, and hence the weight of the person on Mars is less.

NEWTON'S FIRST LAW OF MOTION

An object at rest remains at rest, and an object in motion remains in motion unless acted upon by an unbalanced force.

Newton's first law is also known as the **law of inertia**. **Inertia** is an object's resistance to motion. The more inertia an object has, the harder it is to move the object. Thus, the more mass an object has, the more inertia it has, and the harder it is for you to move that object.

EXAMPLE: When you are in a car driving down the highway going 65 mph, not only is the car going 65 mph, but you and everyone else in the car are also moving at a velocity of 65 mph. The car continues to move at a velocity of 65 mph. Now let's say that the driver runs into a telephone pole, bringing the car to a complete stop. The telephone pole stops the car, but what about the driver and passengers? The pole does not stop the driver and passengers, so they continue moving at 65 mph until something does stop them—usually the steering wheel and the windshield.

NEWTON'S SECOND LAW OF MOTION

The acceleration of an object is directly proportional to the net external force acting on the object, and inversely proportional to the object's mass.

In equation form, Newton's second law of motion can be expressed as

$$\Sigma \mathbf{F} = m\boldsymbol{a}$$

Force = (mass) (acceleration)

Force is measured in units of newtons (N), where $1 \text{ N} = 1 \text{ kg} \cdot \text{m/s}^2$. The Σ is the Greek capital letter sigma and signifies a sum. In this context, the sum of the forces equals an object's mass times its acceleration. If the sum of the forces acting on an object is 0, then the object is balanced and in **equilibrium**. Also, because force is a vector, this equation applies to forces acting along the x and y directions, or

$$\Sigma F_x = ma_x$$
$$\Sigma F_y = ma_y$$

EXAMPLE: Golf ball versus bowling ball: Which hits the ground first? When released from rest from the same height at the same time, which object will strike the ground first—the golf ball or the bowling ball? Any object released from rest and dropped is accelerated at a constant rate by gravity ($g = -9.8 \text{ m/s}^2$). Because g is constant, the force due to gravity is smaller for the golf ball because of the smaller mass of the golf ball in comparison to the bowling ball. In other words,

$$g = \frac{F_{\text{golf ball}}}{m_{\text{golf ball}}} = \frac{F_{\text{bowling ball}}}{m_{\text{bowling ball}}} = \text{constant}$$

21

CHAPTER 1:
Translational
Motion, Forces,
Work, Energy, and
Equilibrium in
Living Systems

Gravity exerts a greater pulling force on the greater mass such that its value remains constant. Therefore, neglecting air resistance, the golf ball and the bowling ball hit the ground at the same time.

NEWTON'S THIRD LAW OF MOTION

For every action force exerted on an object, there is an equal yet opposite reaction force exerted by the object.

This law is also known as the **law of action and reaction**.

EXAMPLE: A person who is standing exerts a force on the ground equal to his or her weight. The ground, in turn, exerts an equal yet opposite force on the person, supporting the weight of the person. The force exerted by the ground on the person is the normal force, as defined previously.

Free-Body Diagrams

An important technique used to solve problems involving forces acting on an object is free-body diagrams. A **free-body diagram** is a diagram in which an object is isolated, and all forces acting on the object are identified and represented on the diagram.

In creating free-body diagrams, you should:

➤ Isolate the object in an imaginary coordinate system in which the object represents the origin.

➤ Identify and represent all forces (with appropriate magnitude and direction) acting on the object.

➤ Resolve all forces in terms of their x and y components.

➤ Substitute into the appropriate Newton's second law of motion, either $\Sigma F_x = ma_x$ or $\Sigma F_y = ma_y$, setting the sum of all forces in each direction equal to ma if the object is accelerating and equal to 0 if the object is not accelerating.

➤ Solve for the unknown variable.

An example of using free-body diagrams to solve a problem is in the case where an object of mass m is stationary on a ramp with a coefficient of static friction μ_s and inclined at an angle θ, as shown in Figure 1-8.

The object is at rest on the inclined plane of $\theta = 30°$, and you are asked to determine the coefficient of static friction, μ_s, between the object and the inclined plane. The coordinate system is rotated such that the x-axis is now along the incline. As noted in the free-body diagram, there are three forces identified from the scenario: the weight of the object acting down (for which there is a component acting in the x direction and a component in the y direction), the normal force acting perpendicular to the inclined plane, and the frictional force that acts opposite to the direction of motion.

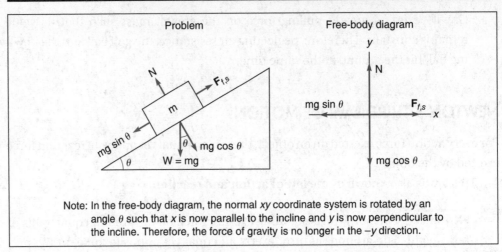

Note: In the free-body diagram, the normal xy coordinate system is rotated by an angle θ such that x is now parallel to the incline and y is now perpendicular to the incline. Therefore, the force of gravity is no longer in the $-y$ direction.

FIGURE 1-8 Example of a free-body diagram. *Source:* From George Hademenos, *Schaum's Outline of Physics for Pre-Med, Biology, and Allied Health Students,* McGraw-Hill, 1998; reproduced with permission of The McGraw-Hill Companies.

Substituting these forces into Newton's second law:

$$\Sigma F_x = ma_x \qquad\qquad \Sigma F_y = ma_y$$
$$\mathbf{F}_{f,s} - mg\sin\theta = 0 \qquad\qquad \mathbf{N} - mg\cos\theta = 0$$

By definition, the kinetic frictional force is $\mathbf{F}_{f,s} = \mu_s \mathbf{N}$, where $\mathbf{N}$ can be found from the forces acting in the y direction: $\mathbf{N} = mg\cos\theta$. So the frictional force is:

$$\mathbf{F}_{f,s} = \mu_s \mathbf{N} = \mu_s mg\cos\theta$$

Substituting this expression back into the equation for the forces acting in the x direction:

$$\mu_s\, mg\cos\theta - mg\sin\theta = 0$$

Eliminating mg and solving for μ_s:

$$\mu_s \cos\theta - \sin\theta = 0$$
$$\mu_s = \frac{\sin\theta}{\cos\theta} = \tan\theta = \tan 30° = 0.58$$

Examples of several common scenarios are presented in the following table:

TABLE 1-3

Scenario	Free-Body Diagram	Application of Newton's Second Law
An object in equilibrium lying on a level surface		Object is in equilibrium, thus $\Sigma \mathbf{F} = m\boldsymbol{a} = 0$ x component: None y component: $\Sigma F_y = m\,a_y = 0$ $N - W = 0$ $N = W = mg$

23

CHAPTER 1:
Translational
Motion, Forces,
Work, Energy, and
Equilibrium in
Living Systems

TABLE 1-3 (cont.)

Scenario	Free-Body Diagram	Application of Newton's Second Law
An object in equilibrium lying on an inclined surface with friction preventing motion	Note: f and N are actually applied at the surface.	Object is in equilibrium, thus $\Sigma \mathbf{F} = m\mathbf{a} = 0$ x component: $\Sigma F_x = ma_x = 0$ $-f + W\sin\theta = 0$ $f = W\sin\theta$ y component: $\Sigma F_y = ma_y = 0$ $N - W\cos\theta = 0$ $N = W\cos\theta$
An object in equilibrium suspended by a string		Object is in equilibrium, thus $\Sigma \mathbf{F} = m\mathbf{a} = 0$ x component: None y component: $\Sigma F_y = ma_y = 0$ $T - W = 0$ $T = W = mg$
An object in equilibrium suspended by two strings of unequal lengths	Note: Tension is **not** proportional to string length.	Object is in equilibrium, thus $\Sigma \mathbf{F} = m\mathbf{a} = 0$ x component: $\Sigma F_x = ma_x = 0$ $-T_1 \sin\theta_1 + T_2 \sin\theta_2 = 0$ $T_1 \sin\theta_1 = T_2 \sin\theta_2$ y component: $\Sigma F_y = ma_y = 0$ $T_1 \cos\theta_1 + T_2 \cos\theta_2 - W = 0$ $T_1 \cos\theta_1 + T_2 \cos\theta_2 = W$
An object is falling and subject to no friction		Object is in motion, thus $\Sigma \mathbf{F} = m\mathbf{a}$ x component: None y component: $\Sigma F_y = ma_y$ $-W(= mg) = ma_y$
An object is falling at constant (terminal) velocity		Object is in equilibrium, thus $\Sigma \mathbf{F} = m\mathbf{a} = 0$ x component: None y component: $\Sigma F_y = ma_y = 0$ $f - W = 0$ $f = W = mg$

Uniform Circular Motion and Centripetal Force

An object moving with constant speed in a circular path undergoes uniform circular motion. Because the object is moving at constant speed does not mean the object is not accelerating—in fact, it is. Although the magnitude of velocity (speed) is constant for an object in uniform circular motion, it is constantly changing direction. If the object is changing direction, it has a changing velocity and thus is accelerating. This acceleration, called **centripetal** (or center-seeking) **acceleration**, is perpendicular to the tangential velocity and is directed toward the center of rotation. The magnitude of centripetal acceleration, a_c, is defined as:

$$a_c = \frac{v^2}{r}$$

and has typical units of acceleration (m/s^2).

Because an object in uniform circular motion has mass and is accelerating, there is a force directed inward toward the center. It is referred to as the **centripetal force** (F_c) defined by:

$$F_c = ma_c = m\frac{v^2}{r}$$

A centripetal force is a vector quantity and has units of newtons.

Translational and Rotational Equilibrium

An object can be in either translational and/or rotational equilibrium, depending on the forces acting on the object. An object is in **translational equilibrium** when the sum of forces is equal to zero, or

$$\Sigma \mathbf{F} = 0$$

or

$$\Sigma F_x = 0, \qquad \Sigma F_y = 0$$

Another type of force, when exerted on an object, causes rotational motion. This type of force is referred to as **torque**, characterized by the symbol τ. It occurs when an external force acts at a given distance from a fixed pivot point (also known as a lever arm, r), as shown in Figure 1-9. Torque is defined as:

$$\text{Torque} = (\text{force})(\text{lever arm}) \sin \theta$$

$$\tau = \mathbf{F}r \sin \theta$$

where θ is the angle between the direction of the force and the direction of the lever arm. Because it is a rotational force, torque can also be expressed analogous to the translational force ($\mathbf{F} = m\mathbf{a}$) by

$$\tau = I\alpha$$

25

CHAPTER 1:
Translational
Motion, Forces,
Work, Energy, and
Equilibrium in
Living Systems

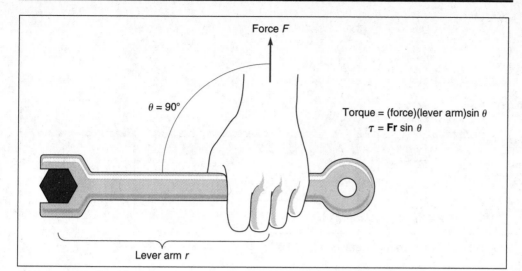

FIGURE 1-9 Torque.

where I is the moment of inertia or an object's resistance to rotational motion and α is the angular acceleration of the rotating object. Torque is a vector quantity with SI units of newton · meter (N · m).

Torque occurs as the result of the rotation of an object, and an object can rotate in either a clockwise or a counterclockwise direction, resulting in τ_{cw} and τ_{ccw}, respectively. To determine the direction of the torque, you must first identify an axis of rotation and the point where each external force acts on the object. Once each torque about the axis of rotation has been calculated, torque is positive if the force causes a counterclockwise rotation; torque is negative if the force causes a clockwise rotation. An object is in **rotational equilibrium** when the sum of torques or rotational forces about any point is equal to zero, or

$$\Sigma \tau = 0$$

or

$$\Sigma \tau_{cw} = \Sigma \tau_{ccw}$$

EXAMPLE: Suppose Tori of mass 42 kg and Cori of mass 70 kg join their sister Lori of mass 35 kg on a seesaw. If Tori and Lori are seated 2.0 and 3.5 m from the pivot, respectively, on the same side of the seesaw, where must Cori sit on the other side of the seesaw in order to balance it?

SOLUTION: The seesaw is in rotational equilibrium, defined by the equation $\Sigma \tau = 0$ or

$$\tau_{Tori} + \tau_{Lori} + \tau_{Cori} = 0$$

or

$$\tau_{Tori} + \tau_{Lori} = -\tau_{Cori}$$

Torque is given as $\tau = \mathbf{F}r \sin \theta$, where θ is 90° because the girls are exerting a force (equal to their weight) perpendicular to the level arm, as shown in Figure 1-10.

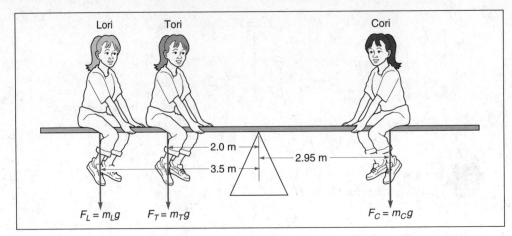

FIGURE 1-10 Seesaw in rotational equilibrium.

Thus,

$$(\mathbf{Fr})_{\text{Tori}} + (\mathbf{Fr})_{\text{Lori}} = -(\mathbf{Fr})_{\text{Cori}}$$

$$(42\text{ kg})(9.8\text{ m/s}^2)(2.0\text{ m}) + (35\text{ kg})(9.8\text{ m/s}^2)(3.5\text{ m})$$

$$= -(70\text{ kg})(9.8\text{ m/s}^2)(r_{\text{Cori}})$$

Solving for r_{Cori}

$$r_{\text{Cori}} = -2.95\text{ m}$$

with the minus sign indicating a position on the opposite side of the seesaw.

Translational and Rotational Motion

Translational motion, or the motion of an object caused by forces exerted in the direction of motion, has already been described through Newton's three laws of motion. These laws of motion can also be extended to describe the **rotational motion** of an object, as noted here:

TABLE 1-4

	Translational Motion	**Rotational Motion**
Newton's First Law	An object at rest or in motion remains at rest or in motion unless acted upon by an unbalanced force.	A body in rotational motion will continue its rotation until acted upon by an unbalanced torque.
Newton's Second Law	The magnitude of force is equal to the product of an object's mass and its acceleration or $F = ma$.	The magnitude of a torque is equal to the product of an object's moment of inertia and its angular acceleration or $\tau = I\alpha$.
Newton's Third Law	For every action force acting on an object, there is a reaction force exerted by the object equal in magnitude and opposite in direction to the original force.	For every torque acting on an object, there is another torque exerted by the object equal in magnitude and opposite in direction to the original torque.

WORK, ENERGY, AND POWER

27

CHAPTER 1:
Translational
Motion, Forces,
Work, Energy, and
Equilibrium in
Living Systems

A force applied to an object results in an acceleration of the object in the direction of the force. This is explained by Newton's second law and, in effect, explains why the object is set into motion. How the object responds to this force, ultimately resulting in motion, is the basis for this section.

Work

Work represents the physical effects of an external force applied to an object that results in a net displacement in the direction of the force. Work is a scalar quantity and is expressed in SI units of joules (J) or newton meters (N · m).

By definition, the work done by a constant force acting on a body is equal to the product of the force **F** and the displacement **d** that occurs as a direct result of the force, provided that **F** and **d** are in the same direction. Thus

$$W = Fd$$

Work = (force)(displacement)

If **F** and **d** are not parallel but **F** is at some angle θ with respect to **d**, then

$$W = Fd\cos\theta$$

because it is only the portion of the force acting in the direction of motion that causes the object to move its displacement **d**. When the entire force is exerted on an object parallel to its direction of motion, then $\theta = 0°$, and thus $\cos 0° = 1$. This in turn results in the formula **W = Fd** (when **F** is parallel to **d**). When **F** is perpendicular to **d**, $\theta = 90°$ and $\cos 90° = 0$. No work is done in this case.

EXAMPLE: Calculate the work done by a mother who exerts a force of 75 N at an angle of 25° below the horizontal (*x*-axis) in pushing a baby in a carriage a distance of 20 meters (m).

SOLUTION: The given information in this problem includes:

$\mathbf{F} = 75\text{ N}$ $\theta = -25°$ $\mathbf{d} = 20\text{ m}$

Substituting this given information into the equation $W = Fd\cos\theta$ yields

$$W = Fd\cos\theta = (75\text{ N})(20\text{ m})\left[\cos(-25°)\right] = 1360\text{ J}$$

EXAMPLE: Work can also be done in stretching a spring. **Hooke's law** describes the force required to stretch a spring by a displacement x and is represented by the equation:

$$F = -kx$$

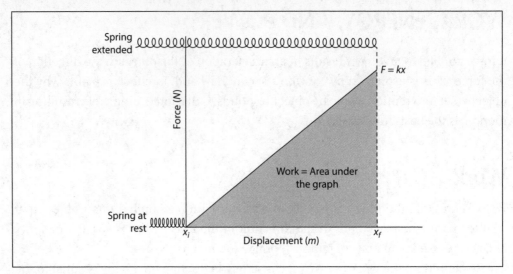

FIGURE 1-11 Work done in stretching a spring.

where k is the spring constant of a spring or the amount of force required to stretch or compress a spring by a defined displacement x. The minus sign corresponds to the opposite direction of the elastic force exerted by a spring in its tendency to return to its normal, unstretched state in response to a stretching force. Since the stretching of a spring requires the application of an external stretching force to pull the spring by a displacement x, work is done in stretching a spring as shown in Figure 1-11.

The work done in stretching a spring can be determined by calculating the area under the graph, which is represented by a triangle of base, x, and height, F. Given that x_i is 0 since the spring position is assumed to be at rest:

$$\text{Area} = \frac{1}{2}(\text{base}) \times (\text{height}) = \frac{1}{2}(x_f) \times (F) = \frac{1}{2}(x_f) \times (kx_f) = \frac{1}{2}kx_f^2 = \frac{1}{2}kx^2$$

$$\text{Area} = \text{work done in stretching spring} = \frac{1}{2}kx^2$$

Pulley Systems

Simple machines are devices that allow people to make work easier by changing the direction of the force applied to the load. One type of simple machine is the **pulley**, which consists of a rope threaded through a groove within the rim of a wheel. As the user applies a force (effort) to one end of a rope threaded over a pulley moving the string a certain distance (effort distance), the other end of the pulley containing the attached load is moved a certain distance (load distance). The pulley reduces the amount of force required to move a load over a given distance. This effect is magnified with the number of pulleys in a pulley system. As the number of pulleys and supporting ropes

29

CHAPTER 1:
Translational
Motion, Forces,
Work, Energy, and
Equilibrium in
Living Systems

increases for a pulley system, a smaller amount of force is required, although the user must pull the rope over a greater distance.

Two terms that describe the capability of a pulley are its mechanical advantage and its efficiency. The **mechanical advantage**, MA, of a pulley is the amount by which the force required to move a load is reduced. It is described by:

$$MA = \frac{F_{out}}{F_{in}}$$

where F_{out} is the output force (force exerted by the pulley system on the load) and F_{in} is the input force (force exerted on the pulley system by the person/machine).

The **efficiency** of a pulley is the ratio comparing the magnitude of the work output, W_{out}, relative to the work input, W_{in}, or

$$\text{Efficiency} = \frac{W_{out}}{W_{in}} = \frac{F_{out}\, d_{out}}{F_{in}\, d_{in}}$$

EXAMPLE: Two movers who are using a pulley system to lift a dining table of mass 230 kilograms (kg) by a distance of 3.5 m exert a force of 750 N. If the pulley system has an efficiency of 72%, determine the length of rope that must be pulled to accomplish the move.

SOLUTION: The equation needed to solve this problem is:

$$\text{Efficiency} = \frac{W_{out}}{W_{in}} = \frac{F_{out}d_{out}}{F_{in}d_{in}}$$

where d_{in} represents the unknown quantity. The force exerted by the pulley system on the dining table is equal to the weight of the dining room table, or

$$F_{out} = \text{weight of the table} = m_{table}g$$

Therefore,

$$d_{in} = \frac{F_{out}d_{out}}{F_{in}(\text{efficiency})} = \frac{(230\ \text{kg})\left(9.81\ \dfrac{\text{m}}{\text{s}^2}\right)(3.5\ \text{m})}{(750\ \text{N})(0.72)} = 14.6\ \text{m}$$

Work Done by Gases

The physical concept of work can also be applied to gases. Consider Figure 1-12, where a piston is moving in a sealed, gas-filled cylindrical chamber.

As heat is applied to the chamber, the thermal energy of the heat source is transferred to the kinetic energy of the atoms of the gas. This causes expansion of the volume of the gas, which in turn does work on the piston, causing it to be displaced by Δy. The result is work done by a gas on a system (in this case, a piston). Using the following

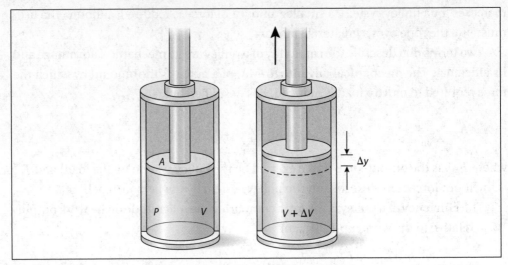

FIGURE 1-12 Piston moving in a sealed, gas-filled cylindrical chamber.

equations:

$$\text{work} = \text{force} \times \text{displacement} \qquad W = F \times d = F \times \Delta y$$

$$\text{pressure} = \frac{\text{force}}{\text{area}} \qquad P = \frac{F}{A} \quad \text{or} \quad F = P \times A$$

then,

$$W = F \times \Delta y = (P \times A) \times \Delta y = P \times (A \times \Delta y) = P\Delta V$$

The work done by the gas on the system is the area under the $P\Delta V$ curve. For the work done by the gas on the piston noted previously, the $P\Delta V$ graph and the calculated work would look like Figure 1-13.

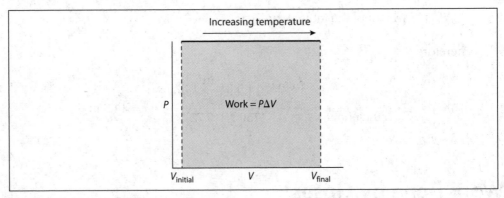

FIGURE 1-13 Work done by the gas on the piston.

Mechanical Energy: Kinetic and Potential

Work describes the effect of a force exerted on an object, causing the object to move a given displacement. Work is performed on a continual basis by athletes when they throw, hit, or kick objects; by children when they slide down a slide, swing on a swing,

31

CHAPTER 1:
Translational
Motion, Forces,
Work, Energy, and
Equilibrium in
Living Systems

or jump off a jungle gym; and by cars when they drive down the road. What is it that allows athletes, children, or cars to perform work? The answer is energy. Energy exists in many different forms, such as mechanical energy, solar energy (energy provided by the sun), chemical energy (energy provided by chemical reactions), elastic potential energy (energy provided by elastic objects such as a spring or rubber band), thermal energy (energy provided as a result of a temperature difference), sound energy (energy transmitted by propagating sound waves), radiant energy (energy transmitted by light waves), electric energy, magnetic energy, atomic energy, and nuclear energy.

Energy is a property that enables an object to do work. In fact, **energy** is defined as the ability of an object to do work. The more energy an object has, the more work the object can perform. The unit of measure for energy is the same as that for work, namely the joule. The next form of energy we discuss is mechanical energy, which exists in two types: kinetic energy and potential energy.

Kinetic energy is the energy of a body that is in motion. If the body's mass is m and its velocity is v, its kinetic energy is:

Kinetic energy (KE) $= \dfrac{1}{2}mv^2$

EXAMPLE: Determine the kinetic energy of a 1500-kg car that is moving with a velocity of 30 m/s.

SOLUTION:

$$\text{KE} = \frac{1}{2}mv^2 = \frac{1}{2}(1500 \text{ kg})(30 \text{ m/s})^2 = 6.75 \times 10^5 \text{ J}$$

The energy that is stored within a body because of its location above the Earth's surface (or reference level) is called **gravitational potential energy**. The gravitational potential energy of a body of mass m at a height h above a given reference level is:

Gravitational potential energy (GPE) $= mgh$

where g is the acceleration due to gravity. Gravitational potential energy depends on the object's mass and location (height above a level surface), but does not depend on how it reaches this height. In other words, gravitational potential energy is path independent. Any force, such as the force due to gravity, that performs work on an object independent of the object's path of motion is termed a **conservative force**.

EXAMPLE: A 4.5-kg book is held 80 centimeters (cm) above a table whose top is 1.2 m above the floor. Determine the gravitational potential energy of the book (1) with respect to the table and (2) with respect to the floor.

SOLUTION:

1. Here, $h = 80 \text{ cm} = 0.8 \text{ m}$, so

$$\text{GPE} = mgh = (4.5 \text{ kg})(9.8 \text{ m/s}^2)(0.8 \text{ m}) = 35.3 \text{ J}$$

2. The book is $h = 0.8 \text{ m} + 1.2 \text{ m} = 2.0 \text{ m}$ above the floor, so its GPE with respect to the floor is:

$$\text{GPE} = mgh = (4.5 \text{ kg})(9.8 \text{ m/s}^2)(2.0 \text{ m}) = 88.2 \text{ J}$$

Work–Kinetic Energy Theorem

Work and energy are interrelated quantities. Energy is the ability to do work, and work can only be done if energy is present. A moving object has kinetic energy and maintains the same kinetic energy if it proceeds at the same speed. However, if the object speeds up or slows down, work is required. The net work required to change the kinetic energy of an object is given by the **work–kinetic energy theorem**:

Net work = change in kinetic energy

$$W_{\text{net}} = \Delta\text{KE}$$

Conservative Versus Nonconservative Forces

The forces mentioned earlier in this chapter are all similar in that they represent a push or a pull and can be expressed in units of Newtons. However, they differ in one respect—forces can be conservative or nonconservative. A **conservative force** describes a force that does work on an object independent of its path of motion between its initial and final positions. An example of a conservative force is the gravitational force. If one lifts a book from the floor (Position A) to a height corresponding to a point directly above the floor (Position B), negative work is being done against the force of gravity. At that point (Position B) above the floor, the work done in raising the book was transferred into gravitational potential energy. The book would have the same amount of gravitational potential energy at Position B, regardless of its path to get to Position B. If the book is then released from Position B, gravity does positive work as the book's gravitational potential energy is transferred into kinetic energy as it falls to the ground. Other examples of conservative forces include the elastic force exerted by a spring and the electric force.

A **nonconservative force** describes a force that does work on an object dependent on its path of motion between its initial and final positions. An example of a nonconservative force is friction. Consider, for example, a book that is pushed across a floor. Friction acts on the book, performing negative work from its initial pushing point (Position A) to the final resting point (Position B). If a greater push is exerted on the book, the book moves a greater distance and hence friction acts on the book for a greater amount of time. In other words, the work done by friction on the moving book depends on the path of the book. Other examples of nonconservative forces include tension, normal force, and air resistance.

33

CHAPTER 1:
Translational
Motion, Forces,
Work, Energy, and
Equilibrium in
Living Systems

Conservation of Energy

Energy is a conserved quantity. According to the **law of conservation of energy**, energy can neither be created nor destroyed, only transformed from one kind to another. Examples of this law can be found in many instances in nature, including the physiology of the human body and the working principles of a car. Consider a child on a swing. At the highest point of the arc, the child's energy is exclusively gravitational potential energy, because the child is not moving. As the child then begins moving downward toward the bottom of the arc, the gravitational potential energy of the child is transformed into kinetic energy. At the bottom point of the arc, the child's energy is exclusively kinetic energy.

In general, the initial mechanical energy (sum of potential energy and kinetic energy before an interaction) is equal to the final mechanical energy (sum of potential energy and kinetic energy after an interaction), or

Initial mechanical energy = final mechanical energy

$$\left(PE_{initial} + KE_{initial}\right) = \left(PE_{final} + KE_{final}\right)$$

EXAMPLE: A child of mass 25.0 kg is at the top of a slide that is 3.8 m high. What is the child's velocity at the bottom of the slide? (Ignore the effects of friction).

SOLUTION: The child's velocity v at the bottom of the slide can be determined from the law of conservation of energy. The gravitational potential energy of the child at the top of the slide is transformed into kinetic energy at the bottom of the slide.

$$GPE_{initial} = KE_{final}$$

or, simplifying,

$$mgh = \frac{1}{2}mv^2$$

Solving for v

$$v = \sqrt{2gh} = \sqrt{(2)\left(9.8 \text{ m/s}^2\right)(3.8 \text{ m})} = \sqrt{74.5} \text{ m/s} = 8.6 \text{ m/s}$$

Power

Power is the rate at which work is done by a force. Thus,

$$P = \frac{W}{t}$$
$$\text{power} = \frac{\text{work}}{\text{time}}$$

The more power something has, the more work it can perform in a given time. The SI unit for power is the **watt**, where 1 watt (W) = 1 joule/second (J/s).

When a constant force **F** does work on a body that is moving at constant velocity *v*, and if **F** is parallel to *v*, the power involved is

$$P = \frac{W}{t} = \frac{Fd}{t} = F\left(\frac{d}{t}\right) = Fv$$

because $d/t = v$, that is,

$$P = Fv$$

power = (force)(velocity)

EXAMPLE: As part of an exercise activity, a 60-kg student climbs up a 7.5-m rope in 11.6 s. What is the power output of the student?

SOLUTION: The problem can be solved with the following equation:

$$P = \frac{W}{t} = \frac{Fd}{t} = \frac{mgh}{t} = \frac{(60 \text{ kg})\left(9.8 \text{ m/s}^2\right)(7.5 \text{ m})}{11.6 \text{ s}} = 380 \text{ W}$$

Importance of Fluids for the Circulation of Blood, Gas Movement, and Gas Exchange

Read This Chapter to Learn About

➤ Fluids at Rest

➤ Fluids in Motion

➤ Circulatory System

➤ Gases

This chapter reviews an important topic of physics: fluids. **Fluids** is a term that describes any substance that flows—a characteristic of both liquids and gases. Fluids possess inertia, as defined by their density, and are thus subject to the same physical interactions as solids. All of these interactions as they pertain to fluids at rest and fluids in motion as well as practical examples related to human physiology are discussed in this chapter.

FLUIDS AT REST

Density and Specific Gravity

Density, ρ, is a physical property of a fluid, given as mass per unit volume, or

$$\rho = \frac{\text{mass}}{\text{unit volume}} = \frac{m}{V}$$

Density represents the fluid equivalent of mass and is given in units of kilograms per cubic meter $\left(\dfrac{kg}{m^3}\right)$, grams per cubic centimeter $\left(\dfrac{g}{cm^3}\right)$, or grams per milliliter $\left(\dfrac{g}{mL}\right)$. Density, a property unique to each substance, is independent of shape or quantity but is dependent on temperature and pressure.

Specific gravity (Sp. gr.) of a given substance is the ratio of the density of the substance ρ_{sub} to the density of water ρ_w, or

$$\text{Sp. gr.} = \frac{\text{density of substance}}{\text{density of water}} = \frac{\rho_{sub}}{\rho_w}$$

where the density of water ρ_w is 1.0 g/cm^3 or 1.0×10^3 kg/m^3. Assuming that equal volumes are chosen, the specific gravity can also be expressed in terms of weight:

$$\text{Sp. gr.} = \frac{\text{weight of substance}}{\text{weight of water}} = \frac{w_{sub}}{w_w}$$

Specific gravity is a pure number that is unitless.

EXAMPLE: Determine the size of container needed to hold 0.7 g of a chemical substance, which has a density of 0.62 g/cm^3.

SOLUTION: The volume of a fluid can be found from the relation for density:

$$V = \frac{m}{\rho} = \frac{0.7\,\text{g}}{0.62\,\dfrac{\text{g}}{\text{cm}^3}} = 1.129\,\text{cm}^3 = 1.129\,\text{mL}$$

Buoyant Force and Archimedes' Principle

Archimedes' principle states: "A body immersed wholly or partially in a fluid is subjected to a **buoyant force** that is equal in magnitude to the weight of the fluid displaced by the body," or

buoyant force = weight of displaced fluid

If the buoyant force is equal to or greater than the weight of the object, then the object remains afloat. However, if the buoyant force is less than the weight of the object, then the object sinks.

But how would you calculate the weight of displaced fluid in a practical scenario? Let's say that you place an object in a graduated cylinder filled with 40 mL of water and, as a result, the water level rises to 44 mL. Placement of the object into the graduated cylinder caused a change in volume of 4 mL. The mass of the displaced fluid can be determined by the equation for density: $\rho = \dfrac{m}{V}$ or $m = \rho V$.

Apply this equation to the problem, $m = \rho V = \left(1.00\,\dfrac{\text{g}}{\text{cm}^3}\right)(4\,\text{cm}^3) = 4.0\,\text{g}$.

The weight of the displaced fluid can be determined by $W = mg = (0.004\,\text{kg})\left(9.8\,\dfrac{\text{m}}{\text{s}^2}\right) = 0.0392\,\text{N}$.

EXAMPLE: A humpback whale weighs 5.4×10^5 N. Determine the buoyant force required to support the whale in its natural habitat, the ocean, when it is completely submerged. Assume that the density of seawater is 1030 kg/m^3 and the density of the whale ρ_{whale} is approximately equal to the density of water (ρ_{water} = 1000 kg/m^3).

SOLUTION: The volume of the whale can be determined from:

$$m = \rho V = \frac{W}{g}$$

Solving for V yields

$$V_{\text{whale}} = \frac{W_{\text{whale}}}{\rho_{\text{whale}}g} = \frac{5.4 \times 10^5 \text{ N}}{\left(1000 \, \frac{\text{kg}}{\text{m}^3}\right)\left(9.8 \, \frac{\text{m}}{\text{s}^2}\right)} = 55.1 \text{ m}^3$$

The whale displaces 55.1 m^3 of water when submerged. Therefore, the buoyant force BF, which is equal to the weight of displaced water, is given by:

$$\text{BF} = W_{\text{seawater}} = \rho_{\text{seawater}} \, g V_{\text{whale}} = \left(1030 \, \frac{\text{kg}}{\text{m}^3}\right)\left(9.8 \, \frac{\text{m}}{\text{s}^2}\right)\left(55.1 \text{ m}^3\right)$$

$$= 5.6 \times 10^5 \text{ N}$$

Pressure: Atmospheric and Hydrostatic

Pressure P is defined as a force F acting perpendicular to a surface area, A, of an object and is given by:

$$\text{pressure} = \frac{\text{force}}{\text{area}} = \frac{F}{A}$$

Pressure is a scalar quantity and is expressed in units of $\frac{\text{N}}{\text{m}^2}$. Two specific types of pressure particularly applicable to fluids include atmospheric pressure and hydrostatic pressure.

Atmospheric pressure P_{atm} represents the average pressure exerted by Earth's atmosphere, and is defined numerically as 1 atm but can also be expressed as 760 millimeters of mercury (mmHg) or 1.01×10^5 pascals (Pa).

Hydrostatic pressure P_{hyd} is the fluid pressure exerted on an object at a depth h in a fluid of density ρ and is given by:

$$P_{\text{hyd}} = \rho g h$$

The total pressure, P, exerted on an object within a contained fluid is the sum of the atmospheric pressure and the hydrostatic pressure:

$$P = P_{\text{atm}} + P_{\text{hyd}} = P_{\text{atm}} + \rho g h$$

EXAMPLE: Given that the density of water is $1.0 \frac{\text{g}}{\text{cm}^3}$, what is the pressure exerted on a swimmer in a swimming pool at a depth of 180 cm? (atmospheric pressure = $1.013 \times 10^5 \frac{\text{N}}{\text{m}}$)

SOLUTION: The pressure exerted on a swimmer at a certain depth within a swimming pool depends on the atmospheric pressure as well as the hydrostatic pressure due to the water above the depth in question. The total pressure exerted on the swimmer at a depth of 180 cm, or 1.8 m, is:

$$P_{\text{total}} = P_{\text{atm}} + P_{\text{hyd}} = P_{\text{atm}} + \rho g h$$

where ρ is the density of water, g is the acceleration due to gravity, and h is the height (or depth) of the column of water.

$$P_{\text{total}} = P_{\text{atm}} + P_{\text{hyd}} = \left(1.013 \times 10^5 \, \frac{\text{N}}{\text{m}^2}\right) + \left(1000 \, \frac{\text{kg}}{\text{m}^3}\right)\left(9.8 \, \frac{\text{m}}{\text{s}^2}\right)(1.8 \, \text{m})$$

$$= 1.19 \times 10^5 \, \frac{\text{N}}{\text{m}^2}$$

Pascal's Principle

Pascal's principle states: "An external pressure applied to a confined fluid will be transmitted equally to all points within the fluid."

EXAMPLE: An example of Pascal's principle is the hydraulic jack, shown in Figure 2-1. If a force of 300 N is applied to a piston of 1-cm^2 cross-sectional area, determine the lifting force transmitted to a piston of cross-sectional area of 100 cm^2.

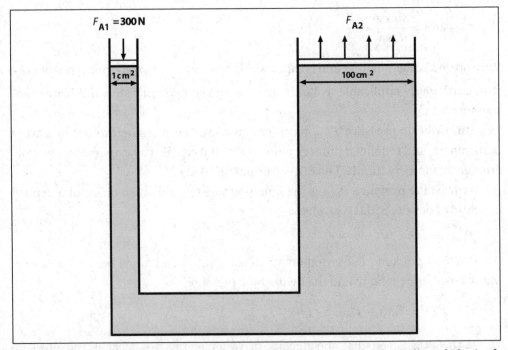

FIGURE 2-1 Hydraulic jack. *Source:* From George Hademenos, *Schaum's Outline of Physics for Pre-Med, Biology, and Allied Health Students*, McGraw-Hill, 1998; reproduced with permission of The McGraw-Hill Companies.

39

CHAPTER 2:
Importance of Fluids
for the Circulation
of Blood,
Gas Movement, and
Gas Exchange

SOLUTION: According to Pascal's principle,

$$P_{1\,cm^2} = P_{100\,cm^2}$$

$$\left(\frac{F}{A}\right)_{1\,cm^2} = \left(\frac{F}{A}\right)_{100\,cm^2}$$

Making the appropriate substitutions yields

$$\frac{300\,N}{1\,cm^2} = \frac{F}{100\,cm^2}$$

Solving for F yields

$$F = 30{,}000\,N$$

FLUIDS IN MOTION

Viscosity and Poiseuille's Law

Viscosity η is a measurement of the resistance or frictional force exerted by a fluid in motion. The SI unit of viscosity is newton seconds per square meter $\left(\dfrac{N \cdot s}{m^2}\right)$. Viscosity is typically expressed in units of poise (P), where

$$1\ \text{poise} = 0.1\frac{N \cdot s}{m^2}$$

Fluid flow, Q, through a rigid, cylindrical tube of radius r and length L subjected to a constant external pressure gradient ΔP can be expressed as:

$$Q = \frac{\pi}{8}\frac{\Delta P r^4}{L\eta}$$

where η is fluid viscosity. This equation is known as **Poiseuille's law**. Fluid flow Q is the rate of volume flow through a pipe and is typically expressed in units of $\dfrac{cm^3}{s}$.

EXAMPLE: Determine the change in fluid flow for (1) a decrease in the pressure gradient by one-half, (2) an increase in viscosity by 2, (3) a decrease in vessel length by one-half, and (4) an increase in vessel radius by 2.

SOLUTION: The effect of the various parameters on fluid flow can be determined by analysis of their qualitative dependence according to Poiseuille's law:

$$Q = \frac{\pi}{8}\frac{\Delta P r^4}{L\eta}$$

1. Fluid flow Q is directly dependent on the pressure gradient ΔP. Thus a decrease in pressure gradient by one-half implies:

$$\Delta P = \frac{\Delta P}{2}$$

Substituting into Poiseuille's law gives:

$$Q = \frac{\pi}{8} \frac{(\Delta P/2)r^4}{L\eta} = \frac{1}{2}\left(\frac{\pi}{8}\frac{\Delta Pr^4}{L\eta}\right) = \frac{Q}{2}$$

Thus a decrease in pressure gradient by one-half results in a decrease in fluid flow by one-half.

2. Fluid flow Q is inversely dependent on the fluid viscosity η. Thus an increase in fluid viscosity by 2 implies:

$$\eta = 2\eta$$

Substituting into Poiseuille's law, you have:

$$Q = \frac{\pi}{8}\frac{\Delta Pr^4}{L(2\eta)} = \frac{1}{2}\left(\frac{\pi}{8}\frac{\Delta Pr^4}{L\eta}\right) = \frac{Q}{2}$$

Thus an increase in fluid viscosity by 2 results in a decrease in fluid flow by one-half.

3. Fluid flow Q is inversely dependent on the vessel length L. Thus a decrease in vessel length by one-half implies:

$$L = \frac{L}{2}$$

Substituting into Poiseuille's law yields:

$$Q = \frac{\pi}{8}\frac{\Delta Pr^4}{(L/2)\eta} = 2\left(\frac{\pi}{8}\frac{\Delta Pr^4}{L\eta}\right) = 2Q$$

Thus a decrease in vessel length by one-half results in an increase in fluid flow by 2.

4. Fluid flow Q is dependent on the vessel radius r to the fourth power. Thus an increase in vessel radius by 2 implies:

$$r = (2r)^4 = 16r^4$$

Substituting into Poiseuille's law, you find:

$$Q = \frac{\pi}{8}\frac{\Delta P(2r)^4}{L\eta} = 16\left(\frac{\pi}{8}\frac{\Delta Pr^4}{L\eta}\right) = 16Q$$

Thus an increase in vessel radius by 2 results in an increase in fluid flow by 16.

Continuity Equation

The **equation of continuity** is, in essence, an expression of the conservation of mass for a moving fluid. Specifically, the equation of continuity states that: (1) a fluid maintains constant density regardless of changes in pressure and temperature, and (2) flow measured at one point along a vessel is equal to the flow at another point along the vessel, regardless of the cross-sectional area of the vessel. Fluid flow Q, expressed in

41

CHAPTER 2:
Importance of Fluids
for the Circulation
of Blood,
Gas Movement, and
Gas Exchange

terms of the cross-sectional area of the vessel A, is given as:

$$Q = Av$$

where v is the velocity of the fluid. Thus the equation of continuity at any two points in a vessel is given as:

$$Q = A_1 v_1 = A_2 v_2 = \text{constant}$$

Laminar and Turbulent Flow

Fluid flow can be characterized according to two different types of flow: laminar flow and turbulent flow. Consider a fluid with density ρ and viscosity η flowing through a tube of diameter d. In **laminar flow,** the fluid flows as continuous layers stacked on one another within a smooth tube and moving past one another with some velocity. However, as the velocity of the fluid increases, fluid particles fluctuate between these ordered layers, causing random motion. When the fluid's velocity exceeds a threshold known as the critical velocity, it now is described as **turbulent flow.** The critical velocity depends on the parameters of the fluid and the vessel according to the relation

$$v = \frac{\eta \text{Re}}{\rho d}$$

where Re is a dimensionless quantity known as the **Reynold's number**.

Surface Tension

Surface tension γ is the tension, or force per unit length, generated by cohesive forces of molecules on the surface of a liquid acting toward the interior. Surface tension is given as force per unit length and defined as the ratio of the surface force F to the length d along which the force acts, or

$$\gamma = \frac{F}{d}$$

Surface tension is given in units of $\frac{\text{N}}{\text{m}}$.

Bernoulli's Principle

Bernoulli's principle, the fluid equivalent of conservation of energy, states that the energy of fluid flow through a rigid vessel by a pressure gradient is equal to the sum of the pressure energy, kinetic energy, and the gravitational potential energy, or

$$E_{\text{tot}} = P + \frac{1}{2}\rho v^2 + \rho g h = \text{constant}$$

An important application of Bernoulli's principle involves fluid flow through a vessel with a region of expansion or contraction. Bernoulli's principle describing fluid flow through a vessel with sudden changes in geometry can be expressed as:

$$\left(P + \frac{1}{2}\rho v^2 + \rho gh \right)_1 = \left(P + \frac{1}{2}\rho v^2 + \rho gh \right)_2$$

where 1 describes the energy of fluid flow in the normal region of the vessel and 2 describes the energy of fluid flow in the enlarged or obstructed region. An illustration of these two different scenarios of Bernoulli's principle as applied to vessel disease is seen in Figures 2-2 and 2-3. Note that Bernoulli's principle assumes a smooth transition between the two regions within a vessel with no turbulence in fluid flow. However, in the practical applications depicted in Figures 2-2 and 2-3, there is turbulence noted in Figure 2-2 about the expansion of the blood vessel, and in Figure 2-3 about the surface of the atherosclerotic plaque. Nevertheless, in many cases the vessel expansion in Figure 2-2 and the atherosclerotic plaque in Figure 2-3 are not significantly pronounced, so Bernoulli's principle can still be applied to these scenarios.

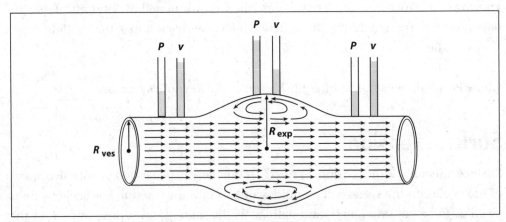

FIGURE 2-2 Bernoulli's principle as applied to the expansion of a blood vessel. *Source:* From George Hademenos, *Schaum's Outline of Physics for Pre-Med, Biology, and Allied Health Students,* McGraw-Hill, 1998; reproduced with permission of The McGraw-Hill Companies.

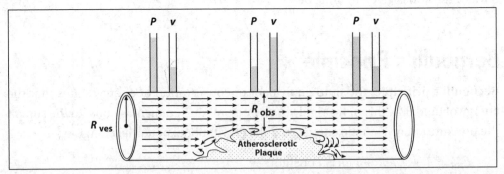

FIGURE 2-3 Bernoulli's principle as applied to an obstruction within a blood vessel. *Source:* From George Hademenos, *Schaum's Outline of Physics for Pre-Med, Biology, and Allied Health Students,* McGraw-Hill, 1998; reproduced with permission of The McGraw-Hill Companies.

43

CHAPTER 2:
Importance of Fluids
for the Circulation
of Blood,
Gas Movement, and
Gas Exchange

APPLICATIONS OF BERNOULLI'S PRINCIPLE: VENTURI EFFECT AND THE PITOT TUBE

Two extensions involving the application of Bernoulli's principle are the Venturi effect and the pitot tube.

The **Venturi effect** can be seen through the working principles of a Venturi meter. A **Venturi meter**, shown in Figure 2-4, is a device that measures fluid flow through a pipe. As the fluid of density ρ moves from the entrance of the pipe with a known cross-sectional area A_1, the fluid's pressure P_1 is at its maximum (causing a greater push and reduced height of the fluid in the U-tube attachment) and its velocity, v, is at its minimum. As the fluid continues through the pipe and encounters a constriction, the cross-sectional area at the narrowed region A_2 is decreased, the velocity increases, causing the fluid's pressure, P_2, to decrease, resulting in an increase in the height of the fluid in the U-tube attachment. The fluid's flow velocity through the constriction of the pipe, v_2, can be determined from the relationship:

$$v_2 = \sqrt{\frac{2g\left(h_1 - h_2\right)}{1 - \left(\dfrac{A_2}{A_1}\right)^2}}$$

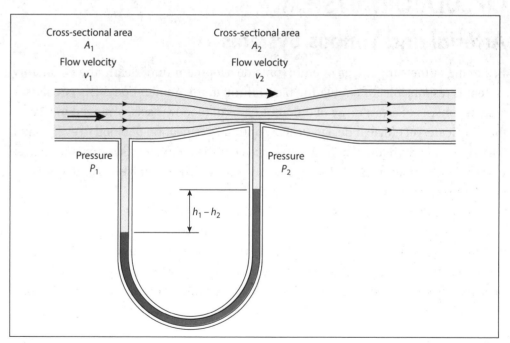

FIGURE 2-4 Venturi meter.

A **pitot tube** is an L-shaped, tubular device used to measure the velocity of airflow through a pipe. The pitot tube has two small holes—one hole is aligned parallel to the direction of the movement of air and is used to measure the stagnation pressure of the airflow. The second hole is located on the side of the parallel portion of the tube

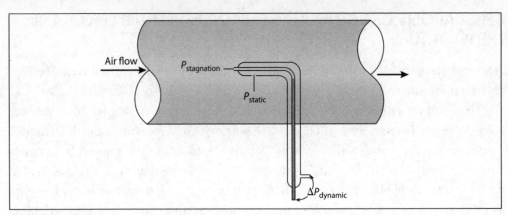

FIGURE 2-5 Pitot tube.

and used to measure the static pressure at that location relative to the airflow. The difference between the stagnation and static pressure values, $\Delta P_{\text{dynamic}}$, recorded at the end of the perpendicular segment of the pitot tube provides a measure of the dynamic pressure, which can then be used to calculate the velocity of airflow using Bernoulli's equation. See Figure 2-5.

CIRCULATORY SYSTEM
Arterial and Venous Systems

Beginning at the early stages of embryonic development until death, the circulatory system is responsible for circulating blood through the human body. The circulatory system consists of a vast array of different types of blood vessels, arranged in a complex, intricate, yet efficient design to allow optimal permeation of blood to every point within the human body. The primary purpose of the circulatory system is to deliver oxygen and nutrients to all of the organs and tissues of the human body and to remove cellular metabolic waste products within the body.

The circulatory system is composed primarily of three types of blood vessels: arteries, veins, and capillaries. **Arteries** transport oxygen-rich blood from the heart under high pressure to beds of **capillary vessels** embedded in tissues and organs of the human body. The role of the **veins** is the exact opposite of arteries in that they transport oxygen-poor blood away from the capillary bed under low pressure and return to the heart.

Pressure and Blood Flow Characteristics of the Circulatory System

Blood is pumped from the left ventricle of the heart into the aorta under a pressure of approximately 120 mm Hg (see Figure 2-6.) As blood moves farther into the circulatory

45

CHAPTER 2:
Importance of Fluids
for the Circulation
of Blood,
Gas Movement, and
Gas Exchange

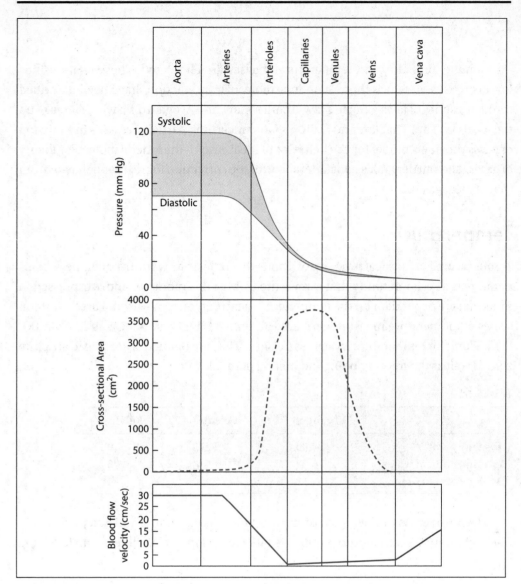

FIGURE 2-6 Pressure and blood flow throughout the human circulatory system.

system, the pressures start to decline steadily. From the aorta, blood flows through the larger arteries at 110 mm Hg, through the medium-sized arteries at 75 mm Hg, and through the smaller arteries or arterioles at 40 mm Hg until it reaches the capillary bed. Blood enters the capillary bed under a pressure of about 30 mm Hg and exits under a pressure of 16 mm Hg. Blood drains from the capillary bed into the smallest veins or venules at 16 mm Hg, continuing into the medium-sized veins under a pressure of 12 mm Hg and into the large veins at 4 mm Hg before returning to the heart.

Velocity of blood flow as blood exits the heart is approximately 30 cm/s and drops to 0.07 cm/s as it moves through the capillary vessels. In the large veins, blood flow maintains a speed of about 10 cm/s. The variation of pressure and blood flow velocity throughout the entire circulatory system is described in Figure 2-6.

GASES

The volume, pressure, and temperature of gases are all related. These relationships for ideal gases, in which there is no intermolecular interaction, have been described through a series of laws—Boyle's law, Charles's law, and Avogadro's law—that make up the Ideal Gas Law. That law and Dalton's law concerning partial pressures in a mixture of gases provide a model for the behavior of ideal gases—the kinetic molecular theory of gases. The van der Waals constants allow for the correction for real gas behavior from that of ideal gases.

Temperature

Temperature is a physical property of a body that reflects its warmth or coldness. Temperature is a scalar quantity that is measured with a thermometer and is expressed in units that are dependent on the temperature measurement scale used. Three common scales of temperature measurement are Fahrenheit (°F), Celsius (°C), and Kelvin (K). (The SI unit for temperature is degrees Celsius.) They are defined according to absolute zero as well as the freezing point and boiling point of water:

TABLE 2-1

	Fahrenheit (°F)	Celsius (°C)	Kelvin (K)
Absolute zero	−460	−273	0
Freezing point of water	32	0	273
Boiling point of water	212	100	373

Absolute zero is the lowest possible threshold of temperature and is defined as 0 K. The temperature scales described in this table are related according to the following equations:

Fahrenheit $\Leftrightarrow$ Celsius: $\qquad T_F = \dfrac{9}{5} T_C + 32° \qquad T_C = \dfrac{5}{9}\left(T_F - 32°\right)$

Celsius $\Leftrightarrow$ Kelvin: $\qquad T_C = T_K - 273° \qquad T_K = T_C + 273°$

EXAMPLE: Normal body temperature is 98.6 °F. Convert this temperature to degrees Celsius.

SOLUTION: To convert degrees Fahrenheit to degrees Celsius, begin with the equation

$$T_C = \frac{5}{9}\left(T_F - 32°\right)$$

Solving for T_C yields

$$T_C = \frac{5}{9}\left(98.6° - 32°\right) = 37\,°C$$

47

CHAPTER 2:
Importance of Fluids
for the Circulation
of Blood,
Gas Movement, and
Gas Exchange

EXAMPLE: Derive a relationship between the Fahrenheit and Kelvin temperature scales.

SOLUTION: The Fahrenheit and Celsius temperature scales and the Celsius and Kelvin temperature scales are related by the equations given previously.

Substituting the first Celsius ⇔ Kelvin equation into the first Fahrenheit ⇔ Celsius equation yields

$$T_F = \frac{9}{5}\left(T_K - 273°\right) + 32° = \frac{9}{5}T_K - \frac{9}{5}\left(273°\right) + 32°$$

$$= \frac{9}{5}T_K - 491.4° + 32° = \frac{9}{5}T_K - 460°$$

So the desired equation is

$$T_F = \frac{9}{5}T_K - 460°$$

Pressure

A gas exerts pressure on the walls of its container. The pressure within a container is measured using a **manometer**. The atmosphere exerts pressure onto the Earth due to gravity. Atmospheric pressure is measured using a mercury **barometer**.

A barometer consists of an evacuated tube in a dish of mercury. The atmospheric pressure pushes the mercury into the tube. At sea level, the mercury rises 760 millimeters (mm). Thus the conversion equation is 1 atmosphere (atm) = 760 mm Hg.

Pressure is a force per unit area. It has various units, including pounds per square inch (psi), Pascal (Pa), or torr.

Ideal Gases

Ideal gases are those in which there is no intermolecular interaction between the molecules. The molecules are many times farther apart than their diameter. Boyle's law, Charles's law, and Avogadro's law describe the relationship between pressure, volume, and temperature in these gases, respectively.

BOYLE'S LAW

Boyle's law derives from experiments done in the 1660s. Robert Boyle determined that the pressure is inversely related to the volume of a gas at constant temperature. In other words, the pressure times the volume equals a constant for a given amount of gas at a constant temperature:

$$PV = \text{constant}$$

CHARLES'S LAW

Charles's law derives from experiments done in the early 1800s. Jacques Charles determined that the volume of a gas is directly related to temperature. The Kelvin scale, with 0 K as the lowest possible temperature, must be used with Charles's law. To obtain a temperature in K, simply add 273.15 to the temperature in degrees Celsius (°C). Charles's law states that the volume divided by the temperature equals a constant for a given amount of gas at a constant pressure:

$$V/T = \text{constant}$$

AVOGADRO'S LAW

Amedeo Avogadro determined that 1 mole (6.022×10^{23} particles) of any gas occupies the same volume at a given temperature and pressure. The use of moles (mol) allows for the counting of particles, thus ignoring the masses of the particles. Moles, with the symbol n, are part of the constant in Boyle's law and Charles's law.

IDEAL GAS CONSTANT

Combining the three laws, one gets

$$PV = n\,\text{constant}\,T$$

The constant is called the **ideal gas constant**. It is given the symbol R and has the value 0.08206 L atm/mol K.

Avogadro used this ideal gas law to determine that 1 mole of any ideal gas would occupy 22.4 L at 0 °C and 1 atm pressure.

APPLICATIONS OF THE IDEAL GAS LAW

There are two major ways to use the ideal gas law. The first method involves changing conditions. If there are initial conditions that are changed, one can solve for any unknown final condition. The mole amount, n, and the gas constant, R, are constant, thus:

$$\frac{P_i V_i}{T_i} = \frac{P_f V_f}{T_f}$$

If five of the six variables are given, the sixth variable can be solved for. If any value remains constant, it falls out of the equation.

EXAMPLE: A sample of gas has volume 3.14 L at 512 mm Hg and 45.6 °C. Calculate the volume at 675 mm Hg and 18.2 °C.

SOLUTION:

1. Change all temperatures to Kelvin

$$45.6\,°\text{C} = 318.8\,\text{K} \qquad 18.2\,°\text{C} = 291.4\,\text{K}$$

49

CHAPTER 2:
Importance of Fluids
for the Circulation
of Blood,
Gas Movement, and
Gas Exchange

2. Rearrange the equation and solve for V_f

$$V_f = \frac{P_i V_i T_f}{T_i P_f} = \frac{(512 \text{ mm Hg}) (3.14 \text{ L}) (291.4 \text{ K})}{(318.8 \text{ K}) (675 \text{ mm Hg})} = 2.18 \text{ L}$$

The second way to use the ideal gas law is under a set of conditions. There are four variables (P, V, T, and n). If three of them are given, the fourth can be solved by using $PV = nRT$.

EXAMPLE: Calculate the molar mass of a gas if a 12.8-gram (g) sample occupies 9.73 L at 21.0 °C and 754 mm Hg.

SOLUTION:

1. Change the temperature to Kelvin and the pressure to atm

$$21.0 \,^\circ\text{C} = 294.2 \text{ K}$$

$$P = 752 \text{ mm Hg}/760 \text{ mm Hg}/\text{atm} = 0.989 \text{ atm}$$

2. Solve for n

$$n = \frac{PV}{RT} = \frac{(0.989 \text{ atm}) (9.73 \text{ L})}{(0.08206 \text{ L atm}/\text{mol K}) (294.2 \text{ K})} = 0.399 \text{ mole}$$

3. Calculate the molar mass

$$\text{mass}/\text{mole} = 12.8 \text{ g}/0.399 \text{ mole} = 32.0 \text{ g}/\text{mole}$$

The Kinetic Molecular Theory of Gases

The **kinetic molecular theory of gases** is a model for gas behavior. It consists of five assumptions concerning ideal gases and explains Boyle's, Charles's, and Avogadro's laws. The five assumptions are:

➤ A gas consists of very small particles that move randomly.

➤ The volume of each gas particle is negligible compared to the spaces between particles.

➤ There are no intermolecular attractive forces between the gas particles.

➤ When gas particles collide with each other or with the walls of the container, there is no net gain or loss of kinetic energy.

➤ The average kinetic energy of each gas particle is proportional to the temperature.

These assumptions are related to Boyle's law, $P \propto 1/V$. Because the pressure is related to the collisions each particle has, the more crowded the particles, the more collisions there are, and the higher the pressure. So as the volume is decreased, crowding and collisions increase, and the pressure increases.

These assumptions are also related to Charles's law, $V \propto T$. Because the particles move faster when the temperature is increased, it follows that there are more collisions when the particles are moving faster. Thus the higher the temperature, the greater the volume required to keep the pressure constant.

The assumptions also relate to Avogadro's law, $V \propto n$. As the number of particles increases, the number of collisions increases (pressure and temperature are constant). Thus the volume must increase to contain the particles.

The kinetic energy of a gas particle is defined by E_k

$$E_k = \frac{1}{2}mv^2$$

where v is the velocity and m is the mass, and v can be shown to be equal to

$$v = (3RT/M)^{1/2}$$

where R is the gas constant 8.314 J/mole K, M is the molar mass, and T is the temperature in K.

The heavier the gas particle, the slower it moves.

HEAT CAPACITY AT CONSTANT VOLUME AND AT CONSTANT PRESSURE

Heat capacity, a quantity unique to a substance, is a measure of the amount of heat energy required (measured in units of joules) to raise the temperature, ΔT, of 1 gram of a substance by 1 degree Celsius. In equation form, the heat energy, Q, generated or released by a change in temperature is given as:

$$Q = mC\Delta T$$

where C is the heat capacity. However, when applied to gases, the heat capacity is different, depending on whether the gas is under constant volume or under constant pressure.

When a gas is under constant volume, the applied heat to the gas cannot result in an expansion of the volume of the gas, so the heat energy is transferred to the internal energy, ΔU, of the gas and the equation noted previously can be rewritten as:

$$\Delta U = mC_V\Delta T$$

where C_V is the heat capacity of a gas at constant volume.

When a gas is under constant pressure, the flow of heat, known as **enthalpy**, H, can be determined by:

$$Q = \Delta H = mC_p\Delta T$$

where C_p is the heat capacity of a gas at constant pressure.

BOLTZMANN'S CONSTANT

The ideal gas law describes the behavior of the pressure (p), volume (V), and temperature (T) of an ideal gas and is typically expressed as:

$$pV = nRT$$

51

CHAPTER 2:
Importance of Fluids
for the Circulation
of Blood,
Gas Movement, and
Gas Exchange

where n is the number of moles and R is a gas constant ($= 8.3145$ J/mol K). However, the ideal gas law can be rewritten to describe a gas in terms of the number of particles of the gas, N, instead of the number of moles by the inclusion of a different constant, k:

$$pV = NkT$$

The constant k, equal numerically to 1.38×10^{-23} J/K, is known as **Boltzmann's constant**.

Real Gases

A real gas deviates somewhat in its behavior from the ideal gas, because the basic assumptions about an ideal gas are not always strictly true.

For example, under conditions of high pressure and/or small volume, gas particles can get close enough to exhibit intermolecular attractive forces. Thus at certain pressures, the actual volume is somewhat smaller than predicted by the ideal gas law.

When pressures get even higher, repulsive forces between particles become important, and the actual volume becomes somewhat larger than predicted by the ideal gas law.

The **van der Waals constants** a and b, which are characteristic for each type of gas, allow for the correction for real gas behavior as follows.

The correction for pressure is $(P + an^2/V^2)$, and the correction for volume is $(V - nb)$. So the van der Waals equation for real gases becomes:

$$(P + an^2/V^2)\,(V - nb) = nRT$$

Partial Pressure of Gases—Dalton's Law

Dalton's law of partial pressures concerns mixtures of gases. It states that each gas in a mixture exerts its own pressure, and the total of each gas's partial pressure equals the total pressure in the container.

At constant V and T, $P_A + P_B + P_C = P_{total}$ for gases A, B, and C in the mixture. Thus $P_{total} = n_{total} RT/V$. Each gas consists of a fraction of the entire amount, n_{total}. Each mole fraction is calculated:

$$X_A = n_A/n_{total} \qquad X_B = n_B/n_{total} \qquad X_C = n_C/n_{total}$$

And each partial pressure is:

$$P_A = X_A P_{total} \qquad P_B = X_B P_{total} \qquad P_C = X_C P_{total}$$

EXAMPLE: Calculate the partial pressure of each gas in a balloon that contains 50.97 g nitrogen, 23.8 g helium, and 19.5 g argon at a total pressure of 2.67 atm.

SOLUTION:

1. Calculate the moles of each gas

$$(50.97 \text{ g } N_2) \, (1 \text{ mole } N_2/28.020 \text{ g}) = 1.819 \text{ mole } N_2$$

$$(23.80 \text{ g He}) \, (1 \text{ mole He}/4.003 \text{ g}) = 5.945 \text{ mole He}$$

$$(19.59 \text{ g Ar}) \, (1 \text{ mole Ar}/39.950 \text{ g}) = 0.488 \text{ mole Ar}$$

2. Sum the moles

Sum = 8.25 mole total

3. Determine the mole fraction X of each gas

$$X_{N_2} = 1.819 \text{ mole}/8.25 \text{ mole} = 0.2200$$

$$X_{He} = 5.945 \text{ mole}/8.25 \text{ mole} = 0.7200$$

$$X_{Ar} = 0.488 \text{ mole}/8.25 \text{ mole} = 0.0591$$

4. Multiply each mole fraction by the total pressure in the balloon

$$P_{N_2} = 0.2200 \times 2.67 \text{ atm} = 0.587 \text{ atm } N_2$$

$$P_{He} = 0.7200 \times 2.67 \text{ atm} = 1.92 \text{ atm He}$$

$$P_{Ar} = 0.0591 \times 2.67 \text{ atm} = 0.158 \text{ atm Ar}$$

CHAPTER 3

Electrochemistry and Electrical Circuits and Their Elements

Read This Chapter to Learn About

➤ Electrostatics

➤ Electric Circuits

➤ Magnetism

➤ Electrochemistry

➤ Specialized Cells—Nerve Cells

ELECTROSTATICS

A simple static shock, the beating of the heart, the operation of household appliances, and the devastating damage inflicted by a lightning bolt—all of these examples in nature involve applications of electrostatics. **Electrostatics** is the study of electrically charged particles—their properties such as mass and charge, their behavior such as conservation of charge, and their interactions such as the repulsive or attractive forces that occur and the calculation of the magnitude of such forces through Coulomb's law. This chapter reviews the fundamental concepts of electrostatics.

Electric Charge and Charge Conservation

Electric charge q is a physical property of the basic building blocks of the **atom**, a fundamental property of all matter. The SI unit of charge is the **coulomb,** abbreviated C. Although charge can be positive or negative, the magnitude of charge is

$e = 1.6 \times 10^{-19}$ C. Considering the particles of the atom, the charge of the positively charged proton is $+1.6 \times 10^{-19}$ C, and the charge of the negatively charged electron is -1.6×10^{-19} C. Two like charges (either two positive charges or two negative charges) repel each other. Positive and negative charges attract each other.

Electric charge is a conserved quantity and thus follows **conservation of charge**:

> Electric charge can neither be created nor destroyed, only transferred. The net charge of a system remains constant.

Conductors and Insulators

As you will read in the following section on electric circuits, it is important to identify materials that will either allow or prevent the flow of electric charge. **Conductors** such as metals are materials that allow the storage of or facilitate the flow of electric charge. **Insulators** such as rubber or wood prevent the storage or flow of electric charge.

Electric Force: Coulomb's Law

Coulomb's law describes the electrostatic force F_{el} between two charged particles q_1 and q_2, separated by a distance r:

$$F_{el} = \frac{1}{4\pi\varepsilon_0}\frac{q_1 q_2}{r^2} = k\frac{q_1 q_2}{r^2}$$

where ε_0 is the permittivity constant, defined as $\varepsilon_0 = 8.85 \times 10^{-12}$ C^2/N$\cdot$m^2. Values for k are:

$$k = \frac{1}{4\pi\varepsilon_0} = 9.0 \times 10^9 \ \frac{\text{N} \cdot \text{m}^2}{\text{C}^2}$$

Electrostatic force, as is the case for all types of forces, is a vector quantity and is expressed in units of newtons (N). The direction of the electrostatic force is based on the charges involved. **Unlike charges** generate an attractive (negative) force, and the direction is toward the other charge; **like charges** generate a repulsive (positive) force, and the direction is away from the other charge.

> **EXAMPLE:** Determine the electrostatic force between two alpha particles of charge $+2e$ $(3.2 \times 10^{-19}$ C) separated by 10^{-13} m.
>
> **SOLUTION:** The electrostatic force can be determined using Coulomb's law,
>
> $$F_{el} = \left(9 \times 10^9 \ \frac{\text{N} \cdot \text{m}^2}{\text{C}^2}\right) \frac{\left(3.2 \times 10^{-19} \text{ C}\right)\left(3.2 \times 10^{-19} \text{ C}\right)}{\left(1 \times 10^{-13} \text{ m}\right)^2}$$
>
> $$= 9.22 \times 10^{-2} \text{ N, repulsive}$$

Electric Field

Electric field E defines the electric force exerted on a positive test charge positioned at any given point in space. A positive test charge, q_o, is similar in most respects to a true charge except that it does not exert an electrostatic force on any adjacent or nearby charges. Thus the electric field of a positive test charge provides an idealized distribution of electrostatic force generated by the test charge and is given by:

$$E = \frac{F_{el}}{q_o}$$

Because E is a vector quantity, the direction is dependent on the identity of the charge. Because the test charge is positive, if the other charge is negative, an attractive force is generated and the direction of E is toward the negative charge. Likewise, if the other charge is positive, a repulsive force is generated and the direction of E is away from the positive charge.

Electric field E is expressed in units of newtons per coulomb. If E is known, it is possible to determine the electrostatic force exerted on any charge q placed at the same position as the test charge using:

$$F_{el} = q_o E$$

An electric field can be produced by one or more electric charges. The electric field of a point charge, which always points away from a positive charge and toward a negative charge, can be calculated by direct substitution of Coulomb's law into the expression for E:

$$E = \frac{F_{el}}{q_o} = \frac{k \dfrac{q q_o}{r^2}}{q_o} = k \frac{q}{r^2}$$

ELECTRIC FIELD LINES

Electric field lines represent a visual display of the electric field that uses imaginary lines to represent the magnitude and direction of the electric field or the distribution of the electrostatic force over a region in space. The lines of force from a positive charge are directed away from the positive charge, whereas the lines of force of a negative charge are directed toward the negative charge, as depicted in Figure 3-1. The magnitude of the force is greater in the region closer to the charge and becomes weaker as the distance from the charge increases.

ELECTRIC FIELD DUE TO CHARGE DISTRIBUTION

For more than one charge in a defined region of space, the total electric field E_{tot}, because it is a vector quantity, is the vector sum of the electric field generated by each charge E_q in the distribution, or

$$E_{tot} = E_{q1} + E_{q2} + E_{q3} + E_{q4} + \cdots$$

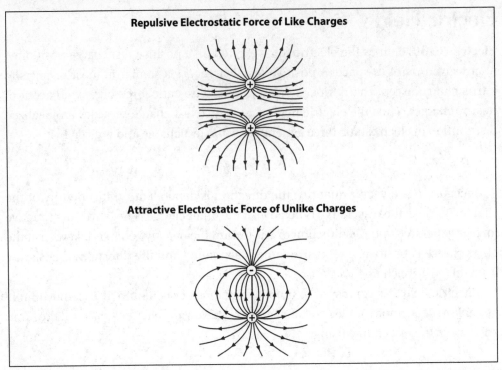

FIGURE 3-1 Electric field lines. *Source:* From George Hademenos, *Schaum's Outline of Physics for Pre-Med, Biology, and Allied Health Students,* McGraw-Hill, 1998; reproduced with permission of The McGraw-Hill Companies.

Electric Potential

The concept of potential in this regard is similar to the potential that was discussed in Chapter 1. It discussed the fact that potential energy becomes stored by an object as a result of work done to raise the object against a gravitational field. The **electric potential** V at some point B becomes stored as a result of work done, W, against an electric field to move a positive test charge from infinity (point A) to that point (point B), or

$$V = \frac{-W}{q_o}$$

$$\text{Electric potential} = \frac{\text{work}}{\text{charge}}$$

The electric potential is a scalar quantity that can be positive, negative, or zero, depending on the sign and magnitude of the point charge as well as the work done. Electric potential is expressed in units of joules per coulomb (J/C) = volts (V).

The **electric potential difference,** ΔV, between any two points A and B in an electric field is related to the work done by the electrostatic force to move the charge from point A to point B as:

$$\Delta V = V_B - V_A = \frac{-W_{AB}}{q_o}$$

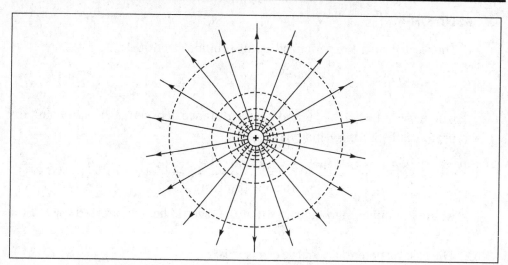

FIGURE 3-2 Equipotential surfaces generated for a positive charge.

The absolute electric potential at a point A that exists at a distance r from a charged particle at point B depends on the magnitude of charge at point B as well as the distance according to the following formula:

$$V = k\frac{q}{r}$$

This is only true if one assumes that $V \to 0$ at a point infinitely far away. Because the electric potential is a scalar quantity, the electric potential for n charges can be determined by adding the electric potential values calculated for each of the n charges:

$$V = \sum_{i=1}^{n} V_i = V_{q_1} + V_{q_2} + V_{q_3} + V_{q_4} + \cdots + V_{q_n}$$

Equipotential surfaces are a graphical method of representing the electric potential of any charge distribution as concentric circles that are normal or perpendicular to electric field lines. Consider the example of a positive charge in Figure 3-2. The electric field vectors are pointed away radially in all directions from the charge. Equipotential surfaces can also be drawn on the diagram to represent the electric potential of a positive charge at any distance r from the charge. Recall that the electric potential of a point charge is given by $V = k\frac{q}{r}$. On the surface of the charge where r is at its minimum, the electric potential is at its greatest, and thus a solid circle is drawn about the point charge to represent the largest magnitude of the potential at the surface of the point charge. As the distance r increases, the electric potential is represented as concentric circles that become larger in circumference.

EXAMPLE: The Bohr model of the hydrogen atom describes electron motion in a circular orbit of radius 0.53 Å (angstrom, where 1 angstrom $= 1 \times 10^{-10}$ m) about the nuclear proton. Determine the following for the orbiting electron:

1. The electric field
2. The electric potential

SOLUTION:

1. The electric field E experienced by the orbiting electron is:

$$E = k\frac{q}{r^2}$$

where $q = -1.6 \times 10^{-19}$ C and r is the distance between the electron and the proton. Substituting values yields:

$$E = \left(9 \times 10^9 \, \frac{\text{N} \cdot \text{m}^2}{\text{C}^2}\right) \frac{-1.6 \times 10^{-19} \, \text{C}}{\left(0.53 \times 10^{-10} \, \text{m}\right)^2} = -5.14 \times 10^{11} \, \frac{\text{N}}{\text{C}}$$

where the minus sign indicates that the electric field is directed toward the electron.

2. The electric potential V of the electron is:

$$V = k\frac{q}{r}$$

Substituting values yields:

$$V = \left(9 \times 10^9 \, \frac{\text{N} \cdot \text{m}^2}{\text{C}^2}\right) \frac{1.6 \times 10^{-19} \, \text{C}}{0.53 \times 10^{-10} \, \text{m}} = 27.2 \, \frac{\text{N} \cdot \text{m}}{\text{C}} = 27.2 \, \text{V}$$

ELECTRIC DIPOLE

An **electric dipole** consists of two point charges, $+q$ and $-q$, typically equal in magnitude but opposite in sign separated by a small distance d, as shown in Figure 3-3.

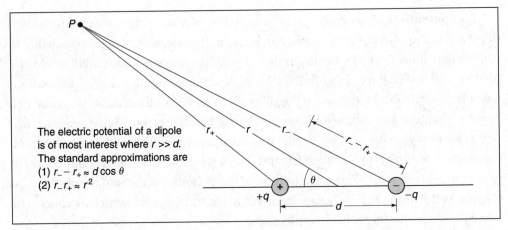

The electric potential of a dipole is of most interest where $r \gg d$.
The standard approximations are
(1) $r_- - r_+ \approx d \cos \theta$
(2) $r_- r_+ \approx r^2$

FIGURE 3-3 Electric dipole.

The electric potential, V, can be found for the electric dipole through the superposition of the two potentials:

$$V = V_{+q} + V_{-q} = k\frac{+q}{r_+} + k\frac{-q}{r_-} = kq\left(\frac{1}{r_+} - \frac{1}{r_-}\right) = kq\left(\frac{r_- - r_+}{r_+ r_-}\right)$$

The objective of this discussion is to calculate the potential of the dipole at a point much farther from the dipole than the distance of separation between the two charges. With such conditions, the following approximations can be made:

1. $r_- r_+ \approx r^2$
2. $r_- - r_+ \approx d\cos\theta$

Substituting these approximations into the equation for electric potential given previously yields an expression for the potential of an electric dipole:

$$V = k\frac{qd\cos\theta}{r^2}$$

where the product qd is referred to as the physical quantity, dipole moment **p**. The dipole moment is a vector quantity, pointing in a direction from the negative charge to the positive charge, with units of coulomb meters (Cm). The equipotential surfaces of an electric dipole are shown in Figure 3-4.

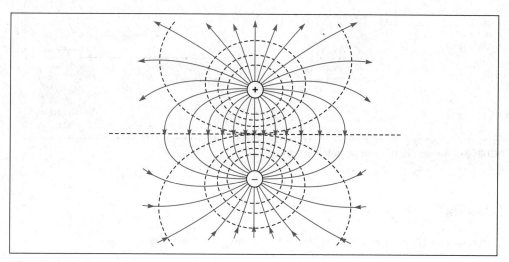

FIGURE 3-4 Equipotential surfaces of an electric dipole.

ELECTRIC CIRCUITS

You do not have to look far to realize the significance of electric circuits: they are involved in providing light to a room and power to an appliance. There are two types of electric circuits: direct current (DC) circuits and alternating current (AC) circuits. This section will focus on DC circuits.

In a **DC circuit**, electricity in the form of an electric charge generated by a voltage source (such as a battery) flows as current through an arrangement of circuit elements or devices (e.g., a lightbulb, an alarm, a motor) that are all connected by a **conductor**, or a material that allows electric charge to flow easily through it. These circuit elements may be connected in series or parallel, as shown in Figure 3-5. In a **series circuit**, two or more circuit elements are connected in sequence, one after the other. In a **parallel circuit**, two or more circuit elements are connected in a branching arrangement, such that a charge may pass through one element or the other. Regardless of the type of circuit, these elements interact with and can directly influence the flow of charge through the circuit.

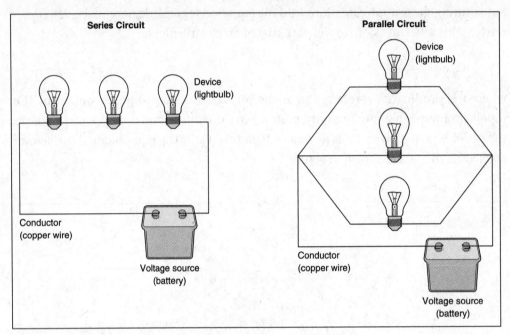

FIGURE 3-5 Series circuit and parallel circuit.

CURRENT

Current, I, is the rate of motion of electric charge and is expressed as:

$$\text{Current} = \frac{\text{electric charge moving through a region}}{\text{time required to move the charge}}$$

$$I = \frac{\Delta q}{\Delta t}$$

where current is measured in SI units of **amperes**, A.

➤ **Current in a series circuit:** Current that flows through one circuit element connected in series must also flow through the remaining elements connected in the series circuit. Therefore, the net or total current that flows through a series circuit remains the same through each of the individual elements or

$$I_{\text{net}} = I_1 = I_2 = I_3 = \cdots = I_n$$

where n refers to the nth element in a series circuit.

➤ **Current in a parallel circuit:** In a parallel circuit, one circuit element branches into two or more connected elements. The current that flows from the voltage source separates, and in the process divides its current among the branch elements. The amount of current that enters each of the branch elements depends on the resistance of that element. In any event, the net or total current in a parallel circuit is equal to the sum of the currents that flow through all connected branching elements, or

$$I_{net} = I_1 + I_2 + I_3 + \cdots + I_n$$

The flow of current in a series and parallel circuit is illustrated in Figure 3-6.

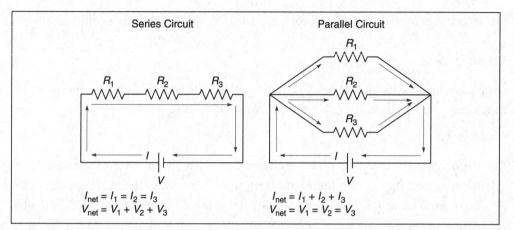

FIGURE 3-6 Flow of current in a series and parallel circuit.

Voltage

Electromotive force, $\mathcal{E}$ (often abbreviated emf), is the voltage or potential difference generated by a battery or power source when no current is flowing. When current is flowing through a circuit with conductive elements of resistance R, the battery generates an internal resistance R_{int}, resulting in a voltage drop through the battery of IR_{int}. The voltage generated by an emf through the circuit is given by:

$$\mathcal{E} - IR_{int} - IR = 0$$

Electromotive force is expressed in units of volts (V).

➤ **Voltage in series.** The net voltage of a circuit with conductive elements connected in series is the sum of the individual voltages across each conductive element of the circuit or

$$V_{net} = V_1 + V_2 + V_3 + \cdots + V_n$$

➤ **Voltage in parallel.** The net voltage of a circuit with conductive elements connected in parallel is identical to the individual voltages across each conductive element of the circuit or

$$V_{net} = V_1 = V_2 = V_3 = \cdots = V_n$$

Resistance

Resistance, R, is the inherent property of a conductor by which it resists the flow of electric current and represents a measure of the potential difference V that must be supplied to a circuit to drive current, I, through the circuit. Resistance is defined as:

$$\text{Resistance} = \frac{\text{potential difference}}{\text{current}}$$

$$R = \frac{V}{I}$$

Resistance is expressed in units of volts per ampere, also known as the **ohm** (Ω).

OHM'S LAW

Ohm's law states that the voltage V across a resistor R is proportional to the current I through it, and can be written in equation form as:

$$V = IR$$

An increase in voltage drives more electrons through the wire (conductor) at a greater rate; thus the current increases. If the voltage remains the same and the wire is a poor conductor, the resistance against the flow of electrons increases, thereby decreasing the current. It is possible to change I by manipulating V and R, but it is not possible to change V by manipulating I because current flow is due to the difference in voltage, not vice versa. The current is a completely dependent variable.

> **EXAMPLE:** The filament of a lightbulb has a resistance of 250 Ω. Determine the current through the filament if 120 V is applied to the lamp.
>
> **SOLUTION:** The current is related to the voltage by Ohm's law.
>
> $$I = \frac{V}{R} = \frac{120 \text{ V}}{250 \text{ }\Omega} = 0.48 \text{ A}$$

As current flows through a resistor, electric power P is dissipated into the resistor according to the following equivalent expressions:

$$P = IV = I^2 R = \frac{V^2}{R}$$

The unit for electric power is the **watt**, abbreviated W.

RESISTORS IN SERIES

In a circuit consisting of three resistors connected in series, as in Figure 3-7, the current must flow through the path presented by the resistors in series. To simplify circuit calculations, the equivalent resistance R_{eq} can be calculated in terms of the resistance of the individual components:

$$R_{eq} = R_1 + R_2 + R_3 + \cdots + R_n$$

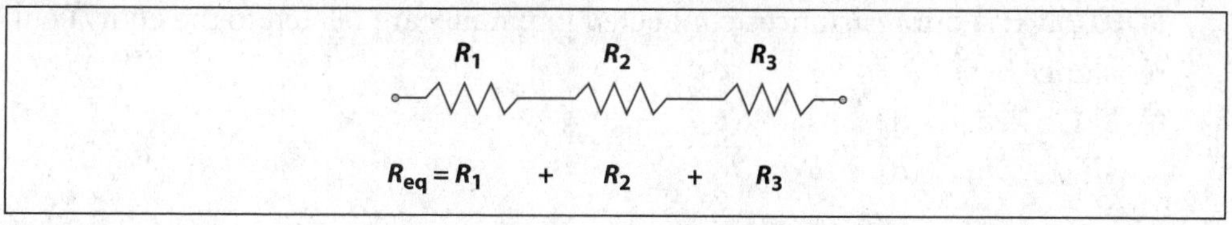

FIGURE 3-7 Resistors in series. *Source:* From George Hademenos, *Schaum's Outline of Physics for Pre-Med, Biology, and Allied Health Students,* McGraw-Hill, 1998; reproduced with permission of The McGraw-Hill Companies.

EXAMPLE: Two resistances $R_1 = 8\ \Omega$ and $R_2 = 6\ \Omega$ are connected in series. Determine the equivalent resistance.

SOLUTION:

$$R_{eq} = R_1 + R_2 = 8\ \Omega + 6\ \Omega = 14\ \Omega$$

RESISTORS IN PARALLEL

In a circuit consisting of three resistors connected in parallel, as in Figure 3-8, the current must flow through the path presented by the resistors in parallel. To simplify circuit calculations, the equivalent resistance R_{eq} can be calculated in terms of the resistance of the individual components:

$$\frac{1}{R_{eq}} = \frac{1}{R_1} + \frac{1}{R_2} + \frac{1}{R_3} + \cdots + \frac{1}{R_n}$$

where the equivalent resistance R_{eq} is always less than the smallest value of resistance of the individual components.

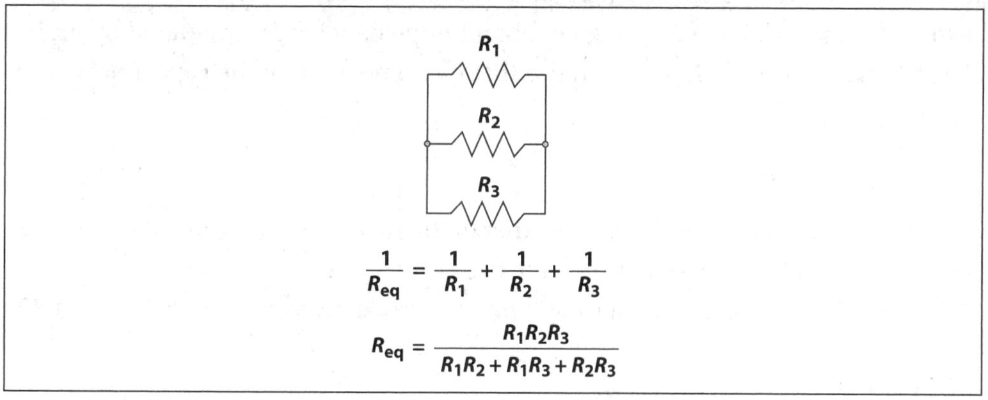

FIGURE 3-8 Resistors in parallel. *Source:* From George Hademenos, *Schaum's Outline of Physics for Pre-Med, Biology, and Allied Health Students,* McGraw-Hill, 1998; reproduced with permission of The McGraw-Hill Companies.

EXAMPLE: A circuit with four resistances connected in parallel yields an equivalent resistance of 1 Ω. If $R_1 = 5\ \Omega$, $R_2 = 5\ \Omega$, and $R_3 = 10\ \Omega$, determine R_4.

SOLUTION: Four resistances connected in parallel are related to the equivalent resistance by:

$$\frac{1}{R_{eq}} = \frac{1}{R_1} + \frac{1}{R_2} + \frac{1}{R_3} + \frac{1}{R_4}$$

$$\frac{1}{1\,\Omega} = \frac{1}{5\,\Omega} + \frac{1}{5\,\Omega} + \frac{1}{10\,\Omega} + \frac{1}{R_4}$$

Solving for R_4 yields $R_4 = 2\,\Omega$.

RESISTIVITY

The resistance R of a conductor depends on the resistivity, ρ, unique to the material, its length, L, and its cross-sectional area, A, or

$$R = \rho \frac{L}{A}$$

Resistivity is given in units of ohm $\cdot$ meter ($\Omega \cdot m$).

> **EXAMPLE:** Given that the resistivity of copper is $1.7 \times 10^{-8}\,\Omega \cdot m$, determine the resistance of a copper wire of 0.30 millimeter (mm) in diameter and 5 m in length.
>
> **SOLUTION:** The resistance of the copper wire is related to its diameter and length by:
>
> $$R = \rho \frac{L}{A} = \rho \frac{L}{\pi r^2} = (1.7 \times 10^{-8}\,\Omega \cdot m) \frac{5.0\,m}{3.14 \left(0.15 \times 10^{-3}\,m\right)^2} = 1.2\,\Omega$$

Capacitance

Capacitors are circuit elements that store charge and consist typically of two conductors of arbitrary shape carrying equal and opposite charges separated by an insulator. **Capacitance**, C, depends on the shape and position of the capacitors and is defined as:

$$C = \frac{q}{V}$$

where q is the magnitude of charge on either of the two conductors and V is the magnitude of potential difference between the two conductors.

The SI unit of capacitance is the coulomb/volt, collectively known as the **farad** (F).

PARALLEL PLATE CAPACITOR

The most common type of capacitor is the parallel-plate capacitor consisting of two large conducting plates of area A and separated by a distance d. The capacitance of a parallel-plate capacitor is:

$$C = \kappa \varepsilon_0 \frac{A}{d}$$

where κ is a dielectric constant (dimensionless) and $\varepsilon_o = 8.85 \times 10^{-12}\ C^2/N \cdot m^2 = 8.85 \times 10^{-12}\ F/m$. For vacuum, $\kappa = 1$.

ENERGY OF A CHARGED CAPACITOR

Because capacitors store positive and negative charge, work is done in separating the two types of charge, which is stored as electric potential energy W in the capacitor, given by:

$$W = \frac{1}{2}qV = \frac{1}{2}CV^2 = \frac{1}{2}\frac{q^2}{C}$$

where V is the potential difference and q is charge.

EXAMPLE: To restore cardiac function to a heart attack victim, a cardiac defibrillator is applied to the chest in an attempt to stimulate electrical activity of the heart and restore the heartbeat. A cardiac defibrillator consists of a capacitor charged to approximately 7.5×10^3 V with stored energy of 500 watt seconds (W·s). Determine the charge on the capacitor in the cardiac defibrillator.

SOLUTION: The energy stored in a capacitor is

$$W = \frac{1}{2}CV^2$$

and the charge on the capacitor is

$$q = CV$$

Solving for C gives

$$C = \frac{q}{V}$$

Substituting into the expression for W, you get

$$W = \frac{1}{2}\left(\frac{q}{V}\right)V^2 = \frac{1}{2}qV$$

Solving for q results in

$$q = \frac{2W}{V} = \frac{2 \cdot 500\ \text{W} \cdot \text{s}}{7.5 \times 10^3\ \text{V}} = 0.13\ \text{C}$$

CAPACITORS IN SERIES

The effective capacitance C_{eff} of capacitors connected in series, as shown in Figure 3-9, is given by:

$$\frac{1}{C_{\text{eff}}} = \frac{1}{C_1} + \frac{1}{C_2} + \frac{1}{C_3} + \cdots + \frac{1}{C_n}$$

where C_n is the nth capacitor connected in series.

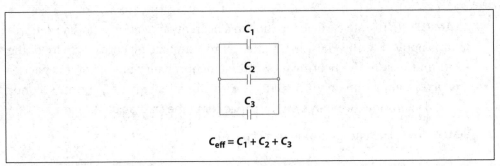

FIGURE 3-9 Capacitors in series. *Source:* From George Hademenos, *Schaum's Outline of Physics for Pre-Med, Biology, and Allied Health Students*, McGraw-Hill, 1998; reproduced with permission of The McGraw-Hill Companies.

$$\frac{1}{C_{\text{eff}}} = \frac{1}{C_1} + \frac{1}{C_2} + \frac{1}{C_3}$$

$$C_{\text{eff}} = \frac{C_1 C_2 C_3}{C_1 C_2 + C_1 C_3 + C_2 C_3}$$

C_1

C_2

C_3

$$C_{\text{eff}} = C_1 + C_2 + C_3$$

FIGURE 3-10 Capacitors in parallel. *Source:* From George Hademenos, *Schaum's Outline of Physics for Pre-Med, Biology, and Allied Health Students*, McGraw-Hill, 1998; reproduced with permission of The McGraw-Hill Companies.

CAPACITORS IN PARALLEL

The effective capacitance C_{eff} of capacitors connected in parallel, as shown in Figure 3-10, is given by:

$$C_{\text{eff}} = C_1 + C_2 + C_3 + \cdots + C_n$$

where C_n is the nth capacitor connected in parallel.

TABLE 3-1

Summary of Circuit Element Quantities of DC Circuits		
Circuit Element	**Series**	**Parallel**
Voltage	$V_{\text{net}} = V_1 + V_2 + V_3 + \cdots + V_n$	$V_{\text{net}} = V_1 = V_2 = V_3 = \cdots = V_n$
Current	$I_{\text{net}} = I_1 = I_2 = I_3 = \cdots = I_n$	$I_{\text{net}} = I_1 + I_2 + I_3 + \cdots + I_n$
Resistance	$R_{\text{eq}} = R_1 + R_2 + R_3 + \cdots + R_n$	$\dfrac{1}{R_{\text{eq}}} = \dfrac{1}{R_1} + \dfrac{1}{R_2} + \dfrac{1}{R_3} + \cdots + \dfrac{1}{R_n}$
Capacitance	$\dfrac{1}{C_{\text{eff}}} = \dfrac{1}{C_1} + \dfrac{1}{C_2} + \dfrac{1}{C_3} + \cdots + \dfrac{1}{C_n}$	$C_{\text{eff}} = C_1 + C_2 + C_3 + \cdots + C_n$

DIELECTRICS

A **dielectric** is an insulator that is usually used to fill the gap between the plates of a capacitor because it increases the capacitance. Dielectric materials are characterized by a dielectric constant, κ, which relates the new capacitance of the capacitor to its original capacitance by the relation:

$$C = \kappa C_o$$

where C_o is the capacitance of a capacitor with an empty gap and C is the capacitance of a capacitor filled with a dielectric. The dielectric constant is equal to 1 for vacuum and slightly greater than 1 for air ($\kappa = 1.00054$).

Conductivity

Conductivity refers to the ability of an object or substance to conduct electricity. Conductivity is a property that can be applied to both metals (metallic conductivity) and substances (electrolytic solutions). **Metallic conductivity** is directly related to the movement of valence or free electrons that can easily be removed from the element's outer shell. Under normal conditions, these valence electrons are randomly spinning in their position. When the element is connected within an electric circuit and subjected to an electrical power source, electric current exerts a push or force on the free electrons, causing them to move between the positive and negative terminals of the battery. In addition to electrons, ions or charged atoms within a solution become free to move under an electric current supplied by a battery. In **electrolytic conductivity**, the electric current causes the positively charged and negatively charged ions to move in opposite directions.

Conductivity Meters

A **conductivity meter** is an instrument equipped with a probe designed to measure the conductivity of a substance within a solution. In performing measurements, as the probe is placed within the solution, an electric voltage is applied between two electrodes within the probe, with the electrical resistance that is provided by the solution causing a reduction in voltage. The voltage change is a reflection of the solution's ionic strength and hence the conductivity of the substance.

MAGNETISM

The working principles of a television monitor, the physical properties of Earth and the basis for the most effective navigational tool in history (the compass) all have a common thread—**magnetism**. A property of matter discovered by the ancient Chinese in the mineral lodestone, magnetism is involved in a wide spectrum of applications in science and technology and represents an important subject in physics. This chapter covers the basics of magnetism.

Magnetic Field

Magnetic field B is an attractive or repulsive force field generated by a moving charged particle. For a standard bar magnet with a north pole (where the lines of force begin) and a south pole (where the lines of force end), the magnetic field is attractive for opposite poles and repulsive for like poles.

Magnetic field is a vector quantity. The unit of magnetic field is the **tesla** (T), where

$$1 \text{ tesla} = 1\frac{\text{newton}}{\text{ampere} \cdot \text{meter}} = 1\frac{\text{weber}}{(\text{meter})^2}$$

Magnetic fields can also be measured in units of **gauss** (G), a unit used for measuring smaller magnetic fields. These two units are related through the conversion ratio $1 \text{ T} = 1 \times 10^4 \text{ G}$.

Magnetic fields are created in the presence of moving charges or current. You can calculate the magnitude of the magnetic field and determine its direction based on the behavior or configuration of the current. Current can flow through a long, straight wire; through a wire loop or coil; through a long solenoid (a long, straight cylinder consisting of many loops of wire wrapped around the cylinder); or through a toroid (a long, cylinder of wire coils that is bent in the form of a doughnut). If current is flowing through each of these four configurations, the magnitude of the magnetic field can be calculated according to the formulas noted in Figure 3-11, where the constant in each of the equations, $\mu_o = 4\pi \times 10^{-7} \text{ T} \cdot \text{m/A}$, is termed the **permeability of free space**. The direction of the magnetic field can be determined using the **right-hand rule**, as depicted in the figure.

EXAMPLE: Earth can produce magnetic fields as high as 600 milligauss (mG). Express this value of magnetic field in terms of teslas.

SOLUTION: The units of tesla and gauss are related according to

$$1 \text{ T} = 10^4 \text{ G}$$

Therefore,

$$600 \text{ mG} = \left(600 \times 10^{-3} \text{ G}\right)\left(\frac{1 \text{ T}}{10^4 \text{ G}}\right) = 6 \times 10^{-5} \text{ T}$$

EXAMPLE: A circular conducting coil of diameter 0.4 m has 50 loops of wire and a current of 3 A flowing through it. Determine the magnetic field generated by the coil.

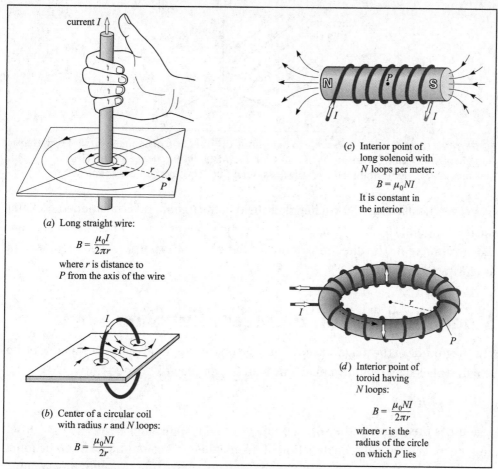

(c) Interior point of
long solenoid with
N loops per meter:

$$B = \mu_0 NI$$

It is constant in
the interior

(a) Long straight wire:

$$B = \frac{\mu_0 I}{2\pi r}$$

where r is distance to
P from the axis of the wire

(d) Interior point of
toroid having
N loops:

$$B = \frac{\mu_0 NI}{2\pi r}$$

where r is the
radius of the circle
on which P lies

(b) Center of a circular coil
with radius r and N loops:

$$B = \frac{\mu_0 NI}{2r}$$

FIGURE 3-11 Calculating the magnitude of a magnetic field. *Source:* From Frederick J. Bueche and Eugene Hecht, *Schaum's Outline of College Physics*, 10th ed., McGraw-Hill, 2006; reproduced with permission of The McGraw-Hill Companies.

SOLUTION: The equation for the magnetic field in the center of a circular loop or coil is

$$B = \frac{\mu_0 NI}{2r} = \frac{\left(4\pi \times 10^{-7} \; \frac{\text{T} \cdot \text{m}}{\text{A}}\right)(50)(3 \text{ A})}{2\,(0.2 \text{ m})} = 4.7 \times 10^{-4} \text{ T}$$

Magnetic Force on a Charged Particle in Motion

The magnitude of the magnetic force, **F**, or the force exerted on a charged particle q moving with a velocity **v** in a uniform magnetic field **B** is defined as:

$$\text{F} = qvB\sin\theta$$

where θ is the angle between the lines of the magnetic field **B** and the direction of the velocity v of the charged particle. The direction of the force can be determined by implementation of the right-hand rule. Given a charged particle moving with a velocity

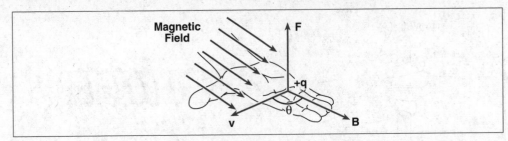

FIGURE 3-12 Using the right-hand rule to determine the direction of a force. *Source:* From George Hademenos, *Schaum's Outline of Physics for Pre-Med, Biology, and Allied Health Students,* McGraw-Hill, 1998; reproduced with permission of The McGraw-Hill Companies.

$q\mathbf{v}$ perpendicular to a uniform magnetic field **B**, the right hand is positioned such that the thumb points in the direction of $q\mathbf{v}$ and the remaining four fingers are aligned in the direction of **B**. The direction of the magnetic force **F** is perpendicular to the palm, as illustrated in Figure 3-12.

Magnetic Force on a Current-Carrying Wire

The magnitude of the magnetic force exerted on a current-carrying wire of current I of length L placed in a uniform magnetic field **B** is defined as

$$F = ILB \sin\theta$$

where L is the length of the wire (conductor) and θ is the angle between the current and the magnetic field. The direction of the magnetic force on the wire can be found by orienting the thumb of the right hand along the axis of the wire with the remaining fingers in the direction of the magnetic field. The magnetic force is directed upward from the aligned palm, as shown in Figure 3-13.

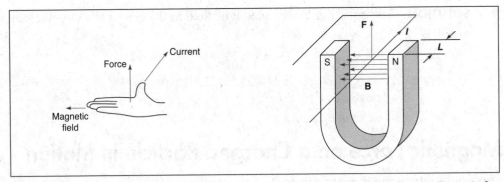

FIGURE 3-13 Determining the magnetic force on a current-carrying wire. *Source:* From Arthur Beiser, *Schaum's Outline of Applied Physics,* 4th ed., McGraw-Hill, 2004; reproduced with permission of The McGraw-Hill Companies.

EXAMPLE: A wire of length 40 centimeters (cm) carrying a current of 30 A is positioned at an angle of 50° to a uniform magnetic field of 10.0×10^{-4} watts per square meter (W/m^2). Determine the magnitude and direction of the force exerted on this wire.

SOLUTION: The magnetic force **F** exerted on the wire of length L with current I placed in a magnetic field **B** is given by:

$$F = ILB \sin \theta$$
$$= (30 \text{ A})(40 \times 10^{-2} \text{ m})(10.0 \times 10^{-4} \text{ W/m}^2)(\sin 50°) = 9.2 \times 10^{-3} \text{ N}$$

Using the right-hand rule where the fingers are aligned with the magnetic field lines and the thumb is aligned with the current direction, the force is directed perpendicularly into the page.

ELECTROCHEMISTRY

Electrochemistry is the study of oxidation–reduction reactions. These are reactions in which electrons are transferred from one species to another. The species that gains electrons is **reduced**; the species that loses electrons is **oxidized**. A reduction-oxidation, or **redox**, reaction that is spontaneous produces electricity. A nonspontaneous redox reaction requires electricity to run. Batteries (**voltaic** or **galvanic cells**) operate by producing electricity via a spontaneous redox reaction. **Electrolytic cells** require electricity to make the reaction occur; they are used in certain industrial processes, such as the purification of aluminum from its ore. These processes are called **electrolysis reactions**.

Electrolytic Cells

ELECTROLYSIS

Electrolysis is the process of splitting or breaking up compounds to stimulate chemical change by passing electricity through the solutions involved in the process.

Electrolytic cells are constructed of nonspontaneous redox reactions that require electricity to make them run. See Figure 3-14.

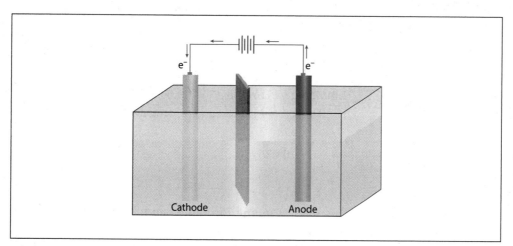

FIGURE 3-14 Electrolytic cell.

In an electrolytic cell, the cathode is negative and the anode is positive. Reduction occurs at the anode, described by the half reaction

$$Y^+ + e^- \rightarrow Y$$

and oxidation occurs at the cathode, described by the half-reaction

$$Z^- \rightarrow Z + e^-$$

FARADAY'S LAWS OF ELECTROLYSIS

Faraday's laws of electrolysis quantify the electrolysis process by establishing a mathematical relationship between the amount of elements deposited at an electrode or the gas liberated as a result of electric current that passes through the solution. The two laws are written as follows:

Faraday's First Law of Electrolysis. During electrolysis within a solution, the mass of any substance deposited or liberated at an electrode is directly proportional to the electric charge that passes through the solution.

Faraday's Second Law of Electrolysis. During electrolysis within a solution, the masses of different substances deposited or liberated at an electrode by the same amount of electric charge are proportional to the equivalent masses of the substances.

To calculate the current (in amperes) required to deposit a certain mass of metal in an electroplating experiment, you must have the following:

➤ Faraday constant, F

➤ n

➤ The time in seconds

➤ The molar mass of the metal

EXAMPLE: Calculate the current needed to deposit 365 milligrams (mg) silver in 216 minutes (min) from aqueous silver ion.

SOLUTION:

➤ From $Ag^{+1} \rightarrow Ag$ is a $1e^-$ change.
➤ Start with the gram amount, and convert it by steps into amperes.
➤ $A = C/s$.

$$(0.365 \text{g Ag}) \left(\frac{1 \text{ mole Ag}}{107.9 \text{ g Ag}} \right) \left(\frac{1 \text{ mole } e^-}{1 \text{ mole Ag}} \right) \left(\frac{9.65 \times 10^4 \text{ C}}{\text{mole } e^-} \right)$$

$$\times \left(\frac{1}{1.30 \times 10^4 \text{ s}} \right) = 0.0251 \text{ A}$$

EXAMPLE: Calculate the mass of iodine formed when 8.52 milliamperes (mA) flows through a cell containing I^- for 10.0 min.

SOLUTION:

➤ From I^- to I_2 is a total of $2e^-$ change.

➤ Start with the amp and convert it by steps into g I_2.

➤ $A \times s = C$.

$$(8.52 \times 10^{-3} \text{ A})(600 \text{ s}) \left(\frac{1 \text{ mole } e^-}{9.65 \times 10^4 \text{ C}} \right) \left(\frac{1 \text{ mole } I_2}{2 \text{ mole } e^-} \right) \left(\frac{254 \text{ g } I_2}{\text{mole } I_2} \right)$$

$$= 6.73 \times 10^{-3} \text{ g } I_2$$

Concentration Cell

A **concentration cell** is a type of electrolytic cell that is composed of two half-cells with the same electrodes separated by a salt bridge but different concentrations. Upon activation, the cell acts to dilute the more concentrated solution and strengthen the more dilute solution. During the process, electrons are transferred from the lower concentration cell to the higher concentration cell, creating a voltage as it approaches equilibrium. The potential of the concentration cell can be determined quantitatively by the **Nernst equation**:

$$E = E^\circ - \frac{RT}{nF} \ln Q$$

where

$R =$ gas constant $= 8.315$ J/K mol

$F =$ Faraday constant

$Q =$ reaction quotient $= \dfrac{[\text{products}]^{coefficient}}{[\text{reactants}]^{coefficient}}$

$E^\circ =$ energy produced by reaction

$T =$ temperature in Kelvin

$n =$ number of electrons exchanged in balanced redox equation

$E =$ cell potential

Voltaic Cells

Voltaic cells (also called **galvanic cells**) are constructed so that a redox reaction produces an electric current. A diagram of a voltaic cell is shown in Figure 3-15.

One half-cell is the **anode**. This is where the oxidation takes place. The electrode wears away as the reaction proceeds, with the metal electrode becoming an ion in the solution.

The other half-cell is the **cathode**. This is where the reduction is taking place. The electrode builds up as the reaction proceeds, with the metal ions in the solution plating out as pure metal.

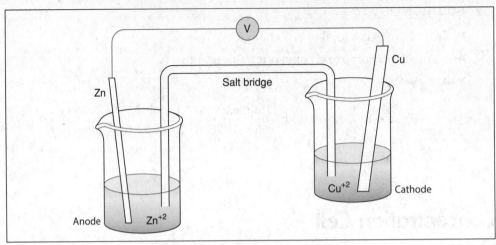

FIGURE 3-15 Voltaic cell with Zn/Zn^{+2} anode and Cu/Cu^{+2} cathode.

The two half-cells are connected by a salt bridge between the solutions and by a wire between the electrodes.

The anode gives up electrons:

$$Zn\ (s) \rightarrow Zn^{+2}\ (aq) + 2e^-$$

The cathode uses the electrons:

$$Cu^{+2}\ (aq) + 2e^- \rightarrow Cu\ (s)$$

BALANCING OXIDATION–REDUCTION REACTIONS

Balancing a redox equation is not the same as balancing a nonredox equation. You have to take the electron change into account.

How to Balance a Redox Equation in an Acidic Solution

1. Divide the equation into two half-reactions, one for oxidation and one for reduction.
2. Balance all the atoms.

   ➤ Start with the main atoms.
   ➤ Then use H_2O to balance O.
   ➤ Then use H^+ to balance H.

3. Determine the total electron change for each half-reaction, using the oxidation numbers of each species that is changing.
4. Determine the lowest common denominator (LCD) of the total electron change.
5. Multiply through each half-reaction so that the electron change equals the LCD.
6. Add the two half-reactions.
7. Cancel where applicable.

How to Balance a Redox Equation in a Basic Solution

1. Balance as for an acidic solution.
2. Change all H^+ to H_2O.
3. Put the same number of OH^- on the other side.
4. Add and cancel where applicable.

EXAMPLE IN ACID SOLUTION:

$Cr_2O_7^{-2} + C_2O_4^{-2} \rightarrow Cr^{+3} + CO_2$ (The phase labels have been left out for clarity.)

SOLUTION:

➤ Divide into two half-reactions.

$$Cr_2O_7^{-2} \rightarrow Cr^{+3}$$
$$C_2O_4^{-2} \rightarrow CO_2$$

➤ Balance the atoms, starting with the main atoms.

$$Cr_2O_7^{-2} \rightarrow 2Cr^{+3}$$
$$C_2O_4^{-2} \rightarrow 2CO_2$$

➤ Use H_2O to balance the oxygen atoms.

$$Cr_2O_7^{-2} \rightarrow 2Cr^{+3} + 7H_2O$$
$$C_2O_4^{-2} \rightarrow 2CO_2$$

➤ Use H^+ to balance the hydrogen atoms.

$$14H^+ + Cr_2O_7^{-2} \rightarrow 2Cr^{+3} + 7H_2O$$
$$C_2O_4^{-2} \rightarrow 2CO_2$$

➤ Determine the oxidation number of each atom that is changing and find the total electron change for each half-reaction.

➤ Cr on the left is +6; Cr on the right is +3. This is a change of 3 electrons, but there are 2 Crs changing, so the total electron change is 6 for this half-reaction.

➤ C on the left is +3; C on the right is +4. This is a change of 1 electron, but there are 2 Cs changing, so the total electron change is 2 for this half-reaction.

➤ Find the LCD of the electron change. The LCD of 6 and 2 is 6.

➤ Balance the electrons; the electron change for both half-reactions must be 6.

➤ The first half-reaction is already a change of 6 electrons, so it stays as is. The second half-reaction is a change of 2, so it must be multiplied by 3.

$$14H^+ + Cr_2O_7^{-2} \rightarrow 2Cr^{+3} + 7H_2O \quad \Delta e^- = 6$$
$$3C_2O_4^{-2} \rightarrow 6CO_2 \quad \Delta e^- = 6$$

➤ Sum the two half-reactions.

$$14H^+ + Cr_2O_7^{-2} + 3C_2O_4^{-2} \rightarrow 2Cr^{+3} + 7H_2O + 6CO_2$$

➤ There is no canceling to do, so this is the final balanced equation.

EXAMPLE IN BASIC SOLUTION:

$Co^{+2} + H_2O_2 \rightarrow Co(OH)_3 + H_2O$ (The phase labels have been left out for clarity.)

SOLUTION:

➤ Divide into two half-reactions.

$$Co^{+2} \rightarrow Co(OH)_3$$
$$H_2O_2 \rightarrow H_2O$$

➤ Balance the atoms, using H_2O to balance oxygen, and H^+ to balance hydrogen.

$$3H_2O + Co^{+2} \rightarrow Co(OH)_3 + 3H^+$$
$$2H^+ + H_2O_2 \rightarrow 2H_2O$$

➤ Determine the electron change for each species that is changing.

   ➤ Co is +2 on the left; it is +3 on the right; this is a 1 electron change, and there is 1 Co atom changing, so the total electron change is 1.

   ➤ O is −1 on the left, it is −2 on the right; this is a 1 electron change, but there are 2 oxygen atoms changing, so the total electron change is 2.

➤ The LCD of 1 and 2 is 2. Therefore the n value is 2.

   ➤ The first half-reaction must be multiplied by 2.

$$6H_2O + 2Co^{+2} \rightarrow 2Co(OH)_3 + 6H^+$$
$$2H^+ + H_2O_2 \rightarrow 2H_2O$$

➤ Sum the two half-reactions.

$$6H_2O + 2Co^{+2} + 2H^+ + H_2O_2 \rightarrow 2Co(OH)_3 + 6H^+ + 2H_2O$$

➤ Cancel out where the same species shows up on both sides.

$$4H_2O + 2Co^{+2} + H_2O_2 \rightarrow 2Co(OH)_3 + 4H^+$$

➤ Change all H^+ to H_2O's and put the same number of OH^- on the other side.

$$4OH^- + 4H_2O + 2Co^{+2} + H_2O_2 \rightarrow 2Co(OH)_3 + 4H_2O$$

➤ Cancel again.

$$4OH^- + 2Co^{+2} + H_2O_2 \rightarrow 2Co(OH)_3$$

CELL NOTATION FOR VOLTAIC CELLS

Rather than draw the voltaic cell, a notation can be used instead. Cell notation is drawn as follows:

anode | anode's ion || cathode's ion | cathode

The **single line** indicates a phase change; the **double line** indicates the salt bridge between the half-cells. The salt bridge is necessary to complete the electrical circuit and allow the reaction to take place. The concentration of the ions is often written directly after the ion.

The cell notation for the cell in Figure 3-12 looks like:

$$Zn \mid Zn^{+2} \mid\mid Cu^{+2} \mid Cu$$

It is read as follows: At the anode

$$Zn\ (s) \rightarrow Zn^{+2}\ (aq)$$

At the cathode

$$Cu^{+2}\ (aq) \rightarrow Cu\ (s)$$

The sum

$$Zn\ (s) + Cu^{+2}\ (aq) \rightarrow Cu\ (s) + Zn^{+2}\ (aq)$$

Sometimes a redox reaction produces a gas or another species that is an ion in solution. In this case, the anode or cathode, being in solution, or being a gas, cannot have a wire attached. A platinum electrode is used to complete the circuit.

EXAMPLE:

$$Zn\ (s) + 2Fe^{+3}\ (aq) \rightarrow Zn^{+2}\ (aq) + 2Fe^{+2}\ (aq)$$
$$Zn \mid Zn^{+2} \mid\mid Fe^{+3}, Fe^{+2} \mid Pt$$

STANDARD CELL POTENTIAL

E°_{cell} is the symbol given to the cell potential under the standard conditions of $25^{\circ}C$, 1 M concentrations for all solutions, and 1 atm pressure for all gases. The E°_{cell} is calculated from the table of reduction potentials, as shown on next page.

TABLE OF REDUCTION POTENTIALS

The table of reduction potentials is used as follows:

➤ This is a table of **reductions**.
➤ For the **oxidation** half-reaction (it is **above** the reduction half-reaction in the table), the reaction is reversed and the sign of the value is reversed.
➤ For a spontaneous reaction, the anode reaction is **above** the cathode reaction.
➤ The anode reaction is the **reverse** of the reduction reaction.

TABLE 3-2

Standard Electrode Reduction Potentials in Aqueous Solution at 25°C	
Reduction Half-Reaction	Standard Potential (V)
$Li^+ (aq) + e^- \rightarrow Li (s)$	−3.04
$Ba^+ (aq) + e^- \rightarrow Ba (s)$	−2.71
$Mg^{+2} (aq) + 2e^- \rightarrow Mg (s)$	−2.38
$Al^{+3} (aq) + 3e^- \rightarrow Al (s)$	−1.66
$Zn^{+2} (aq) + 2e^- \rightarrow Zn (s)$	−0.76
$Cr^{+3} (aq) + 3e^- \rightarrow Cr (s)$	−0.74
$Fe^{+2} (aq) + 2e^- \rightarrow Fe (s)$	−0.41
$Cd^{+2} (aq) + 2e^- \rightarrow Cd (s)$	−0.40
$Ni^{+2} (aq) + 2e^- \rightarrow Ni (s)$	−0.23
$Sn^{+2} (aq) + 2e^- \rightarrow Sn (s)$	−0.14
$Pb^{+2} (aq) + 2e^- \rightarrow Pb (s)$	−0.13
$Fe^{+3} (aq) + 3e^- \rightarrow Fe (s)$	−0.04
$2H^+ (aq) + 2e^- \rightarrow H_2 (g)$	0.00
$Sn^{+4} (aq) + 2e^- \rightarrow Sn^{+2} (aq)$	0.15
$Cu^{+2} (aq) + e^- \rightarrow Cu^+ (aq)$	0.16
$Cu^{+2} (aq) + 2e^- \rightarrow Cu (s)$	0.34
$I_2 (s) + 2e^- \rightarrow 2I^- (aq)$	0.54
$Fe^{+3} (aq) + e^- \rightarrow Fe^{+2} (aq)$	0.77
$Ag^+ (aq) + e^- \rightarrow Ag (s)$	0.80
$Br_2 (l) + 2e^- \rightarrow 2Br^- (aq)$	1.07
$O_2 (g) + 4H^+ (aq) + 4e^- \rightarrow 2H_2O (l)$	1.23
$Cr_2O_7^{-2} (aq) + 14H^+ (aq) + 6e^- \rightarrow 2Cr^{+3} (aq) + 7H_2O (l)$	1.33
$Cl_2 (g) + 2e^- \rightarrow 2Cl^- (aq)$	1.36
$MnO_4^- (aq) + 8H^+ (aq) + 5e^- \rightarrow Mn^{+2} (aq) + 4H_2O (l)$	1.49
$H_2O_2 (aq) + 2H^+ (aq) + 2e^- \rightarrow 2H_2O (l)$	1.78
$S_2O_8^{-2} (aq) + 2e^- \rightarrow 2SO_4^{-2} (aq)$	2.01
$F_2 (g) + 2e^- \rightarrow 2F^- (aq)$	2.87

➤ **Never change the values** except for the sign.

➤ Add the two values to give E°_{cell}.

➤ The weakest reduction reactions are at the top of the table. (They have the most negative potential.)

➤ The strongest reduction reactions are at the bottom of the table. (They have the most positive potentials.)

➤ The E°_{cell} must always be positive for a spontaneous reaction that produces a voltage.

EXAMPLE: Determine E°_{cell} for the following cell:

$| Al | Al^{+3} || I_2 | I^- | Pt$

SOLUTION:

➤ The anode is an oxidation. The table of reduction potentials gives the value −1.66 V for the reduction half-reaction of Al^{+3} to Al. Therefore, the value for the oxidation half-reaction is +1.66 V.

➤ The cathode is the reduction. The table of reduction potentials gives the value +0.54 V for this half-reaction.

➤ Adding the two values gives +2.2 V for the E°_{cell}. It is positive, as it must be for a spontaneous reaction.

STANDARD CELL POTENTIAL AND STANDARD FREE ENERGY CHANGE

The ΔG° can be calculated from E°_{cell} using the following equation:

$$\Delta G^{\circ} = -nFE^{\circ}_{cell}$$

For a spontaneous reaction, E°_{cell} is positive, and ΔG° is negative.

EXAMPLE: Calculate the ΔG° for the cell given previously.

➤ Al to Al^{+3} is a $3e^{-}$ change; I_2 to I^{-} is a $2e^{-}$ change; the $n = 6$.

➤ Plug in the values and calculate ΔG°:

$$\Delta G^{\circ} = -(6)(9.65 \times 10^4 \text{ J/V})(2.2 \text{ V}) = -1.3 \times 10^6 \text{ J}$$

EQUILIBRIUM CONSTANT AND STANDARD CELL POTENTIAL

The equilibrium constant for a reaction can be calculated from E°_{cell} using the equation

$$E^{\circ}_{cell} = (0.0257/n) \ln K$$

EXAMPLE: For the previous cell, with $n = 6$ and $E^{\circ}_{cell} = 2.19$ V, the equilibrium constant is:

$$2.2 = (0.0257/6) \ln K$$

$$513 = \ln K$$

$$K = e^{513} = \text{too large to calculate}$$

NONSTANDARD CELL POTENTIALS

The **Nernst equation** is used to calculate the nonstandard cell potential; this occurs when the concentrations are other than 1 M. The Nernst equation is given as:

$$E_{cell} = E^{\circ}_{cell} - (0.0257/n) \ln Q$$

The equation requires the following:

➤ A balanced equation
➤ The Q expression and the value of Q
➤ The n value
➤ The value of E°_{cell}
➤ The values of E°_{cell}, n, and Q to be plugged in to calculate the nonstandard E_{cell}

EXAMPLE: Calculate the nonstandard cell potential for the cell

Al | Al^{+3} (0.150 M) || Zn^{+2} (0.075 M) | Zn
$3e^-$ $2e^-$

SOLUTION:

➤ Determine the n value which in this case is 6.
➤ Write the balanced equation.

$$2Al\,(s) + 3Zn^{+2}\,(aq) \rightarrow 2Al^{+3}\,(aq) + 3Zn\,(s)$$

➤ Write the Q expression and calculate Q.

$$Q = \frac{[Al^{+3}]^2}{[Zn^{+2}]^3} = \frac{(0.150)^2}{(0.075)^3} = 53.6$$

➤ Calculate the E°_{cell}.

$$
\begin{array}{ll}
Al \rightarrow Al^{+3} & +1.66 \\
Zn^{+2} \rightarrow Zn & -0.76 \\
\hline
 & +0.90
\end{array}
$$

➤ Plug into the Nernst equation.

$$E_{cell} = 0.90 - \left\{(0.0257/6)\ln 53.6\right\}$$

$$E_{cell} = 0.88\,V$$

Batteries

ELECTROMOTIVE FORCE OR VOLTAGE

The **electromotive force**, **emf**, of a cell, or the cell voltage generated by the reaction, is called E_{cell}. If you know the E_{cell} (by measuring it in the lab), you can calculate the work, w, produced by the cell using the equation

$$w_{max} = -nFE_{cell}$$

where $n =$ LCD of the mole e^-, $F = 9.65 \times 10^4$ coulombs (C)/mole e^-, and 1 joule (J) = 1 volt-coulomb (V-C).

EXAMPLE: Calculate the work done by the cell as shown next if the $E_{cell} = 0.650$ V

$$Pt \mid Hg_2{}^{+2} \mid Hg \, (l) \mid\mid H_2 \mid H^+ \mid Pt$$

SOLUTION:

➤ Calculate the n value.

$$n = 2 \quad \text{because } Hg_2{}^{+2} \rightarrow Hg \text{ is a } 2e^- \text{ change}$$
$$H_2 \rightarrow 2H^+ \text{ is a } 2e^- \text{ change}$$

➤ $w_{max} = (-2) \, (9.65 \times 10^4 \text{ C}) \, (0.650 \text{ V}) = -1.25 \times 10^5 \text{ J}$

➤ The sign is negative because work is produced.

Examples of voltaic cells include: (1) lead-storage batteries for cars, which use Pb for an anode, PbO_2 for a cathode, and H_2SO_4 as an electrolyte, and (2) nickel-cadmium batteries, which are drycell batteries where the anode and cathode are rechargeable.

SPECIALIZED CELLS—NERVE CELLS

The functional unit of the nervous system is the **neuron** (see Figure 3-16). The neuron is a highly specialized cell, which contains all of the organelles typically found in eukaryotic cells. It is highly suited for communication because of its wirelike projections, known as **dendrites**, which carry impulses toward the central **cell body**. The cell body is a thicker region of the neuron containing the nucleus and most of the cytoplasm. The **axon** is a projection, generally very long, that carries impulses away from the cell body. A typical neuron has a single axon, which may combine with other axons to form a single nerve.

The neurons are supported by **glial cells**, which are often referred to as **neuroglia** if located in the brain and spinal cord. In the outlying neurons of the peripheral nervous system, which carries impulses to and from the central nervous system, the supporting tissue consists of **Schwann cells**. Schwann cells tend to grow around the axon so that it is wrapped in a multilayered insulating cover called the **myelin sheath**. This fatty, membranous sheath allows for a rapid and highly efficient "insulated wire" for impulse transmission. The myelin sheath is regularly interrupted along the length of the neuron by short stretches of unmyelinated membrane, referred to as the **nodes of Ranvier**.

When a neuron is not conducting an impulse, it is said to be in its **resting state**. In this condition, a **resting potential** or a difference in charge exists between the inside and outside of the membrane. A higher concentration of sodium ions exists outside the membrane, while there is a higher concentration of potassium ions inside. In addition, a number of negatively charged proteins reside on the inside. These concentration

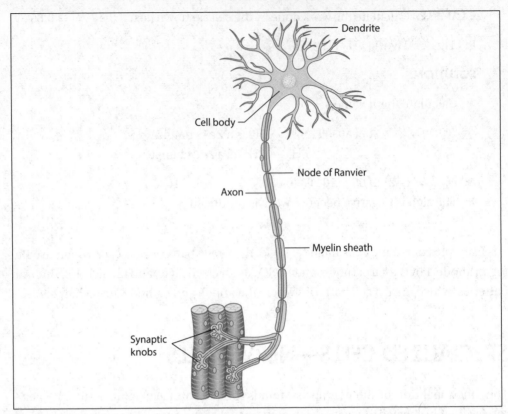

FIGURE 3-16 A model of a typical motor neuron. *Source:* From Sylvia S. Mader, *Biology*, 8th ed., McGraw-Hill, 2004; reproduced with permission of The McGraw-Hill Companies.

gradients are maintained by two factors: the impermeability of the resting membrane to Na^+ and the action of a Na^+/K^+ pump that, driven by ATP, transfers Na^+ to the outside and pumps K^+ inside. Because of these gradients, the inside of the neuron is negative relative to the outside; a potential difference of approximately -60 millivolts exists across the membrane. The natural tendency to correct this energetically unstable imbalance is the driving force behind the nerve impulse.

When a neuron is stimulated, the point of stimulation suddenly becomes permeable to sodium ions, which rush in, depolarizing the membrane as the incoming positive ions balance the negative internal charge. Enough Na^+ rushes in to actually make the inside of the membrane positive for a few milliseconds.

This shift of charge constitutes the **neural impulse**, or **action potential**. Although it occurs at only one place on the neuron, it triggers a depolarization of the adjacent area, thus initiating a new action potential. This process continues as a wave of depolarization down the length of the axon. The impulse is thus not actually transported anywhere but like a wave of water is re-created at each point.

At any point on the neuron when the action potential reaches a maximum (about $+40$ mV) of the interior relative to the exterior, the membrane suddenly again becomes impermeable to Na^+. At the same time, K^+ is pumped out, until it essentially balances the number of sodium ions that rushed in and the membrane is repolarized. This efflux of positive ions restores the resting potential of -60 millivolts (albeit with potassium ions rather than sodium ions). After the resting potential is established, the Na^+/K^+ pumps restore the original sodium and potassium gradients existing before the initiation of the action potential. Until the membrane reaches its resting potential again, it is incapable of developing a new action potential; while this is the case, the membrane is said to be in its **refractory period**.

CHAPTER 4

How Light and Sound Interact with Matter

Read This Chapter to Learn About

➤ Sound

➤ Light

➤ Molecular Structure and Spectra

➤ Geometrical Optics

SOUND

Any sound that you hear—whether it be the whisper of a librarian, a lawnmower your neighbor is using, a car moving down the road, or a jet preparing for takeoff—begins with a vibration, a vibration that moves in space, or a wave. Sound is an example of **longitudinal waves**, or waves that are generated by a disturbance that moves parallel to the direction of motion of the wave. In this chapter, the characteristics and behavior of sound waves are discussed.

Production of Sound

Sound waves are longitudinal waves that can propagate through all forms of matter—solids, liquids, and gases. Sound waves are generated by the motion of molecules or particles of a medium vibrating back and forth in a direction parallel to the direction of wave motion. As an object such as a tuning fork is struck, the vibration of the prong causes the air molecules to vibrate. As the air molecules vibrate, they alternate between being forced together (**compressions**) and then being separated at distances greater than the normal spacing (**rarefactions**). This example of a longitudinal wave is depicted in Figure 4-1.

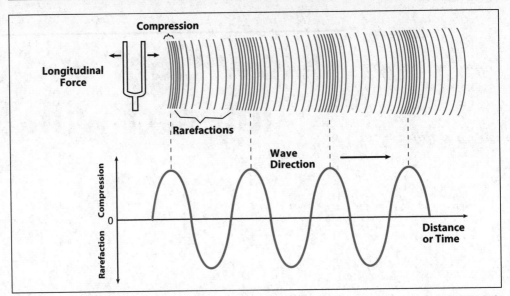

FIGURE 4-1 Longitudinal wave. *Source:* From George Hademenos, *Schaum's Outline of Physics for Pre-Med, Biology, and Allied Health Students,* McGraw-Hill, 1998; reproduced with permission of The McGraw-Hill Companies.

Relative Speed of Sound in Solids, Liquids, and Gases

The movement of sound requires molecules in a medium. The farther apart the molecules in the medium are spaced, the slower the speed of sound through the medium. Conversely, when molecules are tightly spaced, sound travels the fastest. Therefore, the speed of sound is the fastest in solids (where molecules are tightly spaced) and faster in liquids than in gases (where molecules are widely spaced).

The speed of sound through air is approximately 344 meters/second (m/s; 760 miles/hour). In contrast, the speed of sound in water is 1480 m/s.

Sound Intensity

Sound intensity represents the rate of energy transported by a sound wave per unit area perpendicular to its direction of motion. The sound level β, expressed in units of decibels (dB), is defined in terms of sound intensity I as:

$$\beta = 10 \log\left(\frac{I}{I_o}\right)$$

where I_o is the threshold for human hearing [$= 1 \times 10^{-12}$ watts per square meter (W/m^2)] and represents the intensity of the weakest sound detectable by the human ear. The following table lists representative values of sound intensity I and their corresponding sound level β.

TABLE 4-1 Sound Intensity and Sound Level of Representative Sounds

Sound Intensity (W/m²)	Sound Level (dB)	Representative Sounds
1×10^{-12}	0	Threshold of hearing
1×10^{-10}	20	Distant whisper
1×10^{-8}	40	Normal outdoor sounds
1×10^{-6}	60	Normal conversation
1×10^{-4}	80	Busy traffic
1×10^{-2}	100	Siren at 30 m
1	120	Loud indoor rock concert (threshold of pain)
1×10^{2}	140	Jet airplane
1×10^{4}	160	Bursting of eardrums

EXAMPLE: A particular sound level was measured at 75 dB. Determine its sound intensity.

SOLUTION: Using the expression for the sound level intensity, you have:

$$\beta = 10 \log \left(\frac{I}{I_o} \right)$$

$$75 \text{ dB} = 10 \log \left(\frac{I}{1 \times 10^{-12} \frac{W}{m^2}} \right)$$

Solving for I yields:

$$I = \left(1 \times 10^{-12} \frac{W}{m^2} \right) \left(\log^{-1} \frac{75 \text{ dB}}{10} \right) = 3.16 \times 10^{-5} \frac{W}{m^2}$$

Attenuation

Attenuation, also known as **damping**, is a gradual reduction in intensity of the sound wave and a subsequent loss of sound energy. Two primary factors behind attenuation include **scattering** and **absorption**. As it propagates from its source, the sound wave will reflect off of or pass around obstacles as it undergoes diffraction. Also, because sound is a form of energy, sound waves transfer a portion of their energy as they collide with and is absorbed by surrounding molecules in their path including air molecules.

Doppler Effect

The **Doppler effect** refers to the shift in frequency of a transmitted sound that is caused by a change in distance between the source of the sound and the observer. Consider a source emitting a sound of frequency f_s detected by an observer as a frequency f_o. If the source is moving toward the observer, the observer perceives an increase in the sound frequency. If the source is moving away from the observer, the observer perceives a decrease in frequency. The altered frequency detected by the observer is known as the **Doppler-shifted frequency**. These qualitative relationships can be expressed by:

$$f_o = f_s \left(\frac{v \pm v_o}{v \pm v_s} \right)$$

where v is the speed of sound in the given medium.

There are several specific cases of the Doppler effect:

➤ Moving sound source toward a fixed observer

$$f_o = f_s \left(\frac{v}{v - v_s} \right)$$

➤ Moving sound source away from a fixed observer

$$f_o = f_s \left(\frac{v}{v + v_s} \right)$$

➤ Fixed sound source with observer moving toward source

$$f_o = f_s \left(\frac{v + v_o}{v} \right)$$

➤ Fixed sound source with observer moving away from source

$$f_o = f_s \left(\frac{v - v_o}{v} \right)$$

EXAMPLE: A police car, in pursuit of a driver suspected of speeding, is traveling at 30 m/s when the siren is turned on, operating at a frequency of 1.2 kHz. Given that the speed of sound in air is 344 m/s, determine the frequency heard by a stationary or fixed witness as

1. the police car approaches the observer; and,
2. the police car passes the observer.

SOLUTION:

1. For the case of the moving source approaching a stationary observer, the Doppler-shifted frequency detected by the observer is given by:

$$f_o = f_s \left(\frac{v}{v - v_s} \right) = 1200 \text{ Hz} \left(\frac{344 \, \frac{m}{s}}{344 \, \frac{m}{s} - 30 \, \frac{m}{s}} \right) = 1315 \text{ Hz}$$

2. For the case of the moving source passing a stationary observer, the Doppler-shifted frequency detected by the observer is given by:

$$f_o = f_s \left(\frac{v}{v + v_s} \right) = 1200 \text{ Hz} \left(\frac{344 \, \frac{m}{s}}{344 \, \frac{m}{s} + 30 \, \frac{m}{s}} \right) = 1104 \text{ Hz}$$

Pitch

Pitch is often associated with the frequency of a sound wave. On a quantitative level, the pitch is given by the frequency of the sound wave. Pitch is also used to describe qualitatively how the frequency of the sound wave is perceived by an observer. The effect of pitch on an observer can be explained by the approach of an ambulance siren. As the ambulance approaches the observer, the observer notices an increasing pitch; as the ambulance passes the observer, the pitch of the siren decreases.

Resonance in Strings and Pipes

Many objects, such as a tuning fork or plucked string, vibrate at a specific frequency. This frequency is referred to as the object's **natural frequency**. When a periodic, external force strikes the object with a frequency equal to the natural frequency of the object, the amplitude of the object's motion increases and hence energy is absorbed by the object, a condition referred to as **resonance**. Examples of resonance can be found in engineering in the analysis of structure failure in response to severe weather/natural disasters, in medicine with magnetic resonance imaging and lithotripsy of kidney stones, and in music with the tonal qualities of certain string and brass instruments.

Standing Waves

Consider a wave generated on a stretched string with one side connected to a rigid surface. As the wave propagates toward the fixed end, it reflects, inverts, and continues back and forth across the string, causing the string to vibrate. In such instances, two waves (original and reflected waves) of equal frequencies and amplitudes are moving in opposite directions along the string, creating a **standing wave**, as shown in Figure 4-2.

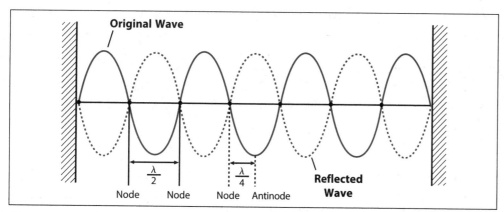

FIGURE 4-2 Standing wave. *Source:* From George Hademenos, *Schaum's Outline of Physics for Pre-Med, Biology, and Allied Health Students,* McGraw-Hill, 1998; reproduced with permission of The McGraw-Hill Companies.

The points with no displacement from the horizontal axis are termed **nodes**, and the points that are maximally displaced from the horizontal axis—that is, points at the peaks and valleys of each wave—are termed **antinodes**. The distance between two adjacent displacement nodes is one-half wavelength and the distance from node to antinode is one-quarter wavelength. The frequency, f, of a standing wave is given by:

$$f = \frac{v}{\lambda}$$

where v is the velocity of the wave.

FREQUENCIES IN A STRETCHED STRING

A stretched string of length L with both ends secured to a rigid surface possesses nodes at both ends. Because the distance between two adjacent nodes is $\lambda/2$, then $\frac{\lambda}{2} = L$ or $\lambda = 2L$. Substituting this value into the expression for the frequency yields:

$$f = \frac{v}{\lambda} = \frac{v}{2L}$$

This is the lowest frequency that the string can accommodate and is termed the **fundamental frequency**, or first harmonic. **Harmonic frequencies**, second and greater, are integer multiples of the first harmonic and can be determined from the generalized relation

$$f = \frac{nv}{2L} \qquad n = 1, 2, 3, \dots$$

The first, second, and third harmonics are illustrated in Figure 4-3.

FREQUENCIES IN A PIPE

The frequencies in a pipe can be derived in a fashion similar to that for the stretched string. However, the pipe offers more conditions to consider, such as both ends open and one end open. A node can be found at the end of a closed pipe whereas an antinode is present toward the open end of the pipe. Given that the distance from node to node is $\lambda/2$ and the distance from node to antinode is $\lambda/4$, the frequencies for a pipe of length L are as follows:

Pipe with both ends open: $\qquad\qquad\qquad L = 2\frac{\lambda}{4} = \frac{\lambda}{2}$

Fundamental frequency: $\qquad f_1 = \frac{v}{2L}$

Harmonics: $\qquad f_n = \frac{nv}{2L} \quad (n = 1, 2, 3, \dots)$

Pipe with one end open: $\qquad\qquad\qquad L = \frac{\lambda}{4}$

Fundamental frequency: $\qquad f_1 = \frac{v}{4L}$

Harmonics: $\qquad f_n = \frac{nv}{4L} \quad (n = 1, 3, 5, \dots)$

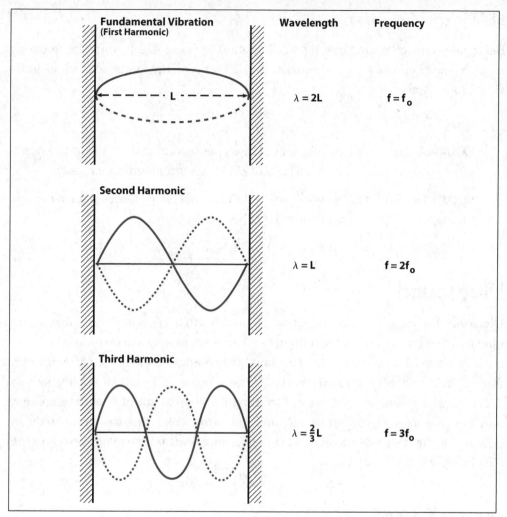

FIGURE 4-3 First, second, and third harmonics of a standing wave in a stretched string. *Source:* From George Hademenos, *Schaum's Outline of Physics for Pre-Med, Biology, and Allied Health Students,* McGraw-Hill, 1998; reproduced with permission of The McGraw-Hill Companies.

EXAMPLE: Determine the velocity of waves in an open pipe of 1.3 m length if the fundamental frequency is 225 Hz.

SOLUTION: For an open pipe, the fundamental frequency is given by:

$$f_1 = \frac{v}{2L}$$

Solving for v gives:

$$v = f_1\,(2L) = (225\ \text{Hz})\,(2)\,(1.3\ \text{m}) = 585\ \frac{\text{m}}{\text{s}}$$

BEATS

Beats are produced during interference by sound waves at slightly different frequencies. The beat frequency f_{beat} is equal to the difference in the frequencies of the individual sound waves f_1 and f_2 or

$$f_{beat} = f_1 - f_2$$

EXAMPLE: Determine the number of beats per second that are heard when two tuning forks of frequencies 256 Hz and 264 Hz are struck simultaneously.

SOLUTION: The beat frequency or the difference between frequencies of the two tuning forks determines the number of beats per second, or

$$f_{beat} = f_1 - f_2 = 264\,\text{Hz} - 256\,\text{Hz} = 8\,\text{Hz}$$

Ultrasound

Ultrasound refers to a region of sound frequencies that are above the range of frequencies that are audible to the human ear. The range of frequencies of human hearing is 20 Hz to 20 kHz (20,000 Hz). Ultrasound encompasses the range of frequencies from 20 kHz to 20 MHz (20,000,000 Hz). Ultrasound has a variety of applications in the medical and biological sciences including the assessment of fetal development and the diagnosis of cardiovascular and cerebrovascular disease, particularly in quantifying the presence and extent of atherosclerosis within the major vessels of the circulatory system.

Shock Waves

Shock waves develop when the speed of an object becomes greater than the speed of sound. In this case, the wavefronts generated by the object surpass the position of the source, resulting in a cone-shaped formation of successive wavefronts referred to as a **Mach zone**. A shock wave occurs along the surface or edge of the cone, resulting in a drastic decrease in air pressure and a very large increase in sound wave amplitude.

LIGHT

We are accustomed to thinking about light in terms of the output of a lamp or a fluorescent lightbulb illuminating a room. This type of light—visible light—represents only a very small subset of the physics definition of light waves, formally known as **electromagnetic waves**. Electromagnetic waves are an example of transverse waves, meaning that the direction of the disturbance is perpendicular to or at right angles to the direction of motion. This section introduces the concept of electromagnetic waves, defines them, and explains their characteristics and behavior as they interact with various surfaces or media, such as mirrors and lenses, to form images (geometrical optics).

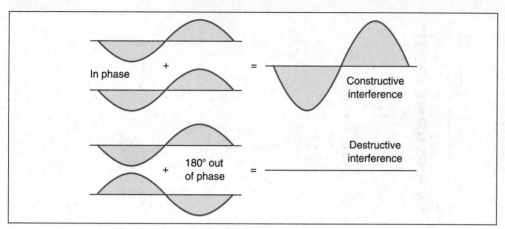

FIGURE 4-4 Wave interference.

Interference

Interference refers to the superposition of two waves traveling within the same medium when they interact. When applied to light waves, interference occurs only when the waves have the same wavelength and a fixed phase difference (i.e., the difference in which the peaks of one wave lead or lag the peaks of the other wave remains constant with time). These types of waves are referred to as **coherent waves**. The **principle of superposition** states that the wave that results from the interaction between two or more waves is the algebraic sum or overlapping of the individual waves, also referred to as superposition. These resultant waves undergo interference, the type of which depends on the phase of the two interacting waves, as shown in Figure 4-4.

When coherent waves with the same amplitude are combined, **constructive interference** occurs when the two waves are in phase and **destructive interference** occurs when the two waves are out of phase (have a phase difference of 180°).

Consider the experimental setup depicted in Figure 4-5, where two coherent light waves of wavelength λ impinge on two narrow slits separated by a distance d. The result is a fringe pattern of alternating bright and dark fringes where the bright fringes represent constructive interference and the dark fringes represent destructive interference. The position of the bright fringes (referred to as **maxima**) and the dark fringes (referred to as **minima**) can be determined from the relations:

Bright fringes (maxima) $d(\sin\theta) = m\lambda$ $m = 0, 1, 2, \ldots$

Dark fringes (minima) $d(\sin\theta) = \left(m + \dfrac{1}{2}\right)\lambda$ $m = 0, 1, 2, \ldots$

where $d\sin\theta$ represents the **path difference**, or the difference between distances that the waves travel to reach the fringe position on the screen.

Diffraction

Diffraction describes the ability of light waves to bend or spread through an aperture (opening) or around an obstacle. Consider a light wave with a wavelength λ that

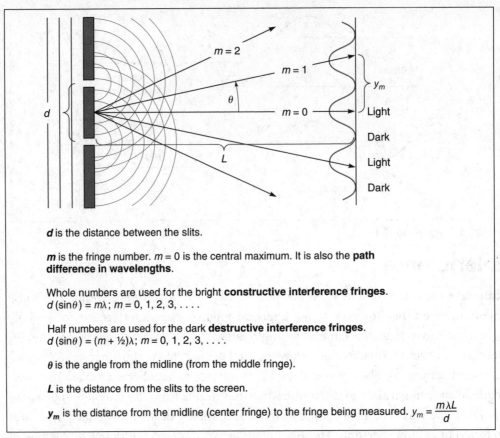

FIGURE 4-5 Experimental setup illustrating an interference pattern.

impinges on a narrow slit of width d. The light spreads out or diverges (a process known as **diffraction**) onto a viewing screen and results in a diffraction pattern consisting of alternating bright fringes and dark fringes. The position of the dark fringes observed at angles θ with respect to the normal or perpendicular of the screen is:

$$n\lambda = d\sin\theta$$

where $n = 1, 2, 3, \ldots$ is the order number of the dark fringe with respect to the central fringe.

Thin Films

The behavior of light as it passes through thin films is based primarily on reflection, refraction, and interference. As light strikes a thin film, the light ray will be partially reflected and partially refracted. The light ray that is refracted will also eventually reflect off of a subsequent film layer as it continues through the thin film. The objective of thin film interference is to determine the phase difference between the reflected first ray and the reflected refracted ray. If the light ray is reflected off of a layer with a higher index of refraction, then the light ray will be 180° out of phase. If the light ray is reflected off of a layer with a lower index of refraction, then the light ray will be in phase.

Constructive interference will occur when the two reflected light rays are shifted by an integer plus $\frac{1}{2}$ multiple of wavelengths. In this case, the path length difference of the light wave through the film can be determined from:

$$2nt = \left(m + \frac{1}{2} \right) \lambda \qquad m = 0, 1, 2, \ldots$$

where n is the index of refraction of the thin film, t is the thickness of the thin film, and λ is the wavelength of the light passing through the thin film.

Destructive interference will occur when the two reflected light rays are shifted by an integer multiple of wavelengths. In this case, the path length difference of the light wave through the film can be determined from:

$$2nt = m\lambda \qquad m = 1, 2, 3, \ldots$$

X-Ray Diffraction and Bragg's Law

In x-ray-diffraction, x-rays are focused on a solid sample in the form of a crystal lattice. The structure of a crystal lattice is an array of atoms positioned an equal distance from each other. The intensity peaks obtained from x-ray diffraction occur as a direct result of (1) **law of reflection**: the angle of incidence of the x-ray is equal to its angle of scatter (as shown in Figure 4-6); and (2) the difference in pathlength occurs as an integer number of wavelengths, demonstrated in the following equation, known as **Bragg's law**, for the constructive interference of the x-rays:

$$n\lambda = 2d \sin \theta$$

where

   $n =$ integer ($= 1, 2, 3, \ldots$)
   $\lambda =$ wavelength of the incident x-rays (measured in angstroms)
   $d =$ interatomic spacing distance (measured in angstroms)
   $\theta =$ angle of incidence (measured in degrees)

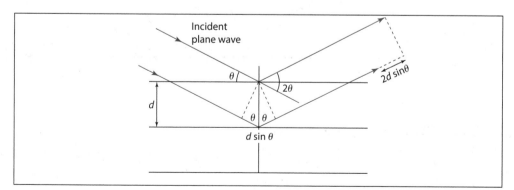

FIGURE 4-6 X-ray diffraction.

Polarization of Light

The disturbance that generates electromagnetic (light) waves is coupled electric and magnetic fields that act in a direction perpendicular to the direction of wave motion. In typical light sources, the electric field vectors are oriented in random directions but still in a direction perpendicular to wave motion. (The same is true for magnetic field vectors, but for the purpose of this discussion on polarization, only the electric field vectors are significant.) A light wave with the electric field vectors oscillating in more than one plane is termed **unpolarized light**.

Polarization is a process by which the electric field vectors of the light waves are all aligned along the same direction; in other words, they are all parallel. Polarization can be accomplished in several ways, with a common one being filters constructed of special materials (such as those found in sunglasses) that are able to block an oscillating plane of electric field vectors that is not moving parallel to the direction of wave motion.

Circular polarization occurs when the two oscillating electromagnetic waves are equal in amplitude but possess a 90° phase difference, as shown in Figure 4-7.

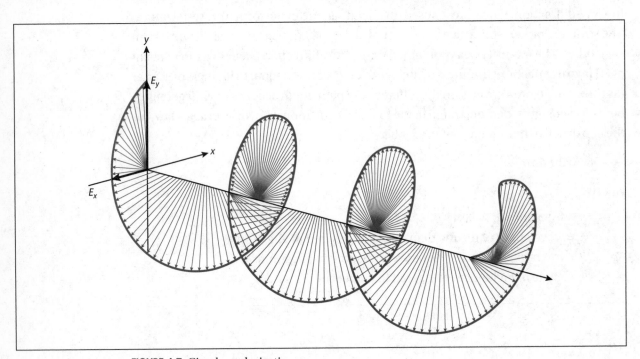

FIGURE 4-7 Circular polarization.

Electromagnetic Radiation

Light is a form of energy that travels as waves in space. But as described in this context, light is much more than just the visible light that one sees emitted from a lightbulb. Visible light is a small part of the **electromagnetic spectrum**, a collection of waves that travel at the same speed [the speed of light in a vacuum, denoted by $c = 3 \times 10^8$

meters/second (m/s)] but have different wavelengths. A **wavelength** of a wave is defined as the distance between two adjacent successive points of the wave.

Electromagnetic waves are transverse waves, meaning they occur as a result of a disturbance acting in a direction at right angles or perpendicular to the direction of wave motion. The disturbance that generates electromagnetic waves is coupled oscillating electric and magnetic fields, as shown in Figure 4-8.

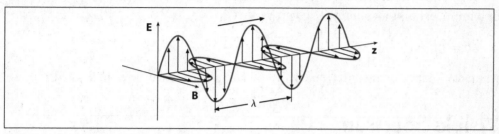

FIGURE 4-8 Electromagnetic waves. *Source:* From George Hademenos, *Schaum's Outline of Physics for Pre-Med, Biology, and Allied Health Students,* McGraw-Hill, 1998; reproduced with permission of The McGraw-Hill Companies.

Electromagnetic Spectrum

The **electromagnetic spectrum** is a compilation of electromagnetic waves, arranged with the larger wavelengths (radio waves) to the left and the smaller wavelengths (gamma rays) to the right, as represented in Figure 4-9 and described in the following table.

TABLE 4-2 Arrangement of Waves in the Electromagnetic Spectrum

Type of Electromagnetic Wave	Range of Frequencies (Hz)	Range of Wavelengths (m)
Radio waves	$< 3 \times 10^9$	$> 1 \times 10^{-1}$
Microwaves	$3 \times 10^9 - 3 \times 10^{11}$	$1 \times 10^{-3} - 1 \times 10^{-1}$
Infrared (IR) waves	$3 \times 10^{11} - 4 \times 10^{14}$	$7 \times 10^{-7} - 1 \times 10^{-3}$
Visible light	$4 \times 10^{14} - 7.5 \times 10^{14}$	$4 \times 10^{-7} - 7 \times 10^{-7}$
Ultraviolet (UV) light	$7.5 \times 10^{14} - 3 \times 10^{16}$	$1 \times 10^{-8} - 4 \times 10^{-7}$
X-rays	$3 \times 10^{16} - 3 \times 10^{19}$	$1 \times 10^{-11} - 1 \times 10^{-8}$
Gamma rays	$> 3 \times 10^{19}$	$< 1 \times 10^{-11}$

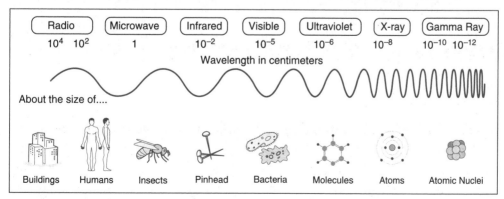

FIGURE 4-9 Electromagnetic spectrum.

Notice as the waves move from radio waves to gamma rays, the frequencies become larger and the wavelengths become smaller. The wavelength is inversely related to the frequency by:

$$v = f\lambda$$

where $v = c$, the speed of light.

In addition, each region of the electromagnetic spectrum, represented by a particle or photon, exhibits an energy, E, given by:

$$E = hf = \frac{hc}{\lambda}$$

where $h = $ Planck's constant ($= 6.63 \times 10^{-34}$ J · s) and $c = $ speed of light ($= 3 \times 10^8$ m/s).

Visible Spectrum

Of particular note is that **visible light**, that region of the electromagnetic spectrum that is visible to the human eye, is the smallest of all of the types of waves. Taken altogether, visible light is seen as white but can be separated into six colors (i.e., violet, blue, green, yellow, orange, and red), with each color defined by its characteristic wavelength. The wavelengths for visible light range from 4.0×10^{-7} m [400 nanometers (nm); 1 nm = 1×10^{-9} m], which represents the color violet, to 7.0×10^{-7} m, which represents the color red.

EXAMPLE: Radio waves have a typical wavelength of 10^2 m. Determine their frequency.

SOLUTION:

$$f = \frac{c}{\lambda} = \frac{3 \times 10^8 \, \frac{m}{s}}{1 \times 10^2 \, m} = 3 \times 10^6 \text{ Hz}$$

EXAMPLE: What is the speed of waves from radio station KQRS that broadcasts at a frequency of 710 kilohertz (kHz)?

SOLUTION: All electromagnetic waves, including radio waves, move with the same speed, the speed of light. Thus, the speed of these waves is 3×10^8 m/s.

MOLECULAR STRUCTURE AND SPECTRA

Absorption Spectroscopy

Spectral properties are used to determine the structure of molecules and ions. Of special importance are ultraviolet (UV), infrared (IR), and nuclear magnetic resonance (NMR). The various types of molecular energy, such as electronic, vibrational, and nuclear spin, are quantized, or in other words, only certain energy states are permitted. The molecule can be raised from its lower energy state (ground state) to a higher energy state (excited state) by the absorption of a photon (quantum of energy) of electromagnetic radiation of the permitted wavelength.

TABLE 4-3

Region of Electromagnetic Spectrum	Type of Excitation	Wavelength of Photon
Far ultraviolet	Electronic	100–200 nm
Near ultraviolet	Electronic	200–350 nm
Visible	Electronic	350–800 nm
Infrared	Molecular vibration	1–300 μm
Radio	Spin (electronic or nuclear)	1 m

Infrared Spectroscopy
BACKGROUND AND THEORY

Molecules have many degrees of freedom, and each electronic state (ground, first excited, second excited, etc.) has an array of energy levels corresponding to various vibrational and rotational states. Just like the electronic transitions, movement among vibrational energy levels is quantized and can be studied through spectrophotometric methods. These energy changes are, of course, much smaller; therefore, the electromagnetic radiation required for excitation is of correspondingly lower energy. For most vibrational excitations, absorption occurs in the infrared region of the spectrum.

Although governed by quantum considerations, many vibrational modes can be modeled using classical physics. For example, a stretching vibration between two nuclei can be characterized using **Hooke's law**, which predicts that the frequency of an absorbance is given by the relationship:

$$\bar{v} = 4.12 \sqrt{\frac{f}{\left(\dfrac{m_1 m_2}{m_1 + m_2}\right)}} \tag{1}$$

where $\bar{v}$ is the frequency in wavenumbers (equal to $1/\lambda$), m_1 and m_2 are the masses of the two nuclei in amu units, and f is the force constant, which can be roughly correlated to bond strength see the following table.

TABLE 4-4 Nominal Force Constant Values for Estimating IR Absorptions

Type of Bond	Nominal Force Constant (f) (dynes/cm)
Single	5×10^5
Double	10×10^5
Triple	15×10^5

Hooke's law provides a useful conceptual framework for predicting the position of various stretches in the IR spectrum. Essentially, there are two deciding terms: the **force constant** and the **reduced mass**, which is given by $m_1 m_2/(m_1 + m_2)$. The former is fairly straightforward—for example, the higher the force constant (i.e., the stronger the bond), the higher the wavenumber of the absorbance. Therefore, the C=C bond is predicted to absorb at a higher wavenumber than the C—C bond, and the C≡C bond higher still. The reduced mass is a bit more subtle. Consider the C—C bond in relation to the C—H bond. The reduced mass for two carbon atoms would be 144/24 = 6. In contrast, a carbon atom and hydrogen atom give a reduced mass of 12/13 = 0.923. Since this term is in the denominator, the lower reduced mass translates into a higher wavenumber.

EXTRACTING INFORMATION FROM IR SPECTRA

These two theoretic factors help understand the overview of IR absorptions given in Figure 4-10. The **IR spectrum** can be broken into four very broad (and fuzzy) categories. At very high frequencies (2500–4000 cm^{-1}), you see what can be dubbed the X—H stretches, positioned at high energy by virtue of the very light hydrogen atom (reduced mass consideration). There are a few features here worth mentioning. First, the almost ubiquitous C—H stretches congregate around 3000 cm^{-1}, but the exact positioning is diagnostic: aromatic C—H stretches tend to be just above 3000 cm^{-1}, and aliphatic stretches tend to be just below that mark. The carbonyl C—H stretch also has a characteristic position, showing up at just less than 2800 cm^{-1}. Another telltale feature in this region belongs to the O—H stretch, which tends to be very broad and dominating. Presence of such a band is a sure sign of an O—H group in your compound (or for the sloppy experimentalist, adventitious water in your IR sample!).

Next move to the region between 1900 and 2500 cm^{-1}, which is home to the triple bond. This area is usually fairly empty, so that absorptions are easy to spot. The alkyne stretch is typically sharp but very weak, and sometimes absent altogether, particularly for symmetrically substituted triple bonds. Nitriles, however, tend to be more

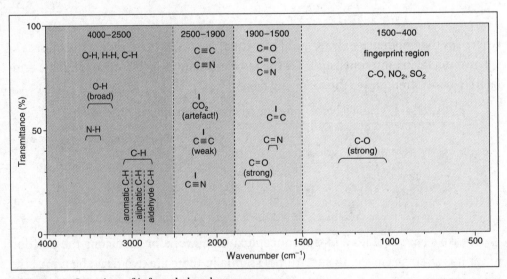

FIGURE 4-10 Overview of infrared absorbance ranges.

prominent, although they still tend toward the weak side. The only thing to watch out for here is that carbon dioxide also absorbs in this vicinity—because most instruments now take measurements in normal atmosphere and subtract out the background CO_2, artifacts can arise from quirky subtraction errors.

The real estate between 1500 and 1900 cm^{-1} houses many of the doubly bonded species, including alkene and carbonyl stretches. Alkenes give rise to a medium-intensity band just higher than 1600 cm^{-1}, whereas the garden-variety carbonyl stretch for a ketone shows up as an intense absorption at about 1715 cm^{-1}. Other carbonyl-containing functional groups wobble around this value: Esters absorb at slightly higher wavenumber (>1730 cm^{-1}), whereas amides have a somewhat lower-frequency absorbance (<1700 cm^{-1}). Often the carbonyl stretch, when present, is the predominant feature of the IR spectrum.

Finally, the portion of the spectrum bounded by 400 and 1500 cm^{-1} is known as the **fingerprint region**. This area tends to be fairly busy, and in fact this preponderance of detail gives rise to its name, because each compound exhibits a characteristic pattern (or fingerprint) in the low-frequency end of the spectrum. Many of these bands are difficult to correlate to particular vibrational modes, but one particular absorption deserves mention. The C—O stretch gives rise to a medium but noticeable band around 1100 cm^{-1}, which is diagnostic of ethers, esters, and alcohols.

There is much more detail that can be extracted from an IR spectrum (e.g., substitution patterns on benzene rings and alkenes), and several other significant modes of vibrational transition (bending, ring breathing, etc.) that have not been treated here. However, by considering just the major stretching vibrations, you are able to obtain a very rich snapshot of the functional group landscape on a molecule. This information complements the other spectroscopic methods, and contributes to the ensemble of data necessary to fully characterize an organic compound.

Ultraviolet-Visible Spectroscopy
BACKGROUND AND THEORY

If a molecule exhibits multiple degrees of unsaturation, the question naturally becomes whether they manifest themselves as rings or double bonds—and if the latter, whether the π (pi) bonds are isolated or in conjugation. To address this dual question, turn to the first of three spectroscopic methods. Recall that π systems arise from the combination of adjacent p orbitals, and that the number of molecular orbitals is determined by the extent of the p orbital array. Furthermore, as the π system encompasses more orbitals, the energy spacing becomes more compact and the distance between the HOMO (highest energy occupied molecular orbital) and LUMO (lowest energy unoccupied molecular orbital) diminishes (Figure 4-11). With simple dienes, this distance is already close enough that absorption of light in the near-UV results in electronic excitation. As conjugation is extended, this absorption moves to longer wavelengths

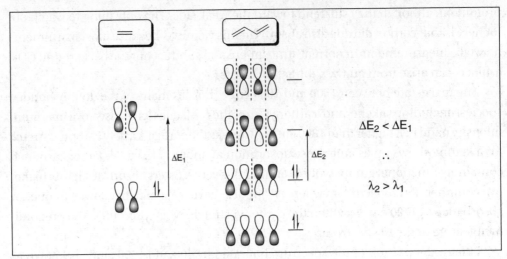

FIGURE 4-11 The impact of extended π systems on absorbance.

(lower energy) and eventually creeps into the visible region. Therefore, these extended π systems are often called **chromophores**, as they are responsible for the color in many organic compounds. In any event, the wavelength of light absorbed is dependent on the degree of conjugation in the chromophore, and so this absorption can tell us much about the nature of the π system in an unsaturated molecule.

INFORMATION FROM WAVELENGTH

It turns out that the π system is also remarkably sensitive to substituent patterns, a phenomenon that can be leveraged for extracting structural information. Through the examination of many experimentally derived values, sets of rules have been developed for predicting the wavelength of maximum absorbance (λ_{max}) for various substrates as a function of structure, work carried out primarily by Woodward, Fieser, and Nielsen. A brief summary of these rules is presented in Figure 4-12. Although not immediately intuitive, they are straightforward to apply once the framework is understood, and they are very powerful predictive tools.

There are a couple of subtleties that tend to be pitfalls for the beginning spectroscopist. First, you must approach the calculation as an accountant, recognizing that you must be very mindful of what is already in the ledger, as well as those items that do not have an impact on the bottom line. Thus, when a double bond is added to the system to extend conjugation, the base value is increased by 30 nanometers (nm), and you have essentially a new chromophore. Also, for carbonyl-containing chromophores, the —R or —OR groups on the other side of the carbonyl group are already accounted for in the base absorbance value, so it is important not to double-count these substituents later on.

Two specialized terminologies also deserve mention. First, a **homoannular diene** refers to any two double bonds that are incorporated into the same ring. Therefore, 1,3-cyclohexadiene would be considered a homoannular diene, but cyclohex-2-enone would not, because only one double bond is incorporated into the ring itself. For every instance of a homoannular component, add 39 nm to the base absorbance. Second, even though the etymology of an exocyclic double bond means "outside the ring," it is best thought of as a double bond that terminates in a ring. Each time this occurs, add 5 nm to the base absorbance.

		dienes	enones and enals			benzophenones, benzaldehydes, and benzoic acids		
base chromophore								
base absorbance λ_{max} (nm)		214	202	215	245 208 (R=H)	246 250 (R=H)		230
modifications to the base absorbance								
	position	all	α	β	γ	δ	o	m	p
substituents	-R	5	10	12	18	18	3	3	10
	-OR	6	35	30	17	31	7	7	25
	-Br	5	25	30	25	25	2	2	15
	-Cl	5	15	12	12	12	0	0	10
	-NR$_2$	60		95			20	20	85
π system architecture	double bond extending conjugation	+ 30 nm					not typically relevant		
	exocyclic character of a double bond	+ 5 nm							
	homoannular diene component	+ 39 nm							

FIGURE 4-12 Abbreviated rules for predicting λ_{max} for UV-Vis absorptions.

To get some practice in applying these rules, consider the tricyclic enone shown in Figure 4-13. Choose the base absorption of 215 (six-membered-ring enone) and tack on three double bonds to extend the conjugation (30 nm each for 90 nm total). You have thus established the domain of the chromophore (shown in bold). It is often helpful to highlight the chromophore for accounting purposes, even by darkening it in with a pencil. Examination of the chromophore thus reveals that ring C houses one

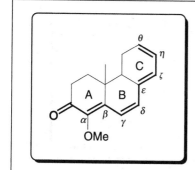

Base chromophore (6-ring enone)	215
3× double bond extensions	+ 90
Homoannular diene (in ring C)	+ 39
2× exocyclic double bonds	+ 10
α-alkoxy substituent	+ 35
β-alkyl substituent	+ 12
ε-alkyl substituent (same as γ)	+ 18
θ-alkyl substituent (same as γ)	+ 18
Predicted λ_{max}	437

FIGURE 4-13 Example of the application of predictive UV-Vis rules.

homoannular diene component, so add 39 nm to the ledger. Careful scrutiny also reveals two occurrences of exocyclic double bonds: both the α,β, and the ε,ζ olefins terminate in ring B. Add 5 nm for each occurrence.

The accounting of substituents is sometimes tricky, particularly for cyclic molecules. First, you must recognize that the substituent connected to the carbonyl group is already accounted for, so you do not double-count it. Start instead with the methoxy substituent in the α position, which adds 35 nm to the chromophore. The rest of the substituents are dealt with in the same manner. To help sort out what are bona fide substituents, imagine the chromophore (bold portion) is a hallway you could walk through—how many doorways would you see, and in what positions? Thus, starting from the carbonyl, you would see a door to your right at the α position, one on your left at the β position, another left door at ε, and finally a left door at θ. For accounting purposes, it matters not that there are substituents attached to those substituents (it also is inconsequential whether the "doors" are on the right or left—it simply helps you visualize the virtual corridor).

INFORMATION FROM INTENSITY

The intensity of the absorbance can also be diagnostic. For example, in the tricyclic enone shown previously we would expect to see at least two bands in the UV-Vis spectrum. The absorbance calculated in Figure 4-14 corresponds to the $\pi \rightarrow \pi^*$ transition from the HOMO to the LUMO. However, the lone-pair electrons on oxygen can also undergo excitation. Because they are technically not connected to the extended π system, they are neither bonding nor antibonding; therefore, they are considered nonbonding (n) electrons. The absorption is thus designated an $n \rightarrow \pi^*$ transition. Because the energy gap is smaller, this absorption occurs at higher wavelengths than the $\pi \rightarrow \pi^*$ transitions.

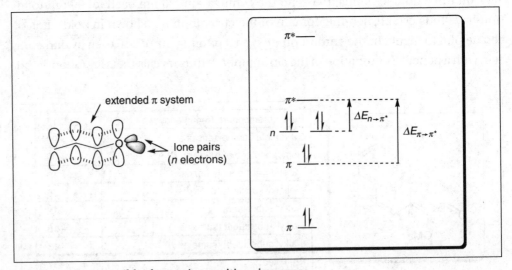

FIGURE 4-14 Two possible electronic transitions in enones.

The two types of excitation events differ not only in the maximum wavelength, but also in intensity. Because the lone pairs are essentially orthogonal to the extended π system, it would seem difficult to imagine how electrons could be promoted from one to the other. Indeed, these $n \to \pi^*$ events are known as **symmetry forbidden electronic transitions**. Like so many other forbidden things, they still happen, but the quantum efficiency is much lower; therefore, the intensity of the absorption is considerably weaker than the $\pi \to \pi^*$ absorption.

The intensity of a specific absorption is usually reported in terms of the molar extinction coefficient (ε), which is given by the relationship:

$$\varepsilon = \frac{A}{cl} \tag{2}$$

where A is the absorbance at the λ_{max}, c is the molar sample concentration, and l is the path length in centimeters (in most instruments, this is 1 cm). For allowed transitions, the molar extinction coefficients are on the order of 10^3 to 10^6. Forbidden transitions are typically in the hundreds.

Nuclear Magnetic Resonance Spectroscopy
BACKGROUND AND THEORY

Nuclear magnetic resonance (NMR) represents the organic chemist's most powerful tool for structure elucidation. The principle of this spectroscopic method is based on the transition of nuclei between spin states, the so-called **spin flip**. Recall from general chemistry that a proton can have a quantum spin number of $+1/2$ or $-1/2$; these two states are also called "spin up" and "spin down." In the absence of a magnetic field, these spin states are of equivalent energy, or degenerate. However, when a strong magnetic field is applied, the energy states differentiate themselves (see Figure 4-15). Nuclei aligned with the magnetic field find a lower energy state (designated α), whereas those opposed to the field are at higher energy (β).

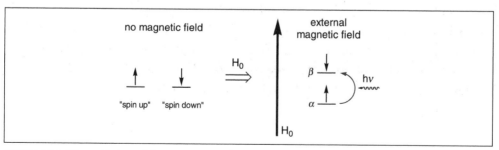

FIGURE 4-15 The splitting of degenerate nuclear spin states.

Analogous to electronic transitions in UV-Vis spectroscopy, nuclei in the lower energy state can be promoted to the next level by the absorption of electromagnetic radiation of the appropriate energy. In the case of spin flips, this absorption occurs in the radio frequency region—in other words, they are relatively low-energy transitions. In principle, this resonance can be observed with any nucleus of odd mass or odd atomic number. Examined here are two of the most indispensable methods, ^{1}H-NMR and ^{13}C-NMR. However, methods for observing other nuclei have become widely available, including ^{11}B, ^{19}F, and ^{31}P (of obvious importance for biochemists).

Very high magnetic fields must be used for useful data, and much of the innovation in NMR hardware centered around magnet technology (e.g., superconducting magnets). For all our efforts, however, the nucleus never experiences the full, unadulterated magnetic strength of the external field (H_0). This is because the electronic cloud surrounding the molecule shields the nuclei from the field. Instead, the α and β levels are split by a somewhat attenuated magnetic field, called the effective magnetic field (H_{eff}). Electron density, however, is a variable parameter. In a local environment in which the electron cloud has been impoverished (e.g., by the inductive effect of an electronegative atom), the nucleus is shielded less and thus experiences a stronger H_{eff} (see Figure 4-16). Consequently, the energy splitting is enhanced and the resonance occurs at correspondingly higher frequency. This phenomenon of higher-frequency absorbances in electron-poor regions is known as **deshielding**.

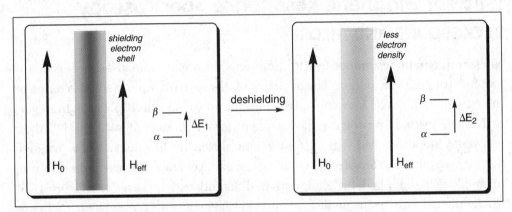

FIGURE 4-16 The shielding effect and deshielding.

Because the resonance frequency is field-dependent, no two spectrometers yield exactly the same resonance values. To alleviate this issue, spectroscopists historically have used an internal standard, against which all other signals are measured. The choice of **tetramethylsilane (TMS) (see Figure 4-17)** as an **NMR standard** was driven by a few practical considerations. First, it is thermally stable and liquid at room temperature; second, it has 12 protons that are identical, so the intensity of absorption is high; and finally, the protons in TMS are quite shielded (silicon is not particularly

$$H_3C\cdots\underset{\underset{H_3C}{|}}{\overset{\overset{CH_3}{|}}{Si}}\diagdown CH_3$$

FIGURE 4-17 The NMR standard, tetramethylsilane (TMS).

electronegative), so almost all other proton resonances you observe occur at higher frequencies relative to TMS.

PRINCIPLE OF CHEMICAL SHIFT

Instruments are characterized by the resonance frequency of TMS in the magnetic field of that instrument. For example, a 400-megahertz (MHz) NMR spectrometer incorporates a superconducting magnet in which TMS resonates at 400 MHz. Stronger magnets lead to higher values (e.g., 600 MHz, 900 MHz); in fact, magnets are so often specified by their TMS frequencies that we sometimes forget that the unit of MHz is a meaningless dimension for a magnetic field. That is, a 400-MHz NMR has a magnetic field strength of about 9.3 Tesla (T), yet for whatever reason, this parameter is almost never mentioned.

Nevertheless, you can use the TMS resonance to talk about the general landscape of the NMR spectrum. Figure 4-18 shows a typical measurement domain for a 400-MHz spectrometer, which is bounded on the right by the resonance frequency of TMS (400,000,000 Hz). The range through which most organic molecules absorb extends to about 400,004,000 Hz, or 4000 Hz relative to TMS. However, these values change as magnetic field strength is altered—an absorbance at 2000 Hz on a 400-MHz NMR would absorb at 1000 Hz on a 200-MHz NMR. To normalize these values, we instead report signals in terms of **parts per million (ppm)**, which is defined as:

$$\text{ppm} = \frac{v}{R} = \frac{\text{Hz}}{\text{MHz}} \tag{3}$$

where v is the signal frequency (in Hz) relative to TMS and R is the base resonance frequency of TMS (in MHz), a parameter known as **chemical shift**. Thus, on a 400-MHz

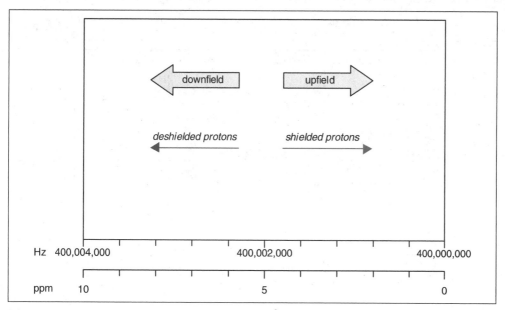

FIGURE 4-18 Important architectural features of the ^{1}H-NMR spectrum.

instrument a signal at 2000 Hz would be reported as having a chemical shift of 5 ppm (2000 Hz/400 MHz). This allows you to establish a universal scale for proton NMR ranging from 0 to about 10 ppm—although it is not terribly uncommon to find protons that absorb outside that range.

Working within this framework, it is important to understand certain features and terminology related to position in the NMR spectrum. First, the ppm scale obscures the fact that frequency increases to the left, so this must be borne in mind. Thus, as protons are deshielded, they are shifted to the left—spectroscopists have dubbed this a "downfield" shift (see Figure 4-18). Similarly, migrating to the right of the spectrum is said to be moving "upfield". Phenomenologically, a downfield shift is evidence of deshielding, and this understanding helps us interpret NMR data.

INFORMATION FROM CHEMICAL SHIFT

Using this idea, you can establish general regions in the NMR spectrum where various proton types tend to congregate (see Figure 4-19). For example, most purely aliphatic compounds (hexane, etc.) absorb far upfield in the vicinity of 1 ppm. The attachment of electron-withdrawing groups (e.g., carbonyls) tends to pull resonances downfield. Thus, the protons on acetone show up at around 2.2 ppm. In general, the region between 0 and 2.5 ppm can be thought of as home to protons attached to carbons attached to carbon (H—C—C). This is also where terminal alkyne protons absorb.

As electronegative elements are attached, however, resonances are shifted even farther downfield. Thus, the methyl protons on methanol resonate at about 3.4 ppm, and the protons on chloromethane appear at about 3.1 ppm. Multiple electronegative elements have an additive effect: compared to chloromethane, dichloromethane resonates at 5.35 ppm, and chloroform (trichloromethane) absorbs at 7.25 ppm. As a

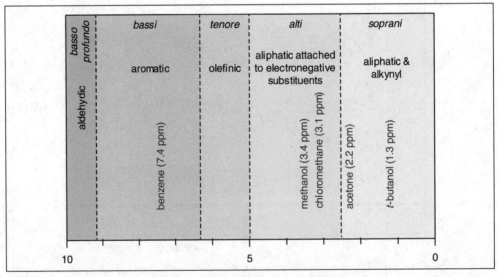

FIGURE 4-19 General regions of the ^{1}H-NMR spectrum, with benchmarks.

rough guideline, the region between 2.5 and 5 ppm belongs to protons attached to carbons that are attached to an electronegative element (H—C—X).

Moving farther downfield, you encounter protons attached to sp^2 carbons, starting with the **olefinic** (alkenyl) variety, which absorb in the region between about 5 and 6.5 ppm. Next come the **aromatic** protons, which range from about 6.5 to 9 ppm. As a benchmark, benzene—the prototypical aromatic compound—absorbs at 7.4 ppm. Just like their **aliphatic** cousins, the olefinic and aromatic protons are shifted downfield as electron-withdrawing groups are attached to the systems. Finally, signals in the region between about 9 and 10 ppm tend to be very diagnostic for **aldehydic** protons—that is, the protons connected directly to the carbonyl carbon.

Now a word of caution. These rough guidelines are just that—they do not represent strict demarcations. Rather, they paint the NMR spectrum in broad brush strokes, so that you can take away an immediate impression from the data to start our thought processes. Think of these regions as voices in a choir, whose ranges often cross each other. Just as tenors often sing the alto line in Early Music, so too can olefins exhibit resonances above 5 ppm.

SPLITTING PATTERNS AND INTEGRATION

It would be enough of a gift if NMR told you only about a given proton's chemical environment—but you can gain much more information from the spectrum. One source of knowledge derives from a phenomenon known as **scalar (or spin–spin) coupling**, through which a proton is influenced by its nearest neighbors. Figure 4-20 explores this effect with the hypothetical situation of one proton (H_x) being next door to a pair of protons (H_a and H_b). The latter two protons are either spin up or spin down, and in fact you can imagine four permutations (2^2) of two nuclei with two states to choose from. If both H_a and H_b are aligned with the external magnetic field, they will serve to enhance H_{eff}, thereby increasing the energy gap between the $H_x\alpha$ and β states, which in turn leads to a higher frequency absorbance (a downfield shift). Conversely, the situation in which both H_a and H_b oppose the external magnetic field diminishes the H_{eff}, leading to an upfield shift. The two remaining permutations have one spin up and the other spin down, thereby canceling each other out. The result is a pattern known as a **triplet**, in which the three prongs of the signal are present in a 1:2:1 ratio.

Had there been only one neighboring proton, there would have been only two possibilities: The neighboring proton is either spin up or spin down. The resulting pattern would have been a **doublet**. By the same token, three neighboring protons would have eight permutations (2^3), which could be all up, all down, two up and one down, or one up and two down. This would lead to a **quartet** pattern. To summarize the trends in these examples, one neighboring proton gives a doublet, two give a triplet, and three give a quartet. In other words, the pattern exhibited (or "multiplicity") has one more prong than the number of neighboring protons. Patterns of this type are said to obey the "**$n+1$ rule**," where n = the number of neighboring protons, and $n + 1$ = the

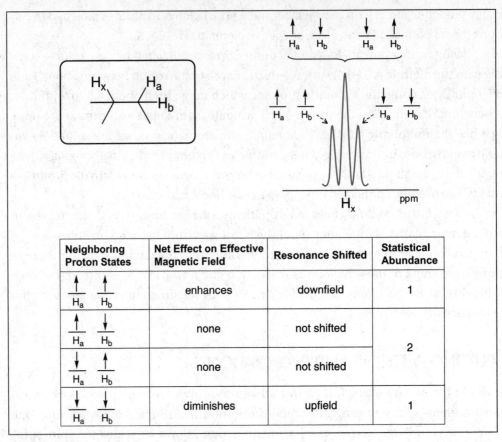

FIGURE 4-20 The origin of scalar splitting.

multiplicity of the signal. The most common splitting patterns and their abbreviations are summarized in the following table. It should be noted here that heteroatomic protons (N—H, O—H) are capricious beasts—in very dilute (and pure) solution, they behave much like any other proton, and obey the $n + 1$ rule, although their chemical shift is hard to pin down. However, the usual state of affairs is to encounter O—H protons as very broad singlets that appear not to couple with adjacent protons. Chemical shift is typically highly variable.

TABLE 4-5 Some Common Splitting Patterns

Abbreviation	Pattern
s	Singlet
d	Doublet
t	Triplet
q	Quartet
quint	Quintet
m	Multiplet

So the chemical shift tells you about a proton's electronic environment, and splitting patterns tell you about the number of neighboring protons—but still the spectrum

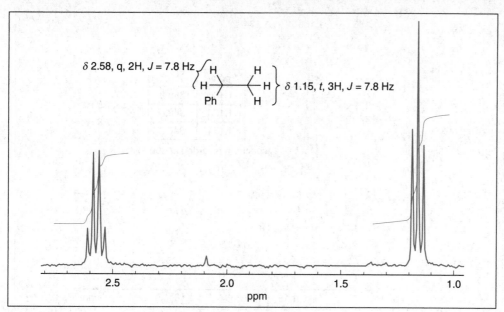

FIGURE 4-21 The ethyl moiety of ethylbenzene.

has further secrets to yield. It turns out that the area under each signal is proportional to the number of protons giving rise to that signal. Therefore, integrating the area under the curves allows you to establish a ratio for all chemically distinct protons in the NMR. As an illustration, Figure 4-21 presents a portion of the NMR spectrum of ethylbenzene corresponding to the ethyl moiety. There are two signals (at 1.15 ppm and 2.58 ppm), corresponding to the two sets of chemically distinct protons on the ethyl substituent (a methyl and methylene group, respectively). The downfield shift of the methylene group is an indication of its being closer to the slightly electron-withdrawing benzene ring. The splitting patterns tell us that the protons resonating at 1.15 (the triplet) are next to two other protons, and the protons at 2.58 (the quartet) are adjacent to three other protons. Furthermore, the integral traces reveal that the two sets of protons are present in a 3:2 ratio. Extract the integration data simply by taking a ruler and measuring the heights of the integral traces. The absolute values mean nothing by themselves, but taken together they establish a ratio of the various protons.

Within a given pattern, the spacing between the peaks is known as the coupling constant, or J-value, usually reported in Hz. Notice in Figure 4-21, the proper way to report NMR data is as follows (explanatory comments in parentheses): δ (indicates the values are in ppm), 1.15 (the chemical shift), t [the multiplicity (here, a triplet)], 3H (the number of protons given by the integration), $J = 7.8$ Hz (the measured coupling constant). This is a very inflexible format, and should always be used when reporting NMR data. A natural question, then, is how to extract the J-values from an NMR spectrum. Again, the ruler is your friend. By carefully measuring against the bottom scale, you can assign ppm values to each prong of the signal (see Figure 4-22). Applying Equation 4.3 (from page 107), if ppm = Hz/MHz, then Hz = (ppm)(MHz). In other words, to convert ppm to Hz, simply multiply by the "field strength," or more accurately, the native

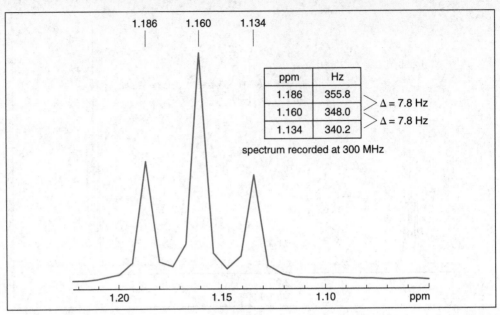

ppm	Hz
1.186	355.8
1.160	348.0
1.134	340.2

Δ = 7.8 Hz

Δ = 7.8 Hz

spectrum recorded at 300 MHz

FIGURE 4-22 Measuring *J*-values from a spectrum.

resonance of TMS. The spectrum in Figure 4-22 was obtained on a 300-MHz instrument, so the prong at 1.186 ppm corresponds to 355.8 Hz (1.186 × 300). Once the peaks are converted to units of Hz, the *J*-value is simply the distance between the peaks. It is worth noting at this point that chemical shifts are reported in ppm because their ppm values do not change with field strength; by the same token, *J*-values in Hz remain constant regardless of magnetic field, so this is how they are reported.

INFORMATION FROM COUPLING CONSTANTS

As luck would have it, the magnitude of the coupling constant can also provide useful information about the structure of a molecule. It is important to understand here, that scalar coupling is not a through-space interaction, but a through-bond effect. In other words, the information about the neighboring nuclear spin states is actually communicated through the electronic network bonding the two sets of nuclei. Also bear in mind that this information must travel through three bonds (H—C, C—C, C—H). Consequently, the orientation relationship between the two C—H bonds is very important. In fact, an empirical relationship has been elucidated between the observed *J*-value and the dihedral angle (ϕ) set up between the two C—H bonds. Figure 4-23 shows this relationship in graphical format, which is known as the **Karplus curve**. The important outcomes are these: When the dihedral angle is at 0° (eclipsed) and 180° (antiperiplanar), the *J*-value is at a maximum (ca. 12 Hz), and at a 90° dihedral angle, the *J*-value is at a minimum (ca. 2 Hz). This makes sense, if one considers that when the two C—H bonds are orthogonal, communication between the σ bonds is practically nonexistent.

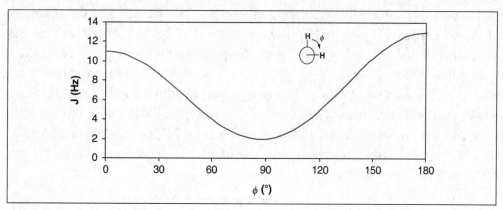

FIGURE 4-23 The Karplus curve.

The impact of the Karplus relationship can be seen in the ring-fusion hydrogens of *cis*- and *trans*-decalin systems (see Figure 4-24). In *cis*-decalin, the dihedral angle is locked at about 60° and the observed coupling constant is relatively low. By contrast, the same hydrogens in *trans*-decalin are antiperiplanar ($\phi = 180°$), and the observed *J*-value is quite large. The Karplus curve also explains the coupling constants in freely rotating systems, which exhibit a time-averaged value of about 7.5 Hz (our garden-variety *J*-value for most acyclic aliphatic protons).

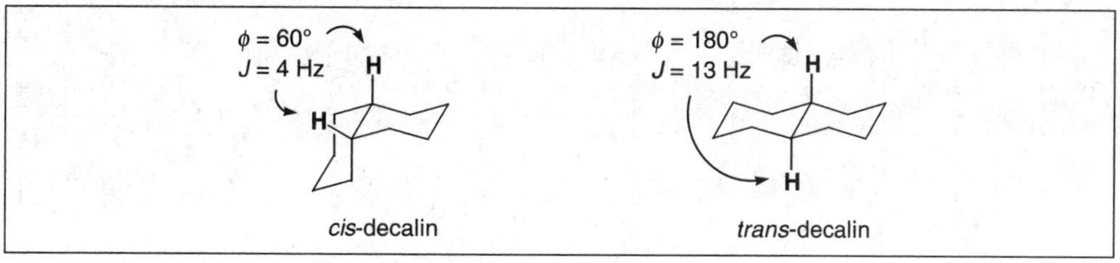

FIGURE 4-24 Impact of the Karplus relationship in constrained systems.

Generally speaking, protons connected to the same carbon (geminal protons) do not split each other—with one significant exception. Figure 4-25 shows three types of geminal protons: homeotopic, enantiotopic, and diastereotopic. To better understand the terminology, consider the imaginary products formed by replacing each of the two geminal protons with another atom, say a chlorine substituent. In the homeotopic example, the two "products" are identical (2-chloropropane); for the enantiotopic protons, two enantiomeric "products" are formed [*R*- and *S*-(1-chloroethyl)benzene]; and replacing H_a versus H_b in the cyclopropane derivative gives diastereomers (*cis*-dichloro vs. *trans*-dichloro).

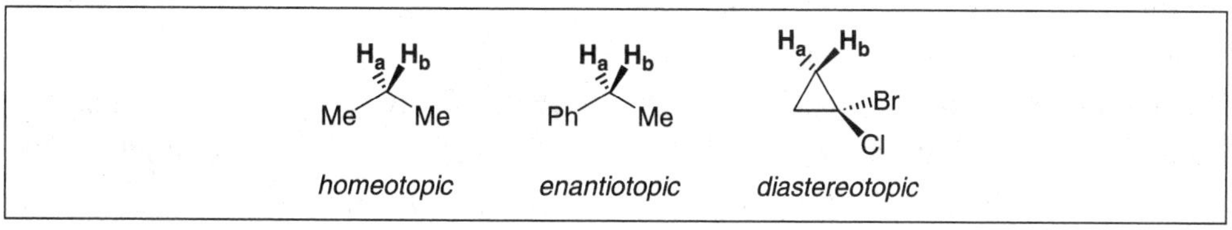

FIGURE 4-25 Three types of geminal protons.

Homeotopic and enantiotopic geminal protons do not split each other, because they are chemically equivalent. In other words, they are identical through a plane of symmetry (the plane of this page). However, **diastereotopic protons** are not chemically equivalent—in the example in Figure 4-25, H_a is in proximity to the chloro substituent, whereas H_b is close to the bromine. In short, they are in different worlds and therefore behave as individuals. Therefore, in these special cases, geminal protons do split each other, and the magnitude of the J-value is relatively large. Figure 4-26 lists this value, along with other representative coupling constants. This summary is useful for the interpretation of spectra.

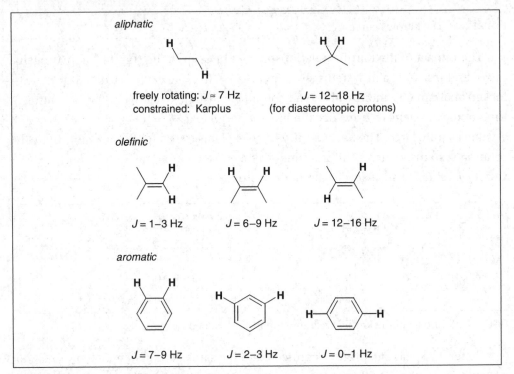

FIGURE 4-26 Some representative coupling constants.

Some interesting patterns arise when a proton is coupled to two different neighbors with divergent J-values. For example, terminal alkenes have three olefinic protons that are related with three different coupling constants (see Figure 4-26). The *trans*-olefinic coupling constant (J_{ac}) is the largest, with typical values ranging from 12 to 16 Hz; the next largest is the *cis*-olefinic value (J_{ab}), which is usually around 6–9 Hz; and finally the *gem*-olefinic coupling constant (J_{bc}) is quite small—about 1–3 Hz.

With this information in hand, consider the excerpt of the NMR spectrum shown in Figure 4-27, which shows the resonances for H_c and H_b. H_a is split into a doublet by H_c (with a large J-value), and again into a doublet by H_b (with a small J-value). This pattern is known as a **doublet of doublets** (or colloquially, as a double doublet) and is designated with the abbreviation "dd." Similarly, H_b is split into a doublet by H_a (with a medium J-value), and again into a doublet by H_c (with a small J-value), to give another

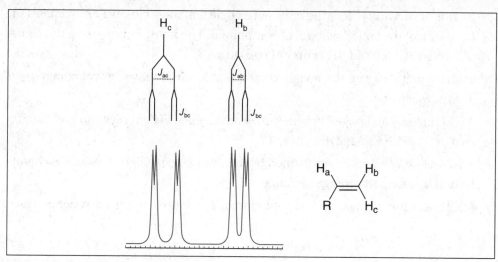

FIGURE 4-27 Multiple splitting patterns.

double doublet. The two double doublets are qualitatively different, and even casual visual inspection reveals that the downfield pattern is a combination of the large and small coupling constants, whereas the upfield pattern incorporates the medium and small coupling constants. This alone would allow you to make a fairly confident assignment of these peaks to H_c and H_b, respectively.

GEOMETRICAL OPTICS

Geometrical optics is a branch of physics concerned with the propagation of light used to form images. In typical problems of geometrical optics, a light source is allowed to strike one of two basic types of optical components: mirrors and thin lenses.

    Mirrors are optical components that reflect light rays from a light source to form an image. Two types of mirrors are **plane mirrors** and **spherical mirrors**. Spherical mirrors can be further subdivided into **concave** (curved inward) mirrors and **convex** (curved outward) mirrors.

    Thin lenses are optical components that refract light rays from a light source to form an image. Thin lenses are generally curved and referred to as spherical thin lenses. Two general forms of spherical thin lenses are concave (curved inward) and convex (curved outward). These two components are discussed in greater detail later.

    Terms describing parameters critical to problems in geometrical optics include the following:

➤ **Object distance**, o, is the distance between the object and the optical component.

➤ **Image distance**, i, is the distance between the image and the optical component.

➤ **Focal length**, f, is the distance between the image and the optical component observed when the source is imaged from an infinite distance. The point at which the incoming light rays converge to form the image is known as the **focal point**, F.

➤ **Radius of curvature**, R, is the radius of a circle that most closely approximates the curvature of the spherical optical component. The point representing the center of this circle is termed the **center of curvature**, C.

Other terms that describe the image formed as a result of these optical components include the following:

➤ A **real image** is an image formed by the convergence of light rays and is characterized by a **positive image distance**, $+i$.

➤ A **virtual image** is an image formed by the divergence of light rays and is characterized by a **negative image distance**, $-i$.

➤ **Magnification**, m, of an optical component (thin lenses or mirror) is defined as:

$$m = -\frac{i}{o} = \frac{h_i}{h_o}$$

$$\text{Magnification} = -\frac{\text{image distance}}{\text{object distance}} = \frac{\text{image height}}{\text{object height}}$$

A **negative magnification value** indicates that the image is smaller than the object and is inverted, whereas a **positive magnification value** indicates that the image is larger than the object and is upright or erect.

In solving problems in geometrical optics, you are presented with an optical component and an object (light source) positioned a given distance from the component and asked to determine the image distance from the component where the image is formed and the type of image formed. This objective can be accomplished using two different techniques: an analytical technique and a graphical technique. The **analytical technique** consists of a mathematical relation between the image distance i, object distance o, focal length f, and radius of curvature R. The **graphical technique** involves ray tracing for the location of the image formed by the optical component. **Ray tracing** graphically follows the path of three principal light rays emitted from the object and interacting with the optical component.

Reflection and Refraction of Light

As light waves propagate through one medium and approach a second medium, they can interact with the boundary between the two media in primarily one of two separate ways: reflection and refraction. Consider a light ray that propagates through one medium and strikes the boundary at an incidence angle of θ_i with the normal (axis perpendicular to the plane surface), as shown in Figure 4-28.

The light ray can reflect or bounce off the surface boundary at an angle of reflection θ_r, also measured with respect to the normal, which is equal in magnitude to the angle of incidence. This is known as the **law of reflection**, represented by:

$$\theta_i = \theta_r$$

angle of incidence = angle of reflection

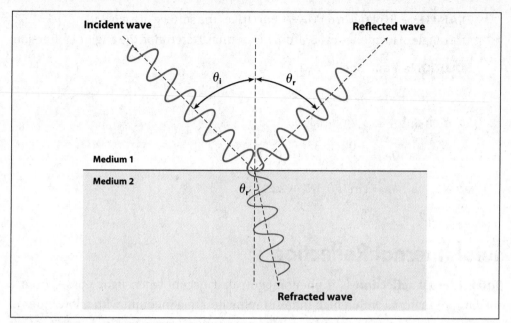

FIGURE 4-28 A light wave propagating through one medium and striking a second medium. *Source:* From George Hademenos, *Schaum's Outline of Physics for Pre-Med, Biology, and Allied Health Students*, McGraw-Hill, 1998; reproduced with permission of The McGraw-Hill Companies.

In addition to reflection, the light ray can bend or refract as it enters the second medium. The angle at which the light ray refracts, $\theta_{r'}$, is dependent on the ratio of the indices of refraction between the two media. The **index of refraction** n for a given material is defined as

$$n = \frac{\text{speed of light in vacuum}}{\text{speed of light in material}} = \frac{c}{v}$$

The index of refraction for common substances is as follows:

Air	$n = 1.00$	Ethyl alcohol	$n = 1.36$
Glass	$n = 1.52$	Polystyrene	$n = 1.55$
Water	$n = 1.33$	Sodium chloride	$n = 1.54$
Diamond	$n = 2.42$	Acetone	$n = 1.36$

The **angle of refraction** $\theta_{r'}$ with respect to the normal is related to the incident angle by the **law of refraction**, also known as **Snell's law**:

$$n_1 \sin \theta_i = n_2 \sin \theta_{r'}$$

where n_1 and n_2 are the indices of refraction of the first medium and second medium, respectively.

> **EXAMPLE:** A ray of light strikes the surface of a swimming pool at an angle of 45° from the normal. Determine the angle of reflection.

> **SOLUTION:** From the law of reflection, the angle of incidence is equal to the angle of reflection. Thus, $\theta_i = \theta_r = 45°$ from the normal.

EXAMPLE: A light ray in air ($n = 1.00$) strikes the surface of a glass pane ($n = 1.52$) at an angle of incidence of 35° from the normal. Determine the angle of refraction.

SOLUTION: From Snell's law:

$$n_1 \sin \theta_i = n_2 \sin \theta_{r'}$$

$$1.00 \sin 35° = 1.52 \sin \theta_{r'}$$

$$\sin \theta_{r'} = \frac{1.00 \sin 35°}{1.52} = 0.377$$

$$\theta_{r'} = \sin^{-1} 0.377 = 22.1°$$

Total Internal Reflection

Total internal reflection is a phenomenon that occurs when light passes from a medium or material with a high index of refraction to a medium with a low index of refraction. For example, consider a light ray passing from glass ($n = 1.52$) to air ($n = 1.00$) at an angle of incidence θ_i, as shown in Figure 4-29. In this case, the angle of refraction is greater than the angle of incidence. In fact, as one increases the angle of incidence, the light ray has an angle of refraction of 90° and is subsequently refracted along the interface between the two media. The angle of incidence that causes light to be refracted at 90° from the normal is called the **critical angle** θ_c, given by:

$$\sin \theta_c = \frac{n_2}{n_1}$$

EXAMPLE: Assuming air as the external medium, determine the critical angle for total internal reflection for diamond ($n = 2.42$).

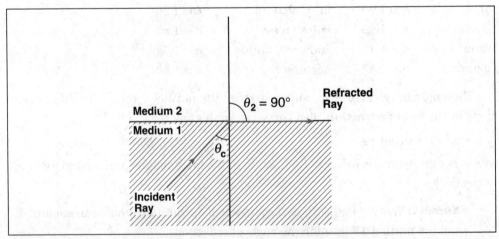

FIGURE 4-29 A light ray passing from glass to air, illustrating total internal reflection. *Source:* From George Hademenos, *Schaum's Outline of Physics for Pre-Med, Biology, and Allied Health Students*, McGraw-Hill, 1998; reproduced with permission of The McGraw-Hill Companies.

SOLUTION: Using the expression for the critical angle

$$\sin \theta_c = \frac{n_2}{n_1} = \frac{n_{air}}{n_{diamond}} = \frac{1.00}{2.42} = 0.413$$

$$\theta_c = \sin^{-1} 0.413 = 24.4°$$

Dispersion of Light

Dispersion is the separation of any traveling wave into separate frequency components. An example of dispersion is the separation of white light into its wavelength components and its corresponding elementary colors as it passes through a prism, as shown in Figure 4-30. As it passes through a prism, white light refracts at different angles with the smallest component wavelength (violet) being bent the farthest and the largest component wavelength (red) being bent the least.

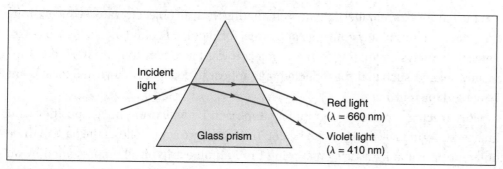

FIGURE 4-30 Separation of white light by dispersion.

Mirrors

PLANE MIRRORS

Light rays emanating from an object toward a plane mirror appear to converge at a point within the mirror, as shown in Figure 4-31. The image created by a plane mirror is always virtual and erect—that is, the image appears to be positioned the same distance from the mirror as the distance from the object to the mirror, but on the other side of the mirror.

SPHERICAL MIRRORS

Spherical mirrors are mirrors that are curved and exist primarily in two forms, depending on their curvature. Concave mirrors are curved inward and convex mirrors are curved outward. The spherical mirrors are represented by their radius of curvature R, which is related to their focal length f by:

Concave mirror $R = +2f$

Convex mirror $R = -2f$

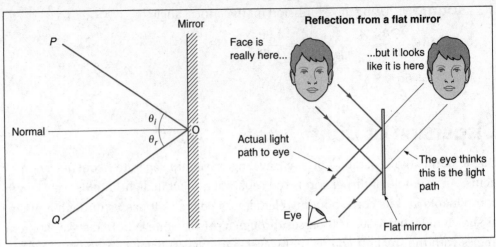

FIGURE 4-31 Image formation in a plane mirror.

In Figure 4-32a, parallel light rays emanating from an object toward a concave mirror reflect and ultimately converge at the real focal point F. Similarly, in Figure 4-32b, parallel light rays emanating from an object toward a convex mirror reflect and ultimately diverge, such that the reflected rays appear to converge at a virtual focal point F' behind the mirror.

Ray tracing represents a graphical approach by which the image position and image size formed by a mirror can be determined. Ray tracing follows the path of three different principal light rays emanating from an object (typically represented by an arrow), interacting with the mirror, and either converging or diverging at the real or virtual focal point, depending on whether the lens is concave or convex, as shown in Figure 4-32c and d.

➤ One principal light ray (Ray 1) travels parallel to the optical axis of the mirror, reflects off the mirror, and passes through the real focal point F of a concave mirror or appears to originate from the virtual focal point F' of a convex mirror.

➤ One principal light ray (Ray 2) travels through the real focal point F and reflected in a direction parallel to the mirror axis.

➤ One principal light ray (Ray 3) travels along a radius of the mirror toward the center of curvature C, striking the mirror perpendicular to its surface. After reflection, the reflected ray travels back along its original path.

The **mirror equation** represents the analytical approach in the determination of the image type and location. The mirror equation relates the object distance o, the image distance i, the focal length f, and the radius of curvature, R, by:

$$\frac{1}{o} + \frac{1}{i} = \frac{1}{f} = \pm\frac{2}{R}$$

where o, i, f, and R are expressed in units of length. The mirror equation and associated parameters are displayed in Figure 4-32e and f.

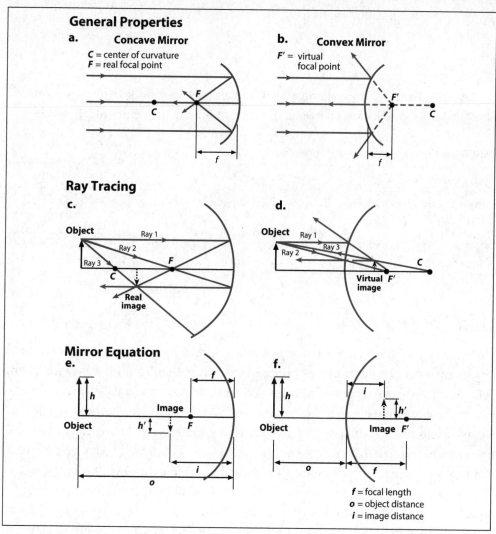

FIGURE 4-32 Spherical mirrors. *Source:* From George Hademenos, *Schaum's Outline of Physics for Pre-Med, Biology, and Allied Health Students,* McGraw-Hill, 1998; reproduced with permission of The McGraw-Hill Companies.

EXAMPLE: The focal length of a concave mirror is 10 centimeters (cm). For an object placed 30 cm in front of the mirror, determine the following:

1. Image distance
2. Magnification

SOLUTION:

1. The image distance is related to the focal length by:

$$\frac{1}{o} + \frac{1}{i} = \frac{1}{f}$$

$$\frac{1}{30 \text{ cm}} + \frac{1}{i} = \frac{1}{10 \text{ cm}}$$

$$i = 15 \text{ cm}$$

2. The magnification is given by:

$$m = -\frac{i}{o} = -\frac{15 \text{ cm}}{30 \text{ cm}} = -0.5$$

Referring to the following table of sign conventions for spherical mirrors, the image is real, inverted, and located between the focal point and the center of curvature.

TABLE 4-6 Sign Conventions for Spherical Mirrors

Parameter	Positive	Negative
Object distance, o	Real object	Virtual object
Image distance, i	Real image	Virtual image
Focal length, f	Concave mirror	Convex mirror
Radius of curvature, R	Concave mirror	Convex mirror
Magnification, m	Erect image	Inverted image

Thin Lenses

Thin lenses, like mirrors, exist as convex or concave lenses. However, lenses form images by refracting light rays, as opposed to mirrors that form images by reflecting light rays. Thin lenses have two surfaces and are thus characterized by two radii of curvature R_1 (side of lens closest to the object) and R_2 (side of lens opposite to the object). A convex lens has a positive R_1 and a negative R_2, whereas a concave lens has a negative R_1 and a positive R_2. For a convex (also referred to as converging) lens, as shown in Figure 4-33a, all light rays emanating from an object refract through the lens and converge to generate an image at the real focal point F on the side of the lens opposing the object. For a concave (also referred to as diverging) lens, as shown in Figure 4-33b, all light rays emanating from an object refract through the lens and diverge to generate an image at the virtual focal point F' on the same side of the lens as the object.

Ray tracing can also be used to determine image position and image size formed by a thin lens. As in the case for mirrors, three particular principal rays of light are followed from the object and ultimately interacting with the lens, as shown in Figure 4-33c and d.

➤ One principal light ray (Ray 1) travels parallel to the optical axis of the lens, refracts through the lens, and passes through a second real focal point F_2 for a convex lens or appears to originate from a second virtual focal point F_2' for a concave lens.

➤ One principal light ray (Ray 2) travels diagonally, directed toward and penetrating through the center of the lens without bending.

➤ One principal light ray (Ray 3) travels through the first real focal point F_1 for a converging lens before it refracts and travels parallel to the optical axis. For a diverging lens, Ray 3 moves through the center of the lens in a straight line.

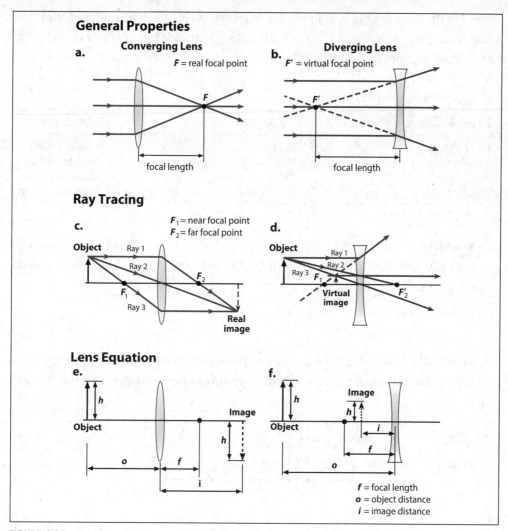

FIGURE 4-33 Thin lenses. *Source:* From George Hademenos, *Schaum's Outline of Physics for Pre-Med, Biology, and Allied Health Students,* McGraw-Hill, 1998; reproduced with permission of The McGraw-Hill Companies.

The **lens equation** relates the object distance o, image distance i, and the focal length f of a lens according to:

$$\frac{1}{f} = \frac{1}{i} + \frac{1}{o}$$

The lens equation and associated parameters are illustrated in Figure 4-33e and f.

Also of importance in creating the lens is the **lens maker's equation**, which can be expressed as:

$$\frac{1}{f} = (n-1)\left(\frac{1}{R_1} - \frac{1}{R_2}\right)$$

where f is the focal length, n is the index of refraction for the lens material, R_1 is the radius of curvature of the lens closest to the object, and R_2 is the radius of curvature of the lens farthest from the object.

TABLE 4-7 Sign Conventions for Spherical Lenses

Parameter	Positive	Negative
Object distance, o	Real object	Virtual object
Image distance, i	Real image	Virtual image
Focal length, f	Converging lens	Diverging lens
Magnification, m	Erect image	Inverted image

EXAMPLE: An object of height 5 cm is positioned 24 cm in front of a convex lens with a focal length of 15 cm. Determine the location and height of the produced image, using the following:

1. Ray tracing
2. The lens equation

SOLUTION: From Figure 4-34, three principal rays emanating from the object are followed through the convex lens, resulting in the formation of a real image.

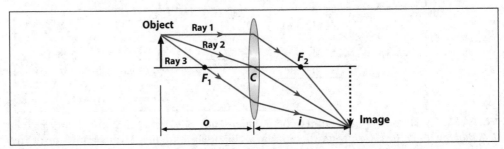

FIGURE 4-34 Three principal rays from an object through a convex lens. *Source:* From George Hademenos, *Schaum's Outline of Physics for Pre-Med, Biology, and Allied Health Students,* McGraw-Hill, 1998; reproduced with permission of The McGraw-Hill Companies.

➤ Ray 1 strikes the lens toward the top and refracts through it. Following refraction, Ray 1 passes through the principal focal point F_2.
➤ Ray 2 passes through the center of the convex lens and continues until it converges with Ray 1.
➤ Ray 3 strikes the lens toward the bottom and refracts through it. Following refraction, Ray 3 continues parallel to the optical axis until it converges with Rays 1 and 2.

The point where all three rays converge represents the size and location of the image. From the ray tracing in Figure 4-34, it can be concluded that the image is real, inverted, magnified, and located farther from the lens than the object.

The lens equation can be used to find the image distance:

$$\frac{1}{i} = \frac{1}{f} - \frac{1}{o} = \frac{1}{15 \text{ cm}} - \frac{1}{24 \text{ cm}} = 0.025 \frac{1}{\text{cm}}$$

so

$$i = \frac{1}{0.025 \dfrac{1}{\text{cm}}} = 40 \text{ cm}$$

A positive value of i indicates the image is real and on the side of the lens opposite the object.

The height of the object h_i can be determined from the magnification m:

$$m = -\frac{i}{o} = -\frac{40 \text{ cm}}{24 \text{ cm}} = -1.67$$

The magnification m is related to the image height by:

$$m = \frac{h_i}{h_o}$$

$$h_i = mh_o = (-1.67)(5 \text{ cm}) = -8.35 \text{ cm}$$

The negative value of h_i indicates that the image is inverted.

Combinations of Lenses

In addition to single lenses, images can be formed from a combination of lenses. Many optical devices, including the compound microscope, use lens combinations to form images. In a system consisting of two lenses, an object is placed in front of the first lens, beyond its focal point (f_{lens1}), as shown in Figure 4-35. The three rays emanate from the object and follow three paths through the lens, with all three rays converging on the opposite side of the lens to form the tip of the image.

When a second lens is placed next to the first lens, Ray 3 refracts upward from the second lens and passes through the focal point of the second lens (f_{lens2}), labeled as 4 (lens 2). Yet a fourth individual ray, labeled 5 (lens 2), begins from the object and passes through the center of the second lens. The intersection of Rays 4 (lens 2) and 5 (lens 2) forms the point for the final image seen by the observer, as shown in Figure 4-36.

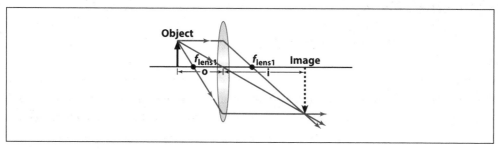

FIGURE 4-35 An object in front of first lens.

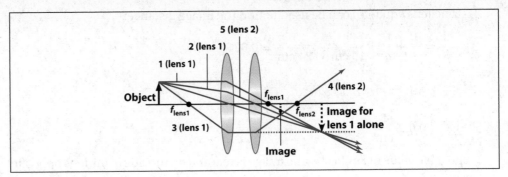

FIGURE 4-36 Combination of two lenses.

Lens Aberrations

A ray diagram that describes the formation of an image with a lens involves three light rays that emanate from an object and refract through the lens at different points, with the rays converging on the opposite side at a point to form an image. This, however, is an ideal case and tends to differ in practice. The deviations from an ideal lens, referred to as **aberrations**, often result in a blurred image. There are two general types of lens aberrations: spherical aberrations and chromatic aberrations.

A **spherical aberration** is related to the geometrical structure of the lens. It occurs when the light rays passing through the lens do not refract as well at the edges of the lens compared to the rays moving through the center of the lens. As a result, the light rays passing through the lens do not converge onto a single point, causing slight blurring of an image. This effect can be addressed by polishing the lens and eventually removing the spherical contours of the lens.

A **chromatic aberration** has to do with the behavior of light. As it strikes the lens, light disperses or separates into its constituent wavelengths, much like it would do with a prism. The separation of the light according to wavelengths prevents the light rays from converging or focusing on a single point. This effect is addressed by using a combination of lenses.

Optical Instruments

COMPOUND MICROSCOPE

The **compound microscope**, shown in Figure 4-37, uses two lenses, an objective lens and an eyepiece lens, separated by an optical tube to produce a magnified image of an object. The object of interest is placed beyond the first focal point f_{o1} of the objective lens. The objective lens produces an intermediate image that is real, inverted, and magnified. This intermediate image serves as the object for the eyepiece lens, which further magnifies the intermediate image to form the final virtual image seen by the observer, as shown in Figure 4-37.

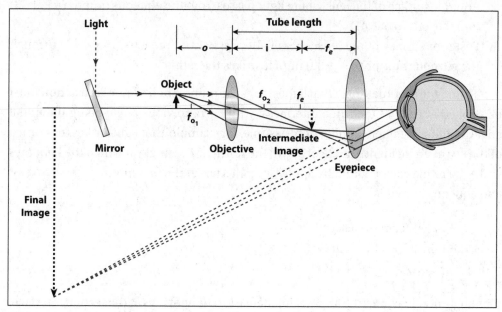

FIGURE 4-37 Compound microscope lenses.

HUMAN EYE

The human eye is a remarkable visual instrument capable of visualizing objects from as far away as infinity to as close as to 20 cm in proximity into focus. The human eye can resolve particles of matter that are held approximately 0.1 mm apart. The ability to focus occurs as the result of **ciliary muscles** that control the curvature of the **cornea**.

Image formation in the human eye occurs on the **retina**, as shown in Figure 4-38, by refraction of light at three separate interfaces:

1. Surface of the cornea where light passes from air ($n = 1.00$) into the cornea (filled with **aqueous humor**) ($n = 1.33$)

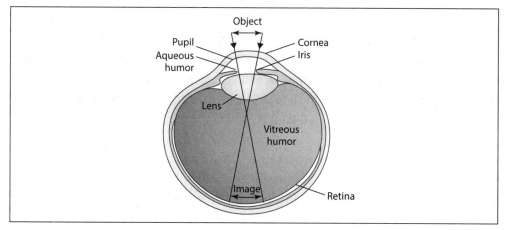

FIGURE 4-38 Image formation in the human eye.

2. Anterior surface of the lens where light passes from the aqueous humor ($n = 1.33$) into the lens ($n = 1.41$)
3. Posterior surface of the lens where light passes from the lens ($n = 1.41$) through the **vitreous humor** ($n = 1.33$) until it strikes the retina.

To find the eventual angle that light strikes the retina, **Snell's law of refraction** must be applied at each of the three interfaces, with each previous angle being the initial angle for the subsequent application. Assume, for example, that light strikes the cornea of the eye at an incidence angle of 35° to the normal. The angle at which the light rays strike the retina can be found by applying Snell's law at the first interface involving air and aqueous humor:

$$n_{\text{air}} \sin \theta_i = n_{aq \text{ humor}} \sin \theta_{r'}$$
$$(1.00) \sin 35° = (1.33) \sin \theta_{r'}$$
$$\sin \theta_{r'} = 25.5°$$

This angle now becomes the angle of incidence for the light rays at the second interface. At the second interface involving aqueous humor and the lens:

$$n_{aq \text{ humor}} \sin \theta_i = n_{\text{lens}} \sin \theta_{r'}$$
$$(1.33) \sin 25.5° = (1.41) \sin \theta_{r'}$$
$$\sin \theta_{r'} = 23.9°$$

This angle now becomes the angle of incidence for the light rays at the third interface. At the third interface involving the lens and vitreous humor:

$$n_{\text{lens}} \sin \theta_i = n_{vi \text{ humor}} \sin \theta_{r'}$$
$$(1.41) \sin 23.9° = (1.33) \sin \theta_{r'}$$
$$\sin \theta_{r'} = 25.4°$$

Common visual impairments of the eye include myopia (nearsightedness) and hyperopia (farsightedness), both of which can be readily corrected with the proper choice of eyeglass or contact lens. In **myopia**, focused vision is achieved for objects that are near, while vision becomes blurred for distant objects. The exact opposite is true in **hyperopia**, where distant objects can be seen clearly and close objects appear blurry. The nature of these impairments involves the point of convergence for parallel rays of light from the object. In the normal eye, parallel rays from an object enter through the lens and converge on the retina where the image is formed.

A myopic person can easily see close objects clearly, but vision becomes blurry for distant objects. The myopic eye focuses light in front of the retina due in part to a lens with too short a focal length. The shortened focal length occurs as a result of either an elongated eyeball or excessive curvature of the cornea. The objective in treating myopia is to reduce the converging power of the lens, which can be accomplished with the placement of a diverging (concave) lens in front of the eye.

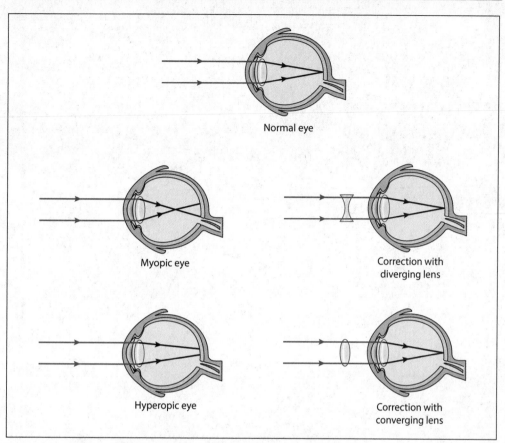

FIGURE 4-39 Common visual impairments and their related solutions.

A hyperopic person can easily see distant objects clearly, but vision becomes blurry for close objects. The hyperopic eye focuses light behind the retina due in part to inadequate curvature of the cornea or too flat a lens or too short an eyeball. The objective in treating hyperopia is to increase the converging power of the lens, which can be accomplished with the placement of a converging (convex) lens in front of the eye. These common visual impairments and their related solutions are illustrated in Figure 4-39.

Atoms, Nuclear Decay, Electronic Structure, and Atomic Chemical Behavior

> ### Read This Chapter to Learn About
>
> ➤ Atomic Nucleus
> ➤ Electronic Structure
> ➤ The Periodic Table: Classification of Elements into Groups by Electronic Structure
> ➤ The Periodic Table: Variations of Chemical Properties with Group and Row

ATOMIC NUCLEUS

The smallest building block, or unit, of all matter is the **atom**. All atoms consist of three basic particles: **protons**, **neutrons**, and **electrons**. The protons and neutrons are tightly packed in a positively charged nucleus situated at the center of the atom, and the electrons are in continual orbit around the nucleus. The protons and neutrons, collectively known as **nucleons**, account for the majority of the mass of the atom. The proton charge is identical in magnitude to that of the electron but is positive, whereas the electron is negatively charged. The neutron is neutrally charged (uncharged) and is slightly heavier than the proton.

Mass of the proton $\qquad m_p = 1.67 \times 10^{-27} \text{ kg}$
Mass of the neutron $\qquad m_n = 1.68 \times 10^{-27} \text{ kg}$
Mass of the electron $\qquad m_e = 9.11 \times 10^{-31} \text{ kg}$

Atomic Number and Atomic Weight

Elements are categorized according to the following properties based on the numbers of protons and neutrons:

Mass number A = number of protons and neutrons (collectively known as nucleons)

Atomic number Z = number of protons (which is equal to the number of electrons)

The mass number is representative of the weight of an atom and is often referred to as **atomic weight**.

Another symbol, N, is used to represent the number of neutrons in the nucleus and can be determined by:

$$N = A - Z$$

The quantities, A, Z, and N are related by the equation:

$$A = N + Z$$

In symbolic form, an atom is represented by:

$$^A_Z X$$

For example, consider the elements carbon $^{12}_6 C$, sulfur $^{32}_{16} S$, and potassium $^{39}_{19} K$. Carbon has 12 protons and neutrons ($A = 12$), 6 protons ($Z = 6$), and 6 neutrons ($N = 12 - 6 = 6$). Sulfur has 32 protons and neutrons ($A = 32$), 16 protons ($Z = 16$), and 16 neutrons ($N = 32 - 16 = 16$). Potassium has 39 protons and neutrons ($A = 39$), 19 protons ($Z = 19$), and 20 neutrons ($N = 39 - 19 = 20$).

Isotopes

Isotopes represent a class of nuclei with the same number of protons (Z) but different number of neutrons (N) and thus of nucleons (A). They usually do not decay into different nuclei. As an example, the nuclides $^1_1 H$, $^2_1 H$ (deuterium), and $^3_1 H$ (tritium) are all isotopes of hydrogen. The nuclides $^{10}_6 C$, $^{11}_6 C$, $^{12}_6 C$, $^{13}_6 C$, $^{14}_6 C$, and $^{15}_6 C$ are all isotopes of carbon.

Nuclear Binding Energy

Applied to the atomic nucleus, the conservation of mass implies that the mass of the nucleus is equal to the sum of the masses of protons and neutrons, the particles that are housed in the nucleus. However, this is not the case with the **rest mass** of a nucleus, which is less than the sum of the rest masses of the protons and neutrons. The reason for this difference in mass, referred to as the **mass defect**, is that negative energy is required to bind the individual proton and neutron particles within the nucleus. This energy, referred to as the **nuclear binding energy**, is given by Einstein's

133

CHAPTER 5:
Atoms, Nuclear
Decay, Electronic
Structure, and
Atomic Chemical
Behavior

equation that describes the conversion between mass and energy, or

$$\text{Nuclear binding energy} = \left\{ (Zm_p)c^2 + (Nm_n)c^2 \right\} - M_{nuc}c^2$$

where $M_{nuc}c^2$ is the mass defect.

Radioactive Decay

Radioactive decay is a nuclear phenomenon exhibited by radioactive isotopes or elements with an atomic number Z greater than that of lead ($Z = 82$). In these elements, which contain generally more neutrons (N) than protons (Z), the repulsive electric forces in the nucleus become greater than the attractive nuclear forces, making the nuclei unstable. In nature, the radioactive element strives toward a stabilized state of existence and, in the process, spontaneously emits particles (photons and charged and uncharged particles), and in so doing transforms to a different nucleus and hence a different element. This process is referred to as radioactive decay and is dependent on the amount and identity of the radioactive element.

ALPHA, BETA, GAMMA DECAY

Radionuclides typically undergo radioactive decay of three common types.

➤ **Alpha decay**, caused by the repulsive electric forces between the protons, involves the emission of an alpha particle (or a helium nucleus that consists of two protons and two neutrons) by nuclei with many protons. In alpha decay, the radioactive nucleus **decreases** in A (mass number) by 4 and **decreases** in Z (number of protons) by 2.

➤ **Beta decay**, which occurs in nuclei that have too many neutrons, can occur by emission of a β particle. A β^- particle is an electron, and a β^+ particle is a positively charged electron, known as a **positron**. In β^- decay, the radioactive nucleus **remains unchanged** in A and **increases** in Z by 1. In β^+ decay, the radioactive nucleus **remains unchanged** in A and **decreases** in Z by 1.

➤ **Gamma decay** occurs by the emission of highly energetic photons. In gamma decay, the radioactive nucleus **remains unchanged** in A and **remains unchanged** in Z.

> **EXAMPLE:** The isotope radium-226 decays according to the reaction $^{226}_{88}\text{Ra} \rightarrow$ $^{222}_{86}\text{Rn} + {}^A_Z\text{X}$. What is the identity of the unknown element ${}^A_Z\text{X}$?
>
> **SOLUTION:** By the conservation of mass, the mass number, A, and the atomic number, Z, must be equal on either side of the reaction. Thus,
>
> $$226 = 222 + A_{unk} \quad \text{or} \quad A_{unk} = 226 - 222 = 4$$
> $$88 = 86 + Z_{unk} \quad \text{or} \quad Z_{unk} = 88 - 86 = 2$$

The unknown element has a mass number of $A = 4$ and an atomic number of $Z = 2$, which is a helium atom or ^4_2He.

HALF-LIFE AND EXPONENTIAL DECAY

Given a radioactive element originally with N_o number of atoms, the number of atoms present at any time t is:

$$N(t) = N_o e^{-\lambda t}$$

where λ is a decay constant, defined by:

$$\lambda = \frac{0.693}{T_{1/2}}$$

Here, $T_{1/2}$ is the **half-life** of the radioactive element and represents the time required for one-half of the radioactive atoms to remain unchanged. Half-lives for radioactive elements range from fractions of seconds (e.g., polonium-212 [^{212}Po], $T_{1/2} = 3 \times 10^{-7}$ s) to billions of years (e.g., uranium-238 [^{238}U], $T_{1/2} = 4.5 \times 10^9$ yr). Radioactive decay is an exponential curve and is illustrated in Figure 5-1.

EXAMPLE: Oxygen-15 is a radioisotope with a half-life of 2.1 min. What is the decay constant λ of oxygen-15?

SOLUTION: The decay constant is related to the half-life of a radioactive element by:

$$\lambda = \frac{0.693}{t_{1/2}} = \frac{0.693}{(2.1 \text{ min}) \cdot \left(\dfrac{60 \text{ s}}{1 \text{ min}} \right)} = 5.5 \times 10^{-3} \text{ s}^{-1}$$

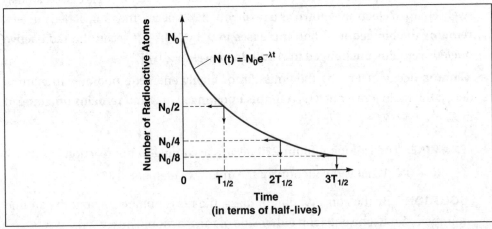

FIGURE 5-1 Radioactive decay. *Source:* From George Hademenos, *Schaum's Outline of Physics for Pre-Med, Biology, and Allied Health Students*, McGraw-Hill, 1998; reproduced with permission of The McGraw-Hill Companies.

135

CHAPTER 5:
Atoms, Nuclear
Decay, Electronic
Structure, and
Atomic Chemical
Behavior

Mass Spectrometry

Mass spectrometry is based on the principle of differentiating molecules by accelerating charged species through a strong magnetic field or across a voltage potential, in which behavior is dictated by the charge-to-mass ratio of the ions. In a common technique, a sample is bombarded with very high-energy electrons, which transfer energy into the molecules, much like photons of visible light induce the formation of an excited state. However, these excited species are so energetic that the only way to relax is by releasing an electron, thereby forming a **radical cation**, known as the **molecular ion**.

Once formed, these ions are accelerated through some differentiating field. The classic approach for differentiation is to pass the beam of charged particles through a magnetic field, which refracts the ions based on their charge-to-mass ratios and velocities. In a very broad sense, this is analogous to the refraction of white light into a spectrum of colors based on the differential interaction of variously energetic photons with the medium of the prism.

ELECTRONIC STRUCTURE

The electron of the hydrogen atom is known to have a wavelike nature. When hydrogen atoms are heated to glowing, they emit light in a quantized series of discrete lines. The wavelike nature of the hydrogen atom is described fully by the **Schrödinger wave equation**, which has four solutions called **wave functions**, represented by ψ.

When ψ is squared, a three-dimensional probability map for finding the electron around the nucleus results. This map shows where the likelihood of finding the electron is 95% or greater. This area is called an **orbital**.

There are four orbitals, one for each of the ψ^2 areas. The orbitals are called s, p, d, and f. These orbitals are described by four variables, which are called **quantum numbers**, contained in each wave function. A quantum number indicates the energy of the orbital.

Quantum Numbers
PRINCIPAL QUANTUM NUMBER, *n*

The **principal quantum number, *n***, is a positive integer that describes the size and energy level of the orbital. Orbitals are grouped according to their n value. All orbitals with the same n value are said to be in the **n shell**. The total number of orbitals per energy level is given by n^2.

ANGULAR MOMENTUM QUANTUM NUMBER

The **quantum number l** is called the **angular momentum quantum number**. It describes the three-dimensional shape of an orbital. It can be any integer value from 0 up to $n-1$. A given n shell contains all the orbitals from $l=0$ up to $l=n-1$.

The $l=0$ orbital is called the **s orbital**. It is spherical with the nucleus at the center of the sphere. The s orbital can hold up to 2 electrons.

The $l=1$ orbital is called the **p orbital**. It is dumbbell shaped with 2 lobes and a node (0% probability) at the nucleus. The p orbital can hold up to 6 electrons.

The $l=2$ orbital is called the **d orbital** and it has various shapes, including 4 lobes. The d orbital can hold up to 10 electrons.

The $l=3$ orbital is called the **f orbital** and it also has various shapes, including 8 lobes. The f orbital can hold up to 14 electrons.

MAGNETIC QUANTUM NUMBER

The **quantum number m_l** is called the **magnetic quantum number**. It describes the orientation of the orbital about an x, y, z coordinate system. Each possible orientation can hold up to 2 electrons maximum. For each orbital, there are $2l+1$ different orientations. The quantum number m_l is all integer values from $-l$ up to $+l$.

For the **s orbital**, $l=0$ and $m_l=0$. There is one orientation; it is labeled $m_l=0$ and it can hold up to 2 electrons maximum.

For the **p orbital**, $l=1$ and $m_l=-1, 0, +1$. There are three orientations, one along the x axis, one along the y axis, and the third along the z axis. Each orientation has an m_l label, and each orientation can hold 2 electrons, for a total of 6 electrons.

For the **d orbital**, $l=2$ and $m_l=-2, -1, 0, +1, +2$. There are 5 orientations and each has an m_l label. The d orbital can hold a total of 10 electrons.

For the **f orbital**, $l=3$ and $m_l=-3, -2, -1, 0, +1, +2, +3$. There are 7 orientations and each has an m_l label. The f orbital can hold a total of 14 electrons.

SPIN QUANTUM NUMBER

Two electrons can occupy the individual orientations of each orbital. Both electrons in an orientation have a -1 charge. They do not repel each other, as might be expected, because of the spin quantum number.

When a charged particle spins, it acts like a bar magnet. When an electron spins in a clockwise manner, it acts like a magnet with, say, North up. If the other electrons spins in a counterclockwise manner, it has the opposite orientation—say, North down. So the 2 electrons pair up in a very stable manner. One of the electrons has spin $+1/2$, and the other has spin $-1/2$.

Electrons are often designated by an arrow, using $\uparrow$ for spin $+1/2$ and $\downarrow$ for spin $-1/2$ (although this is arbitrary).

137

CHAPTER 5:
Atoms, Nuclear
Decay, Electronic
Structure, and
Atomic Chemical
Behavior

Thus for 2 electrons to occupy the same orbital orientation, they must have opposite spins.

Ground State, Excited States

Each orbital has a specific energy level associated with it. The energy levels of the orbitals are **quantized**—that is, only certain energy levels exist. If an electron that is in a low-energy orbital (**ground state**) absorbs light energy, it can use the energy to reach a higher-energy orbital, which is called an **excited state**. Which orbital it can reach depends on how much energy is absorbed.

Once in the excited state, the electron drops back to its original ground state. When it does this, it releases the energy as light energy. Figure 5-2 shows an electron in the 2-shell absorbing enough energy to reach the 5-shell, then dropping back down to the 2-shell. This process is called the **5 → 2 transition**.

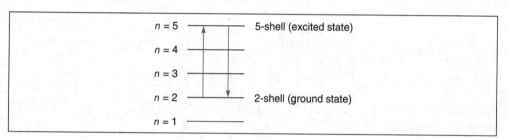

FIGURE 5-2 The 5 → 2 transition of the hydrogen atom.

When the 5 → 2 transition occurs, the electron emits light. It is a narrow band of blue light that can be seen in the visible spectrum of the light emitted by a glowing sample of hydrogen.

Absorption and Emission Line Spectra

Consider a hypothetical atom that has just three energy levels: 0 eV, 2 eV, and 5 eV. The 0 eV energy level is the ground state; the 2 eV energy level is the first excited state; and the 5 eV energy level is the second excited state. When this atom absorbs an energetic photon, the possible transitions that can occur are noted in Figure 5-3, depending on the atom's initial energy level and the energy of the photon. The emission of an energetic photon follows similar possible transitions in reverse to those reflecting the absorption of a photon as depicted in the energy-level diagram.

Photon energy is determined by the difference of the energy values of the two states involved in the transition. **Photon wavelength** can be calculated from the equation:

$$E = \frac{hc}{\lambda}$$

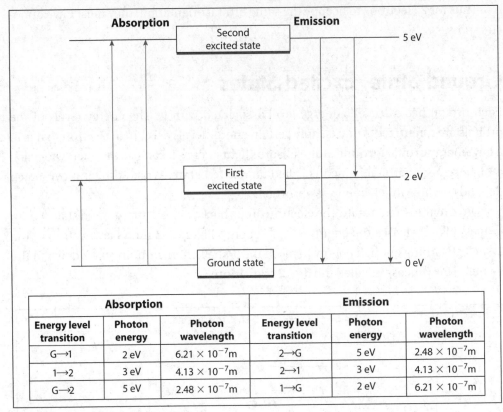

Absorption			Emission		
Energy level transition	Photon energy	Photon wavelength	Energy level transition	Photon energy	Photon wavelength
G→1	2 eV	6.21×10^{-7} m	2→G	5 eV	2.48×10^{-7} m
1→2	3 eV	4.13×10^{-7} m	2→1	3 eV	4.13×10^{-7} m
G→2	5 eV	2.48×10^{-7} m	1→G	2 eV	6.21×10^{-7} m

FIGURE 5-3 Energy level diagram.

or rearranging the equation to solve for λ yields:

$$\lambda = \frac{hc}{E}$$

If photon energy = 2 eV, then:

$$\lambda = \frac{hc}{E} = \frac{(4.135 \times 10^{-15}\ eV \cdot s)\left(3.0 \times 10^8\ \frac{m}{s}\right)}{2\ eV} = 6.21 \times 10^{-7}\ m$$

If photon energy = 3 eV, then:

$$\lambda = \frac{hc}{E} = \frac{(4.135 \times 10^{-15}\ eV \cdot s)\left(3.0 \times 10^8\ \frac{m}{s}\right)}{3\ eV} = 4.13 \times 10^{-7}\ m$$

If photon energy = 5 eV, then:

$$\lambda = \frac{hc}{E} = \frac{(4.135 \times 10^{-15}\ eV \cdot s)\left(3.0 \times 10^8\ \frac{m}{s}\right)}{5\ eV} = 2.48 \times 10^{-7}\ m$$

The **visible emission spectrum** of the hydrogen atom consists of four distinct lines (collectively known as the **Balmer series**), with all transitions involving $n = 2$ as the ground state. The emitted photon wavelength for each of the four transitions within a hydrogen atom is noted in the following table:

139

CHAPTER 5:
Atoms, Nuclear
Decay, Electronic
Structure, and
Atomic Chemical
Behavior

TABLE 5-1

Energy Level Transition	Wavelength of Emitted Photon (nm)	Color
6 → 2	410.2	Violet
5 → 2	434.1	Violet
4 → 2	486.1	Cyan (Blue-green)
3 → 2	656.3	Red

An expression for the energy of each of these transitions can be characterized by the following equation, expressed in terms of inverse wavelength:

$$\frac{1}{\lambda} = R_H \left(\frac{1}{n_i^2} - \frac{1}{n_f^2} \right)$$

where R_H = Rydberg constant = $1.09 \times 10^7 \text{ m}^{-1}$, n_i = initial state, and n_f = final state.

Pauli Exclusion Principle

Every electron can be described by a unique set of quantum numbers n, l, m_l, and m_s.

> **EXAMPLE:** Write all the possible quantum numbers for a $5p$ electron.
>
> $n = 5$ $l = 1$ $m_l = -1, 0, +1$ $m_s = \pm 1/2$
>
> **SOLUTION:** A $5p$ electron can have one of six possible sets of quantum numbers, as shown in Figure 5-4.

If the $5p$ orbital is full, it will contain 6 electrons. Each electron has a different set of quantum numbers. This is called the **Pauli exclusion principle**—no two electrons in an atom can have the same set of quantum numbers.

Paramagnetism and Diamagnetism

Elements can exhibit magnetic behavior when placed in an external magnetic field. The magnetic behavior is based on the element's electronic configuration of orbital shells. Elements such as helium ($1s^2$), beryllium ($1s^2 2s^2$), and neon ($1s^2 2s^2 2p^6$) that have **filled orbital shells** are not affected by and do not respond to an external magnetic field. These elements are referred to as **diamagnetic elements**.

n	5	5	5	5	5	5
ℓ	1	1	1	1	1	1
m_ℓ	−1	0	+1	−1	0	+1
m_s	+1/2	+1/2	+1/2	−1/2	−1/2	−1/2

FIGURE 5-4 The six possible sets of quantum numbers for a $5p$ electron.

Elements such as hydrogen ($1s^1$), lithium ($1s^2 2s^1$), and carbon ($1s^2 2s^2 2p^2$) that have **unfilled orbital shells** are strongly affected and thus do respond to an external magnetic field. These elements are referred to as **paramagnetic elements**.

Conventional Notation for Electronic Structure

THE SHELLS

The seven shells contain orbitals based on the quantum numbers. The **1-shell** contains the $1s$ orbital for a total of 2 electrons. The **2-shell** contains the $2s$ and the $2p$ orbitals for a total of 8 electrons. The **3-shell** contains the $3s$, $3p$, and $3d$ orbitals, for a total of 18 electrons.

The **4-shell** contains the $4s$, $4p$, $4d$, and $4f$ orbitals. The **5-shell** contains the $5s$, $5p$, $5d$, and $5f$ orbitals. There is room for a $5g$ orbital, but an element with this many electrons has not yet been discovered.

The **6-shell** contains the $6s$, $6p$, and $6d$ orbitals. The **7-shell** contains the $7s$ and $7p$ orbitals. Higher orbitals are also possible for these two shells, but elements with that many electrons are unknown.

The order of the orbitals from lowest to highest energy can be determined by using a mnemonic device made by listing the orbitals in each shell, then following the arrows as shown in Figure 5-5. This is called the **Aufbau principle**.

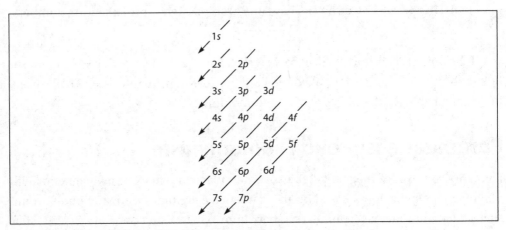

FIGURE 5-5 The order of the orbitals, in terms of increasing energy level.

ORBITAL DIAGRAMS OF MULTIELECTRON ATOMS

Going beyond hydrogen in the periodic table, an electron must be added for each subsequent element. Thus helium has two electrons, lithium has three, etc.

The first orbital is the lowest energy orbital, and the first electron always occupies this orbital. Because the first orbital is $1s$, it holds two electrons. The second electron goes into the $1s$ orbital as well, but with an opposite spin to the first electron. The $1s$ orbital is now full. Figure 5-6 illustrates the filling of the $1s$ orbital.

141

CHAPTER 5:
Atoms, Nuclear
Decay, Electronic
Structure, and
Atomic Chemical
Behavior

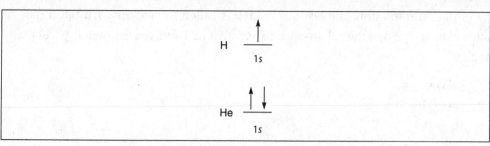

FIGURE 5-6 The orbital diagrams of hydrogen and helium.

The next higher energy orbital is the 2s orbital. Lithium's third electron must go into this orbital. Going on to boron, which has five electrons, the next orbital, 2p, is utilized. Figure 5-7 illustrates the orbital diagram of lithium and of boron.

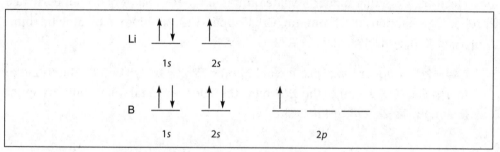

FIGURE 5-7 The orbital diagrams of lithium and boron.

With carbon, there are two electrons in the 2p orbital. The second electron goes into the second orientation, and it has the same spin as the first electron, as per **Hund's rule**, which states that each orientation must get one electron before any is filled. This maximizes the number of parallel spins, as shown in Figure 5-8.

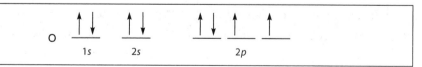

FIGURE 5-8 The orbital diagram of carbon.

Oxygen has four electrons in the 2p orbital. Each orientation gets a single electron, and then the first orientation gets the fourth, as shown in Figure 5-9.

FIGURE 5-9 The orbital diagram of oxygen.

ELECTRON CONFIGURATIONS

The **electron configuration** of an element lists the orbitals in order of energy level and states how many electrons are in each orbital as a superscript. In most cases, all the orbitals are full until the last one, which is called the **valence orbital**. It may or may not be full. When the valence orbital is full or half-full, the element is particularly stable.

EXAMPLES

H is $1s^1$

He is $1s^2$

O is $1s^2 2s^2 2p^4$

Anomalous Electron Configurations. Very large orbitals, such as d and f, are especially stable when full or even when half-full. Some metals such as the **transition metals**, which have a higher n value s orbital preceding the valence orbital, can use the s electrons from that higher n value orbital in order to fill or half-fill the valence d orbital. This happens to Chromium (Cr), Copper (Cu), Niobium (Nb), Molybdenum (Mo), Lead (Pd), and Silver (Ag).

> **EXAMPLE:** Copper looks like it would be $1s^2 2s^2 2p^6 3s^2 3p^6 4s^2 3d^9$. But if one of the $4s$ electrons goes into the $3d$ orbital, the valence orbital will be full. So copper is actually $1s^2 2s^2 2p^6 3s^2 3p^6 4s^1 3d^{10}$.

Bohr's Model of the Hydrogen Atom

In 1913, physicist Niels Bohr advanced a model of the hydrogen atom in which an electron moves in a circular orbit around the proton in the nucleus. It was explained that the attractive electric force between the positively charged proton and the negatively charged electron kept the electron in circular orbit. In Bohr's model of the atom, the electron could be found only in stable orbits or discrete energy states where no electromagnetic radiation was emitted by the atom. According to Bohr, radiation energy was emitted by the atom when the electron jumped between energy states. This model provided an explanation of atomic spectra.

In the Bohr atom, the lowest energy level, or **ground state** (characterized by the integer $n = 1$), required for the electron to maintain a circular orbit closest to the nucleus is -13.6 electron volts (eV). In order for an electron to orbit in excited energy states about the nucleus, energy must be given to the electron. Energy is provided in the form of electromagnetic radiation or light. When an electron absorbs electromagnetic radiation of a certain frequency, it jumps to the corresponding excited ground state with an energy equivalent to the frequency. When the electron returns to its ground state, the electron emits electromagnetic radiation of frequency equal to the energy difference between the two energy states. The relation for energy levels in a Bohr atom is given by:

$$E = -\left(13.6\,\text{eV}\right)\frac{Z^2}{n^2} \qquad n = 1, 2, 3, \ldots$$

and is depicted for the hydrogen atom ($Z = 1$) in Figure 5-10.

143

CHAPTER 5:
Atoms, Nuclear
Decay, Electronic
Structure, and
Atomic Chemical
Behavior

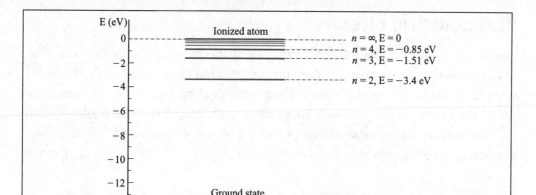

FIGURE 5-10 Energy levels in the Bohr atom. *Source:* From Frederick J. Bueche and Eugene Hecht, *Schaum's Outline of College Physics*, 10th ed., McGraw-Hill, 2006; reproduced with permission of The McGraw-Hill Companies.

Heisenberg Uncertainty Principle

The ability to accurately describe the energy level transitions of an atom depends on one's ability to quantify the motion of the orbiting atomic electron. The **Heisenberg uncertainty principle** states that it is not possible to simultaneously determine the position and momentum of the electron with a high degree of accuracy. This statement can be combined in equation form as the product of the uncertainties of measurement of position, Δx, and momentum, Δp, as:

$$\Delta x \Delta p > \frac{\hbar}{2}$$

where $\hbar = \dfrac{h}{2\pi}$ (h = Planck's constant). A similar statement can be made with regard to the product of the uncertainties of measurement of energy, ΔE, and time, Δt, as:

$$\Delta E \Delta t > \frac{\hbar}{2}$$

Effective Nuclear Charge

The **nuclear charge** of an atom would appear to be the same as its atomic number, or number of protons. However, the electrons in the innermost orbitals can have a shielding effect, so that the effective nuclear charge, Z_{eff}, is less than the atomic number Z, by the electron shielding effect. If this shielding were perfect, the maximum number of electrons in the innermost two shells would be 10. So any electrons in the third shell (such as a $3s$ electron) would be attracted to the nucleus by a charge equal to $Z - 10$ for an atom of atomic number Z.

Z_{eff} increases going across a row and up a column on the periodic table.

Photoelectric Effect

Electrons are bound to the surface of a metal with an energy known as the work function. The **work function**, W_{min}, represents the minimum amount of work required to liberate the electron from the surface. When a beam of light strikes the surface of the metal, the energy of the photon is transferred to the electron. If the photon energy ($E = hf$) is greater than the work function of the bound electron, electrons (or photoelectrons) are ejected from the surface with a maximum kinetic energy, KE_{max}, given by

$$KE_{max} = hf - W_{min}$$

This is referred to as the **photoelectric effect**.

THE PERIODIC TABLE: CLASSIFICATION OF ELEMENTS INTO GROUPS BY ELECTRONIC STRUCTURE

Alkali Metals

The group IA metals are called the **alkali metals** and their valence shell electron configuration is ns^1. Hydrogen is in this group, but it has properties rather different from those of the other elements in the group. The other elements which include lithium, sodium, potassium, rubidium, and cesium are soft, low-melting, lustrous metals. They react violently with water, forming a +1 ion as a hydroxide salt and hydrogen gas. They become more reactive with increasing atomic number. Almost all of the compounds made with these metals are soluble in water.

Alkaline Earth Metals

The group IIA metals are called the **alkaline earth metals**. Their valence shell electron configuration is ns^2. Beryllium is in this group, but it has properties rather different than the others because it is a nonmetal. The other elements which include magnesium, calcium, strontium, barium, and radium are fairly soft with low density. They readily form oxides and hydroxides; they usually give up their valence electrons to form +2 ions. The oxides and hydroxides of this group are insoluble in water for the most part and do not decompose when heated. Barium hydroxide is soluble and is also a strong base.

Halogens

The group VIIA elements are called the **halogens**. This group includes fluorine, chlorine, bromine, iodine, and astatine. Their valence shell electron configuration is ns^2np^5. They have a tendency to gain one electron to form a −1 ion. They can make ionic bonds as a −1 ion, or they can share electrons in covalent bonds with other nonmetals. The elemental halogens exist as diatomic molecules, except for astatine. Most of the chemistry of the halogens involves oxidation–reduction reactions in water solution. Fluorine is the strongest oxidizing agent in the group and it is the most readily reduced.

145

CHAPTER 5:
Atoms, Nuclear
Decay, Electronic
Structure, and
Atomic Chemical
Behavior

Noble Gases

The elements in group VIIIA are called the **noble gases**. This group includes helium, neon, argon, krypton, xenon, and radon. Their valence shell electron configuration is ns^2np^6; in other words, their valence orbital is full.

Transition Metals

The **transition metals** have a d orbital as their valence orbital. Some of them use higher n value s orbital electrons in order to fill or half-fill their d orbital, thus stabilizing it.

The transition metals lose electrons easily and readily form ionic compounds. With the transition metals, it is the d orbital that gives the element its physical and chemical properties. They can form various different ionic states, ranging from +1 to +8. They tend to lose electrons from a higher n value shell first. Cations that have a half-full or full d orbital are especially stable.

Many transition metals form more than one stable oxide. Usually, the oxide that has a higher percentage of oxygen forms most easily.

Representative Elements

The **representative**, or **main-group**, **elements** consist of all p-block elements except helium. This includes all nonmetals (except hydrogen and helium) and all metalloids.

Metals and Nonmetals

The elements can be divided into two major categories, the metals and the nonmetals. The dividing line between them is a stairline that starts at boron and goes down to astatine. The elements to the left of the stairline are metals; those to the right of it are the nonmetals.

Metals have certain properties in common. They have luster, are malleable, and can conduct electricity and heat. They lose electrons easily to form cations, and most of their bonding is ionic in nature.

The **nonmetals** have certain properties in common as well. The ones with lower molar masses tend to be gases in the elemental state. The elements from groups V, VI, and VII can gain electrons to form anions, although most of the bonding of nonmetals, including hydrogen, is covalent.

The **metalloids** are the compounds along the stairline that share properties of both metals and nonmetals. Silicon, for instance, has luster and malleability. Others in this group include germanium, arsenic, antimony, tellurium, polonium, and astatine. As one goes down a column, the main group elements of groups III through VII increase their metallic character. These elements are often used as **semiconductors**.

Oxygen Group

The group VIA elements are in the **oxygen group**. This group contains oxygen, sulfur, selenium, and tellurium. Their valence shell electron configuration is ns^2np^4. They tend to form -2 ions, and they often have a -2 oxidation state in covalent compounds. The number of oxidation states increases with atomic number. Oxygen reacts readily with most metals; this reactivity decreases going down the column. Selenium and tellurium are semiconductors, whereas sulfur is an electrical insulator.

THE PERIODIC TABLE: VARIATIONS OF CHEMICAL PROPERTIES WITH GROUP AND ROW

Electronic Structure
THE REPRESENTATIVE ELEMENTS

Groups IA through VIIIA are called the **representative**, or **main-group**, **elements**. They have either s or p orbitals for their valence orbital. The total number of electrons in the valence shell of each A group is equivalent to the group number. For instance, carbon in group IVA has the electron configuration $2s^22p^2$ and has 4 electrons in its 2-shell.

NOBLE GASES

Noble gases have complete valence orbitals, which make them very stable elements and, for the most part, they are nonreactive. They do not form ions. Xenon, krypton, and radon react with the very electronegative elements oxygen and fluorine to make a few covalent compounds. The noble gases are monatomic in the elemental form.

TRANSITION METALS

The B groups are called the **nonrepresentative elements**, or **the transition metals**. They are found in the middle of the periodic table. They have a d orbital for their valence orbital.

The **lanthanides** and the **actinides** are found at the bottom of the table. They have an f orbital for their valence orbital.

Valence Electrons

The chemical properties of elements are closely associated with the electron configuration of their outermost shells. The elements are arranged into groups (the columns)

147

CHAPTER 5:
Atoms, Nuclear
Decay, Electronic
Structure, and
Atomic Chemical
Behavior

and periods (the rows). Within a group, every atom has the same number of electrons (valence electrons) in its valence orbital, and they share similar chemical properties. Within a period, electrons are added sequentially from left to right to fill the orbitals within the shells. The period number (1–7) corresponds exactly to the shell number for the *s* and *p* orbitals within that period (see Figure 5-11). The number of electrons in the valence orbital is what gives a group its characteristic chemical properties.

Ionization Energy

The **ionization energy**, *I*, of an atom is the energy required to remove an electron from the valence shell, making it an ion.

VARIATION OF IONIZATION ENERGY WITH GROUP AND ROW

The ionization energy for the hydrogen atom is 1312 kJ/mole. Elements that have fewer electrons in their valence orbital have lower ionization energies. The elements in group I have the lowest first ionization energies in their respective periods; those in group VIII have the highest. It is more difficult to remove an electron from a full orbital than from one that is not full. If the removal of an electron results in a full valence orbital, the ionization energy is lower.

As shown in the following table, the ionization energy decreases as one goes down a group, because electrons that are held in higher *n* value shells are farther from the nucleus and held less tightly.

TABLE 5-2 The Ionization Energies (kJ/mol) of the First 20 Elements

Z	Element	First	Second	Third	Fourth	Fifth	Sixth
1	H	1,312.0					
2	He	2,373.0	5,251				
3	Li	520.0	7,300	11,815			
4	Be	899.0	1,757	14,850	21,005		
5	B	801.0	2,430	3,660	25,000	32,820	
6	C	1,086.0	2,350	4,620	6,220	38,000	47,261
7	N	1,400.0	2,860	4,580	7,500	9,400	53,000
8	O	1,314.0	3,390	5,300	7,470	11,000	13,000
9	F	1,680.0	3,370	6,050	8,400	11,000	15,200
10	Ne	2,080.0	3,950	6,120	9,370	12,200	15,000
11	Na	495.9	4,560	6,900	9,540	13,400	16,600
12	Mg	738.1	1,450	7,730	10,500	13,600	18,000
13	Al	577.9	1,820	2,750	11,600	14,800	18,400
14	Si	786.3	1,580	3,230	4,360	16,000	20,000
15	P	1,012.0	1,904	2,910	4,960	6,240	21,000
16	S	999.5	2,250	3,360	4,660	6,990	8,500
17	Cl	1,251.0	2,297	3,820	5,160	6,540	9,300
18	Ar	1,521.0	2,666	3,900	5,770	7,240	8,800
19	K	418.7	3,052	4,410	5,900	8,000	9,600
20	Ca	589.5	1,145	4,900	6,500	8,100	11,000

1 IA	2 IIA	3	4	5	6	7	8	9	10	11	12	13 IIIA	14 IVA	15 VA	16 VIA	17 VIIA	18 VIIIA
1 H 1.0079																	2 He 4.0026
3 Li 6.941	4 Be 9.0122											5 B 10.81	6 C 12.011	7 N 14.007	8 O 15.999	9 F 18.998	10 Ne 20.179
11 Na 22.989	12 Mg 24.305											13 Al 26.981	14 Si 28.086	15 P 30.974	16 S 32.06	17 Cl 35.453	18 Ar 39.948
19 K 39.098	20 Ca 40.08	21 Sc 44.956	22 Ti 47.88	23 V 50.941	24 Cr 51.996	25 Mn 54.938	26 Fe 55.847	27 Co 58.933	28 Ni 58.69	29 Cu 63.546	30 Zn 65.38	31 Ga 59.72	32 Ge 72.59	33 As 74.922	34 Se 78.96	35 Br 79.904	36 Kr 83.80
37 Rb 85.468	38 Sr 87.62	39 Y 88.906	40 Zr 91.22	41 Nb 92.905	42 Mo 95.94	43 Tc (98)	44 Ru 101.07	45 Rh 102.91	46 Pd 106.42	47 Ag 107.87	48 Cd 112.41	49 In 114.82	50 Sn 118.69	51 Sb 121.75	52 Te 127.60	53 I 126.90	54 Xe 131.29
55 Cs 132.91	56 Ba 137.33	57 *La 138.90	72 Hf 178.49	73 Ta 180.95	74 W 183.85	75 Re 186.21	76 Os 190.2	77 Ir 192.22	78 Pt 195.08	79 Au 196.97	80 Hg 200.59	81 Tl 204.38	82 Pb 207.2	83 Bi 208.98	84 Po (209)	85 At (210)	86 Rn (222)
87 Fr (223)	88 Ra 226.0	89 #Ac 227.03	104 Rf (261)	105 Db (262)	106 Sg (263)	107 Bh (262)	108 Hs (265)	109 Mt (266)	110 Uun (269)	111 Uuu (272)	112 Uub (277)						

*Lanthanides

58 Ce 140.12	59 Pr 140.91	60 Nd 144.24	61 Pm (145)	62 Sm 150.36	63 Eu 151.96	64 Gd 157.25	65 Tb 158.92	66 Dy 162.50	67 Ho 164.93	68 Er 167.26	69 Tm 168.93	70 Yb 173.04	71 Lu 174.97

#Actinides

90 Th 232.03	91 Pa 231.03	92 U 238.03	93 Np 237.05	94 Pu (244)	95 Am (243)	96 Cm (247)	97 Bk (247)	98 Cf (251)	99 Es (254)	100 Fm (257)	101 Md (257)	102 No (255)	103 Lr (256)

FIGURE 5-11 The periodic table.

149

CHAPTER 5:
Atoms, Nuclear
Decay, Electronic
Structure, and
Atomic Chemical
Behavior

The first ionization energy is the lowest because subsequent electrons are more difficult to remove because of the positive charge produced. It is easiest to remove an electron from a partially-filled orbital, and more difficult from a filled valence orbital.

Electron Affinity

Ionization energy is the energy required to form a cation. **Electron affinity** is the energy change that occurs when electrons are added to the valence orbital, producing an anion.

VARIATION OF ELECTRON AFFINITY WITH GROUP AND ROW

Energy is given off when anions are formed; thus, a negative sign accompanies the energy difference to indicate its direction of flow. The greater the electron affinity of an atom, the more stable the anion that is formed. It would be expected that group VII elements would have the largest (most negative) electron affinity, because only 1 electron is required to fill the valence orbital.

Generally, the electron affinity increases going across a period to group VII. It then drops, and then increases again going across the next period. Within a group, the electron affinities are approximately equal. Electron affinity is lower to produce a half-full or a full valence orbital, and it is higher if one is adding an electron to an already half-full or full orbital.

Electronegativity

Electronegativity is the ability of an atom in a molecule to pull electron density of a bond toward itself. It is used most often with covalently-bonded atoms.

VARIATION OF ELECTRONEGATIVITY WITH GROUP AND ROW

Electronegativity generally increases going across a period and decreases going down a group. Fluorine has the highest electonegativity, at 4.0 on the **Pauling scale**, followed by oxygen at 3.5, then chlorine and nitrogen at 3.0. These numbers are averages of the absolute values for the ionization energy for an atom.

Atomic Radius

The size of atoms is related to the number of electrons and shells that it has. Generally, the size decreases going across a period, because as the electron number increases, the attraction to the nucleus increases (Z_{eff} increases), thus the atomic radius decreases.

Going down a group, the shell number increases and Z_{eff} decreases, thus the atomic radius increases (see Figure 5-12).

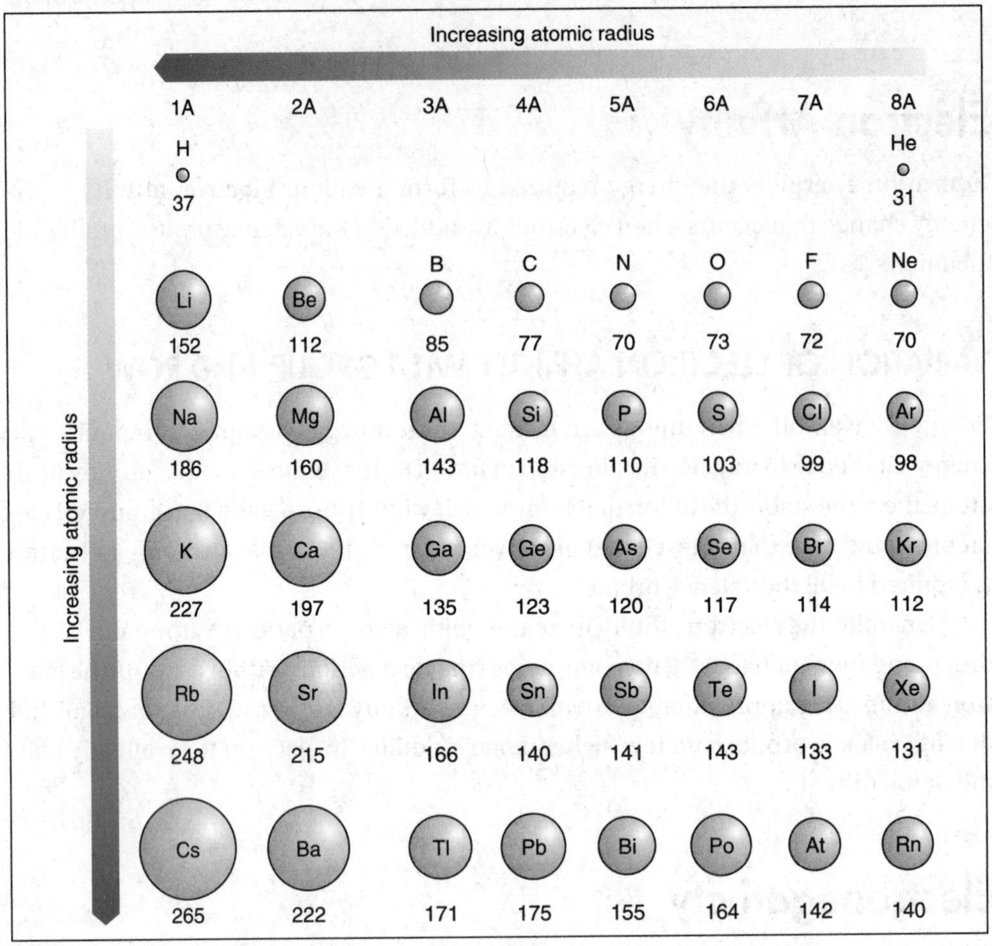

FIGURE 5-12 Atomic radii (in picometers) of the main group elements.

Ionic Radius

The sizes of ions depend on whether they have lost or gained electrons. The more electrons an ion has, the larger its radius. Thus Fe^{+2} is larger than Fe^{+3}, but both are smaller than an Fe atom. If two ions are **isoelectronic** (have the same number of electrons), then the radius decreases across a row and increases down a column, as do neutral atoms.

BONDING BETWEEN IONS

Bonds between atoms that have an electronegativity difference of more than 2 are ionic. An **ionic bond** consists of an electrostatic attraction between a positive ion and a negative ion. It occurs when an element with a low ionization energy encounters an

151

CHAPTER 5:
Atoms, Nuclear
Decay, Electronic
Structure, and
Atomic Chemical
Behavior

element with a high electron affinity, such as when sodium encounters chlorine:

$$2Na + Cl_2 \rightarrow 2NaCl$$

Ions arrange themselves into a lattice network, where no two like ions are neighbors. The energy required to break up the lattice into individual ions is called the **lattice energy**, U. The energy given off when a lattice is created is $-U$, where $U = kz_1z_2/d$.

In this equation, k is a proportionality constant, z_1 is the charge on the cation, z_2 is the charge on the anion, and d is the average distance between their nuclei. The lattice energy is greatest when the charges are large and the diameters are small. Thus LiF has a greater lattice energy than LiI, because F is smaller than I. By the same reasoning, AlI_3 has a greater lattice energy than NaI because the charges are greater.

Unit I Minitest

This minitest is designed to assess your mastery of the content in Chapters 1 through 5 of this volume. The questions have been designed to simulate actual MCAT questions in terms of format and degree of difficulty. They are based on the content categories associated with the Foundational Concept that is the theme of this unit. They are also designed to test the scientific inquiry and reasoning skills that the test makers have identified as essential for success in medical school.

In this test, most of the questions are based on short passages that typically describe a laboratory experiment, a research study, or some similar process. There are also some questions that are not based on passages.

Use this test to measure your readiness for the actual MCAT. Try to answer all of the questions within the specified time limit. If you run out of time, you will know that you need to work on improving your pacing.

Complete answer explanations are provided at the end of the minitest. Pay particular attention to the answers for questions you got wrong or skipped. If necessary, go back and review the corresponding chapters or text sections in this unit.

Now turn the page and begin the Unit I Minitest.

Directions: *Choose the best answer to each of the following questions. Questions 1–5 are based on the following passage.*

Passage I

In October 2012, Felix Baumgartner attempted a world record sky-diving jump from just over 128,000 ft (39,014 m) above the Earth's surface. He was fitted with a customized, pressurized spacesuit that brought his total weight to 260 lbs (1156 N). The spacesuit was designed to collect and transmit important monitoring, communications, and tracking information throughout the jump. Mr. Baumgartner then ascended to the jumping altitude housed within a pressurized capsule of weight = 2900 lbs (12900 N) attached to a 30×10^6 cubic feet (8.5×10^8 L) helium-filled weather balloon. The weather balloon with the attached capsule ascended at a rate of 1000 ft/min (5.1 m/s), reaching the jumping altitude in approximately 2 hours.

Once the capsule reached the jumping altitude, the door to the capsule was opened and Mr. Baumgartner stepped out and fell forward, beginning his free fall descent. He continued falling until he reached a maximum speed of 834 mph (373 m/s), which exceeded the speed of sound. This speed was Mr. Baumgartner's terminal velocity—the velocity attained in which he was no longer being accelerated downward due to gravity. Once he reached this speed, Mr. Baumgartner deployed his parachute and glided safely to Earth's surface.

1. The terminal velocity of a skydiver can be determined in large part by the orientation of the skydiver in free fall. Which orientation would be MOST likely to result in the largest terminal velocity for the skydiver?

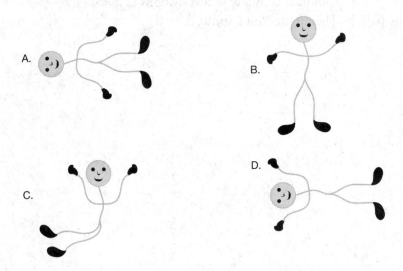

2. Assuming the density of helium is 0.1785 g/cm^3, the weight of the helium used to inflate the balloon was:

   A. 1.5×10^8 N

   B. 1.5×10^7 N

   C. 1.5×10^6 N

   D. 1.5×10^5 N

3. The distance traversed by Mr. Baumgartner before he reached maximum velocity was approximately:

   A. 4800 m

   B. 5480 m

   C. 6350 m

   D. 7100 m

4. The drag force, F_{drag}, can be expressed in terms of the terminal velocity, v_t, as $F_{\text{drag}} = Cv_t^2$, where C is a drag constant. The value of the drag constant for Mr. Baumgartner is:

   A. 0.008 kg/m

   B. 0.680 kg/m

   C. 1.320 kg/m

   D. 5.640 kg/m

5. Once the skydiver has reached terminal velocity, the free body diagram that BEST describes the forces acting on a skydiver at terminal velocity is:

A.
F_g

B.
F_d
F_g

C.
F_d
F_g

D.
F_d
F_g

Questions 6 and 7 are not based on a passage.

6. When hydrogen is heated, the atoms that are formed enter an excited state and energy is released in the form of light. The electrons can move between the various principal energy levels as shown in the following diagram:

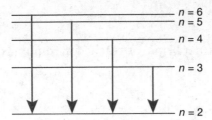

As a result of the electron transitions to the ground state, four bands of light called the Balmer Series are produced. Which of the four possible transitions to $n = 2$ in the visible spectrum of hydrogen has the longest wavelength?

A. 3 to 2

B. 4 to 2

C. 5 to 2

D. 6 to 2

7. Thirty milliliters of a solution drawn into a 5-g syringe has a total mass of 80 g. The density of the solution in the syringe is:

A. $1.8 \dfrac{g}{cm^3}$

B. $2.5 \dfrac{g}{cm^3}$

C. $4.2 \dfrac{g}{cm^3}$

D. $5.7 \dfrac{g}{cm^3}$

Questions 8–12 are based on the following passage.

Passage II

Bromine, discovered in the early 1800s, has an atomic number of 35 and is located in group 17. Besides being able to exist as a diatomic liquid, bromine can frequently be found in salts and is useful in preparing organic molecules with a range of functions. Some of these uses include pesticides, water purification, prescription drugs, photochemicals, and flame retardants. In some sodas, one can find brominated vegetable oil added as an emulsifying agent. In addition to its strong odor, bromine is a dark, brown-orange liquid at room temperature. Bromine has two stable isotopes, Br-79 and

Br-81, and a relative atomic abundance which causes the atomic mass of bromine to be 79.904. Bromine-80 is one of the many unstable isotopes of bromine. It readily undergoes beta decay to form Kr-80. Bromine can also undergo other modes of decay to form Kr-80. When analyzing organic compounds that have bromine in them, the mass spectrometric analysis of the compound frequently shows a peak of equal intensity at m/z = 79 and m/z = 81 or M^+ and M^{+2} peaks of equal height as well.

8. From the masses of the isotopes and the atomic mass of bromine, you can conclude that the relative abundances of the isotopes are approximately:
    A. 35.0% Br-79 and 75.0% Br-81
    B. 50.7% Br-79 and 49.3% Br-81
    C. 100% Br-80
    D. 33.3% Br-79, 33.3% Br-80, and 33.3% Br-81

9. When a sample of Br_2 is analyzed using a mass spectrometer, the most prominent features of the analysis will be:
    A. one peak at m/z = 80 (100%)
    B. one peak at m/z = 160 (100%)
    C. two peaks at m/z = 79 (50%) and m/z = 81 (50%)
    D. three peaks at m/z = 158 (25%), m/z = 160 (50%), and m/z = 162 (25%)

10. Br_2 is expected to be:
    A. diamagnetic
    B. paramagnetic
    C. polar
    D. more dense than diatomic iodine

11. The effective nuclear charge experienced by the valence electrons of bromine will increase the most as you:
    A. move from top to bottom in group 17.
    B. move from bottom to top in group 17.
    C. move from left to right in period 4.
    D. move from right to left in period 4.

12. If Br-80 were to emit a positron, $_{+1}^{0}e$, instead of a beta particle, it would still be possible to form Kr-80 via other modes of decay. This would need to include:
    A. one mode of beta decay
    B. two modes of beta decay
    C. one mode of alpha decay
    D. two modes of positron decay

Questions 13–15 are not based on a passage.

13. In a direct current circuit, a voltage gradient, ΔV, generates and pushes current, I, through a wire of resistance, R, according to Ohm's law or $\Delta V = IR$. Ohm's law can analogously be applied to blood flow, Q, through a vessel of length, L, by the presence of a pressure gradient, ΔP. In this case, the variables involved in blood flow are related by Poiseuille's law or $Q = \dfrac{\pi r^4}{8\eta L}\Delta P$. Given this, which of the following scenarios would result in the greatest resistance of blood flow?

    A. Double the length and double the radius.

    B. Double the length and halve the radius.

    C. Halve the length and double the radius.

    D. Halve the length and halve the radius.

14. For an individual who is myopic or nearsighted, the eyeball is longer than normal, causing visual images to be focused in front of the retina. Myopia can be corrected by:

    A. using a concave lens, which increases the focal length

    B. using a convex lens, which increases the focal length

    C. using a concave lens, which reduces the focal length

    D. using a convex lens, which reduces the focal length

15. The hydrogen atom consists of a single electron of charge $q_e = -1.6 \times 10^{-19}$ C and a single proton of charge $q_p = +1.6 \times 10^{-19}$ C separated by a distance, $r_{ep} = 5.3 \times 10^{-11}$ m. The electrostatic force that exists between the proton and the electron is:

    A. 3.1×10^{-8} N

    B. 4.5×10^{-8} N

    C. 6.8×10^{-8} N

    D. 8.2×10^{-8} N

Questions 16–20 are based on the following passage.

Passage III

Electromagnetic radiation is often described in physics textbooks as a transverse wave that travels in a vacuum at a speed of $c = 3 \times 10^8$ m/s. Formed by coupled oscillating electric and magnetic fields, electromagnetic radiation comprises all of the types of waves represented within the electromagnetic spectrum, varying in frequency, f, and wavelength, λ, according to the equation, $c = f\lambda$. In addition to its wavelike properties, electromagnetic radiation also behaves as waves do. However, classic experiments in quantum physics have also discovered that light behaves as a particle. The particle of light, known as a photon, has energy $E = hf$ where h is Planck's constant ($h = 6.63 \times 10^{-34}$ J · s) and f is frequency. This apparent contradiction is accepted as the "wave-particle duality of light." Two classical experiments that substantiated the "wave-particle duality of light" were Fraunhofer single-slit diffraction and the Compton effect (see figure).

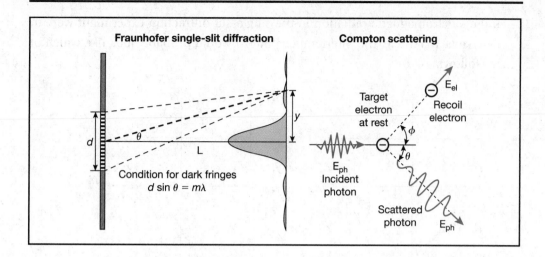

In Fraunhofer single-slit diffraction, monochromatic light is incident parallel to a diffraction grating with a single slit of width d. The light rays will bend around the opening of the slit and project onto a flat screen located a distance, L, from the diffraction grating as a pattern of bright and dark fringes. The pattern of dark fringes (minima) are described by $d\sin\theta = m\lambda$, $m = 1, 2, 3, \ldots$ as the integer value of the particular fringe.

In Compton scattering, a photon of initial energy E_{ph} and wavelength λ_I is incident upon an electron of mass m_e, initially at rest. Upon the collision, the photon is deflected with a scattered energy E'_{ph} at an angle θ with respect to the incident axis as well as an increased wavelength, λ_f, given by $\lambda_f = \lambda_i + \left(\dfrac{h}{m_e c}\right)(1 - \cos\theta)$ where h is Planck's constant, c is the speed of light, and m_e is the rest mass of the electron $(9.1 \times 10^{-31}$ kg). The Compton-scattered electron scatters with an energy E_{el} at an angle ϕ.

16. According to the nature and description of the two experiments in the passage, you can conclude that:

  A. single-slit diffraction supports the wave nature of light, while Compton scattering supports the particle nature of light.

  B. single-slit diffraction supports the particle nature of light, while Compton scattering supports the wave nature of light.

  C. both single-slit diffraction and Compton scattering support the wave nature of light.

  D. both single-slit diffraction and Compton scattering support the particle nature of light.

17. If the electromagnetic radiation in the single-slit diffraction experiment were to behave as a particle, the interference pattern would probably look like which of the following?

A.

B.
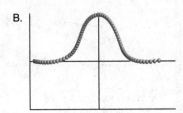

C.
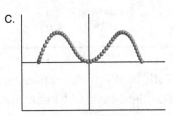

D.
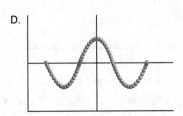

18. The Compton-scattered photon, compared to the incident photon, possesses:
   A. higher energy, higher frequency, smaller wavelength
   B. higher energy, lower frequency, smaller wavelength
   C. lower energy, higher frequency, longer wavelength
   D. lower energy, lower frequency, longer wavelength

19. In the Compton scattering experiment, the energy of the Compton-scattered electron, E_{el}, can be expressed in terms of the energies of the incident, E_{ph}, and Compton-scattered, E'_{ph} photons by:

   A. $E_{el} = \dfrac{\left[E_{ph} - E'_{ph}\cos(\theta)\right]}{\cos(\phi)}$

   B. $E_{el} = \dfrac{\left[E_{ph} - E'_{ph}\cos(\theta)\right]}{\sin(\phi)}$

   C. $E_{el} = \dfrac{\left[E_{ph} - E'_{ph}\sin(\theta)\right]}{\cos(\phi)}$

   D. $E_{el} = \dfrac{\left[E_{ph} - E'_{ph}\sin(\theta)\right]}{\sin(\phi)}$

20. An expression for the momentum of a Compton-scattered photon in terms of Planck's constant, h, is:
   A. h/λ
   B. $h\nu$
   C. λh
   D. λ/h

Questions 21–26 are based on the following passage.
Passage IV

A group of students were assigned the task of assembling a slingshot constructed from rubber bands secured with clamps at the edge of a tabletop that is a known distance, Δy, from the floor and then predicting the horizontal range distance, Δx, that a launched projectile (marble) will land from the base of the table. A schematic of the rubber band slingshot is shown in the following illustration:

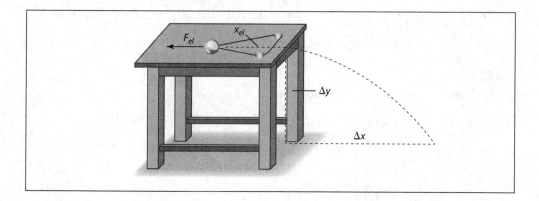

Before the slingshot was constructed, a series of measurements were performed on the rubber band to determine the stretching distance, x_{el}, as a function of an elastic force, F_{el}, applied to the rubber band. The data are shown here:

F_{el} (N)	2	3	4	5
x_{el} (cm)	14	21	26	30

The students used the data above to theoretically determine the landing distance of a marble. To compare the effectiveness of their theoretical calculations, the students then launched a marble by stretching the rubber band slingshot to four different values of x_{el}, and recorded the corresponding landing distances, Δx. The data are shown in the following table:

Stretch Distance, x_{el}	2.00 cm	4.00 cm	6.00 cm	8.00 cm
Predicted Value, Δx_{pr}	3.94 m	5.63 m	7.18 m	8.45 m
Observed Value, Δx_{ob}	2.64 m	4.55 m	6.01 m	8.04 m

21. The spring constant for the rubber band used as a slingshot is:
    A. 18.8 N/m
    B. 1.88 N/m
    C. 0.188 N/m
    D. 0.0188 N/m

22. The velocity that the marble leaves the table upon release of the stretched rubber band is:

   A. kmx_{el}

   B. $\dfrac{k}{m}x_{el}$

   C. $\sqrt{km}x_{el}$

   D. $\sqrt{\dfrac{k}{m}}x_{el}$

23. The percent error between the values collected for a stretch distance of 2.0 cm is:

   A. 12%

   B. 26%

   C. 33%

   D. 42%

24. The horizontal landing distance, Δx, can be expressed according to:

   A. $\left[\sqrt{\dfrac{k}{m}}x_{el}\right]\left[\sqrt{\dfrac{g}{2\Delta y}}\right]$

   B. $\left[\sqrt{\dfrac{m}{k}}x_{el}\right]\left[\sqrt{\dfrac{2\Delta y}{g}}\right]$

   C. $\left[\sqrt{\dfrac{k}{m}}x_{el}\right]\left[\sqrt{\dfrac{\Delta y}{2g}}\right]$

   D. $\left[\sqrt{\dfrac{k}{m}}x_{el}\right]\left[\sqrt{\dfrac{2\Delta y}{g}}\right]$

25. If the students pull the slingshot back to 10 cm, the horizontal landing distance, Δx_{ob}, they might expect to see is:

   A. 9.7 m

   B. 10.4 m

   C. 11.9 m

   D. 13.1 m

26. If the marble were doubled in mass, the effect on the horizontal landing distance would be:

   A. decrease by $\sqrt{2}$

   B. increase by $\sqrt{2}$

   C. decrease by 2

   D. no change

Question 27 is not associated with a passage.

27. Which of the following is the MOST stable conformation of chlorocyclohexane?

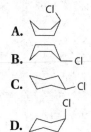

    A.

    B. ‑Cl

    C. ‑Cl

    D.

Questions 28–32 are based on the following passage.
Passage V

A standard imaging procedure in the investigation and evaluation of patients with cardiovascular disease is nuclear stress testing. Nuclear stress testing is often used to determine the extent of coronary artery blockage and assess the damage of heart muscle that arises as a result of a heart attack. In a typical nuclear stress test, the patient first walks on a treadmill to elevate the heart rate. Several minutes into the exercising period, a radiotracer or a drug tagged with a radioactive element known to target the heart is injected into the patient's vein and allowed to circulate. As the radiotracer circulates through the blood flow within the heart, the radioactive element decays, emitting gamma radiation that is collected by a gamma ray detector. If a part of the heart's muscle is damaged and not receiving blood flow, the amount of gamma rays detected from this area is less than normal regions of heart muscle. The collected gamma rays are used to produce images of the functional capacity of the heart, allowing the physician to identify any regions of the heart that are functioning below normal capacity.

    A common radioactive element used in this testing procedure is thallium-201 (Tl-201). With a half-life of 73 hours, Tl-201 decays to mercury-201 (Hg-201) by electron capture according to:

$$^{201}_{81}\text{Tl} + {}^{0}_{-1}e \rightarrow {}^{201}_{80}\text{Hg} + {}^{0}_{0}\nu$$

The radioactive emissions from Tl-201 are primarily x-rays in the energy range 69–83 keV with gamma rays of energy 135 keV and 167 keV emitted less frequently.

28. In the radioactive decay process of Tl-201, which of the following is true?

    A. A is constant; N increases; Z increases
    B. A is constant; N increases; Z decreases
    C. A increases; N increases; Z is constant
    D. A increases; N is constant; Z is constant

29. The wavelength of the 167 keV gamma ray emitted from Tl-201 is: (NOTE: $h = 4.15 \times 10^{-15}$ eV $\cdot$ sec; 1 angstrom (Å) $= 1 \times 10^{-10}$ m)

    A. 0.074 Å

    B. 0.183 Å

    C. 0.259 Å

    D. 0.362 Å

30. When compared to x-rays (68–83 keV), gamma rays (167 keV) have:

    A. lower frequency, shorter wavelength, but the same speed

    B. higher frequency, shorter wavelength, but the same speed

    C. lower frequency, longer wavelength, and greater speed

    D. higher frequency, shorter wavelength, and slower speed

31. In a typical nuclear stress test procedure, the percentage of the initial Tl-201 dose that would be present after 24 hours is:

    A. 40%

    B. 55%

    C. 67%

    D. 80%

32. The amount of time required for Tl-201 to decay to 10% of its original dosage is:

    A. 2 days

    B. 5 days

    C. 10 days

    D. 14 days

This is the end of the Unit I Minitest.

Unit I Minitest Answers and Explanations

1. **The correct answer is B.** Terminal velocity occurs when the drag force exerted on the skydiver becomes equal in magnitude and opposite in direction to the weight of the skydiver. The drag force develops as the air molecules interact with the surface area of the falling skydiver. The greater the surface area of the skydiver that acts perpendicular to the direction of the skydiver's fall, the greater force will be exerted on the skydiver, resulting in a smaller terminal velocity. To the contrary, the smaller the surface area of the skydiver that acts perpendicular to the direction of the skydiver's fall, the smaller force will be exerted on the skydiver, resulting in a larger terminal velocity. From the orientations presented in the options, the one orientation that translates to the smallest surface area and hence the greatest terminal velocity is given by choice B.

2. **The correct answer is C.** Using the relationship

$$\text{density} = \frac{\text{mass}}{\text{volume}},$$

you can determine the mass of the helium used to inflate the balloon from

$$\text{mass} = (\text{density}) \times (\text{volume})$$

where density = 0.1785 g/cm^3 and volume = 8.5×10^8 mL or since 1 mL = 1 cm^3, volume = 8.5×10^8 cm^3. Thus,

$$\text{mass} = \left(0.1785 \ \frac{\text{g}}{\text{cm}^3}\right) \times \left(8.5 \times 10^8 \ \text{cm}^3\right)$$

$$= 1.52 \times 10^8 \ \text{g}$$

$$= 1.52 \times 10^5 \ \text{kg}$$

The weight of the helium used to inflate the balloon can be determined from

$$\text{weight} = (\text{mass}) \times (\text{acceleration due to gravity})$$

$$= (1.52 \times 10^5 \ \text{kg}) \times (9.8 \ \text{m/s}^2)$$

$$= 14.9 \times 10^5 \ \text{N}$$

$$= 1.49 \times 10^6 \ \text{N} \approx 1.5 \times 10^6 \ \text{N}$$

given by choice C.

3. **The correct answer is D.** The initial velocity (v_i) of Mr. Baumgartner in the vertical direction is 0, his final velocity (v_f) is 373 m/s, and the acceleration due to gravity is 9.8 (although in reality it is probably slightly lower because of the significantly large jumping altitude). The equation of motion that can be used to determine the distance traversed by Mr. Baumgartner is:

$$\text{displacement} = \frac{(\text{final velocity})^2 - (\text{initial velocity})^2}{2 \times (\text{acceleration due to gravity})}$$

$$= \frac{\left(373\,\frac{m}{s}\right)^2 - \left(0\,\frac{m}{s}\right)^2}{19.6\,\frac{m}{s^2}}$$

$$= \frac{139,129\,\frac{m^2}{s^2} - 0}{19.6\,\frac{m}{s^2}}$$

$$= 7098\,m$$

4. **The correct answer is A.** When an object in free fall reaches terminal velocity, it is in equilibrium. In other words, the drag force acting upward becomes equal in magnitude yet opposite in direction to the object's weight or:

$$F_d = F_g$$
$$Cv_t^2 = mg$$
$$C = \frac{mg}{v_t^2} = \frac{1,156\,N}{\left(373\,\frac{m}{s}\right)^2} = \frac{1,156\,N}{139,129\,\frac{m^2}{s^2}} = 0.008\,\frac{kg}{m}$$

5. **The correct answer is C.** Terminal velocity occurs for a free-falling object when the drag force (F_d) becomes equal in magnitude yet opposite in direction to the object's weight or force due to gravity (F_g). This is depicted by the free body diagram with the two forces, F_d and F_g, drawn as arrows of equal size in opposite directions, given by choice C.

6. **The correct answer is A.** The longest wavelength will have the lowest frequency and the lowest energy. This lowest energy occurs from the transition from $n = 3$ to $n = 2$. The relationship can be found in the equation $E = \frac{hc}{\lambda}$. The energy, E, of a photon is equal to Planck's constant times the speed of light, divided by the wavelength. As the wavelength increases, the value of the denominator increases, decreasing the value of E.

7. **The correct answer is B.** The density of a solution can be determined from:

$$\rho = \frac{m}{V}$$

where ρ is the density of the solution (in units of $\frac{g}{cm^3}$), m is the mass of the solution (in units of g), and V is the volume of the solution (in units of cm^3). The mass of the solution, m_{sol}, is the total mass of the solution and the syringe, m_{tot}, minus the mass of the syringe, m_{syr}, or:

$$m_{tot} = m_{sol} + m_{syr}$$

$$m_{sol} = m_{tot} - m_{syr} = 80\text{ g} - 5\text{ g} = 75\text{ g}$$

The volume of the solution in the syringe is $V_{syr} = 30\text{ mL} = 30\text{ cm}^3$. The density of the solution is:

$$\rho = \frac{m}{V} = \frac{75\text{ g}}{30\text{ cm}^3} = 2.5\ \frac{g}{cm^3}$$

8. **The correct answer is B.** Realizing that the atomic mass is almost at the midpoint value of the two isotopes, you can conclude that the approximate abundance is about 50% for each isotope. This comes closest to choice B. To check, take the relative abundance for each isotope and multiply by the mass number for that isotope. Doing so gives the following: $(0.507)(79) + (0.493)(81) = 40.053 + 39.933 = 79.986$. Considering that there will always be some error in analysis, this is the closest choice to the atomic mass of bromine.

9. **The correct answer is D.** There are four combinations for the bromine atoms: Br-79 and Br-79 ($= 158$), Br-79 and Br-81 ($= 160$), Br-81 and Br-79 ($= 160$), and Br-81 and Br-81 ($= 162$). An m/z ratio of 160 will be detected 50% of the time while the other two m/z ratios occur 25% of the time each.

10. **The correct answer is A.** The electron configuration for bromine is $1s^2 2s^2 2p^6 3s^2 3p^6 4s^2 3d^{10} 4p^5$. While a bromine atom has an unpaired electron, Br_2 does not. Because there are no unpaired electrons, it will be diamagnetic. Br_2 will not be polar as it is diatomic and both atoms have the same electronegativity. Finally, looking at the trend down the halogen family, F_2 will be a gas as will Cl_2 because of their low atomic masses and low dispersion force attractions. Because I_2 has the greater mass, its dispersion forces allow it to be a solid at room temperature. As per the passage, bromine is a liquid and will be less dense than iodine.

11. **The correct answer is C.** The general trend is that Z_{eff} will increase moving down a family and from left to right across a period. However, because the number of core electrons remains constant while one goes from left to right in a period, the nuclear charge will increase and have a greater effect on the valence electrons. The impact of effective nuclear charge will be greater when moving left to right than from top to bottom on the periodic table.

12. **The correct answer is B.** When $_{35}^{80}$Br undergoes positron decay, the result is $_{+1}^{0}e +$ $_{34}^{80}$Se. In order to achieve $_{36}^{80}$Kr, two more modes of beta decay need to occur as per the following:

$$_{34}^{80}\text{Se} \rightarrow _{-1}^{0}e + _{35}^{80}\text{Br} \quad \text{and} \quad _{35}^{80}\text{Br} \rightarrow _{-1}^{0}e + _{36}^{80}\text{Kr}$$

13. **The correct answer is B.** This problem can be solved by substituting the results of each scenario into Poiseuille's law and searching for the smallest value. Choice A yields a 8-fold increase in flow. Choice B results in a 32-fold decrease in flow. Choice C yields a 32-fold increase in flow, while choice D results in a 8-fold decrease in flow.

14. **The correct answer is A.** By definition of the two types of lenses, a concave lens increases the focal length of an image, while a convex lens reduces the focal length of an image. Therefore, choices B and C are incorrect and can be immediately excluded. Since myopia results in image formation in front of the retina, the appropriate corrective lens would be a concave lens which increases the focal length of the image, causing the image to focus past this point and on the retina. Choice A is the correct response. Choice D represents the corrective approach for hyperopia or farsightedness.

15. **The correct answer is D.** The electrostatic force can be calculated using Coulomb's law:

$$F = k\frac{q_e q_p}{r_{ep}^2} = \left(9 \times 10^9 \ \frac{\text{N} \cdot \text{m}^2}{\text{C}^2}\right) \frac{(-1.6 \times 10^{-19}\,\text{C})(+1.6 \times 10^{-19}\,\text{C})}{(5.3 \times 10^{-11}\text{m})^2}$$

$$= -8.2 \times 10^{-8}\,\text{N}$$

represented by choice D.

16. **The correct answer is A.** In single-slit diffraction, light (electromagnetic radiation) passes through a small slit within a diffraction grating and moves toward a screen as wavefronts. As the wavefronts strike the screen, points within the wavefronts will either amplify as a result of constructive interference or cancel each other as a result of destructive interference. The alternating patterns of constructive and destructive interference will result in a pattern of bright and dark fringes on the screen. This observation is indicative of the wavelike behavior of light. Compton scattering involves a two-dimensional elastic collision that can take place only if particles are involved. An electron is a particle and thus in order to observe the Compton effect, light (electromagnetic radiation) must also behave as a particle as well.

17. **The correct answer is A.** The interference pattern described in Fraunhofer single-slit diffraction is based on the fact that light behaves as waves. Wavefronts passing through the slit move toward the screen and, depending on the position of the wavefronts, an interference pattern consisting of alternating maxima and minima will result. If the source were composed of particles, the resultant image will depict a linear array of points, consistent with the geometrical constraints of the slit, as illustrated in Option A.

18. **The correct answer is D.** In Compton scattering, a two-dimensional elastic collision occurs between a photon with an incident energy, E_{ph}, and an electron at rest. As the photon collides with the electron, it scatters at some angle θ after transferring a portion of its energy to the electron, which in turn causes it to scatter with an energy, E_{el}, at some angle ϕ. The energy of the scattered photon, E'_{ph}, is less than the original energy of the photon. From the relation

$$E = hv = h\frac{c}{\lambda},$$

you can see that a reduced energy implies a lower frequency (because energy is directly proportional to frequency) and a longer wavelength (because energy is inversely proportional to wavelength).

19. **The correct answer is A.** This problem requires the application of the conservation of energy:

$$(\text{total energy})_{\text{before collision}} = (\text{total energy})_{\text{after collision}}$$

$$(E_{ph} + E_{el})_{\text{before collision}} = (E'_{ph} + E'_{el})_{\text{after collision}}$$

Although the collision is two-dimensional, only the conservation of energy in the x-direction allows one to develop a relationship between the energy of the Compton-scattered electron and the energy of the incident and scattered photon:

$$(E_{ph} + 0)_{\text{before collision}} = (E'_{ph}\cos(-\theta) + E'_{el}\cos(\phi))_{\text{after collision}}$$

$E_{el} = 0$ because the electron before the collision is at rest. Because cosine is an even function, $\cos(-\theta) = \cos(\theta)$. Therefore,

$$E_{ph} = E'_{ph}\cos(\theta) + E'_{el}\cos(\phi)$$

Solving for E'_{el} yields

$$E_{el} = \frac{\left[E_{ph} - E'_{ph}\cos(\theta)\right]}{\cos(\phi)}$$

20. **The correct answer is A.** This problem can be solved through the use of unit analysis. The units for Planck's constant, h, are $J \cdot s$, wavelength, λ, is m, and frequency, v, is $\frac{1}{s}$. The question is which combination of these units will yield the units of momentum $\left(\frac{kg \cdot m}{s}\right)$. The term that has units of momentum is $\frac{h}{\lambda}$.

21. **The correct answer is A.** The spring constant, k, which is a constant unique to an elastic object that describes the amount of force required to stretch or compress the elastic object by a known distance, can be determined from the data displayed in the first table. Plotting the data with the elastic force, F_{el}, on the y-axis and stretching distance, x_{el}, on the x-axis, the spring constant can be found by taking the slope of the graph. Since the data indicate a linear graph, the slope and thus the spring constant can be found by using the endpoints:

$$k = \text{slope} = \frac{\text{rise}}{\text{run}} = \frac{\Delta F_{el}}{\Delta x_{el}} = \frac{5N - 2N}{0.3m - 0.14m} = \frac{3N}{0.16m} = 18.75\frac{N}{m}$$

22. **The correct answer is D.** The work done in pulling back the slingshot is stored as elastic potential energy, which in turn is transferred to kinetic energy of the moving projectile. Applying the work-kinetic energy theorem:

Work = Elastic Potential Energy = Change in Kinetic Energy

$$= \frac{1}{2}kx_{el}^2 = \frac{1}{2}mv_f^2 - \frac{1}{2}mv_o^2$$

$$v_f^2 = \frac{k}{m}x_{el}^2 \qquad v_f = \sqrt{\frac{k}{m}}x_{el}$$

23. **The correct answer is C.** The percent error can be found from the following equation and substituting in the appropriate values:

$$\%\text{Error} = \left[\frac{\text{Predicted Value} - \text{Observed Value}}{\text{Predicted Value}}\right] \times 100\%$$

$$= \left[\frac{3.94\text{m} - 2.64\text{m}}{3.94\text{m}}\right] \times 100\% = 32.9\% \approx 33\%$$

24. **The correct answer is D.** The horizontal landing distance, Δx, can be determined from the equation:

$$\Delta x = v_x \Delta t$$

From the response to Question 21, the horizontal velocity that the marble leaves the tabletop with is given by:

$$v_f = v_x = \sqrt{\frac{k}{m}}x_{el}$$

The time can be found using the equation for displacement in the y-direction for accelerated motion:

$$\Delta y = \frac{1}{2}g\Delta t^2$$

Solving for Δt yields:

$$\Delta t = \sqrt{\frac{2\Delta y}{g}}$$

Substituting into the expression above for the horizontal landing distance gives:

$$\Delta x = v_x \Delta t = \left[\sqrt{\frac{k}{m}}x_{el}\right]\left[\sqrt{\frac{2\Delta y}{g}}\right]$$

25. **The correct answer is A.** The students are being asked to extrapolate from the data points already collected and displayed in the second table. Performing simple linear regression analysis, the graphed data reveal the following graph of a line:

$$y = 88.3x + 0.895$$

Substituting the value of 10 cm or 0.1 m into the regression line for x, the y-value or the observed value the students should expect to see when the slingshot is pulled back to 10 cm is:

$$y = 88.3 \, (0.10) + 0.895 = 9.73 \, \text{m}$$

26. **The correct answer is A.** Using the expression for the horizontal landing distance:

$$\Delta x = v_x \, \Delta t = \left[\sqrt{\frac{k}{m}} x_{\text{el}} \right] \left[\sqrt{\frac{2\Delta y}{g}} \right]$$

If the mass of the marble were doubled,

$$\Delta x = v_x \, \Delta t = \left[\sqrt{\frac{k}{2m}} x_{\text{el}} \right] \left[\sqrt{\frac{2\Delta y}{g}} \right]$$

So, in comparison to the original mass of the marble, the horizontal landing distance would decrease by $\sqrt{2}$.

27. **The correct answer is C.** The answer choices are best considered as two sets of two: two boat conformations and two chair conformations. Boat conformations in general are almost always of higher energy owing to the so-called flagpole interactions shown here:

The distinguishing characteristic between the two chair conformations is that one (choice C) places the chlorine substituent in an equatorial attitude, whereas the other (choice D) forces the substituent to occupy an axial position. An equatorial orientation is almost always energetically preferable.

28. **The correct answer is B.** In the decay process of Thallium-201, given in the passage as $^{201}_{81}\text{Tl} + \, ^{0}_{-1}e \rightarrow \, ^{201}_{80}\text{Hg} + \, ^{0}_{0}\nu$, it can be seen that the mass number of Tl-201 ($A = 201$) is identical to the mass number of Hg-201 ($A = 201$); the atomic number of Tl-201 ($Z = 81$) is greater than the atomic number of Hg-201 ($Z = 80$); and the neutron number of Tl-201 ($N = 201 - 81 = 120$) is smaller than the neutron number of Hg-201 ($N = 201 - 80 = 121$). Thus, A remains constant, N increases by one and Z decreases by one. Choice B is the correct choice.

29. **The correct answer is A.** The wavelength of the gamma ray is equal to its energy by the relation:

$$E = h\frac{c}{\lambda}$$

where E is the energy of the electromagnetic radiation (in units of eV), h is Planck's constant ($= 4.15 \times 10^{-15}$ eV $\cdot$ sec), c is the speed of light in vacuum ($= 3.0 \times 10^8$ m/s), and 1 is the wavelength.

$$\lambda = h\frac{c}{E} = (4.15 \times 10^{-15} \, eV \cdot s)\frac{\left(3.0 \times 10^8 \, \text{m/s}\right)}{(167 \times 10^3 \, eV)} = 0.074 \times 10^{-10} \, m = 0.074 \, \text{Å}$$

30. **The correct answer is B.** The energy, wavelength, frequency, and speed are related by:

$$E = hv = h\frac{c}{\lambda}$$

Because gamma rays have higher energy than x-rays and frequency is linearly proportional to the energy, the frequency is larger as well. Because the wavelength is inversely proportional to energy, the wavelength decreases as the energy increases. The speed of the x-rays, which is the same speed for the gamma ray, is the speed of light in a vacuum and is constant. Thus, choice B is the correct answer.

31. **The correct answer is D.** This problem is solved using the radioactive decay equation:

$$N = N_o e^{-\left(\frac{0.693}{T_{1/2}}\right)\cdot t}$$

$$\frac{N}{N_o} = e^{-\left(\frac{0.693}{73 hr}\right)\cdot 24 \, hr} = e^{-0.22} = 0.80$$

Expressed in percentage, the fraction $\frac{N}{N_o}$ is 80%.

32. **The correct answer is C.** This problem is solved using the radioactive decay equation:

$$N = N_o e^{-\left(\frac{0.693}{T_{1/2}}\right)\cdot t}$$

$$\frac{N}{N_o} = 0.10 = e^{-\left(\frac{0.693}{73 hr}\right)\cdot t} = e^{-(0.0095/hr)\cdot t}$$

Taking the natural logarithm of both sides yields:

$$-2.3 = -(0.0095/\text{hr}) \cdot t$$
$$t = \frac{2.3}{0.0095/\text{hr}} = 242 \, \text{hr} \approx 10.1 \, \text{days}$$

UNIT II

Chemical Foundations of Biological Systems

Foundational Concept: The principles that govern chemical interactions and reactions form the basis for a broader understanding of the molecular dynamics of living systems.

CHAPTER 6 The Unique Nature of Water and Its Solutions

CHAPTER 7 The Nature of Molecules and Intermolecular Interactions

CHAPTER 8 Separation and Purification Methods

CHAPTER 9 Structure, Function, and Reactivity of Biologically Relevant Molecules

CHAPTER 10 Principles of Chemical Thermodynamics and Kinetics

Unit II MINITEST

The Unique Nature of Water and Its Solutions

Read This Chapter to Learn About

➤ Acid–Base Reactions

➤ Ions in Solutions

➤ Solubility

➤ Acid–Base Titrations

ACID–BASE REACTIONS

An acid reacts with a base to form an ionic compound, often called a **salt**, plus water.

Brønsted–Lowry Definition of Acids and Bases

ACIDS

An **acid** is a compound that produces H^+ (**hydronium ion**) in water solution. There are strong acids and weak acids. A **strong acid** is defined as an acid that dissociates fully into two ions in water solution.

The six strong acids are HCl, HBr, HI, HNO_3, H_2SO_4, and $HClO_4$.

All other acids are **weak acids**, defined as an acid that dissociates only to a very small extent in water solution. Some examples are HF, HCN, H_2CO_3, H_3PO_4, acetic acid, and oxalic acid.

BASES

A **base** is a compound that produces **OH⁻ (hydroxide ion)** in water solution. There are strong bases and weak bases. A **strong base** fully dissociates into its ions in water solution. Among the strong bases are hydroxides of groups IA and IIA that are fully soluble in water. They are $LiOH$, $NaOH$, KOH, and $Ba(OH)_2$.

There are many **weak bases**, but most of them are organic analogs of ammonia, NH_3. Ammonia dissolves in water, but only a very small percentage of NH_3 molecules produce NH_4OH, which then dissociates into NH_4^+ and OH^-.

TYPES OF ACID–BASE REACTIONS

When a strong acid reacts with a strong base, the ionic compound that forms is **neutral** in water solution. The ionic compound is formed by taking the cation from the base and the anion from the acid.

$$HCl + KOH \rightarrow KCl + H_2O \qquad \text{KCl is neutral.}$$
$$H_2SO_4 + NaOH \rightarrow NaHSO_4 + H_2O \qquad \text{NaHSO}_4 \text{ is neutral.}$$

When a strong acid reacts with a weak base, the ionic compound that forms is **acidic** in water solution.

$$HCl + NH_4OH \rightarrow NH_4Cl + H_2O \qquad \text{NH}_4\text{Cl is acidic.}$$
$$HClO_4 + NH_4OH \rightarrow NH_4ClO_4 + H_2O \qquad \text{NH}_4\text{ClO}_4 \text{ is acidic.}$$

When a weak acid reacts with a strong base, the ionic compound that forms is **basic** in water solution.

$$HF + NaOH \rightarrow NaF + H_2O \qquad \text{NaF is basic.}$$
$$HCN + KOH \rightarrow KCN + H_2O \qquad \text{KCN is basic.}$$

Compounds, such as water, that can serve as an acid (donates a proton) or base (accepts a proton) are referred to as **amphiprotic compounds**.

Ionization of Water

Acidity is a measure of the concentration of H^+ in a dilute water solution. It is measured using the **pH scale**, which is based on a process that water undergoes called **autoionization**:

$$H_2O\ (l) \rightleftharpoons H^+(aq) + OH^-\ (aq) \qquad K_w = 1 \times 10^{-14}$$

This is an **equilibrium process** that lies very far to the left. The K for this, in other words, is very small. It is called K_w (for water) and $K_w = 1 \times 10^{-14}$ at 25 °C. This means that approximately 1 out of every 10^{14} molecules dissociates into ions in this manner.

An acid produces H^+ in water solution. A base produces OH^- (hydroxide) in water solution. When an acid reacts with a base, a salt is formed. This chapter discusses these compounds and their interactions.

The pH Scale

The pH scale is from 0 to 14. It is a logarithmic scale (powers of 10). Each pH is 10-fold less acidic than the next lower pH value.

At pH 7, a solution is neutral.

$$[H^+] = [OH^-]$$

Writing the K expression,

$$K_w = [H^+][OH^-] = 1 \times 10^{-14}$$

At pH 7,

$$[H^+] = [OH^-] = 1 \times 10^{-7} \text{ M}$$

From this, you can see that the pH = $-\log [H^+]$ and that pOH = $-\log [OH^-]$. When the pH is 7, the pOH is 7 as well.

$$pH + pOH = 14$$

When $[H^+] = 1 \times 10^{-3}$ M, the pH = 3; and when $[OH^-] = 1 \times 10^{-11}$ M, the pOH = 11.

EXAMPLE: Calculate the pH if $[H^+]$ is 3.5×10^{-5} M.

SOLUTION:

➤ Because the exponent is −5, the pH is near 5.
➤ pH = $-\log (3.5 \times 10^{-5}) = 4.5$

EXAMPLE: Calculate $[H^+]$ when pH = 8.4.

SOLUTION:

➤ $8.4 = -\log [H^+]$
➤ $[H^+] = 10^{-8.4} = 4 \times 10^{-9}$ M

EXAMPLE: Calculate $[OH^-]$ when pH = 10.6.

SOLUTION:

➤ pOH = $14 - 10.6 = 3.4$
➤ $[OH^-] = 10^{-3.4} = 4 \times 10^{-4}$ M

Conjugate Acids and Bases

A Brønsted–Lowry acid, which is a **proton donor**, can be represented in general as **HX** and a Brønsted–Lowry base, which is a **proton acceptor**, can be represented as **X⁻**. The general reaction of an acid placed in water would be described in the following form:

$$HX + H_2O \rightarrow X^- + H_3O^+$$

acid + base → base + acid

where the acid (HX) donates a proton to water (which acts as a base) to yield H_3O^+, which is a hydronium ion (a water molecule that has accepted a donated proton). HX and X^- are often referred to as a **conjugate acid–base pair** defined as a pair of compounds that differ in structure by one proton. HX is a conjugate acid while X^- is the conjugate base. The acid, which has the proton to donate, is the conjugate acid, while the base, which is ready to accept the proton, is the conjugate base.

An example of a reaction involving an acid is:

$$HCl + H_2O \rightarrow Cl^- + H_3O^+$$

(hydrochloric acid) + (water) → (chloride ion) + (hydronium ion)

acid + base → base + acid

The same process applies when a base is placed in water, which yields the general reaction:

$$X^- + H_2O \rightarrow HX + OH^-$$

base + acid → acid + base

where the base (X^-) accepts a proton from water (which acts as an acid) to yield the conjugate acid of the base and OH^- (hydroxide ion). An example of a reaction involving a base is:

$$NH_3 + H_2O \rightarrow NH_4^+ + OH^-$$

(ammonia) + (water) → (ammonium ion) + (hydroxide ion)

base + acid → acid + base

Strong Acids and Bases

STRONG ACIDS

A strong acid is an acid where every molecule dissociates into H^+ and the counter ion (the conjugate base). There are six strong acids—HCl, HBr, HI, HNO_3, H_2SO_4, and $HClO_4$.

The equation for the dissociation of HCl is written:

$$HCl\ (aq) \rightarrow H^+\ (aq) + Cl^-\ (aq)$$

Because there is no reverse reaction taking place, strong acids do not involve any equilibrium process. Simple stoichiometry suffices. The concentration of the proton and the concentration of the conjugate base Cl^- are equal to the initial concentration of the acid.

If 1,000 HCl molecules are dissolved in water, they dissociate into 1,000 H^+ and 1,000 Cl^- ions.

STRONG BASES

If the base is a strong base, every molecule dissociates into ions in water solution. The most common strong bases are LiOH, NaOH, KOH, and $Ba(OH)_2$.

$$KOH\ (aq) \rightarrow K^+\ (aq) + OH^-\ (aq)$$

$$Ba(OH)_2\ (aq) \rightarrow Ba^{2+}\ (aq) + 2\ OH^-\ (aq)$$

There is no equilibrium here; stoichiometry suffices to determine $[OH^-]$ and, thus, pH. For LiOH, KOH, and NaOH, the base concentration equals the hydroxide concentration.

$$[KOH] = [OH^-]$$

For $Ba(OH)_2$, the base concentration is half of the hydroxide concentration.

$$[Ba(OH)_2] = \frac{1}{2}\ [OH^-]$$

EXAMPLE: Calculate the pH of 0.065 M KOH. This is a strong base with 1 : 1 stoichiometry.

SOLUTION:

➤ $[KOH] = [OH^-] = 0.065$ M.
➤ $pOH = -\log 0.065 = 1.2$
➤ $pH = 14 - 1.2 = 12.8$

EXAMPLE: Calculate the pH of 0.065 M $Ba(OH)_2$. This is a strong base with 1 : 2 stoichiometry.

SOLUTION:

➤ $[Ba(OH)_2] = \frac{1}{2}\ [OH^-] = 0.065$
➤ $[OH^-] = 0.13$ M
➤ $pOH = -\log 0.13 = 0.9$
➤ $pH = 14 - 0.9 = 13.1$

Weak Acids and Bases

WEAK ACIDS

Weak acids have the word *acid* as part of their name, and they are not one of the six strong acids.

For weak acids, only 1 out of every 10,000–100,000 molecules undergoes dissociation to proton and conjugate base or

$$HA\ (aq) \rightleftarrows H^+\ (aq) + A^-\ (aq)$$

Most of the molecules are still in the HA form. This is an equilibrium process, with a very small K_a (for acid). The K_a values are typically in the range of 10^{-4} to 10^{-6}. The K_a expression is written as:

$$K_a = \frac{[H^+] [A^-]}{[HA]}.$$

EXAMPLE: Calculate the pH of 0.15 M HNO_3.

SOLUTION:

➤ This is a strong acid, so the proton concentration is equal to the acid concentration: $[H^+] = [HNO_3] = 0.15$ M.

➤ $pH = -\log 0.15 = 0.8$

EXAMPLE: Calculate the pH of 0.15 M HF. For this problem, $K_a = 6.7 \times 10^{-4}$.

SOLUTION: This is a weak acid. The steps for solving this problem are:

➤ Write the equation.

$$HF\ (aq) \rightleftharpoons H^+\ (aq) + F^-\ (aq)$$

➤ Fill in the table.

	HF	$\leftrightarrows$	H^+	+	F^-
At equilibrium	0.15 M		x		x

(Small K so the initial HF concentration equals the HF concentration at equilibrium.)

➤ Write the K expression.

$$K_a = \frac{[H^+] [F^-]}{[HF]}$$

➤ Fill in the equilibrium values.

$$6.7 \times 10^{-4} = \frac{x^2}{0.15}$$

➤ Solve the $[H^+]$ for x.

$$x = [H^+] = 1 \times 10^{-2}\ M$$

➤ Calculate the pH.

$$pH = -\log (1 \times 10^{-2}) = 2$$

WEAK BASES

We use ammonia for the weak base problems because almost all weak bases are organic derivatives of ammonia. When ammonia is dissolved in water, approximately 1 out of every 100,000 molecules produces an OH^- (hydroxide ion).

The equation is:

$$NH_3\ (aq) + H_2O\ (aq) \rightleftharpoons NH_4^+\ (aq) + OH^-\ (aq)$$

This is an equilibrium process and the K_b (for base) is 1.8×10^{-5}. The K_b expression is written:

$$K_b = \frac{[NH_4^+][OH^-]}{[NH_3]}$$

EXAMPLE: Calculate the pH of 0.065 M NH_3. In this example, $K_b = 1.8 \times 10^{-5}$.

SOLUTION: This is a weak base; there are certain steps to follow.

➤ Write the equation.

$$NH_3\ (aq) + H_2O\ (l) \leftrightharpoons NH_4^+\ (aq) + OH^-\ (aq)$$

➤ Fill in the table.

	NH_3	$\leftrightharpoons$	NH_4^+	+	OH^-
At equilibrium	0.065 M		x		x

➤ Write the K expression.

$$K_b = \frac{[NH_4^+][OH^-]}{[NH_3]}$$

➤ Fill in the equilibrium values.
➤ Solve for x, i.e., $[OH^-]$.

$$1.8 \times 10^{-5} = \frac{x^2}{0.065}$$

$$x = [OH^-] = 1.1 \times 10^{-3}\ M$$

➤ Calculate the pOH.

$$pOH = 3$$

➤ Calculate the pH.

$$pH = 11$$

POLYPROTIC ACIDS

Polyprotic acids are acids that have more than one proton; therefore, they have more than one K_a. There is just one K_a per proton removed. In the following equations, all substances are in aqueous solution.

➤ Carbonic acid has 2 protons (both weak):

$$H_2CO_3$$

➤ For the removal of the first proton,

$$H_2CO_3 \rightleftharpoons H^+ + HCO_3^{-1}$$

➤ For the removal of the second proton,

$$HCO_3^{-1} \rightleftharpoons H^+ + CO_3^{-2}$$

➤ K_{a1} for the first proton $= 4.3 \times 10^{-7}$ Weak acid

➤ K_{a2} for the second proton $= 4.8 \times 10^{-11}$ Weaker acid

➤ Phosphoric acid has 3 protons (all weak):

$$H_3PO_4$$

➤ Removal of first proton,

$$H_3PO_4 \rightleftharpoons H^+ + H_2PO_4^{-1} \quad K_{a1} = 6.9 \times 10^{-3}$$

$$3H \rightarrow 2H$$

➤ Removal of second proton,

$$H_2PO_4^{-1} \rightleftharpoons H^+ + HPO_4^{-2} \quad K_{a2} = 6.2 \times 10^{-8}$$

$$2H \rightarrow 1H$$

➤ Removal of third proton,

$$HPO_4^{-2} \rightleftharpoons H^+ + PO_4^{-3} \quad\quad K_{a3} = 4.8 \times 10^{-13}$$

$$1H \rightarrow 0H$$

pH OF A POLYPROTIC ACID SOLUTION

If you are calculating the pH of a solution of carbonic acid or phosphoric acid, only the first (and largest) K_{a1} is used. The amount of proton produced by the subsequent K_a values is negligible compared to the first. In all of the equations that follow, every substance is in aqueous solution except the water, which is liquid.

SALTS OF POLYPROTIC ACIDS

$NaHCO_3$ is the salt of NaOH and H_2CO_3. It is a basic salt (K_b); thus, it produces OH^- and a conjugate acid:

$$HCO_3^{-1} + H_2O \rightleftharpoons OH^- + H_2CO_3 \quad K_{b1} = 2.3 \times 10^{-8}$$

Na_2CO_3 is also a salt of NaOH and H_2CO_3. It is a basic salt (K_b); thus, it produces OH^- and a conjugate acid:

$$CO_3^{-2} + H_2O \rightleftharpoons OH^- + HCO_3^{-1} \quad K_{b2} = 2.1 \times 10^{-4}$$

There are three salts of phosphoric acid:

$$NaH_2PO_4$$

$$Na_2HPO_4$$

$$Na_3PO_4$$

All of these are basic salts; they produce OH^- and a conjugate acid

$$H_2PO_4^{-1} + H_2O \rightleftharpoons OH^- + H_3PO_4 \quad\quad K_{b1} = 1.4 \times 10^{-12}$$

$$HPO_4^{-2} + H_2O \rightleftharpoons OH^- + H_2PO_4^{-1} \quad\quad K_{b2} = 1.6 \times 10^{-7}$$

$$PO_4^{-3} + H_2O \rightleftharpoons OH^- + HPO_4^{-2} \quad\quad K_{b3} = 2.1 \times 10^{-2}$$

EXAMPLE: Calculate the pH of 0.1185 M phosphoric acid solution.

SOLUTION:

➤ For the pH of a polyprotic acid, we use only the K_{a1}.

$$K_{a1} = 6.9 \times 10^{-3}$$

➤ Write the equation.

$$H_3PO_4 \rightleftarrows H^+ + H_2PO_4^{-1}$$

➤ Fill in the table.

H_3PO_4	$\leftrightarrows$	H^+	$+$	$H_2PO_4^{-1}$
0.1185 M		x		x

➤ Write K_a expression.

$$K_a = \frac{[H^+]\,[H_2PO_4^{-1}]}{[H_3PO_4]}$$

➤ Fill in values and solve for x.

$$6.9 \times 10^{-3} = \frac{x^2}{0.1185\,M}$$

$$x = [H^+] = \sqrt{8.2 \times 10^{-4}} = 2.9 \times 10^{-2}\,M$$

➤ Calculate the pH.

$$pH = -\log[H^+] = 1.5$$

EXAMPLE: Calculate the pH of 0.0165 M sodium hydrogen phosphate.

SOLUTION:

➤ Write the formula.

$$Na_2HPO_4$$

➤ Recognize that this is a basic salt, so it is a base. So you need a K_b.
➤ Write the equation.

$$HPO_4^{-2} + H_2O \rightleftarrows OH^- + H_2PO_4^{-1}$$

➤ Fill in the table.

HPO_4^{-2}	$\leftrightarrows$	OH^-	$+$	$H_2PO_4^{-1}$
0.0165 M		x		x

➤ Determine which K_b is needed.

K_{b1} involves $2H \rightarrow 3H$

K_{b2} involves $1H \rightarrow 2H$

K_{b3} involves $0H \rightarrow 1H$

➤ Because our salt has 1H and is going to the conjugate acid with 2H, we need K_{b2}.

$$K_{b2} = 1.6 \times 10^{-7}$$

➤ Write the K_b expression.

$$K_{b2} = \frac{[OH^-] [H_2PO_4^-]}{[HPO_4^{-2}]}$$

➤ Fill in the values and solve for x.

$$1.6 \times 10^{-7} = \frac{x^2}{0.0165 \text{ M}}$$

$$x = [OH^-] = 5.1 \times 10^{-5} \text{ M}$$

➤ Calculate pOH and pH.

$$pOH = 4.3$$

$$pH = 9.7$$

SOLUTIONS OF SALTS

When an acid reacts with a base, in stoichiometric quantities, an ionic compound (a salt) is formed, along with water:

$$\text{acid} + \text{base} \rightarrow \text{salt} + H_2O$$

The ionic compound is neutral, acidic, or basic (when dissolved in water), depending on which acid and base were used to make it.

CASE 1:

$$\text{Strong acid} + \text{Strong base} \longrightarrow \text{Neutral salt} \quad pH = 7$$

CASE 2:

$$\text{Strong acid} + \text{Weak base} \longrightarrow \text{Acidic salt} \quad pH < 7$$

CASE 3:

$$\text{Weak acid} + \text{Strong base} \longrightarrow \text{Basic salt} \quad pH > 7$$

We look next at salts from cases 2 and 3 only. In the following equations, all substances are in aqueous solution except water, which is liquid.

CASE 2 EXAMPLES:

$$HCl + NH_4OH \longrightarrow NH_4Cl + H_2O$$

$$HNO_3 + NH_4OH \longrightarrow NH_4NO_3 + H_2O$$

CASE 3 EXAMPLES:

$$HF + LiOH \longrightarrow LiF + H_2O$$

$$HCN + KOH \longrightarrow KCN + H_2O$$

$$CH_3COOH + KOH^- \longrightarrow CH_3COO^-K^+ + H_2O$$

ACIDIC SALTS

Acidic salts are formed when a strong acid reacts with a weak base, as in case 2.

EXAMPLE: Calculate the pH of 0.078 M ammonium nitrate. For this problem, $K_a = 5.6 \times 10^{-10}$.

SOLUTION:

➤ Recognize that NH_4NO_3 is an acidic salt.
➤ Therefore, it is an acid (produces H^+).
➤ Write the equation.

$$NH_4^+ \ (aq) \rightleftharpoons NH_3 \ (aq) + H^+ \ (aq)$$

➤ Fill in the table.

	NH_4^+	$\rightleftarrows$	NH_3	+	H^+
At equilibrium	0.078 M		x		x

➤ Write the K expression.

$$K_a = \frac{[NH_3]\,[H^+]}{[NH_4^+]}$$

➤ Fill in the values and solve for x, the $[H^+]$.

$$5.6 \times 10^{-10} = \frac{x^2}{0.078\,M}$$

$$x = [H^+] = 6.6 \times 10^{-6}\,M$$

➤ Calculate pH.

$$pH = 5.2$$

BASIC SALTS

Basic salts are formed when a strong base reacts with a weak acid, as in case 3.

EXAMPLE: Calculate the pH of 0.035 M KCN. For this problem, $K_b = 1.6 \times 10^{-5}$.

SOLUTION:

➤ Recognize that KCN is a basic salt.
➤ Therefore, it is a base (produces OH^-).
➤ Write the equation. The only ion here that can produce OH^- from water is the cyanide. You must have a negative ion to remove the H^+ from H_2O, leaving OH^-.

$$CN^- \ (aq) + H_2O \ (l) \rightleftharpoons HCN \ (aq) + OH^- \ (aq)$$

➤ Fill in the table.

	CN^-	$\rightleftarrows$	HCN	+	OH^-
At equilibrium	0.035 M		x		x

➤ Write the K expression.

$$K_b = \frac{[HCN]\,[OH^-]}{[CN^-]}$$

➤ Fill in the values and solve for x, the $[OH^-]$.

$$1.6 \times 10^{-5} = \frac{x^2}{0.035\,M}$$

$$x = [OH^-] = 7.5 \times 10^{-4}\,M$$

➤ Calculate pOH.

$$pOH = 3.1$$

➤ Calculate pH.

$$pH = 10.9$$

Equilibrium Constants

You have just examined the **equilibrium constants** K_a and K_b for various acids and bases. Now see how they work together to produce the ionization constant for water, K_w. First consider the K_a expression for an acid and the K_b expression for a base:

$$K_a = \frac{[H_3O^+][A^-]}{HA} \quad \text{and} \quad K_b = \frac{[HA][OH^-]}{[A^-]}$$

When you multiply K_a by K_b, you get $K_a \times K_b = [H_3O^+][OH^-] = K_w = 1 \times 10^{-14}$. Prove it to yourself by multiplying the K_a value of HF (7.2×10^{-4}) by the K_b value of F^- (1.4×10^{-11}).

One other equilibrium constant to be examined in this chapter is the **solubility product constant** of a slightly soluble salt, K_{sp}. Keep in mind that this is an equilibrium constant between the ionic compound and a saturated solution of the ions that it forms. Consider the slight ability of AgCl (s) to dissolve in water. The equation for this is AgCl $(s) \rightarrow Ag^+$ $(aq) + Cl^-$ (aq). When you write the equilibrium constant expressions for a reaction, solids, liquids, and solvents are not included. This expression is written as $K_{sp} = [Ag^+][Cl^-]$ and has a value of 1.8×10^{-10}. When comparing this to the K_{sp} for $CaSO_4$ (2.4×10^{-5}), you see that the calcium sulfate is more soluble than the silver chloride.

Buffers

DEFINITION OF COMMON BUFFER SYSTEMS

A **buffer** is a solution that resists change in pH when small amounts of acid or base are added. It is usually a solution that is made of approximately equal concentrations of an acid and its conjugate base. The calculation of the pH of a buffer uses exactly the same method as for a common ion.

EXAMPLE: Calculate the pH of a buffer made by mixing 60.0 milliliters (mL) of 0.100 M NH_3 with 40.0 mL of 0.100 M NH_4Cl. The equilibrium constant, K_a, is

$$K_a = 5.6 \times 10^{-10}$$

SOLUTION:

➤ Calculate the molarity of each component in the mixture.

$$(0.0600 \text{ L}) (0.100 \text{ M}) = 0.006 \text{ mole}/0.100 \text{ L} = 0.060 \text{ M } NH_3$$

$$(0.0400 \text{ L}) (0.100 \text{ M}) = 0.004 \text{ mole}/0.100 \text{ L} = 0.040 \text{ M } NH_4Cl$$

➤ Write the equation and fill in the values.

	NH_4	$\rightleftharpoons$ H^+	+	NH_3
Initial	0.040 M	0		0.060 M
Δ	$-x$	$+x$		$+x$
At equilibrium	0.040 M $- x$	x		0.060 M $+ x$

➤ Assume the change is negligible.
➤ Write the K_a expression.

$$K_a = \frac{[H^+] [NH_3]}{[NH_4^+]}$$

➤ Plug in the values and solve for x.

$$5.6 \times 10^{-10} = \frac{x (0.060)}{0.040}$$

$$x = [H^+] = 3.7 \times 10^{-10} \text{ M}$$

➤ Calculate the pH.

$$pH = 9.4$$

INFLUENCE OF BUFFERS ON A TITRATION CURVE

While titration curves will be covered in more detail later in this chapter, you can use a titration curve to show the impact of a buffer on a solution and how it resists changes in pH. Buffers resist change in pH because they contain an acidic component to neutralize OH^- ions and a basic component to neutralize H^+ ions. Consider the following situation where a different number of moles of HCl in 1 liter of solution produce various pH values (see Figure 6-1). If a buffer is made from 0.2 M acetic acid and 0.2 M sodium acetate, you can see that adding a small amount of the acid has little effect on the pH, causing the line to remain more horizontal. In order for the line to remain horizontal, the buffer concentration must be sufficiently larger than the amount of acid being added.

Even if the buffer were made with half the concentration of acetic acid and sodium acetate, 0.1 M each, the 0.1 M HCl solution would have a pH of 2.72—still shy of the pH of 1 if there was no buffer present at all.

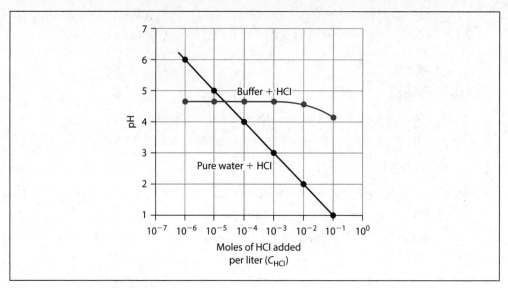

FIGURE 6-1 Influence of buffers on a titration curve.

IONS IN SOLUTIONS

Anions and Cations

When an ionic compound is dissolved in a solution, there is a formation of both negative and positive ions. The negative ions are called **anions**, while the positive ions are called **cations**. For example, when a salt such as sodium chloride is added to water, you get Na^+ and Cl^- as the cation and anion, respectively.

NOMENCLATURE OF IONIC COMPOUNDS

Ionic compounds consist of cations and anions. The name of the cation comes first, and it is named as the **element**. There are a few complex cations, but the most important one is ammonium ion, which has the formula NH_4^{+1}.

The main group elements form cations in a systematic manner. Elements from group I always form +1 cations. Elements from group II always form +2 cations. The metals Al and Ga from group III always form +3 cations. In general, the metals always form cations.

Anions are generally formed from nonmetals, or groups of nonmetals that are covalently bonded. The simple cations and anions and many of the complex anions are listed in the following table.

To name a compound such as Na_3N, the cation Na^{+1} is called **sodium** and the anion N^{-3} is called **nitride**. Therefore, the compound is sodium nitride. AlN is aluminum nitride; Mg_3N_2 is magnesium nitride; and MgO is magnesium oxide.

To write the formula of calcium hydride, the calcium cation is Ca^{+2} and the anion hydride is H^{-1}. Two hydrides are required to balance the +2 charge on the calcium ion, in order to net out to zero overall. So the formula is CaH_2.

TABLE 6-1 Simple and Complex Anions and Cations

Main Group Cations and Simple Anions						
Group IA	**IIA**	**IIIA**	**IVA**	**VA**	**VIA**	**VIIA**
H^+ Hydrogen						H^- Hydride
Li^+ Lithium	Be^{2+} Beryllium	Al^{3+} Aluminum		N^{3-} Nitride	O^{2-} Oxide	F^- Fluoride
Na^+ Sodium	Mg^{2+} Magnesium	Ga^{3+} Gallium			S^{2-} Sulfide	Cl^- Chloride
K^+ Potassium	Ca^{2+} Calcium	In^{3+} Indium			Se^{2-} Selenide	Br^- Bromide
Rb^+ Rubidium	Sr^{2+} Strontium				Te^{2-} Telluride	I^- Iodide
Cs^+ Cesium	Ba^{2+} Barium					

Complex Anions							
Cyanide	CN^-						
Hydroxide	OH^-						
Peroxide	O_2^{-2}						
Permanganate	MnO_4^-						
Chromate	CrO_4^{-2}						
Dichromate	$Cr_2O_7^{-2}$						
Carbonate	CO_3^{-2}	Hydrogen carbonate	HCO_3^-				
Phosphate	PO_4^{-3}	Hydrogen phosphate	HPO_4^{-2}	Dihydrogen phosphate	$H_2PO_4^-$		
Phosphite	PO_3^{-3}	Hydrogen phosphite	HPO_3^{-2}	Dihydrogen phosphite	$H_2PO_3^-$		
Sulfate	SO_4^{-2}	Hydrogen sulfate	HSO_4^-				
Sulfite	SO_3^{-2}	Hydrogen sulfite	HSO_3^-				
Nitrate	NO_3^-						
Nitrite	NO_2^-						
Perchlorate	ClO_4^-	Perbromate	BrO_4^-	Periodate	IO_4^-		
Chlorate	ClO_3^-	Bromate	BrO_3^-	Iodate	IO_3^-		
Chlorite	ClO_2^-	Bromite	BrO_2^-	Iodite	IO_2^-		
Hypochlorite	ClO^-	Hypobromite	BrO^-	Hypoiodite	IO^-		

Complex Cation	
Ammonium	NH_4^+

A good method to determine how many cations and how many anions are in a formula is the **lowest common denominator method**. The lowest common denominator of the charges is determined (ignoring the signs). This gives the total + charges and the total − charges necessary.

EXAMPLE: Determine the formula of sodium oxide.

SOLUTION: Sodium is Na^{+1} and oxide is O^{-2}. The lowest common denominator of 1 and 2 (the charges) is 2. Thus, the positive charges must total +2 and the negative charges must total −2. So there must be 2 sodium cations and 1 oxide anion, and the formula is Na_2O.

Transition metal cations vary in their possible charges; the charge of the metal must be written in the name as a roman numeral. Thus, copper (II) oxide means that the copper cation is Cu^{+2}. Because oxide is always O^{-2}, the charges balance, and the formula is CuO.

Copper (I) oxide means that the copper cation is Cu^{+1}. Oxide is O^{-2}. The lowest common denominator is 2; thus, there must be two Cu^{+1} cations for every oxide anion. The formula is Cu_2O.

The complex anions must be memorized. Their names, formulas, and net charge are given in the previous table.

EXAMPLE: Write the formula of sodium phosphate.

SOLUTION: The sodium cation is Na^{+1} and the phosphate anion is PO_4^{-3}. The lowest common denominator of the charges is 3. Thus, there must be 3 sodium cations and 1 phosphate anion to result in a net zero charge for the molecule. So the formula is Na_3PO_4.

HYDRATION AND THE HYDRONIUM ION

When a water solution contains cations and anions, the water molecules will orient themselves depending on whether an anion or cation is nearby. Because water is a polar molecule where oxygen is the negative end, the oxygen of a water molecule will be oppositely attracted to a cation. When a water molecule is oriented toward an anion, the hydrogen atoms of the water molecule will be attracted to the anion. This is because the hydrogen atoms of the water molecule are the positive ends of the molecule and will be attracted to the negative anions. When the ions are surrounded or solvated by water molecules, they are called **hydrated ions**.

Hydrogen ions can also interact with a water molecule. This is found in acid–base chemistry when a proton is in solution. When in solution, the hydrogen ions (protons) will form a coordinate covalent bond to a free pair of electrons on the oxygen atom of a water molecule. This forms the hydronium ion as shown in the reaction $H^+ + H_2O \rightarrow H_3O^+$.

SOLUBILITY

Concentration Units

There are various concentration units that can be used to describe how much solute is dissolved in a certain amount of solution. This section deals with reactions that take place in solution. The concentration unit that is used to make solutions for reaction is **molarity**, which has the symbol **M**, and is defined as:

M = mole solute/liter (L) solution

This definition is also a working equation. There are three variables; if two are known, the third can be calculated.

> **EXAMPLE:** Calculate the molarity of a solution that is prepared by dissolving 1.192 grams (g) of oxalic acid ($C_2H_2O_4$) in water to a total of 100.0 milliliters (mL) of solution.

SOLUTION:

1. Convert the mass of oxalic acid to moles.

   $(1.192$ g$)$ $(1$ mole$/90.04$ g$) = 0.01324$ mole oxalic acid

2. Convert the milliliters to liters.

   $(100.0$ mL$)$ $(1$ L$/1000$ mL$) = 0.1000$ L

3. Calculate the molarity.

   M $= 0.01324$ mole$/0.1000$ L $= 0.1324$ M

Solubility Product Constant

Insoluble ionic compounds are actually soluble to a very small extent. These solubilities are equilibrium-based processes, with a very small equilibrium constant K.

The solubility equation is written with the solid on the left and the ions in solution on the right, as shown in the following examples:

$$CaC_2O_4(s) \leftrightarrows Ca^{+2} (aq) + C_2O_4^{-2} (aq)$$
$$PbI_2(s) \leftrightarrows Pb^{+2} (aq) + 2I^- (aq)$$
$$Ca_3(PO_4)_2(s) \leftrightarrows 3Ca^{+2} (aq) + 2PO_4^{-3} (aq)$$

The K expression for solubility product constant—called K_{sp}—is written as:

$$K_{sp} = [Ca^{+2}] [C_2O_4^{-2}]$$
$$K_{sp} = [Pb^{+2}] [I^-]^2$$
$$K_{sp} = [Ca^{+2}]^3 [PO_4^{-3}]^2$$

The solubility of the compound (in M units) can be calculated from the K_{sp} data.

➤ Write the equation.

   $$CaF_2 (s) \leftrightarrows Ca^{+2} (aq) + 2F^- (aq)$$

➤ Fill in the values.

	Ca^{+2}	+	$2F^-$
Initial	0		0
Δ	$+x$		$+2x$
At equilibrium	x		$2x$

➤ Write the K_{sp} expression.

   $$K_{sp} = [Ca^{+2}] [F^-]^2$$

➤ Plug in value for K_{sp} (found in the following table) and solve for x.

$$4.0 \times 10^{-11} = x(2x)^2 = 4x^3$$
$$x = [Ca^{+2}] = 2.2 \times 10^{-4} \text{ M}$$

TABLE 6-2 Solubility Products of Some Slightly Soluble Ionic Compounds at 25 °C

Compound	K_{sp}
Aluminum hydroxide [Al(OH)$_3$]	1.8×10^{-33}
Barium carbonate (BaCO$_3$)	8.1×10^{-9}
Barium fluoride (BaF$_2$)	1.7×10^{-6}
Barium sulfate (BaSO$_4$)	1.1×10^{-10}
Bismuth sulfide (Bi$_2$S$_3$)	1.6×10^{-72}
Cadmium sulfide (CdS)	8.0×10^{-28}
Calcium carbonate (CaCO$_3$)	8.7×10^{-9}
Calcium fluoride (CaF$_2$)	4.0×10^{-11}
Calcium hydroxide [Ca(OH)$_2$]	8.0×10^{-6}
Calcium phosphate [Ca$_3$(PO$_4$)$_2$]	1.2×10^{-26}
Chromium (III) hydroxide [Cr(OH)$_3$]	3.0×10^{-29}
Cobalt (II) sulfide (CoS)	4.0×10^{-21}
Copper (I) bromide (CuBr)	4.2×10^{-8}
Copper (I) iodide (CuI)	5.1×10^{-12}
Copper (II) hydroxide [Cu(OH)$_2$]	2.2×10^{-20}
Copper (II) sulfide (CuS)	6.0×10^{-37}
Iron (II) hydroxide [Fe(OH)$_2$]	1.6×10^{-14}
Iron (III) hydroxide [Fe(OH)$_3$]	1.1×10^{-36}
Iron (II) sulfide (FeS)	6.0×10^{-19}
Lead (II) carbonate (PbCO$_3$)	3.3×10^{-14}
Lead (II) chloride (PbCl$_2$)	2.4×10^{-4}
Lead (II) chromate (PbCrO$_4$)	2.0×10^{-14}
Lead (II) fluoride (PbF$_2$)	4.1×10^{-8}
Lead (II) iodide (PbI$_2$)	1.4×10^{-8}
Lead (II) sulfide (PbS)	3.4×10^{-8}
Magnesium carbonate (MgCO$_3$)	4.0×10^{-5}
Magnesium hydroxide [Mg(OH)$_2$]	1.2×10^{-11}
Manganese (II) sulfide (MnS)	3.0×10^{-14}
Mercury (I) chloride (Hg$_2$Cl$_2$)	3.5×10^{-18}
Mercury (II) sulfide (HgS)	4.0×10^{-54}
Nickel (II) sulfide (NiS)	1.4×10^{-24}
Silver bromide (AgBr)	7.7×10^{-13}
Silver carbonate (Ag$_2$CO$_3$)	8.1×10^{-12}
Silver chloride (AgCl)	1.6×10^{-10}
Silver iodide (AgI)	8.3×10^{-17}
Silver sulfate (Ag$_2$SO$_4$)	1.4×10^{-5}
Silver sulfide (Ag$_2$S)	6.0×10^{-51}
Strontium carbonate (SrCO$_3$)	1.6×10^{-9}
Strontium sulfate (SrSO$_4$)	1.6×10^{-9}
Tin (II) sulfide (SnS)	1.0×10^{-26}
Zinc hydroxide [Zn(OH)$_2$]	1.8×10^{-14}
Zinc sulfide (ZnS)	3.0×10^{-23}

Conversely, the K_{sp} can be calculated using solubility data.

EXAMPLE: Calculate the K_{sp} of lead (II) iodide if the solubility is 1.2×10^{-3} M.

SOLUTION: The solubility equals x; therefore, $x = 1.2 \times 10^{-3}$.

➤ Write the equation.

$$PbI_2(s) \leftrightharpoons Pb^{+2}\ (aq) + 2I^-\ (aq)$$

➤ Fill in the values.

	Pb^{+2}	+	$2I^-$
Initial	0		0
Δ	$+1.2 \times 10^{-3}\ (x)$		$+2.4 \times 10^{-3}\ (2x)$
At equilibrium	$+1.2 \times 10^{-3}$		$+2.4 \times 10^{-3}$

➤ Write the K_{sp} expression.

$$K_{sp} = [Pb^{+2}]\ [I^-]^2$$

➤ Plug in values and solve for K_{sp}.

$$K_{sp} = (1.2 \times 10^{-3})\ (2.4 \times 10^{-3})^2$$

$$K_{sp} = 6.9 \times 10^{-9}$$

Common Ion Effect

When one of the ions is added to a solution at equilibrium, the equilibrium shifts to remove the added ion; thus the solubility lessens and more precipitate forms.

EXAMPLE: Calculate the solubility of calcium oxalate in 0.15 M calcium chloride. The equilibrium constant, K_{sp}, is:

$$K_{sp} = 2.3 \times 10^{-9}$$

SOLUTION:

➤ Write the equation.

$$CaC_2O_4(s) \leftrightharpoons Ca^{+2}\ (aq) + C_2O_4^{-2}\ (aq)$$

➤ Fill in the values.

	Ca^{+2}	+	$C_2O_4^{-2}$
Initial	0.15		0
Δ	$+x$		$+x$
At equilibrium	$0.15 + x$		x

➤ Assume the change is negligible.
➤ Write the K_{sp} expression.

$$K_{sp} = [Ca^{+2}]\ [C_2O_4^{-2}]$$

➤ Plug in values and solve for x.

$$2.3 \times 10^{-9} = (0.15)x$$
$$x = [C_2O_4{}^{-2}] = 1.5 \times 10^{-8} \text{ M}$$

The common ion effect occurs when you add strong acid or strong base to a solution of weak acid or weak base at equilibrium. The added base or acid reacts to form more of one of the components in equilibrium.

EXAMPLE: Calculate the concentration of acetate ion in a solution that is 0.10 M HAc and 0.010 M HCl. The equilibrium constant, K_a, is:

$$K_a = 1.8 \times 10^{-5}$$

SOLUTION:

➤ Write the equation.

$$\text{HAc } (aq) \rightleftarrows \text{H}^+ (aq) + \text{Ac}^- (aq)$$

➤ Fill in the table.

	HAc	$\rightleftarrows$	H$^+$	$+$	Ac$^-$
Initial	0.10		0.010		0
Δ	$-x$		$+x$		$+x$
At equilibrium	$0.10 - x$		$0.010 + x$		x

➤ Assume the change is negligible.
➤ Write the K_a expression.

$$K_a = \frac{[\text{H}^+]\,[\text{Ac}^-]}{[\text{HAc}]}$$

➤ Plug in values.

$$1.8 \times 10^{-5} = \frac{(0.010)\,x}{0.10}$$

➤ Solve for x.

$$x = [\text{Ac}^-] = 1.8 \times 10^{-4} \text{ M}$$

COMPLEX ION FORMATION

Many metal ions can accept electron pairs from other molecules (Lewis bases), causing the metal ions to act as Lewis acids. When these metal ions accept these electron pairs, a complex ion forms. Some examples are:

$$\text{Ag}^+ (aq) + 2\text{NH}_3 (aq) \rightarrow \text{Ag(NH}_3)^{2+} (aq)$$
$$\text{Cu}^{2+} (aq) + 4\text{CN}^- (aq) \rightarrow \text{Cu(CN)}_4^{2-} (aq)$$
$$\text{Cd}^{2+} (aq) + 4\text{Br}^- (aq) \rightarrow \text{CdBr}_4^{2-} (aq)$$

Accompanying these complexes are equilibrium constants of formation, or formation constants, K_f. The greater the value of K_f, the more stable the complex of ions will be in aqueous solution.

COMPLEX IONS AND SOLUBILITY

The addition of a Lewis base can drive an equilibrium and allow a slightly soluble salt to be more soluble. For example, AgCl will be only slightly soluble in water according to the reaction:

$$AgCl\ (s) \rightarrow Ag^+\ (aq) + Cl^-\ (aq)$$

However, should an electron pair be introduced into the preceding reaction, the equilibrium can be shifted toward the right. If cyanide ion were then added to the preceding reaction, CN^- would bond to Ag^+ to form the complex ion $Ag(CN)_2^-$. This complex ion has an equilibrium constant of formation, which is on the order of 10^{21}. The cyanide ion does a terrific job of removing the silver ions from solution, driving the reaction to the right and increasing the solubility of AgCl.

SOLUBILITY AND pH

Lowering the pH increases the solubility of basic ionic compounds. If you calculate the solubility of a basic compound in pure water as a reference, you can compare the solubility at a lower pH.

> **EXAMPLE:** (Part I—Reference): Calculate the solubility of nickel (II) hydroxide in pure water. The solubility constant, K_{sp}, is:
>
> $$K_{sp} = 2.0 \times 10^{-15}$$

SOLUTION:

➤ Write the equation.

$$Ni(OH)_2(s) \leftrightarrows Ni^{+2}\ (aq) + 2OH^-\ (aq)$$

➤ Fill in the values.

	Ni^{+2}	+	$2OH^-$
Initial	0		0
Δ	$+x$		$+2x$
At equilibrium	x		$2x$

➤ Write the K_{sp} expression.

$$K_{sp} = [Ni^{+2}]\ [OH^-]^2$$

➤ Plug in values and solve for x.

$$2.0 \times 10^{-15} = x(2x)^2$$

$$x = [Ni^{+2}] = 7.9 \times 10^{-6}\ M$$

EXAMPLE: (Part II): Calculate the solubility of nickel (II) hydroxide at pH 8.

SOLUTION:

➤ The pOH = 6; therefore, $[OH^-] = 1 \times 10^{-6}$ M.
➤ Plug in values using this concentration of OH^-.

$$2.0 \times 10^{-15} = x(1 \times 10^{-6})^2$$

$$x = [Ni^{+2}] = 2 \times 10^{-3} \text{ M}$$

EXAMPLE: (Part III): What is the pH of a saturated solution of nickel (II) hydroxide in pure water?

SOLUTION:

$$[OH^-] = 2x = 2(7.9 \times 10^{-6}) = 1.6 \times 10^{-5} \text{ M}$$

$$pOH = 4.8$$

$$pH = 9.2$$

This says that at any pH less than 9.2, the solubility is $> 7.9 \times 10^{-6}$ M, and as shown previously, at pH 8, the solubility is 2×10^{-3} M.

ACID–BASE TITRATIONS

An **acid–base titration** is the addition of a quantity of base of known concentration, using a burette, to a known volume of acid of unknown concentration, until the endpoint is reached. An **indicator compound**, such as phenolphthalein, is added so that a color change occurs at the endpoint. At that point, an equivalent amount of base has been added, and the volume that contains that amount is determined from the initial and final volumes on the burette. The concentration of the acid solution can then be calculated.

EXAMPLE: A 25.0-mL sample of HCl is titrated with 0.0750 M NaOH. The titration requires 32.7 mL of base to reach the endpoint. Calculate the molarity of the HCl.

SOLUTION:

➤ Write the equation for the reaction.

$$HCl + NaOH \rightarrow NaCl + H_2O$$

➤ The stoichiometry of HCl to NaOH is 1 : 1.
➤ Calculate the moles of base added in the titration.

$$(0.0750 \text{ M}) (0.0327 \text{ L}) = 0.00245 \text{ mole NaOH added}$$

➤ Calculate the moles of acid in the solution.

$$(0.00245 \text{ mole base}) (1 \text{ mole acid}/1 \text{ mole base}) = 0.00245 \text{ mole acid}$$

➤ Calculate the molarity of the acid.

$$M = \text{mole}/L = 0.00245 \text{ mole}/0.0250 \text{ L} = 0.098 \text{ M acid}$$

There are two major types of acid–base titrations. One is the addition of strong base to strong acid; the other is the addition of strong base to weak acid. The pH of the endpoint solution can be calculated for the second case.

Addition of Strong Base to Strong Acid

➤ The initial pH is the pH of the strong acid solution.

$$[H^+] = [HA]$$

➤ At the midpoint, calculate the moles of acid left.
➤ Then calculate the M of the acid solution.
➤ Calculate the pH at the midpoint.
➤ At the endpoint, the pH is 7, because the salt is neutral.

Addition of Strong Base to Weak Acid

➤ The initial pH is the pH of the weak acid solution.

$$K_a = x^2/[HA]$$
$$x = [H^+]$$
$$pH = -\log [H^+]$$

➤ At the midpoint, use the **Henderson–Hasselbach equation** after calculating the molarity of each component.

$$pH = pK_a + \log \frac{[A^-]}{[HA]} \quad \text{where } pK_a = -\log K_a$$

➤ At the endpoint, it's the pH of a basic salt solution.

➤ Calculate the molarity of the salt.
➤ Calculate the K_b.

$$K_b = x^2/[A^-]$$
$$x = [OH^-]$$

➤ Calculate pOH.
➤ Calculate pH.

EXAMPLE: A 25.0-mL sample of 0.0875 M acetic acid is titrated with 0.150 M NaOH. Consider the following given values:

$$K_a = 1.8 \times 10^{-5} \quad pK_a = 4.74$$

SOLUTION:

➤ Calculate the pH of the initial acid solution.

$$HA\ (aq) \rightleftarrows H^+\ (aq) + A^-\ (aq)$$

$$K_a = \frac{[H^+]\ [A^-]}{[HA]}$$

$1.8 \times 10^{-5} = x^2/0.0875$

$x = [H^+] = 1.25 \times 10^{-3}$ M

pH $= 2.9$

➤ Calculate the pH at the point when 5.0 mL of base has been added.

(0.005 L) (0.150 M NaOH) $= 7.5 \times 10^{-4}$ mole base added

➤ Reacts with 7.5×10^{-4} mole acid.

(0.0250 L) (0.0875 M acid) $= 2.188 \times 10^{-3}$ mole acid initially

➤ Subtract 7.5×10^{-4} mole acid that is now gone to get:

1.438×10^{-3} mole acid in 30 mL $= 0.0479$ M acid, and

7.5×10^{-4} mole conj base in 30 mL $= 0.0250$ M base

➤ Plug into the Henderson–Hasselbach equation.

$$pH = 4.74 + \log\frac{0.0250}{0.0479}$$

pH $= 4.5$

➤ Calculate the pH at the endpoint of the titration.

Here, you have added 2.188×10^{-3} mole NaOH to completely neutralize the initial amount of acid. This requires 2.188×10^{-3} mole/0.150 M $= 0.0146$ L NaOH solution.

$[A^-] = 2.188 \times 10^{-3}$ mole/0.0396 L total $= 0.055$ M conj base

➤ Calculate $K_b = K_w/K_a = 5.6 \times 10^{-10}$

$K_b = x^2/0.055$ M $= 5.6 \times 10^{-10}$

$x = [OH^-] = 5.5 \times 10^{-6}$ M

pOH $= 5.3$

pH $= 8.7$

Indicators

The easiest way to tell the approximate pH value of a solution is via the use of an indicator. **Universal indicators** are usually made from a blend of indicators and can have more than six distinct colors to give more exact pH values. Other indicators, such as **litmus**, have just two colors. When choosing an indicator for a titration, there is much to consider.

Indicators such as **phenolphthalein** are useful during a titration because their change in color tells you when the endpoint has been reached. The reaching of the endpoint is the reaching of the equivalence point as well. Not all indicators turn color at the same pH. This is why you need to pick an indicator with a pK that is close to the equivalence point. For example, the equivalence point in a titration between NaOH and acetic acid is about 9.2. You would choose phenolphthalein for this reaction because it has a pK of 9.3. If you were to titrate a strong acid and a weak base, then **methyl orange** might be used as an indicator. The pK of this indicator is about 3.7, and it changes color at a pH range of 3.1–4.4.

Neutralization

Neutralization is the process by which an acid and base are mixed together to form a salt and water. A classic example is the reaction between HCl and NaOH to form NaCl and H_2O. Because the three ionic compounds in the reaction are all completely soluble electrolytes, the net ionic reaction for the neutralization of these substances will be:

$$H^+ + OH^- \rightarrow H_2O$$

However, this is not the only type of neutralization that you can find. For example, if you were to have an acid spill in the laboratory, you would use sodium bicarbonate ($NaHCO_3$) or sodium carbonate (Na_2CO_3) to neutralize the spill. In these cases, the acid is neutralized and carbon dioxide is formed. The equations for the reactions are:

$$HCl + NaHCO_3 \rightarrow NaCl + H_2O + CO_2$$
$$2HCl + Na_2CO_3 \rightarrow 2NaCl + H_2O + CO_2$$

Interpretation of Titration Curves

As a base or acid is titrated, the pH can be measured and plotted to form a **titration curve**. In general, there are three more common shapes to be familiar with and one that is less popular. In Figure 6-2, you can see the titration curve of a strong acid and a strong base. As the strong base is titrated with the strong acid, the pH for the most part stays relatively high until the equivalence point is reached. At the equivalence point, the slope will be the steepest and the pH will be 7.

When a weak base is titrated with a strong acid, the pH will start at a lower basic value and the endpoint will occur at a pH that is on the acidic side of the pH scale. The opposite will occur when a strong base is titrated with a weak acid; the pH will start very basic and the pH at the equivalence point will be in the basic range.

One more case to consider is when a diprotic or polyprotic acid is involved (see Figure 6-3.). In the case of acids such as H_2CO_3 or H_3PO_4, the curves will have more than one equivalence point. Consider the titration of 25 mL of 0.100 M H_2CO_3 with 0.100 M NaOH. The pH starts low as there is just acid present. When the first H^+ ion is completely removed from the acid, you have the first equivalence point, which takes place after 25 mL of base are added. Now the base is titrating against the HCO_3^-. The second equivalence point at 50 mL of base added shows another equivalence point and a steep part of the curve. This shows the complete removal of the H^+ ion from the HCO_3^- to form CO_3^{2-}.

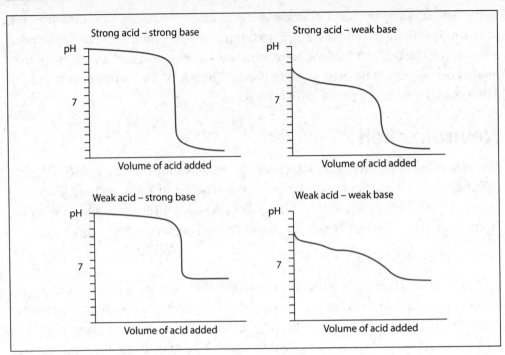

FIGURE 6-2 Titration curves.

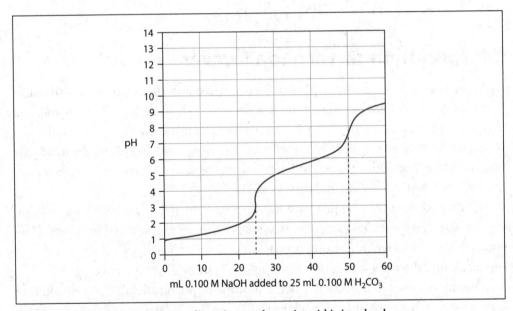

FIGURE 6-3 Titration curve when a diprotic or polyprotic acid is involved.

Oxidation–Reduction Reactions

Oxidation–reduction reactions, the third type of reaction in solution (next to precipitation reactions and acid-base reactions), involve the transfer of one or more electrons from one species in the reaction to another.

Any species that loses electrons is **oxidized**. Any species that gains electrons is **reduced**. Oxidation and reduction can be tracked using the oxidation number of each atom. Each atom in a formula has an oxidation number. It is similar to a charge; for simple ions, the charge and the oxidation number are the same. For atoms of an element, the oxidation number is always zero.

RULES FOR OXIDATION NUMBERS

➤ The oxidation number of an atom in a pure element is zero.

➤ The oxidation number of a simple ion is the same as its charge.

➤ The oxidation number of oxygen is usually -2, except in peroxides, where it is -1.

➤ The oxidation number of hydrogen in a covalent compound is $+1$ unless it is bonded to boron, where it is -1.

➤ The oxidation number of hydrogen in an ionic compound is -1.

➤ The oxidation number of fluorine is always -1.

➤ The sum of all the oxidation numbers in a neutral compound is always zero.

When the oxidation number of an atom decreases from one side of the equation to the other side, that atom is reduced. If an oxidation number increases, that atom is oxidized.

EXAMPLE: State which atom is oxidized and which is reduced in the following equation:

$$Fe + Cu^{+2} \rightarrow Fe^{+2} + Cu$$

SOLUTION:

1. Because Fe is an element, its oxidation number is 0.
2. Because Cu^{+2} is a simple ion, its oxidation number is $+2$.
3. Fe^{+2} is a simple ion; its oxidation number is $+2$.
4. Cu is an element; its oxidation number is 0.
5. Therefore, Fe is going from 0 to $+2$; Fe is being oxidized.
6. Cu is going from $+2$ to 0; Cu is reduced.

EXAMPLE: Try another problem. Which atom is oxidized and which is reduced?

$$2Sb + 3Cl_2 \rightarrow 2SbCl_3$$

SOLUTION:

1. Because Sb is an element; its oxidation number is 0.
2. Because Cl_2 is an element; its oxidation number of each Cl is 0.
3. Sb in $SbCl_3$ is the ion Sb^{+3}; oxidation number $+3$.
4. Cl in $SbCl_3$ is the ion Cl^{-1}; oxidation number -1.
5. Therefore,

$$Sb^0 \rightarrow Sb^{+3} \quad \text{oxidation}$$
$$Cl^0 \rightarrow Cl^{-1} \quad \text{reduction}$$

COMMON TYPES OF OXIDATION–REDUCTION REACTIONS

A few of the more common classifications of oxidation–reduction reactions are combination reactions, decomposition reactions, single displacement reactions, and combustion reactions.

A **combination reaction** occurs when two substances combine to form a third substance.

$$CaO \ (s) + SO_2 \ (g) \rightarrow CaSO_3 \ (s)$$

A **decomposition reaction** occurs when a single substance decomposes to two or more substances.

$$2KClO_3 \rightarrow 2KCl + 3O_2$$

A **single displacement reaction** occurs when an element reacts with an ionic compound and replaces the cation in the compound. The original cation becomes an element.

$$Cu + 2AgNO_3 \rightarrow 2Ag + Cu(NO_3)_2$$

A **combustion reaction** occurs when a substance reacts with oxygen to produce one or more oxides.

$$4Fe + 3O_2 \rightarrow 2Fe_2O_3$$

OXIDATION–REDUCTION TITRATIONS

Oxidation–reduction titration typically does not require an indicator compound to be added, because there is often an automatic color change on reaction.

EXAMPLE: A 25.0 mL sample of MnO_4^- is titrated with 0.0485 M I^- solution. To reach the endpoint, 18.7 mL of the I^- solution is required. Calculate the molarity of the MnO_4^- solution. The balanced equation is:

$$10I^- + 16H^+ + 2MnO_4^- \rightarrow 5I_2 + 2Mn^{+2} + 8H_2O$$

➤ Calculate the moles of I^- added.

$$(0.0485 \ mole/L) \ (0.0187 \ L) = 9.07 \times 10^{-4} \ mole \ I^- \ added$$

➤ Calculate the moles of MnO_4^-.

$$(9.07 \times 10^{-4} \ mole \ I^-) \ (2 \ mole \ MnO_4^-/10 \ mole \ I^-)$$
$$= 1.81 \times 10^{-4} \ mole \ MnO_4^-$$

➤ Calculate the molarity of MnO_4^-.

$$M = 1.81 \times 10^{-4} \ mole/0.0250 \ L = 0.00726 \ M \ MnO_4^-$$

The Nature of Molecules and Intermolecular Interactions

Read This Chapter to Learn About

➤ The Chemical Bond

➤ Molecular Shape

➤ Molecular Orbitals

➤ Noncovalent Bonds

THE CHEMICAL BOND

Without chemical bonds, molecules would not exist. Therefore, rationalizing chemical phenomena must begin with an understanding of bonding.

Types of Bonds

Nobel laureate Roald Hoffmann described molecules as "persistent groupings of atoms." Such assemblies are held together by chemical bonds, which conventionally fall into one of two categories: ionic and covalent. Both bonds involve electrostatic forces: **ionic bonds** are present between a positively-charged cation and a negatively charged anion (as in sodium chloride), whereas **covalent bonds** arise from the mutual attraction of two positively charged nuclei to negatively-charged electron density shared between them (as in diatomic nitrogen). However, covalent and ionic bonds are just two ends of a bonding continuum.

When the electronegativity difference between the atoms is quite small, the electron density is equitably distributed along the internuclear axis, and it reaches a maximum at the midpoint of the bond. Such a bond is said to be purely covalent. On the other hand, when the two nuclei have widely divergent electronegativities, the electron density is not "shared" at all: two ionic species are formed and the electron density approaches zero along the internuclear axis at the edge of the ionic radius.

However, organic chemistry rarely operates at the boundaries of purely covalent or purely ionic bonding. Instead, most examples lie along a continuum between these two extremes (see Figure 7-1). For example, **polar covalent bonds** result from an uneven sharing of electron density, a situation that sets up a permanent dipole along the bond axis. The O—H and C—F bonds are examples of polar covalent bonds. Such bonds are stronger than you would expect, because the covalent attraction is augmented by the coulombic forces set up by the dipole.

Conversely, there are many examples of essentially ionic compounds that exhibit covalent character. In other words, even though there are practically two ionic species bound together, electron density is still shared between them. Almost all carbon-metal bonds fall into this category. For example, methyllithium (H_3CLi) can be thought of as a methyl anion (H_3C^-) with a lithium counterion (Li^+). Even though this is not a strictly accurate representation (i.e, there is indeed shared electron density), it still allows you to make sound predictions about its chemical behavior.

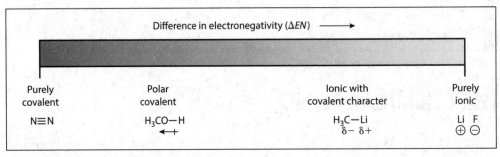

FIGURE 7-1 Types of bonding in organic molecules.

Lewis Structures and Resonance Forms

Examining electronegativity trends can allow you to make predictions about bond polarity, but you also need to understand the larger bonding picture: how many bonds are formed with each atom? The **Lewis dot diagram** represents a surprisingly simple device for representing global molecular bonding on a primary level. These diagrams are built up by considering the valence electrons brought to the table by each atom (conveniently remembered by counting from the left on the periodic table) and then forming bonds by intuitively combining unpaired electrons. For example, methane (CH_4) and formaldehyde (H_2CO) are constructed as shown in Figure 7-2.

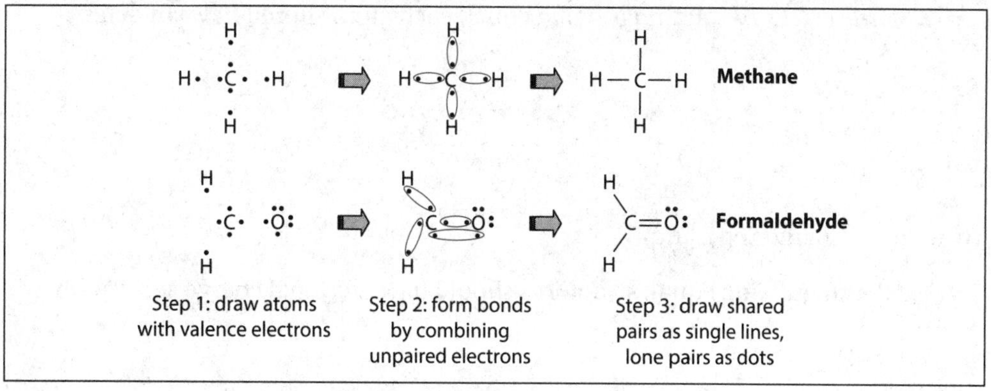

205

CHAPTER 7:
The Nature of
Molecules and
Intermolecular
Interactions

FIGURE 7-2 Lewis structures for methane and formaldehyde.

Notice that there are two types of electron pairs in the molecules in Figure 7-2: (1) **shared pairs (or bonds)**, which are represented by lines (each line representing two shared electrons), and (2) **lone pairs**, which are depicted using two dots. When calculating formal charges—which, incidentally, should always be done—assign to a given atom all of its lone pair electrons and half of each shared pair; then compare the sum to the number of valence electrons normally carried. For example, consider the amide species (see Figure 7-3). The nitrogen atom is surrounded by two lone pairs (nitrogen "owns" all four) and two shared pairs (nitrogen "owns" only one in each pair), giving a total of six electrons assigned to nitrogen. Compared to the five valence electrons normally carried by nitrogen, this represents an excess of one electron; therefore, a formal charge of -1 is given to the nitrogen atom.

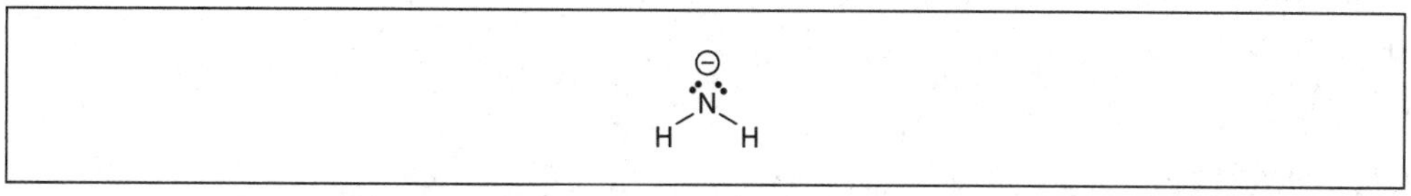

FIGURE 7-3 Lewis structure for the amide species.

Occasionally, the Lewis structures don't coalesce right away into such tidy packages. Therefore, you must often select the most reasonable Lewis representation from a collection of candidates. These are known as **resonance forms**, and while all reasonable candidates tell you something about the nature of the molecule they represent, some resonance structures are more significant contributors than others. In making such an assessment, the following guidelines are helpful:

A. Octet Rules

  1. *Big octet rule*: no row 2 element can accommodate more than 8 electrons.

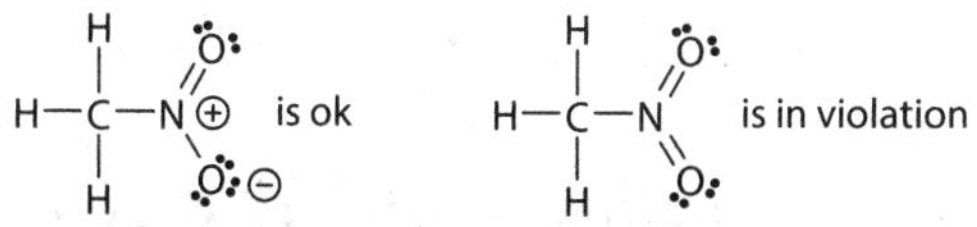

2. *Little octet rule*: all things being equal, each atom should have an octet.

is better than

B. Rules of Charge Separation

1. All things being equal, structures should have minimal charge separation.

is better than

2. Any charge separation should be guided by electronegativity trends.

is better than

Of all these, only the big octet rule is inviolable. Structures that break the latter three rules are less desirable—those that break the first one are unreasonable and unsupportable. Keep in mind that Lewis structures are gross simplifications of a more complex reality, and sometimes no one representation is adequate to describe the total bonding within a molecule. Even when a structure satisfies all the rules—as with the first depiction of formaldehyde—other structures (resonance forms) may need to be considered to predict the properties of a molecule. The concept of resonance is considered later in this chapter.

The Condensed Formula and Line Notation

Another useful principle for constructing a structural representation from a molecular formula involves the idea of **valency**, or the number of bonds typically formed by a given element. For example, carbon normally has a valency of four; nitrogen, three; oxygen, two; hydrogen and the halogens, one. It is valency that underlies the hidden code of the so-called condensed formula, as illustrated in Figure 7-4 for the compound 3-hydroxypentanal. A **condensed formula** can appear to be ambiguous about structure, but in fact it is rich in structural information as long as you are aware of a few simple rules:

1. A condensed formula is read from left to right.
2. Each carbon atom in the formula is connected to the next carbon in the formula.
3. Everything to the right of a carbon (but before the next) is connected to that carbon.
4. Parentheses are used to indicate whole groups attached to a carbon.
5. Normal valencies must be satisfied (C = 4; N = 3; O = 2; H = 1; etc.).

207

CHAPTER 7:
The Nature of
Molecules and
Intermolecular
Interactions

As the example in Figure 7-4 shows, the first step in converting a condensed formula into a **structural formula** is to lay out the **carbon backbone**—in this case a five-carbon chain. You then connect all the indicated substituents: three hydrogens to the first carbon, two hydrogens to the second, and so on, recognizing that the hydroxy (OH) moiety is treated as an entire group attached to the third carbon. The tricky part is the expansion of the CHO group. It is tempting to imagine a structure in which the carbon is attached to the hydrogen, which in turn is attached to the oxygen (lower left depiction). However, this would violate three valency guidelines: oxygen has only one bond, carbon only two, and hydrogen one too many. A proper reading of the condensed formula would be, "hydrogen belongs to the fifth carbon, and so does oxygen." With a bit of thought, the only reasonable arrangement would be the one shown in the lower right, which includes a carbon-oxygen double bond.

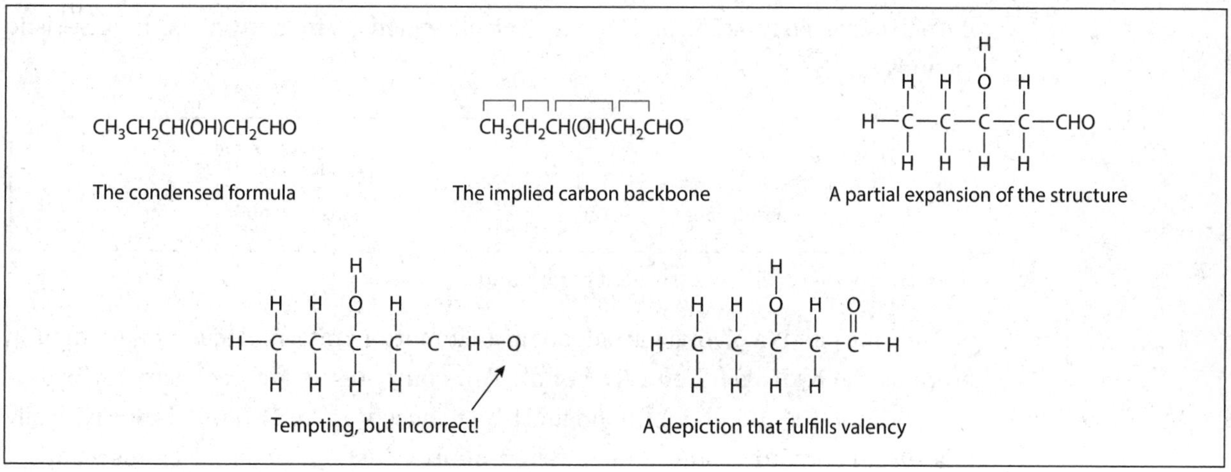

FIGURE 7-4 Converting a condensed formula to a full formula.

A condensed formula is one type of shortcut for depicting structure—its claim to fame is that it can be produced using a keyboard even when graphical software is unavailable. However, an even more important and widespread shortcut is **line notation**, which is universally used by organic chemists when they sketch compounds, its advantage being that the salient features of complex structures can be quickly and conveniently depicted. Figure 7-5 shows 3-hydroxypentanal in line notation. The assumptions underlying the simplification are these:

1. Every unlabeled vertex or terminus is a carbon atom.
2. Any unused valency of carbon is filled by hydrogen.

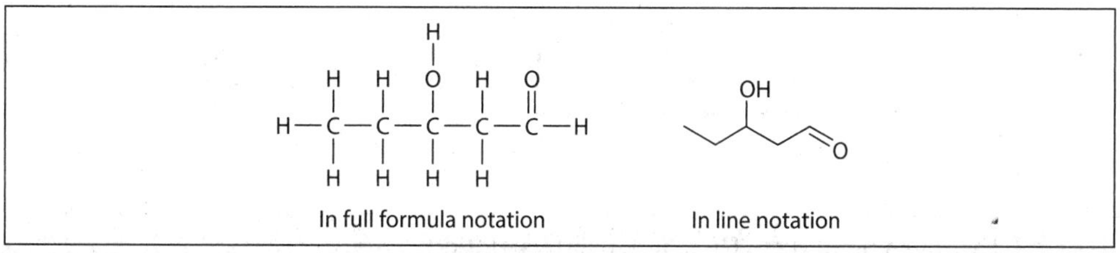

FIGURE 7-5 Two valid depictions of 3-hydroxypentanal.

Keeping Track of Lone Pairs

You may have noticed that the preceding depictions do not include **lone pairs**—in fact, the depiction of lone pairs is an arbitrary matter, and they are often neglected in drawings. However, it is absolutely crucial to know where they are, as the presence or absence of lone pairs can define the chemistry of a species. For example, consider the two seemingly similar compounds, diethylborane and diethylamine (see Figure 7-6)—both have row 2 central atoms, which are trivalent, but their behaviors could not be more different. There is no lone pair on diethylborane—the central boron has only six electrons around it, thereby breaking the little octet rule. The molecule is starved for electron density, and it therefore reacts with electron-rich substrates. On the other hand, diethylamine does have a lone pair on the nitrogen, even though some depictions may not include this detail. Thus nitrogen fulfills the little octet rule, and the lone pair can even function as a source of electron density in many of its characteristic reactions.

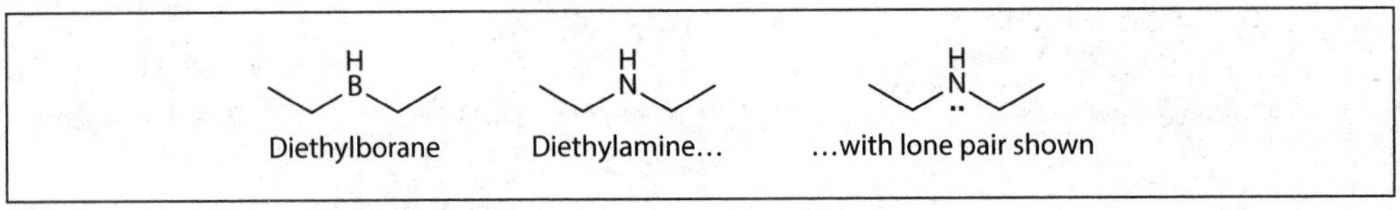

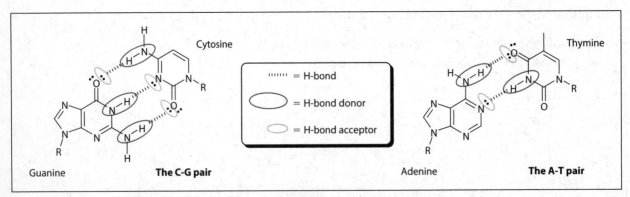

Diethylborane   Diethylamine...   ...with lone pair shown

FIGURE 7-6 Two very different trivalent compounds.

The lone pair is a pivotal participant in an important intermolecular phenomenon known as the **hydrogen bond (H-bond)**. Two components are necessary for hydrogen bonding: an H-bond donor and an H-bond acceptor. An **H-bond donor** typically comes from a hydrogen bound to a **heteroatom**, which for organic chemists almost always means nitrogen, oxygen, or sulfur (and sometimes fluorine). These $N-H$, $O-H$, and $S-H$ bonds are quite polar, with most of the electron density being hoarded by the heteroatom. As a result, the hydrogen starts to look rather like a proton (H^+) in need of extra electron density. Thus an **H-bond acceptor** is anything that can provide this electron density—and more often than not it comes in the form of a lone pair. This is nicely illustrated by the familiar H-bonding motif in DNA base pair recognition (see Figure 7-7). Three H-bonds are set up between cytosine and guanine, whereas

FIGURE 7-7 Hydrogen bonding in DNA base pair recognition.

209

CHAPTER 7:
The Nature of
Molecules and
Intermolecular
Interactions

two are enjoyed by thymine and adenine. In each case, the H-bond donors are N—H bonds, while the H-bond acceptors are lone pairs on nitrogen or oxygen. Inspection reveals that the degree of H-bonding would be far less with a G-T pair or an A-C pair.

MOLECULAR SHAPE

With an understanding of connectivity among atoms within molecules, it is now appropriate to consider the three-dimensional arrangement of these atoms, since molecular shape is one of the chief factors determining the functionality and reactivity of a given molecule.

Geometry of Atoms Within Molecules

There are three frequently encountered geometries in organic chemistry: **digonal** (or linear), **trigonal**, and **tetrahedral** (see Figure 7-8). Each atom within a molecule is almost always characterized by one of these geometries, the chief hallmark of which is the associated bond angle: 180° for linear arrays, 120° for trigonal planar centers, and 109.5° for tetrahedral arrangements. Deviation from these ideal bond angles does occur, but significant deformation usually has a destabilizing effect known as **bond angle strain**.

Geometry	Arrangement	Bond angle	Hybridization of x
Digonal	a—x—b	180°	sp
Trigonal	a⋯x—b c	120°	sp^2
Tetrahedral	a d⋯x—b c	109.5°	sp^3

FIGURE 7-8 Common central atom geometries in organic chemistry.

There are at least three ways to conceptualize molecular geometry. One classical approach is through the **hybridization of atomic orbitals**. If orbitals are derived from wave functions, then these functions can be combined mathematically to obtain hybrid descriptions. Thus if you combine an *s* orbital, which is spherically symmetrical, with a single *p* orbital, which has directionality along a single axis, it stands to reason that the outcome (two equivalent *sp* orbitals) should also have directionality along one dimension. Likewise, the combination of an *s* orbital with two *p* orbitals gives a result (three equivalent *sp²* orbitals) that defines a plane (see Figure 7-9).

Another framework is conceptually more straightforward. Known as **valence shell electron pair repulsion (VSEPR) theory**, this approach asks the question of how

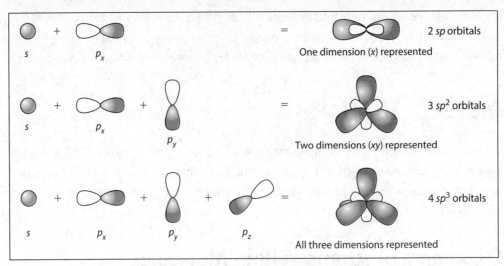

FIGURE 7-9 Central atom geometry as described by orbital hybridization.

negatively charged electron clouds can most effectively stay out of each other's way. If there are only two electron clouds, then the happiest arrangement is to be diametrically opposed to each other; for three clouds, a trigonal planar array; and for four clouds, a tetrahedral arrangement provides the maximum distance among them. Interestingly, these considerations predict exactly the same outcomes as hybrid orbital theory, although they are fundamentally different approaches. Strictly speaking, neither are theoretically accurate as compared to a strict **quantum mechanical analysis**—a third method not addressed here—however, they are useful predictive models nonetheless.

Thus to predict the geometry about a central atom, you must ask only how many things surround it—where "things" are understood to be either atoms or lone pairs. Figure 7-10 offers an illustration of this method, and experimental evidence backs up the predictions (e.g., the $C-C-C$ bond angle is practically $120°$). A generalization can also be derived from this example: since carbon is almost always tetravalent, then if only single bonds are attached to a carbon, it must have four other atoms surrounding it; if a double bond is attached to that carbon, then only three atoms can surround

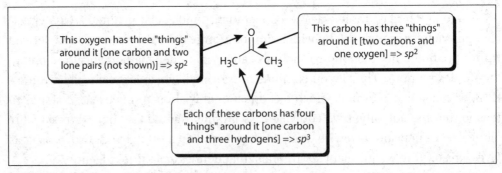

FIGURE 7-10 Prediction of geometry for acetone.

211

CHAPTER 7:
The Nature of
Molecules and
Intermolecular
Interactions

it; and so on. As a consequence, carbons with only single bonds tend to be tetrahedral (sp^3), carbons that are part of a double bond tend to be trigonal (sp^2), and triply bonded carbons are always digonal (sp).

There are three special cases for carbon that deserve mention: carbanions, carbocations, and radicals. Carbanions are carbons bearing a negative charge, as in the methyl anion (see the following table). **Carbanions** have lone pairs on carbon, even though they are rarely shown explicitly. Using the rules described previously, you would predict an sp^3 geometry about the carbon, and indeed most carbanions exhibit a pyramidal shape. **Carbocations** are carbon centers with only three bonds and a positive formal charge (e.g., methyl cation). Since the only things to accommodate are the three substituents (in this case, hydrogen atoms), the predicted geometry of carbon is sp^2—and experimental evidence supports the idea that carbocations are planar. **Radicals** lie somewhere between these two extremes. Since the p orbital is only half filled, it doesn't demand the same space that a doubly filled orbital would, but still requires more than an empty one. The most accurate way to think about such centers is as a shallow pyramid, which very rapidly inverts. A time-averaged representation would approximate a planar species; therefore, frequently radicals are depicted as being planar.

TABLE 7-1 Geometries of Some Special Carbon Centers

Species	Formula	Structure
methyl anion	$^{\ominus}CH_3$	
methyl cation	$^{\oplus}CH_3$	
methyl radical	$^{\ominus}CH_3$	

Asymmetric Centers and Enantiomerism

Since they are inherently three-dimensional, tetrahedral carbons can impart a special characteristic to molecules, a property known as **asymmetry**. But before you can understand asymmetry, you first have to examine the idea of symmetry. The uninitiated think of symmetry as a binary state—that an object is either symmetrical or not symmetrical. However, there are degrees of symmetry, and many so-called elements of symmetry. This is a topic best treated in the domain of mathematics, but we shall very briefly scratch the surface here to gain some underpinnings for practical application. First, consider methane (CH_4)—a molecule that is unassuming, yet full of symmetry. Figure 7-11 shows three types of symmetry elements (there are others not shown here) belonging to methane. The sigma (σ) plane is an imaginary mirror that slices through the molecule—reflection through the plane results in an image identical to the starting depiction. Methane actually has six such planes: one with H_1 and H_2 in the plane; one with H_1 and H_3; one with H_1 and H_4; one with H_2 and H_3; one with H_2 and H_4; and one with H_3 and H_4. There are also two types of rotational axes. A C_2 axis has two "clicks" in a 360° rotation—180° each turn; methane has six of these, much like the sigma planes. A C_3 axis has three "clicks" in a full rotation—120° each turn; methane has four of these, one coinciding with each of the C—H bonds.

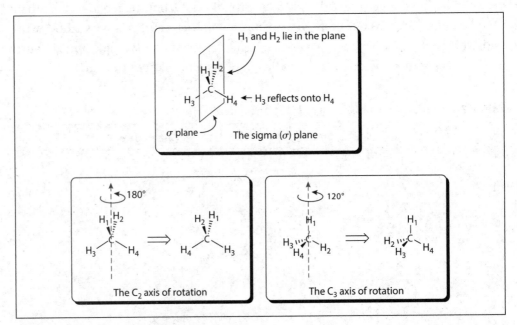

FIGURE 7-11 Symmetry elements of methane.

As you add substituents to methane, however, symmetry starts to drop off rapidly. For example, the addition of a single substituent, such as fluorine (see Table 7-2) reduces the number of sigma planes by half (each sigma plane must include the fluorine), slashes the number of C_3 axes to one (the axis which coincides with the C—F bond), and eliminates the C_2 axes altogether. A second substituent results in an even more impoverished symmetry environment, such that chlorofluoromethane has only a single sigma plane. After a third substituent is introduced (i.e., bromochlorofluoromethane), there are no symmetry elements left. Therefore, such a molecule is said to be **asymmetric**.

213

CHAPTER 7:
The Nature of
Molecules and
Intermolecular
Interactions

TABLE 7-2 Symmetry Elements of Methane Derivatives

Compound	Structure	σ Planes	C_2 Axes	C_3 Axes
methane		6	6	4
fluoromethane		3	0	1
chlorofluoromethane		1	0	0
bromochlorofluoromethane		0	0	0

In other words, if a tetrahedral center is surrounded by four different groups, then the center is asymmetric. Furthermore, if a molecule contains an asymmetric center, it must exist as one of two enantiomers, or antipodes (literally, "opposite feet"). **Enantiomers** are nonsuperimposible mirror images, just like hands and feet (see Figure 7-12), and they represent two distinct compounds. Consequently, asymmetric centers are also called **stereogenic** centers and **chiral** (handed) centers.

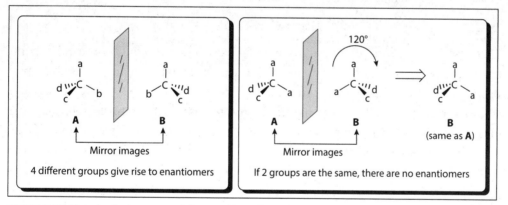

FIGURE 7-12 Tetrahedral centers and enantiomerism.

If any two or more groups are the same, then the center possesses a sigma plane, and the mirror image becomes a replica of the same molecule, so no enantiomerism exists. In other words, the mirror image is the compound itself, and there is only one chemical entity. Thus the presence of a sigma plane in a molecule destroys **chirality** (asymmetry). With more complex molecules, multiple chiral centers may be present; however, even in these cases a global sigma plane may be present.

Chiral compounds may be found in either of two enantiomeric forms. The enantiomers are identical in almost all physical properties: melting point, boiling point,

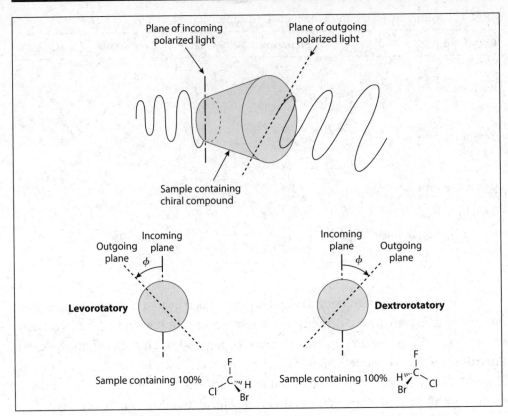

FIGURE 7-13 The phenomenon of optical rotation.

dielectric constant, and so on, with one notable exception. A solution of a chiral compound interacts with light in such a way that the plane of polarized light is rotated upon passing through a sample of the compound, a phenomenon known as **optical rotation** (see Figure 7-13, top). The other enantiomer rotates light to the same degree, but in the opposite direction (see Figure 7-13, bottom). Enantiomers that rotate light clockwise (i.e., to the right) are known as **dextrorotatory isomers**, and those that rotate light in a counterclockwise direction (i.e., to the left) are known as **levorotatory isomers**. It is important to understand that there is no straightforward way to correlate structure to behavior. In other words, you cannot tell just by looking at a molecule whether it would be dextrorotatory or levorotatory. By the same token, optical rotation tells you nothing about a molecule except that it is chiral.

A sample that rotates plane-polarized light is said to be optically active. The degree to which the sample rotates light is called the optical rotation (in degrees). If a sample is **optically inactive** (i.e., it does not rotate plane-polarized light), it could mean one of two things: either (1) the sample does not contain chiral molecules, or (2) the sample contains exactly equal quantities (50/50) of two enantiomers. The latter situation, known as a **racemic mixture**, produces no optical activity, because for each levorotatory molecule there is a dextrorotatory counterpart—equal numbers pulling in opposite directions maintain the status quo.

215

CHAPTER 7:
The Nature of
Molecules and
Intermolecular
Interactions

The term **racemic** refers to the composition of an enantiomeric mixture in which the components are exactly equal. Another term related to composition is **optically pure**, which means that only one enantiomer is present with no contamination from the other enantiomer. Of course, there are other compositions possible (e.g., a 60/40 mixture), which are neither racemic nor optically pure. Such lopsided mixtures are called **scalemic**; another term is **enantiomerically enriched**, since there is more of one enantiomer than another. Such scalemic mixtures can be defined by **enantiomeric excess** (or % ee), which is a quantitative term derived by subtracting the percentage of the lesser component from that of the greater. Therefore, a 55/45 mixture would have a 10% ee, a 95/5 mixture would have a 90% ee, and so forth.

All the vocabulary that surrounds this topic can easily get muddled. Always remember that chirality is a property of a **molecule** (it is a geometric reality derived from the molecular shape), whereas optical activity is a property of a **sample** (i.e., a macroscopic collection of molecules). In other words, molecules can be chiral or achiral, and samples can be optically active or inactive. Furthermore, the ideas of optical purity and optical activity are often confused. Here it is useful to keep in mind that optical purity is a **state** of a sample (i.e., a reflection of its composition), whereas optical activity is a **behavior** of a sample. Optically pure samples are always optically active, but not all optically active samples are optically pure, since scalemic mixtures are also optically active. The following table correlates these various properties and behaviors of enantiomeric mixtures.

TABLE 7-3 Properties and Behaviors of Enantiomeric Mixtures

State of Purity	Optically Pure	Scalemic	Racemic	Scalemic	Optically Pure
optical behavior					
% dextrorotatory enantiomer	0	25	50	75	100
% levorotatory enantiomer	100	75	50	25	0
enantiomeric excess (%)	100	50	0	50	100
optical rotation (°)	$-2x$	$-x$	0	x	$2x$
optically active?	yes	yes	no	yes	yes

Molecular Conformations

From this cursory inspection, it is clear that a fair amount of complexity surrounds the environment of a single carbon atom. But what about larger arrays of atoms? Since most molecules have considerable flexibility, it is important to understand what kinds of shapes are most stable and the energetics involved in their interconversion. Before doing this, however, it is necessary to come to terms with two additional methods of depiction for molecular structure: the **sawhorse (dash-wedge) projection**, and the **Newman projection**.

Consider a two-carbon array with three substituents on each carbon. Figure 7-14 shows such an array in two different depictions. The sawhorse projection views the molecule from the side. Substituents that come out of the plane toward us are depicted with wedges; those that go away from you are shown with dashes. If there is neither dash nor wedge, a plain line (and attached substituent) is assumed to lie in the plane of the paper. "Plain bonds lie in the plane," is a good mnemonic device in this regard.

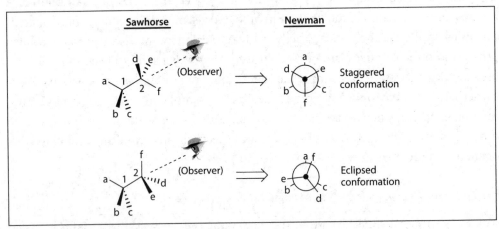

FIGURE 7-14 Sawhorse and Newman projections.

A Newman projection simply looks at the molecule from a different angle, namely down a carbon-carbon bond (indicated by the observer's eye). This is a much more straightforward way of showing the spatial relationship of substituents. Just remember that the small dot represents the front carbon, while the large circle represents the back carbon. Thus in the projections shown, the small dot is carbon-2 and the large circle is carbon-1; in other words, a C2→C1 Newman projection has been drawn. However, it could have just as easily been drawn as a C1→C2 variant, in which the small dot would be carbon-1.

Since there can be rotation about carbon-carbon bonds, this molecule can adopt a variety of conformations. In general, these conformations fall into one of two categories: staggered and eclipsed. Note that in the sawhorse depictions, the plain bonds (i.e., neither dash nor wedge) in the staggered conformation describe a "Z" or zigzag pattern, whereas in the eclipsed conformation they form a "U." This is a quick and easy way to distinguish one from another.

In staggered conformations, any two substituents are characterized by one of two relationships. Substituents are said to be **gauche** with respect to each other if they are

217

CHAPTER 7:
The Nature of
Molecules and
Intermolecular
Interactions

side-by-side. In the illustration, there are six gauche relationships: a-e, e-c, c-f, f-b, b-d, and d-a. The other relationship is **antiperiplanar**, in which case the two substituents are as far away as possible from each other. In the same depiction, there are three antiperiplanar relationships: a-f, e-b, and d-c. In eclipsed conformations, there is only one type of relationship between substituents to care about, namely eclipsed. In the eclipsed Newman projection, there are three pairs of eclipsed substituents: a-f, c-d, and b-e. Don't be confused by the double duty of the term **eclipsed**—there are staggered and eclipsed **conformations**, which describe the global molecular attitude, and there are gauche, antiperiplanar, and eclipsed **relationships** between substituents. There are only gauche and antiperiplanar relationships in staggered conformations, and there are only eclipsed relationships in eclipsed conformations.

It should come as no surprise that eclipsed conformations are of higher energy than staggered conformations. This is due to the steric interactions that result from the very close proximity of substituents in the eclipsed relationships. By the same token, staggered conformations that place large groups in a gauche arrangement are of higher energy than those that have those groups antiperiplanar with respect to each other. Using these basic principles, you can construct a diagram showing the relative energies of a conformational ensemble, as illustrated in Figure 7-15 for butane ($CH_3CH_2CH_2CH_3$). This is a process known as **conformational analysis**.

To begin the conformational analysis, all the possible conformations for the molecule, both eclipsed and staggered, must be drawn. This might seem more difficult than it really is—first, just jot down any conformation and then methodically convert it to the remaining possibilities. For example, in Figure 7-15 the first conformation (A) is chosen arbitrarily. Conformation A is converted to C by rotating the front carbon (small dot) clockwise—notice that the back carbon does not change. This maneuver has the net effect of bringing the front methyl (CH_3) group from the 6 o'clock position to the 10 o'clock position. To get from A to C, the molecule must pass through the high-energy eclipsed conformer B. The remaining conformations are derived by continuing to rotate the front carbon in a clockwise fashion until you arrive back at A.

The next step is to assess all the group interactions in each conformer. For the sake of simplicity, neglect $H-H$ interactions, since the hydrogen atom is so small. Thus in conformer A, observe four methyl-hydrogen gauche interactions (in other words, each methyl group has a hydrogen to either side—each flanking hydrogen counts as an interaction). In conformer C, there are only two methyl-hydrogen gauche interactions, but there is also a methyl-methyl gauche interaction. These interactions are used to estimate the relative placement of the conformers on the energy diagram.

The diagram can be constructed easily through a three-step approach. First, keep in mind that all eclipsed conformations will be higher than the staggered conformations, so there are two separate collections of conformers (i.e., staggered and eclipsed). Then estimate the relative placement of the conformers within each set. For example, in comparing the energetics of the staggered conformers A and C, you could say two methyl hydrogen gauche interactions (2 vs. 4) have been traded for one methyl-methyl

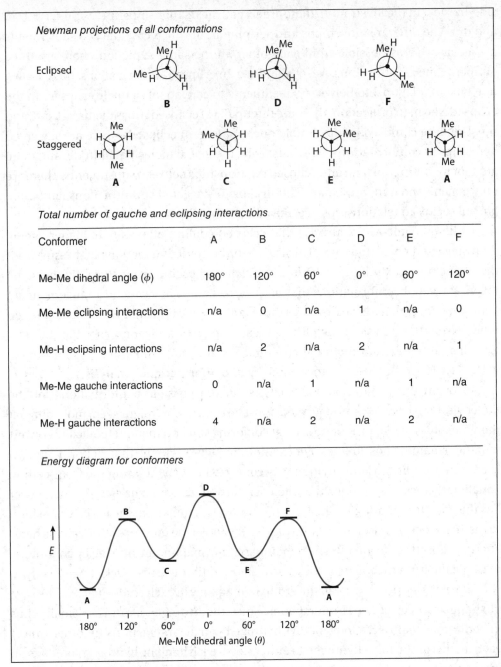

FIGURE 7-15 Conformational analysis of butane.

gauche interaction. Realizing that the methyl group is considerably larger than the hydrogen, it seems reasonable that the cost of having the two large groups next to each other outweighs the benefit of two less small-large interactions. This is the rationale for placing C higher on the diagram than A. Inspection of conformer E reveals that it exhibits the same type and number of gauche interactions as C; therefore, C and E are at the same energy level. Through similar analysis, the placement of the eclipsed conformations is estimated.

219

CHAPTER 7:
The Nature of
Molecules and
Intermolecular
Interactions

Conformations of Cycloalkanes

There are special conformational issues for cyclic molecules. As a general rule, **cycloalkanes** are less flexible than open-chain analogs, and they can adopt far fewer conformations. However, both types have predictable low-energy conformations. For example, consider hexane (see Figure 7-16): inasmuch as there is free rotation about all the carbon-carbon bonds, you could envision the six conformational option described in butane for each of the internal C—C bonds (i.e., C2-C3, C3-C4, and C4-C5). The most stable conformation is the one that has all antiperiplanar relationships, as shown in Figure 7-16. Similarly, cyclohexane can and does adopt many conformations, but the most stable arrangement is the so-called **chair conformation**.

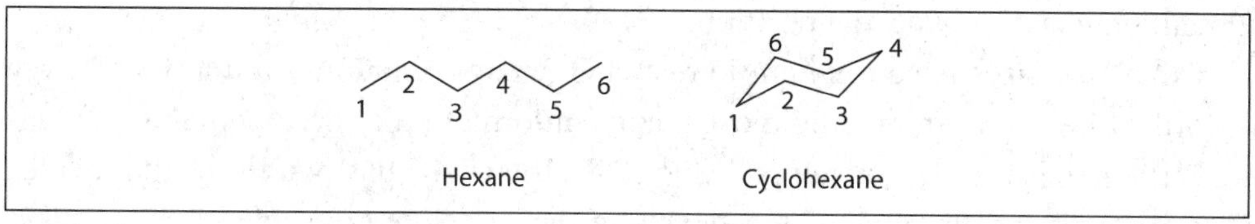

FIGURE 7-16 Stable conformations of hexane and cyclohexane.

Although it may not be evident, there are two alternate chair forms that are related by the **chair flip**. It is important to understand that the flip is not a rotation of the molecule, but a reconformation. As the top depiction in Figure 7-17 shows, carbon 1 flips from pointing downward to pointing upward, carbon 4 does the reverse, and the entire molecule reconforms in place. As a side note, always keep in mind that the chair projection is a side view of the ring, and the lower bond (i.e., C2-C3) is assumed to be in front.

When substituents are added to the cyclohexane, the chair flip takes on special significance. To understand this, first come to terms with some characteristics of the substituents on a cyclohexane ring. Examination of Figure 7-17 (lower depiction) reveals that substituents can adopt one of two attitudes: **axial** (shown as triangles in the left chair) or **equatorial** (shown as squares)—every chair conformation has six of each

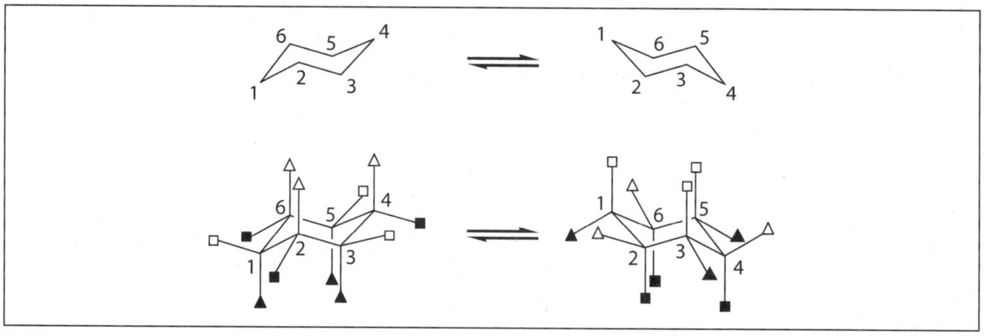

FIGURE 7-17 The chair flip of cyclohexane.

type. Note that a chair flip interchanges axial and equatorial substituents, so that all of the triangles become equatorial on the right side. It is a good idea to construct a model and physically induce a ring flip to see how this works.

It is equally important to understand what does *not* change during a ring flip. Any ring has two faces—as these depictions are drawn, they can be called the top and bottom faces. Any substituent points toward either the top or the bottom face. Again, each chair cyclohexane has six of each type—the six white substituents are all pointing toward the top face, and the six black ones are pointing toward the bottom face. Note that there are three axial and three equatorial substituents pointing up, and three of each pointing down. Also note that a ring flip does not change whether a substituent points up or down. So in other words the triangle substituent on carbon 4 always points up, although it may convert from axial to equatorial. As a general rule, the bulkiest substituent prefers the equatorial position.

Other ring sizes have different lowest energy conformations, and a brief survey is worthwhile. For example, the most stable conformation of cyclopentane (see Figure 7-18) is the so-called **envelope**, which (like the chair) has two forms that equilibrate through the flipping of the envelope flap. Cyclobutane adopts a so-called **puckered conformation**, which again has two forms that equilibrate through a ring flip. Notice that the same rules for cyclohexanes hold true for these cycloalkanes—namely, that there are two types of substituent attitudes (here, called pseudoaxial and pseudoequatorial) that interconvert upon ring flips; also, the substituents point toward a certain face, and that face remains constant throughout conformational changes. Finally, cyclopropanes have practically no conformational flexibility—there is really only one possibility, and all substituents have equivalent attitudes. However, of course, there are still two faces to the molecule, so substituents can point toward the top face or the bottom face.

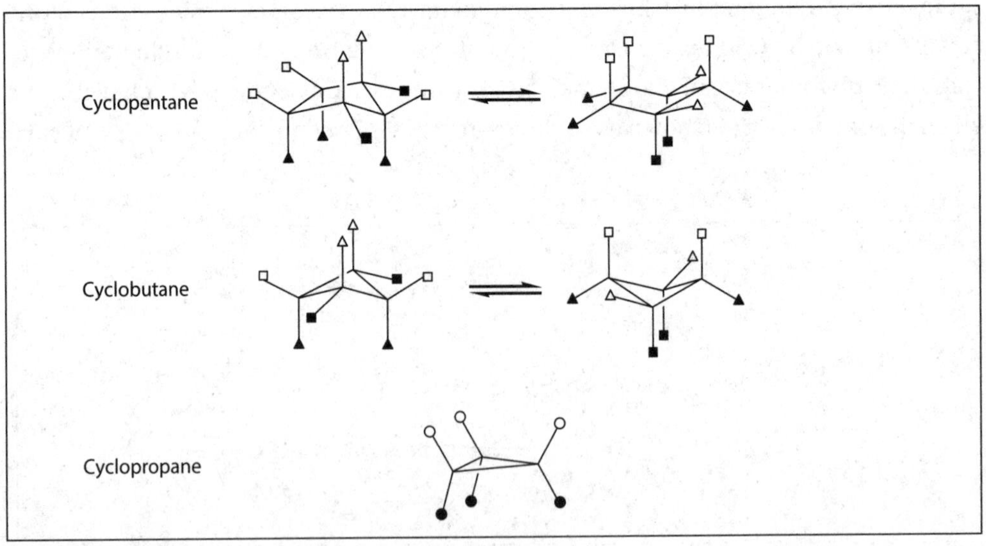

FIGURE 7-18 Stable conformations of other cycloalkanes.

221

CHAPTER 7:
The Nature of
Molecules and
Intermolecular
Interactions

So what factors govern the adoption of a given stable conformation? The main determinant is the minimization of ring strain. In cyclic molecules, there are essentially two sources of strain: bond angle strain and torsional strain. **Bond angle strain** derives from a compression of the ideal sp^3 bond angle (109.5°) to accommodate a cyclic array. Not surprisingly, this is worst for the three-membered ring, and is almost nil for the five- and six-membered rings. The other source of strain is less obvious. **Torsional strain** derives from the torque on individual bonds from eclipsed substituents trying to get out of each other's way. Again, this is most pronounced in cyclopropane (compare Figure 7-18), and all the other cycloalkanes twist in ways to minimize or eliminate this strain. For example, inspection of a molecular model of chair cyclohexane will reveal that all carbon-carbon bonds have a perfectly staggered conformation. Interestingly, the five-membered ring is not so lucky. Even in the envelope conformation, substituents tend toward eclipsing each other. The following table summarizes the individual components, but a good overall take-home message is that ring strain decreases according to the trend: 3 > 4 ≫ 5 > 6. This has implications in reactivity of cyclic molecules.

TABLE 7-4 Ring Strain in Cycloalkanes

Cycloalkane	Torsional Strain	Bond Angle Strain
cyclopropane	a lot	a lot
cyclobutane	some	a lot
cyclopentane	a little	practically none
cyclohexane	none	none

Reconciling Visual Meaning

Coming to terms with the three-dimensionality of organic chemistry is often a challenge for students, yet this is possibly the most important transferable cognitive skill developed by the study of the subject. The novice is confronted with a jumble of alternative depictional devices that appear to be interchangeable. However, a structural drawing is a way of communicating, and specific information is carried in these depictions. For example, if you are presented with a simple line drawing (see the following table), you can quickly see the landscape of the molecule—what the **regiochemistry** is (that is, *where* the atoms are) and which functional groups are present—but you are told nothing about the **stereochemistry** (that is, the three-dimensional arrangement of the atoms). On the other hand, the **Fischer projection** was developed specifically for quickly conveying the absolute stereochemistry (configuration) of a molecule. You must carefully choose the right depiction for the information you wish to convey, and you must also be able to fully interpret the messages given by specific structures.

One particularly thorny depictional issue centers around relative and absolute stereochemistry. For example, you can draw a structure for *cis*-5-methylcyclohex-2-enol, which is unequivocal and easily distinguishable from the corresponding

TABLE 7-5 Summary of Structural Depictions

Type of Depiction	Example	Best for Depicting
line structure	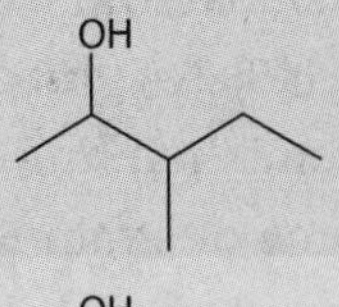	constitution and connectivity
sawhorse	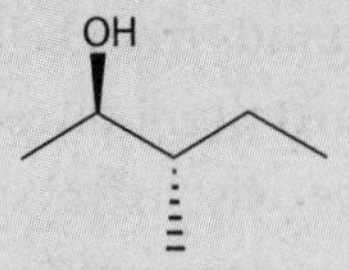	relative and absolute stereochemistry
Newman	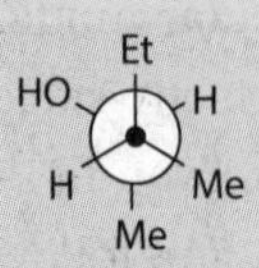	conformation
Chair	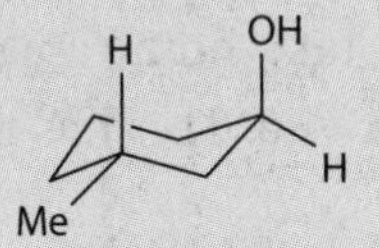	conformation
Fischer	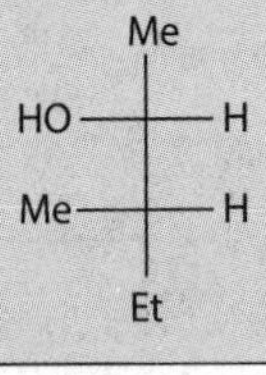	configuration (absolute stereochemistry)

trans-isomer (see Figure 7-19). However, it has been arbitrarily chosen to draw the substituents with two wedges—a structure with two dashes would have been equally valid. In this example, the only intent was to show that the two substituents are on the same side of the molecule, that is, their relative stereochemistry. Whether carbon-1 is an *R* or *S* center is unknown.

Unfortunately, the same kind of depiction has been used to show absolute stereochemistry. For example, if you were to draw specifically the 1*S*, 5*S* enantiomer of *cis*-5-methylcyclohex-2-enol, both substituents would be attached with wedges (see the following table)—but here their *absolute* placement in space are depicted, not just their positions relative to each other. Conversely, the *R*, *R* enantiomer would be drawn with dashes. Note that when the configuration is included in the name, *cis/trans* designation

cis-5-methylcyclohex-2-enol   *trans*-5-methylcyclohex-2-enol

FIGURE 7-19 Relative stereoisomers.

223

CHAPTER 7:
The Nature of
Molecules and
Intermolecular
Interactions

is unnecessary. Converting a name to a structure is relatively easy—if *R/S* information is given, simply represent it accurately in the structure; if only relative (*cis/trans*) stereochemical information is given, you have a couple of choices for the dashes and wedges; if no stereochemical information is provided, then you can draw only a simple line structure. However, the reverse operation is trickier: properly interpreting a sawhorse structure requires context. A good rule of thumb is that any sawhorse structure containing chiral centers is *assumed to be a racemic mixture* unless somehow identified as a single enantiomer. This context can be in the form of optical rotation data or explicit statements such as "single enantiomer" or "optically pure."

TABLE 7-6 Relative Versus Absolute Stereochemistry

Structural Depiction	Corresponding Name	*cis/trans*
OH ... Me (Optically pure)	(1*S*, 5*S*)-5-methylcyclohex-2-enol	*cis*
OH ...Me (Optically pure)	(1*R*, 5*R*)-5-methylcyclohex-2-enol	*cis*
OH ...Me (Optically pure)	(1*S*, 5*R*)-5-methylcyclohex-2-enol	*trans*
OH Me (Optically pure)	(1*R*, 5*S*)-5-methylcyclohex-2-enol	*trans*

Occasionally, you need to be deliberately ambiguous about the stereochemistry of a compound—for example, if the stereochemical arrangement has not been determined or if you know that there is a mixture of stereoisomers. For this there is a device known colloquially as the "squiggly line," which indicates the orientation of the substituent can be up, down, or both. In cyclic structures, the use of the squiggly line has the same effect as using plain line structure (see Figure 7-20, left). However, for alkenes there is really no other alternative to show a mixture of *cis* and *trans* isomers than to employ this handy depictional device (see Figure 7-20, right).

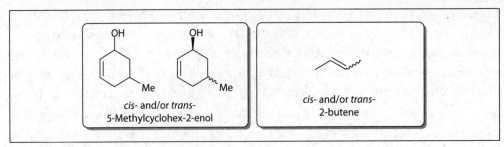

FIGURE 7-20 Deliberately ambiguous stereochemistry.

With this in mind, your choice of depiction must be carefully chosen to reflect what you know about a particular molecule or collection of molecules, and it must be suited to the task of representing this information. In addition, a given structural representation has specific meaning which you must properly interpret. As an organizing principle, it is very useful to think of structure (and representation) as layers of detail (see Figure 7-21), the lowest level of detail being constitutional (how the atoms are connected), then stereochemical, and ultimately conformational (the particular shape a molecule adopts)—not unlike the primary, secondary, and tertiary structure of proteins.

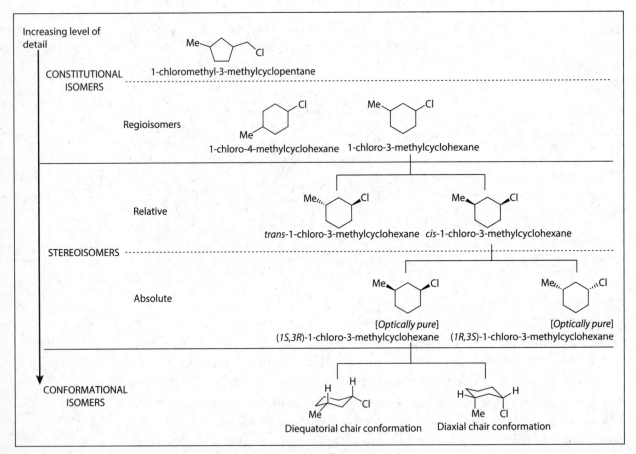

FIGURE 7-21 Levels of detail in structural representation.

225

CHAPTER 7:
The Nature of
Molecules and
Intermolecular
Interactions

MANIPULATING STRUCTURES IN THREE-DIMENSIONAL SPACE

It is frequently necessary to compare two structures or convert one type of depiction into another. To do this one needs to have a clear understanding of the depictions themselves and the three-dimensional objects they represent. Ultimately, the challenge lies in being able to manipulate the two-dimensional drawings in ways that are three-dimensionally competent. For example, consider the chair form of *trans*-3-methylcyclohexanol shown in Figure 7-22. The six depictions shown are simply reorientations of the molecule by rotating in a plane perpendicular to the page, a process which can be thought of as "spinning the plate." Note that the molecule has not been reconfigured—these are not ring flips, but a static structure viewed from different angles, as if perusing it in the hands.

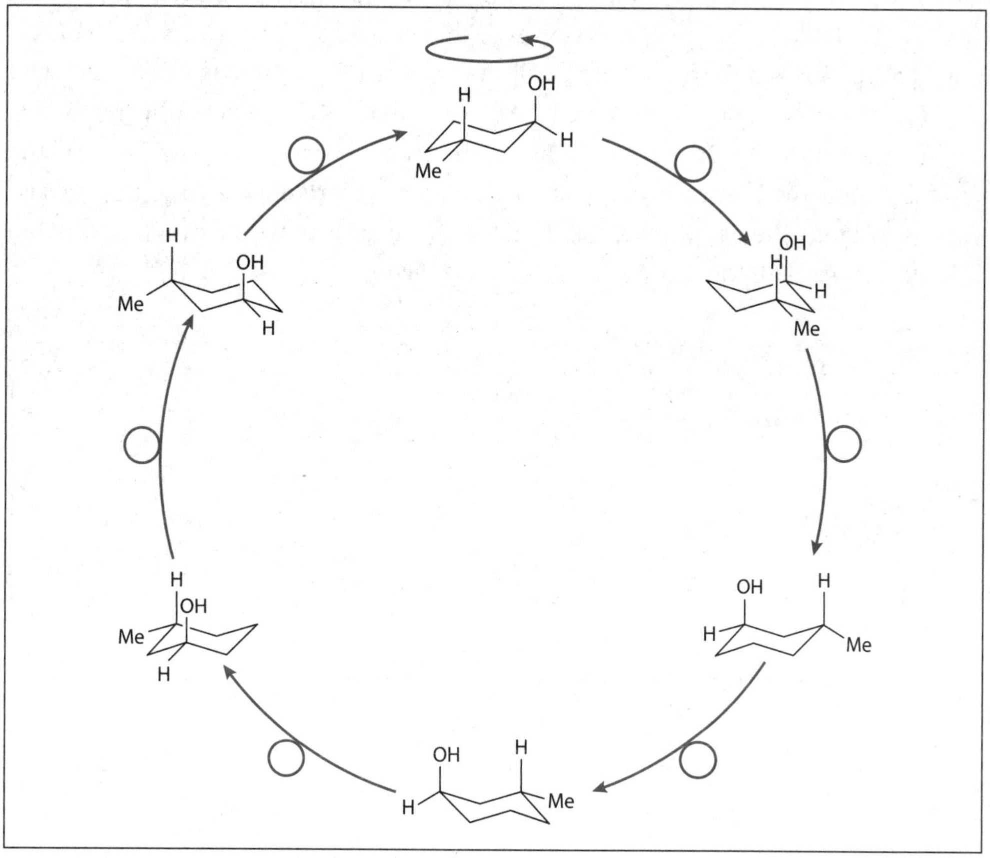

FIGURE 7-22 The spinning plate maneuver.

Similar things can be done with sawhorse structures, as shown in Figure 7-23. Here the molecule is first flipped horizontally, then vertically, and finally rotated 180° in plane, which here is called the **pinwheel turn**. Note that when a molecule is flipped, dashes become wedges (and vice versa), but they remain the same during an in-plane rotation. This is an obvious statement, but it is critical to be conscious of the fact as

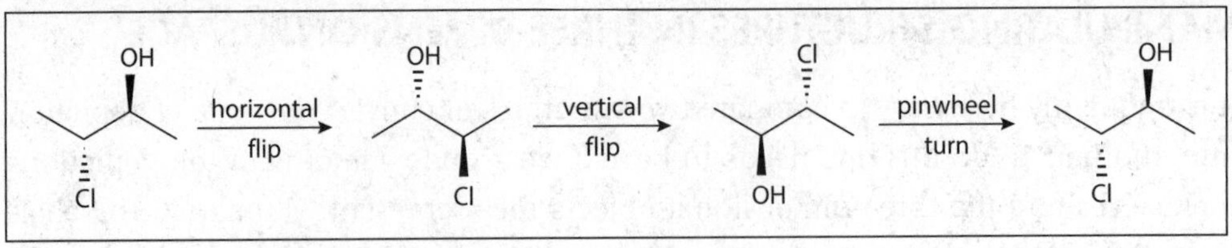

FIGURE 7-23 Some manipulations of sawhorse structures.

you manipulate structures later on. You can also perform these maneuvers on chair cyclohexanes as well.

When converting specialized depictions—like Newman or Fischer projections—to more conventional drawings (e.g., sawhorse structures), bear in mind that this is ultimately a change in point of view. So for a Newman projection, you sight the molecule down a carbon-carbon bond, but in a sawhorse you view the same bond side-on. An easy way to think about the conversion is to imagine that the Newman projection is hinged at the back carbon and you push the structure into the page much like you would shut an open door (see Figure 7-24); thus the bond that points directly toward you in structure A (the C2—C3 bond) lies in the plane in structure B. You can use the same technique with Fischer projections, as long as you remember that the stylized representation (C) really implies the dashes and wedges shown in structure D. Note that two-centered Fischer projections are always eclipsed.

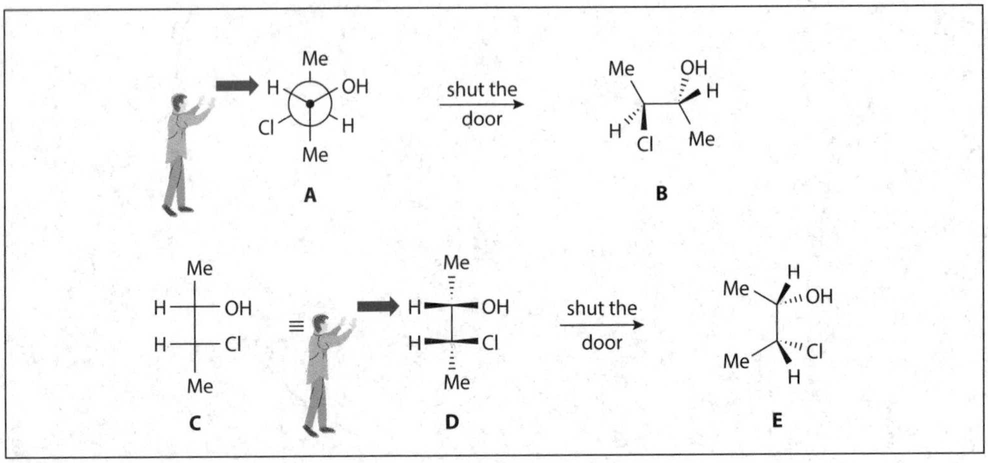

FIGURE 7-24 Shutting the door.

RAPID COMPARISON OF DEPICTIONS

Now imagine that you were asked to evaluate the two representations A and C, and decide whether they are enantiomers, diastereomers, or the same thing. First, review the difference between enantiomers and diastereomers. Both fall under the broader umbrella term of **stereoisomers**, which refers to different spatial orientation of

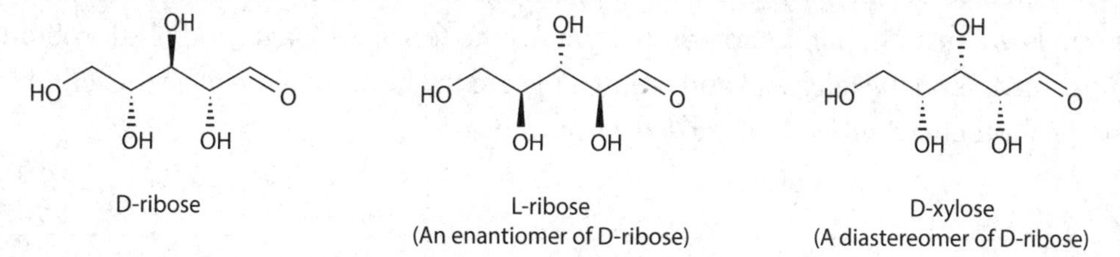

227

CHAPTER 7:
The Nature of
Molecules and
Intermolecular
Interactions

D-ribose

L-ribose
(An enantiomer of D-ribose)

D-xylose
(A diastereomer of D-ribose)

FIGURE 7-25 Enantiomers versus diastereomers.

substituents. As an illustration, consider the naturally occurring sugar D-ribose (see Figure 7-25), which has three chiral centers bearing hydroxy groups. Each group could be oriented in one of two ways—a dash or a wedge; so in essence it is a binary outcome. Since there are three centers, then the total number of unique permutations is $2^3 = 8$. D-ribose represents one such permutation, which here is called the "down-up-down" isomer (referring to the orientation of the hydroxy groups). The enantiomer of D-ribose is L-ribose (the D and L designations are peculiar to carbohydrate nomenclature), and you will notice that *each and every chiral center is inverted*—this is true for any set of enantiomers. So L-ribose accounts for one stereoisomer of D-ribose, but there are six others—all of them diastereomers of D-ribose. Figure 7-25 shows only one of the diastereomers, namely D-xylose, which has a down-down-down arrangement of hydroxy substituents. Therefore, you can define a **diastereomer** as a stereoisomer in which one or more, *but not all*, chiral centers have been inverted.

A common temptation for the novice is to assign *R* and *S* designations to each of the chiral centers and make the comparison in an algorithmic way. Indeed, you would find that the configuration for D-ribose is $(2R, 3R, 4R)$ and for L-ribose is $(2S, 3S, 4S)$, thus confirming the designation of enantiomer. However, this method is time consuming and error-prone. For each chiral center, you must assign the CIP priorities, orient the center correctly, and decide whether a→b→c is clockwise or counterclockwise. This means that to compare ribose with another structure, 36 discrete operations must be made, and if an error occurs in any one, the whole comparison breaks down. Instead, you should become skilled in analyzing these problems from a three-dimensional standpoint. In other words, manipulate the structures in your mind's eye so you can compare them visually.

With this backdrop, return to the question of comparing Newman projection A to Fischer projection C in Figure 7-24. The first order of business is to convert them to sawhorse representations (B and E, respectively). Then the question is how to compare the two very different sawhorses. To make a reliable comparison, you must first reorient the structures so they share elements of commonality. It is generally easier to simply take one as a reference and reorient the other—for example, to arbitrarily take structure B as a reference and manipulate E to adopt the elements of commonality (see Figure 7-26). So what are these elements? Examining structure B, you find that (1) it is a staggered conformation, (2) C1, C2, C3, and C4 are all in the plane, (3) the hydroxy group is on the right hand and pointed toward the top of the page, and (4) the chloro substituent is on the left hand and pointed toward the bottom of the page (never mind for the moment whether they are dashes or wedges).

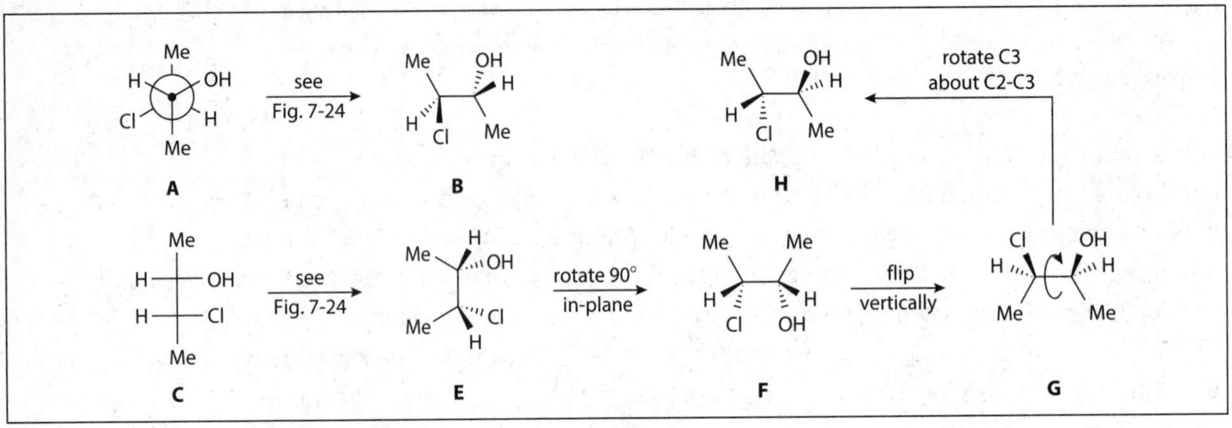

FIGURE 7-26 Comparing two representations.

Now set about the task of reorienting E to adopt these four elements, starting with an in-plane rotation to get structure F, followed by a vertical flip to obtain structure G. Notice that the dashes and wedges remain the same during the rotation, but change during the vertical flip. The motivation for this maneuver was to place the hydroxy group on the right side and pointing toward the top of the page. Notice, however, that the conformation is eclipsed (as indeed all Fischer projections must be). To make a comparison, you must then rotate about the C2—C3 bond 180° to arrive at structure H. Unlike the previous operations, this is a reconformation of the molecule—but the identity of the compound remains the same. Now you are in a position to evaluate the two structures (B and H). Notice that every chiral center in H is the opposite of that in B; therefore, the two must be enantiomers.

Similar operations can be carried out on cyclic molecules. Again, it is generally easier to convert all representations into dash-wedge drawings before making manipulations and comparisons. Figure 7-27 demonstrates two mnemonics for re-envisioning chair cyclohexane depictions. Imagine that the back carbon-carbon bond (highlighted in blue) is a hinge and that the cyclohexane ring is a flat surface, like a table or ironing board. You can push the molecule up on the hinge, much like a foldaway ironing board, in which case the hydroxy group becomes a dash at the 3 o'clock position and the methyl group is a wedge at the 10 o'clock position. Alternatively, you can let the surface fall suspended by the hinge, as if letting down a drop-leaf table. Here the hydroxy group would still be at 3 o'clock, but as a wedge, and the methyl group would be a dash at 8 o'clock.

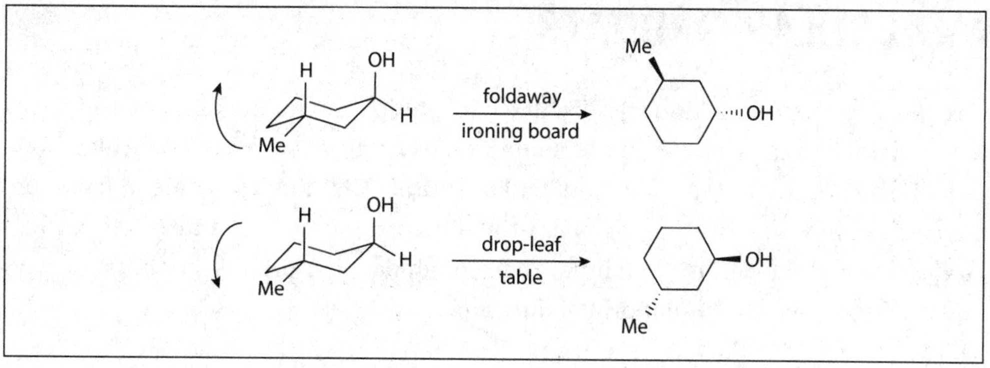

229

CHAPTER 7:
The Nature of
Molecules and
Intermolecular
Interactions

FIGURE 7-27 Converting chairs into dash-wedge representations.

You can apply these techniques to the comparison of a chair representation to a two-dimensional dash-wedge cyclohexane drawing, for example, structures A and B in Figure 7-28. You can use B as a reference structure and manipulate A to adopt the required orientation. Here the elements of commonality are quite straightforward: methyl is at 2 o'clock and chloro is at 4 o'clock. First use the drop-leaf table maneuver on A to obtain the dash-wedge structure C, which has methyl at 11 o'clock and chloro at 1 o'clock. Then recognize that a simple in-plane rotation of the molecule will put the substituents in the proper attitude for comparison. Inspection reveals that A and B are indeed the same thing.

Again, your goal should be the ability to carry out these manipulations in your mind's eye. As you practice this skill, sketching out intermediate steps with pencil and paper can be helpful, as shown in the previous figures. Also, molecular models are great support devices to help you see the three-dimensional reality of two-dimensional drawings. Once you develop this facility, comparing different representations becomes extremely rapid and reliable. Moreover, you hone the valuable (and increasingly rare) skill of three-dimensional visualization.

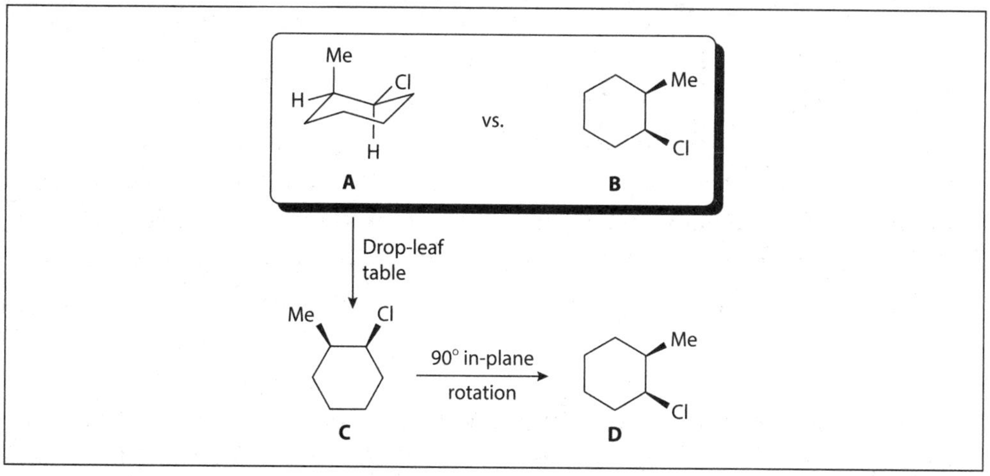

FIGURE 7-28 Comparing chair cyclohexane derivatives.

MOLECULAR ORBITALS

The concept of hybridization was discussed earlier in this chapter and is a useful way to predict molecular shape. To understand the electronic behavior of molecules, however, it is necessary to introduce **molecular orbital (MO) theory**. While in fact there are many manifestations of molecular orbital theory, the basic premise is that when atoms are close enough to each other to form bonds, their orbitals combine in ways that produce a new molecular orbital outcome.

Alkenes

MO theory is very similar to the concept of **hybridization**, in which s and p orbitals combine to form new hybrid orbitals. For example, the unhybridized carbon atom has a $2s$ orbital and three identical $2p$ orbitals in its valence shell. To accommodate three things (atoms or lone pairs) around carbon, two of the $2p$ orbitals and the $2s$ orbital combine to form three identical sp^2 orbitals, leaving one $2p$ orbital untouched (see Figure 7-29).

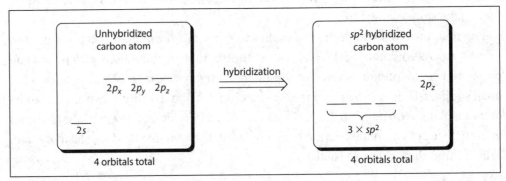

FIGURE 7-29 Atomic orbital hybridization.

While useful, the idea of hybridization is a simplification. It's tempting to imagine (and in fact some textbooks propose) that these hybrid orbitals interact in predictable ways to make new molecules. In reality, molecular orbitals are governed by complex quantum chemical considerations that can be predicted fully accurately only by sophisticated computer calculations. However, that is not to say that molecular orbitals are devoid of conceptual power. To explore some of these principles, examine the molecular orbital scenario for ethene (see Figure 7-30).

Ethene is constituted from two carbon atoms and four hydrogen atoms. Each carbon atom has four atomic orbitals (think of them as being sp^2 hybridized), and each of the four hydrogen atoms has a single 1s orbital, for a total of 12 atomic orbitals. These atomic orbitals combine to form 12 new and unique molecular orbitals, all of different energies. **Hund's rule** and the **Pauli exclusion principle** apply to molecules

231

CHAPTER 7:
The Nature of
Molecules and
Intermolecular
Interactions

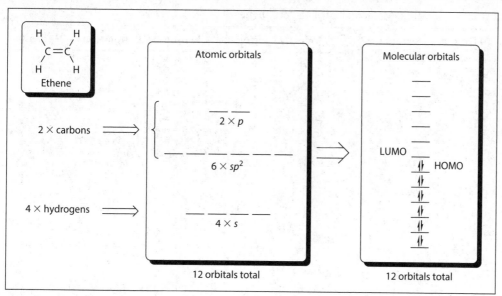

FIGURE 7-30 Molecular orbitals of ethene.

as well as atoms, so once these molecular orbitals are formed, they fill up from bottom to top. Since ethene has 12 electrons total (4 valence electrons from each carbon and 1 electron from each hydrogen), the bottommost 6 molecular orbitals are filled, and the topmost six are empty.

In general, the shapes of these orbitals (as calculated by computer algorithms) are complex and nonintuitive. However, there are special cases that can be very accurately predicted using **frontier molecular orbital (FMO) theory**. Here the frontier can be thought of as separating the filled from the unfilled orbitals—the frontier orbitals are thus the **highest occupied molecular orbital (HOMO)** and the **lowest unoccupied molecular orbital (LUMO)**. It turns out that these orbitals govern much of the reactivity of molecules, and moreover their shape can be predicted by manipulating the unhybridized p orbitals using a method called the **linear combination of atomic orbitals (LCAO)**.

The principle of LCAO is that adjacent p orbitals mix in predictable ways. If each orbital is a mathematical wave function, then they can be combined by addition and subtraction to result in new molecular orbitals. This principle is illustrated in the following table. If the wave function of the first p orbital (φ_1) is added to that of the second p orbital (φ_2), then a new molecular orbital is formed in which the two p orbitals are in-phase (lower row). A **constructive relationship** results, in which the electron density is shared between the two carbon atoms, providing a bonding interaction. This type of bond is designated a π bond. Conversely, if one p orbital is subtracted from the other, then a **destructive relationship** results, and the electron density drops to zero between the carbon atoms—this point of no electron density is called a **node** (designated by the dashed line in the schematic). In general, a node occurs every time the sign of the phase ($+/-$) occurs.

TABLE 7-7 Frontier Molecular Orbitals for Ethene

LCAO	Schematic	Model	Nodes	Symm	Population	Frontier
$+\varphi_1 - \varphi_2$			1	A	—	LUMO
$+\varphi_1 + \varphi_2$			0	S	⇅	HOMO

Extended π (pi) Systems

These π molecular orbitals arise anytime there are contiguous arrays of unhybridized p orbitals. **Extended π (pi) systems** develop when more than two adjacent p orbitals are present, as is the case with butadiene (see the following table), a molecule that has two adjacent double bonds. Historically, such double bonds have been called **conjugated**, a term that stems from their tendency to undergo chemistry together, rather than as isolated double bonds. This behavior is explained by FMO theory: each carbon bears an unhybridized p orbital, and this contiguous array interacts to give four new π molecular orbitals. Since they've been constructed using only the p orbitals, each of which housed a single electron, there are only four electrons to accommodate. Therefore, only the first two molecular orbitals are filled.

As it turns out, the two lowest energy molecular orbitals in butadiene have a net constructive effect, so they are called **bonding orbitals** and designated π. The two highest energy molecular orbitals, on the other hand, are overall destabilizing; therefore, they are called **antibonding orbitals** and designated π^*. Notice that increasing energy correlates with increasing number of nodes—this is a general trend. There is another guideline that derives from symmetry. An outcome of the mathematics behind LCAO dictates that all π molecular orbitals must be either symmetric (S) or antisymmetric (A). Symmetric, the more familiar term, means that the orbital reflects upon itself across a vertical center line, with phases matching exactly. **Antisymmetric** means that reflection across a center line results in the exact *opposite* phase for each and every point. When the π molecular orbitals are arranged properly, the progression usually alternates between symmetric and antisymmetric orbitals.

Generally speaking, the larger the extended π (pi) system, the lower the energy. Therefore, molecules with multiple double bonds are more stable if those bonds are arranged in alternating arrays. For example, 1,3-pentadiene is more stable than

233

CHAPTER 7:
The Nature of
Molecules and
Intermolecular
Interactions

TABLE 7-8 **Π** Molecular Orbitals for Butadiene

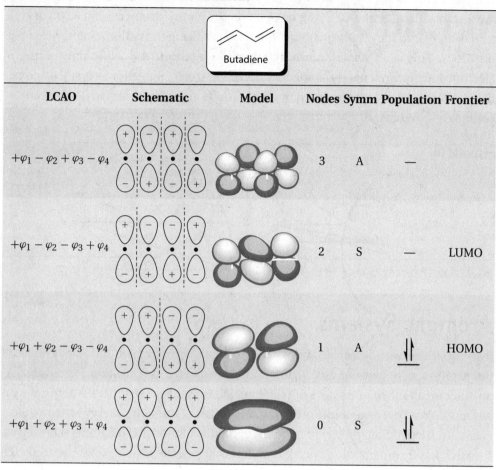

LCAO	Schematic	Model	Nodes	Symm	Population	Frontier
$+\varphi_1 - \varphi_2 + \varphi_3 - \varphi_4$			3	A	—	
$+\varphi_1 - \varphi_2 - \varphi_3 + \varphi_4$			2	S	—	LUMO
$+\varphi_1 + \varphi_2 - \varphi_3 - \varphi_4$			1	A	⇅	HOMO
$+\varphi_1 + \varphi_2 + \varphi_3 + \varphi_4$			0	S	⇅	

1,4-pentadiene, and 2-cyclohexanone is more stable than 3-cyclohexanone (see Figure 7-31). This is a phenomenon known as **conjugation**. Since you know that the origin of the effect can be described by MO theory, it comes as no surprise that conjugated double bonds often behave as a collective, whereas nonconjugated double bonds behave as two isolated species.

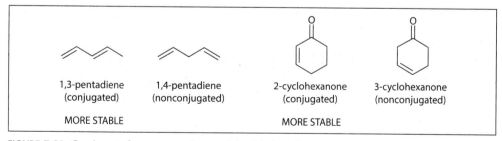

FIGURE 7-31 Conjugated vs. nonconjugated double bonds.

True conjugation arises from a mixing of adjacent p orbitals. A similar (but weaker) effect can arise from the interaction of p orbitals with adjacent bonds. For example, the methyl cation is not a very stable species, largely owing to the empty p orbital on carbon and the resulting violation of the octet rule. However, the ethyl cation is a bit more stable, because the C—H sigma bond on the methyl group can spill a bit of electron density into the empty p orbital, thereby stabilizing the cationic center (see Figure 7-32). This is an effect known as **hyperconjugation**, and while the sharing of electron density is not nearly as effective here as in true conjugation, it is still responsible for the following stability trend in carbocations and radicals: methyl < primary ≪ secondary < tertiary.

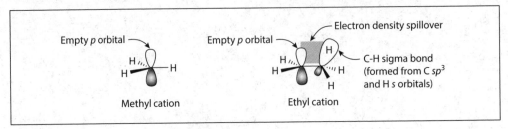

FIGURE 7-32 Hyperconjugation in the ethyl cation.

Aromatic Systems

In comparison with linear arrays, when p orbitals are arranged in a circle without interruption, as in benzene (see Figure 7-33), unexpected stabilization can emerge. As an outcome of the mathematics of LCAO (which is not discussed here), there are usually multiple sets of degenerate orbitals (i.e., orbitals of the same energy level). While it is not intuitively straightforward to construct molecular orbital diagrams themselves, there is a handy mnemonic device known as **Frost's circle**, which allows you to sketch out the relative energy levels of such molecules.

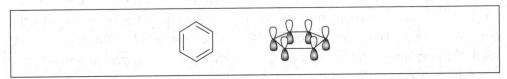

FIGURE 7-33 Contiguous p orbitals in benzene.

Frost's circle is really quite simple—it starts by drawing a regular polygon of the appropriate size with one point down. A circle is then drawn around the polygon, and each point of contact represents a molecular orbital energy level. For example, benzene is a six-membered ring, so its array of molecular orbitals starts with a single lowest-energy MO, followed by two sets of two MOs of the same energy, and then a single highest-energy MO (see Figure 7-34). Since benzene has 6π electrons, only the three lowest-energy orbitals are filled. This electronic arrangement accounts for the fact that benzene is particularly stable, a phenomenon known as aromaticity.

Aromaticity arises only from molecules possessing a cyclic, contiguous, and coplanar array of p orbitals. But this arrangement can also result in **antiaromaticity**,

235

CHAPTER 7:
The Nature of
Molecules and
Intermolecular
Interactions

whereby molecules are less stable than expected. The difference between aromaticity and antiaromaticity lies in the number of π-electrons that must be accommodated. This can be predicted using **Hückel's rule**, which states that systems having $4n\pi$ electrons, (i.e., 4, 8, 12 electrons) tend to be antiaromatic, and those having $(4n+2)\pi$ electrons (i.e., 2, 6, 10 electrons) tend to be aromatic.

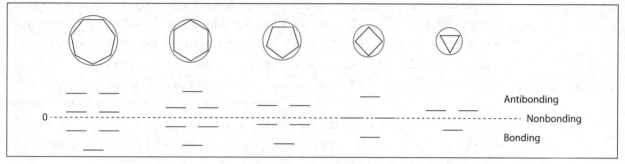

FIGURE 7-34 Frost's circle for determining aromatic MO energy levels.

Figure 7-35 demonstrates the molecular orbital basis of Hückel's rule using cyclopentadienyl ions. The molecular orbital energy levels are drawn using Frost's circle, and then populated with the appropriate number of p electrons. The cyclopentadienyl cation has only 4 electrons in the π (pi) system, whereas the corresponding anion has 6 (the negative charge represents a lone pair of electrons on carbon). Using Hückel's rule, you would predict the anion to be stable (aromatic) and the cation to be unstable (antiaromatic), which is indeed the experimentally observed result. However, the MO picture provides more insight into why the cation is so unstable—the molecule has 2 unpaired electrons. Finally, cyclopentadiene itself (far right), is considered nonaromatic. Since to be aromatic or antiaromatic, there must be a cyclic, contiguous, coplanar array of p orbitals, cyclopentadiene is out of the running because there is no p orbital at the methylene (CH_2) center, which interrupts the π (pi) system. Therefore,

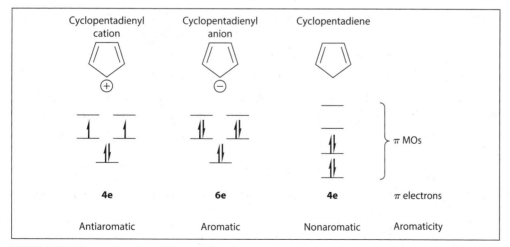

FIGURE 7-35 The molecular orbital origin of aromaticity.

its MO diagram is analogous to that of butadiene (see the earlier table "Π Molecular Orbitals for Butadiene" on page 233).

MO Description of Resonance

MO theory also provides a more thorough understanding of resonance. For example, the acetaldehyde anion (see Figure 7-36) is stabilized by resonance delocalization, whereby the negative charge is distributed between the carbon and the oxygen. Resonance forms do not "equilibrate"—that is, the molecule does not oscillate between forms A and B—rather, the two resonance structures are an attempt to represent a more complete truth than any single Lewis structure can. However, if you apply simple geometrical rules to each form, you would predict an sp^3 hybridization for the anionic carbon in form A, but form B clearly indicates an sp^2 geometry. How do you accurately predict the geometry of the molecule?

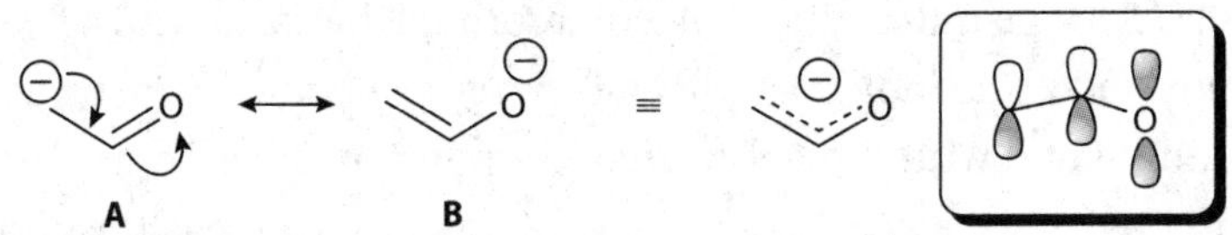

FIGURE 7-36 Resonance stabilization of the acetaldehyde anion.

Molecular orbital theory shows that an extended π system can be established by housing the negative charge in a p orbital. Thus the three-orbital array gives rise to a set of molecular orbitals in which the electron density is distributed throughout the molecule and the overall energy is minimized. For this reason, you expect both the anionic carbon and the oxygen to exhibit sp^2 hybridization, since this is the only way that all three atoms have unhybridized p orbitals. This is at variance with the predictions for the methyl anion (see earlier table "Geometries of Some Special Carbon Centers" on page 211), which was based on minimizing steric interactions; here the energy benefit of an extended π-system compensates for the steric cost. Therefore, the acetaldehyde anion is a completely planar molecule.

A similar anomaly can be seen with cations, as well. Thus the dimethylamino-methyl cation (see Figure 7-37) can be shown as two resonance forms (A and B), in which the nitrogen lone pair participates in stabilizing the adjacent positive charge on carbon. However, you are faced with a dilemma similar to the acetaldehyde anion: form A would predict an sp^3 hybridization for nitrogen, whereas form B appears to have sp^2 geometry. The only way for form B to have meaning is if a π bond is established between the 2 p orbitals on carbon and nitrogen (inset). Therefore, the species is planar.

Aside from the geometrical considerations, these two examples show the action of two specific types of functional groups. The carbonyl group (C=O) is an

FIGURE 7-37 Resonance stabilization of the dimethylaminomethyl cation.

electron-withdrawing group (designated **EW**), while the amino group (NR_2) is an **electron-donating group (ED)**. This idea is important for a variety of chemical reactivities, but the easiest way to keep the categories straight is to examine whether the group would best stabilize a cation or an anion. Generally speaking, electron density can be pushed *into* EW groups, thus stabilizing a negative charge, whereas electrons can be pushed *from* ED groups, which stabilizes adjacent positive charges. For this reason, ED groups generally have lone pairs.

There are two components of electron-withdrawing and electron-donating behavior: resonance and induction. As the term suggests, the **resonance effect** can be represented by electron-pushing arrows to give different resonance forms. This effect may be weak or strong, but it can exert influence over very large distances through extended π-systems. The **inductive effect** stems primarily from electronegativity; it can be quite strong, but its influence is local—the magnitude drops off sharply as distance from the functional group increases. The following table summarizes these effects for some common functional groups. In most cases the inductive and resonance effects work in concert, while in some instances they are at odds. The amino and methoxy substituents are almost always classified as ED groups, even though the central atoms are electronegative—the activity of the lone pairs dominates their behavior. The halogens are more subtle (e.g., chlorine). Generally speaking, they are grouped with the EW substituents.

TABLE 7-9 Some Common ED and EW Groups

Functional	Group Formula	Resonance Effect	Inductive Effect
Electron-withdrawing (EW) groups			
acetyl	$-COCH_3$		
carbomethoxy	$-CO_2CH_3$		
chloro	$-Cl$		
cyano	$-CN$		
nitro	$-NO_2$		
phenylsulfonyl	$-SO_2Ph$		
Electron-donating (ED) groups			
amino	$-NH_2$		
methoxy	$-OCH_3$		
methyl	$-CH_3$		
		← more EW | more ED →	← more EW | more ED →

NONCOVALENT BONDS

In addition to the fixed covalent bonds that hold molecules together, there are a host of so-called intermolecular forces that play a significant role in the properties of molecules.

Types of Intermolecular Forces

The magnitude of intermolecular forces spans a wide range, as depicted in Figure 7-38. Unlike covalent bonds, which are permanent and relatively easy to study thermodynamically, these noncovalent interactions are often fugitive, making unequivocal determination of their energies very difficult. Consequently, published values vary widely and are dependent upon the method of measurement (or calculation) and the types of systems studied. For the purposes of this overview, examples will be limited to organic molecules in solution.

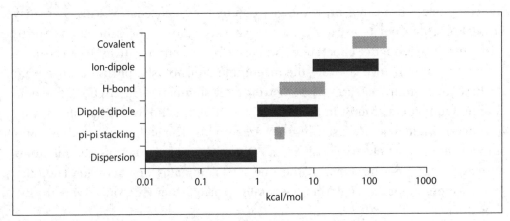

FIGURE 7-38 Comparison of intermolecular interaction energies.

ION-DIPOLE INTERACTIONS

Ion-dipole interactions are largely responsible for the dissolution of ionic compounds in water. For example, lithium chloride has a lattice enthalpy of 206 kcal/mol and a melting point of 605 °C, yet it dissolves rather easily in water. Remarkably, relatively weak ion-dipole forces (see Figure 7-39) overcome the strong ionic bonds holding the salt together. Obviously, this is an outcome of the sheer numbers of interactions in play: although small individually, these forces are quite significant in sum. Two effects are noteworthy in this interaction: the ions themselves are stabilized by the multiple interactions, and the water (or other solvent) is organized around the ions. This well-defined organization of solvent around a solute is often called the **solvent shell**.

Not surprisingly, the degree of organization around the ions is dependent upon the amount of charge. For example, the calcium ion (Ca^{2+}) exhibits a solvation enthalpy

239

**CHAPTER 7:
The Nature of
Molecules and
Intermolecular
Interactions**

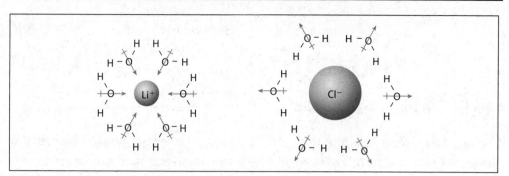

FIGURE 7-39 Ion-dipole forces around aqueous lithium chloride.

(ΔH_{solv}) in water of 416 kcal/mol, twice that of the similarly-sized sodium cation (Na^+). Conversely, with constant charge, the strength of solvation increases as ionic radius decreases. In other words, as the electrostatic charge is confined to a smaller space, its effect on the surrounding solvent is more pronounced. As one illustration of this effect, Figure 7-40 charts the dependence of solvation enthalpy on ionic radius among the alkali metal cations.

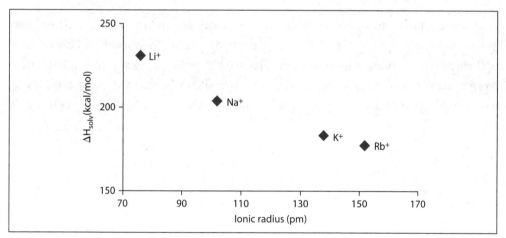

FIGURE 7-40 Solvation enthalpy as a function of ionic size.

HYDROGEN BONDING

The **hydrogen bond** is perhaps the most wide-ranging intermolecular force among biological molecules, and it remains a bit of an enigma. The classical view of the hydrogen bond (see Figure 7-41) is that of an interaction between an electron-rich lone pair (i.e., the hydrogen bond acceptor) and a highly polarized covalent bond involving hydrogen (i.e., the hydrogen bond donor).

Most textbooks relegate hydrogen bonds to compounds containing nitrogen, oxygen, and fluorine. However, there is considerable evidence that thiols (RSH) can serve as hydrogen bond donors, and one study suggests that more than 70 percent of

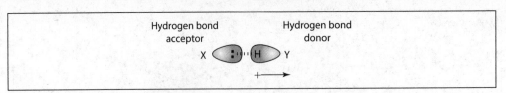

FIGURE 7-41 Model of hydrogen bonding.

cysteines in proteins have the thiol proton within hydrogen-bonding distance of a nitrogen or oxygen. The role of sulfur as a hydrogen bond acceptor is more controversial, however. In a very recent investigation using atomic force microscopy, 8-hydroxyquinoline was found to exhibit hydrogen bonds involving OH, NH, and CH bonds (see Figure 7-42).

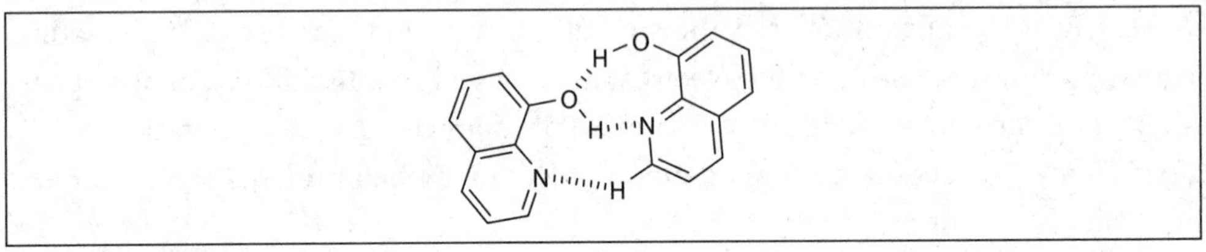

FIGURE 7-42 Hydrogen bonds observed in 8-hydroxyquinoline.

A particularly strong type of hydrogen bond occurs in proteins when two oppositely-charged amino acid residues are involved, a phenomenon known as a **salt bridge**. These interactions can be crucial in establishing the structure and function of proteins. For example, salt bridges in the active site of *Escherichia coli* aminopeptidase N (see Figure 7-43) have recently been shown to play a critical role in that enzyme's stability and activity.

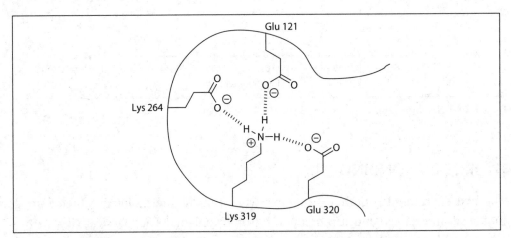

FIGURE 7-43 Salt bridges in the active site of *E. coli* aminopeptidase N.

DIPOLE-DIPOLE INTERACTIONS

Dipole-dipole forces arise when polar molecules are in proximity to each other. The force can be either attractive or repulsive, depending upon the relative directions of the

241

CHAPTER 7:
The Nature of
Molecules and
Intermolecular
Interactions

two dipoles, with an antiparallel arrangement providing the greatest stabilizing effect. Thus, for example, when *p*-dichlorobenzene (a common ingredient in mothballs) is dissolved in acetone, much of the solvent power is provided by dipole-dipole forces (see Figure 7-44). One characteristic of the dipole-dipole interaction is its sensitivity to distance—the force drops off as a function of the distance cubed.

FIGURE 7-44 Dipole-dipole forces in acetone solution.

PI-PI STACKING

An often neglected contributor to intramolecular forces is the **pi-pi stacking** interaction. Aromatic compounds such as benzene have molecular orbitals that are in a circular array, and the particular arrangement leads to anisotropic electron densities. The areas above and below the ring (i.e., the faces) are slightly electron rich, while the perimeter (or edge) is slightly electron poor. This sets the stage for favorable electrostatic interactions between aromatic rings. Figure 7-45 shows two common motifs found in pi-pi interactions. One is an **off-center parallel arrangement**, in which electron-rich and electron-poor layers align so that there is a small amount of coulombic attraction at the edges. Another is an **edge-to-face alignment**, whereby the electron-poor edge of one aromatic ring aligns perpendicular to the electron-rich face of another. The strength of these interactions is on the order of weak dipole-dipole forces, but in large biopolymers such as DNA, the sum of these interactions can be substantial.

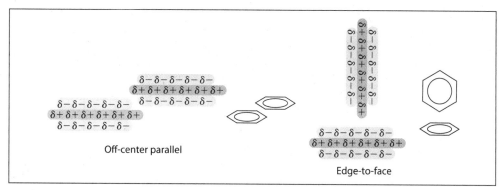

FIGURE 7-45 Two common pi-stacking motifs.

DISPERSION FORCES

The weakest of the intermolecular forces, **London dispersion forces (LDF)**, are found in all molecules. In the case of nonpolar species, where stronger interactions are absent, LDFs are usually the sole cohesive principle between molecules. Were it not for the dispersion effect, noble gases would not exist in liquid form. Dispersion forces even account for about one-quarter of the attractive force between water molecules.

The basis of LDF lies in fairly complex quantum mechanical outcomes, but it is often described as the favorable coalignment of instantaneous dipoles that are randomly generated by momentary unequal distributions of electron density in a molecule. While these instantaneous dipoles average out to zero over time for a given molecule, the continual coordination of these microdipoles between molecules provides a net attractive force.

Effects of Intermolecular Forces
PHYSICAL PROPERTIES

One of the most obvious and pervasive impacts of intermolecular forces on molecules is seen in their boiling points. This is illustrated in the three molecules 2-methyl-1-butene, ethyl acetate, and propionic acid (see Figure 7-46), which have almost identical molecular weights. For the 2-methyl-1-butene, LDFs are the predominant intermolecular force. However, in the case of ethyl acetate, the introduction of the oxygen atoms results in polar bonds (between carbon and oxygen), leading to a net dipole. In the condensed phase, these dipoles align between molecules (left inset), providing a greater cohesive force, which is revealed in a higher boiling point (77 °C vs. 31 °C).

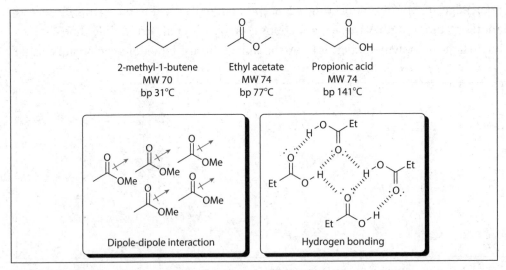

FIGURE 7-46 Impact of intermolecular forces on boiling points.

243

CHAPTER 7:
The Nature of
Molecules and
Intermolecular
Interactions

With propionic acid, there are not only dipole-dipole interactions, but also opportu-nities for hydrogen bonding. In fact, most carboxylic acids in the condensed phase form strong dimeric structures with complementary hydrogen bonds (see Figure 7-46, right). Because of these additional intermolecular forces, propionic acid has a boiling point of 141 °C vs. 77 °C for ethyl acetate.

Molecular geometry can play an important role, as exemplified by the two geomet-ric isomers of 1,2-dichloroethene (see Figure 7-47). In the *cis*-isomer, both of the polar C—Cl bonds are pointed in the same direction, so there is a net dipole for the whole molecule. In the *trans*-isomer, these bonds are antiparallel and the bond dipoles tend to cancel each other out, leading to a molecule with a very small net dipole. This is consequently reflected in the lower boiling point of the *trans*-isomer.

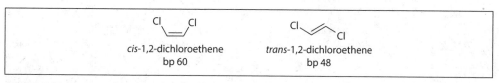

cis-1,2-dichloroethene
bp 60

trans-1,2-dichloroethene
bp 48

FIGURE 7-47 Impact of intermolecular forces on boiling points.

Intermolecular forces are additive, and since hydrogen bonds are relatively strong, polyols tend to have exceedingly high boiling points. Figure 7-48 provides a useful set of examples. In a series of nonpolar molecules, progressing from ethane to butane to 3-methylpentane results in a steady increase in boiling points, due to increased mass and a larger electronic cloud (i.e., greater LDFs). When one CH_2 group is replaced with an OH group (ethane to ethanol), the boiling point jumps from −88°C to 65°C, a 153°C difference. Additional OH groups magnify this effect, so the difference in boiling points between 3-methylpentane and glycerol is 226°C. Taking this to an extreme, the straight-chain hydrocarbon eicosane ($C_{20}H_{42}$, MW 283) has a boiling point of 343°C, as opposed to the much smaller, but much more polar, glucose molecule ($C_6H_{12}O_6$, MW 180), which has a calculated boiling point of 527° C (in practice, glucose burns before it boils).

CONFORMATIONAL IMPLICATIONS

Noncovalent forces can play a major role in many aspects of molecular shape and behavior. For example, in *trans*-1,2-dichlorohexane (see Figure 7-49, left), the chair conformer in which the two chloro substituents are diequatorial is preferred on steric grounds. However, the equilibrium is not as right-handed as you might expect, since the diaxial conformer allows the two polar bonds to be antiparallel, which avoids the unfavorable dipole-dipole interactions in the diequatorial conformer. Similarly, in *cis*-cyclohexanediol (see Figure 7-49, right), the equilibrium is less right-handed than steric considerations would predict, since the diaxial conformer can take advantage of an intramolecular hydrogen bond.

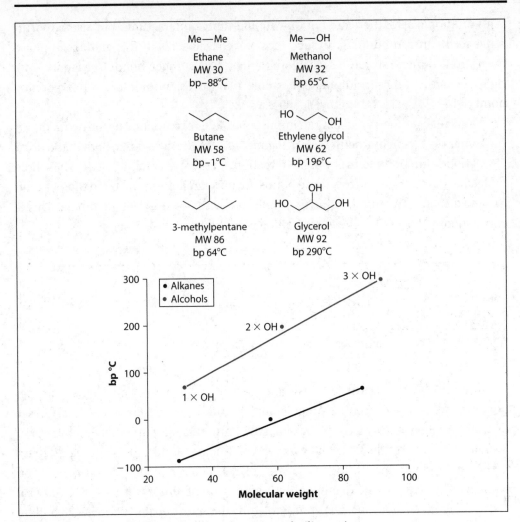

FIGURE 7-48 Impact of multiple functional groups on boiling points.

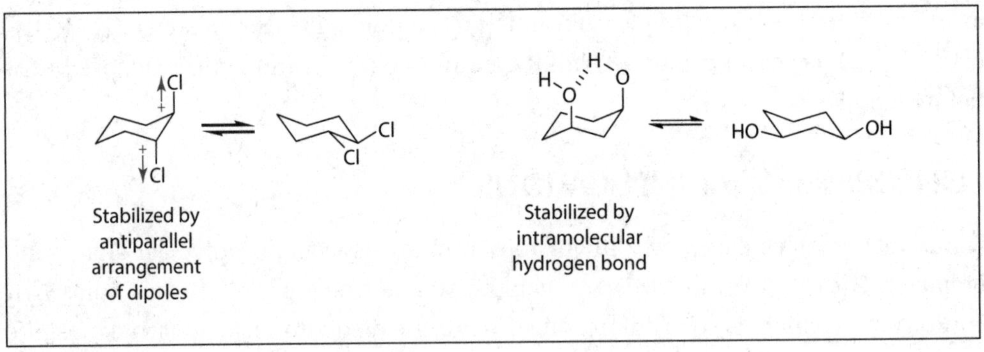

FIGURE 7-49 Conformational stabilization by noncovalent forces.

These factors even play out in chemical equilibria. For example, ketones are known to be in tautomeric equilibrium with their enol counterparts, but the keto form is generally the far more thermodynamically stable option. Thus 2-butanone exists almost exclusively in the keto form. However, pentane-2,4-dione exists as a mixture of keto

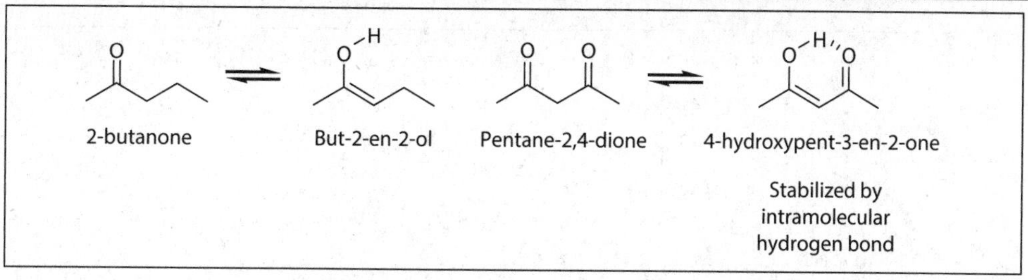

245

CHAPTER 7:
The Nature of
Molecules and
Intermolecular
Interactions

FIGURE 7-50 Stabilization of a β-ketoenol tautomer by hydrogen bonding.

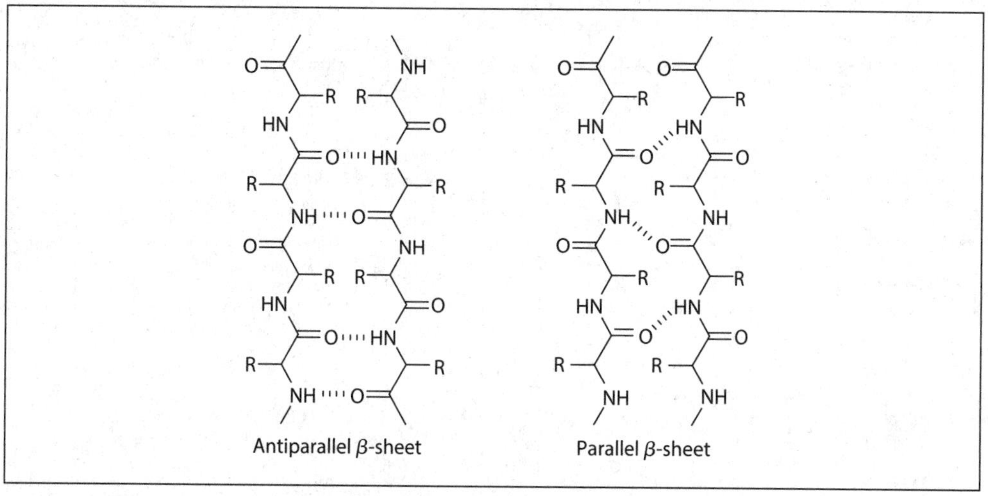

FIGURE 7-51 Two protein β-sheet geometries stabilized by hydrogen bonding.

and enol forms due to (among other things) the stabilization of the enol tautomer by an intramolecular hydrogen bond (see Figure 7-50).

Most significant for biomolecules, noncovalent forces are responsible for essential structural motifs found in macromolecular arrays. In addition to the familiar nucleotide base pairings through complementary hydrogen bonds (see Figure 7-7 on page 208), the α-helices and β-sheets found in proteins are the outcome of noncovalent forces (most significantly hydrogen bonding). Figure 7-51 illustrates two β-sheet patterns, both of which feature repeating hydrogen bonds between the amide carbonyl oxygen and the NH proton.

Material chemists can also take advantage of these interactions when designing molecules. For example, the polycyclic aromatic molecule shown in Figure 7-52 self-assembles into a repeating hexameric array, which forms an intriguing macromolecular honeycomb structure. The forces leading to this behavior have been traced to the dipole-dipole interactions between the trifluoromethylphenyl moieties on adjacent molecules, which are electron deficient on one end of the benzene ring due to the strong electron-withdrawing effects of the trifluoromethyl group.

Thus, while the chemical bond is the primary determinant in the structure of individual small molecules, intermolecular forces are of equal importance in dictating the structure of much larger biomolecules and macromolecular assemblies.

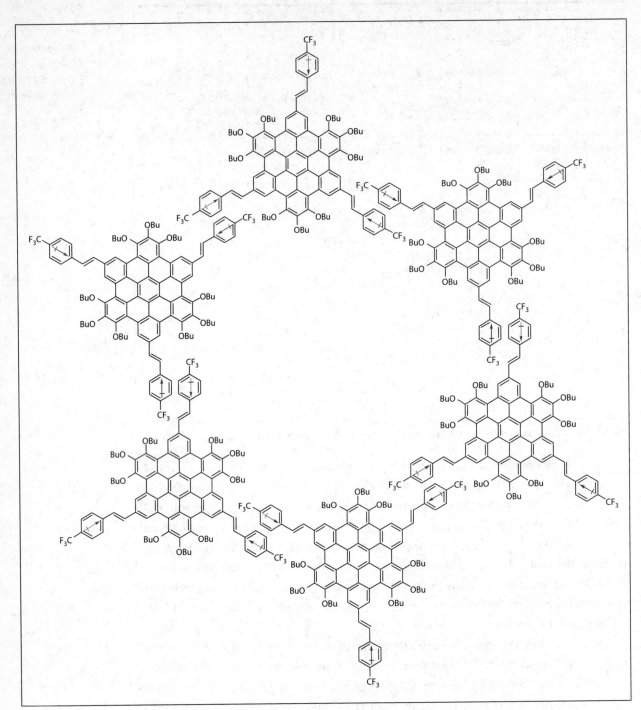

FIGURE 7-52 Molecular self-assembly driven by dipole-dipole interactions.

CHAPTER 8

Separation and Purification Methods

Read This Chapter to Learn About

➤ Principal Techniques

➤ Special Applications for Biomolecules

PRINCIPAL TECHNIQUES

The separation of mixtures is important for two reasons. First, separatory techniques are required for analyzing any number of complex mixtures—from contaminants in well water to forensic DNA samples to pharmaceutical formulations. Second, it is often necessary to purify compounds for further use—for example, the isolation of morphine from poppy seeds or the purification of intermediates in a multistep organic synthesis.

The most common techniques fall into three broad categories—**extraction**, **chromatography**, **distillation**. Each are based on slightly different chemical principles—in some respects overlapping, in others complementary. From a practical standpoint, a significant point of differentiation is scalability. For example, distilling 1 kg of solvent poses no particular technical challenges. However, purifying even 20 g of a reaction mixture by **chromatography** is an expensive and laborious proposition. Extending this to an industrial scale (on the order of 100 kg or more) is no less of a challenge, although it can be done.

TABLE 8-1 General Methods for Separation and Purification

	Extraction	Chromatography	Distillation
Principle of Separation	Differential solubility between two or more solvent systems (e.g., water and dichloromethane)	Differential affinity between a stationary phase (e.g., silica or cellulose) and a mobile phase	Differential vapor pressures
Common Applications	Initial aqueous workup of reactions; separation of inorganic salts from organic products	Final purification of reaction mixtures (e.g., flash columns); analysis of products (e.g., HPLC and GC)	Purification of solvents and volatile products; concentration of reaction mixtures
Scope and Limitations	Broadly applicable; can be used with any two immiscible solvents	Can be used on a wide variety of compounds and mixtures	Limited to products with appreciable vapor pressure at or below 300°C
Scalability	Excellent	Limited	Very good
Relative Expense	Low	High	Moderate

By the same token, the various methods also differ in their scope and range of application. Clearly, a compound must exhibit some degree of volatility under reasonable conditions to be distilled. However, column chromatography can be used to purify a wide array of compounds, whether solid or liquid, polar or nonpolar, volatile or nonvolatile. It is sometimes advantageous to use combinations of methods—for example, a "quick and dirty" chromatography column to remove baseline impurities from a complex reaction mixture, followed by a careful distillation to obtain an analytically pure sample.

Extraction

The basis of extractive techniques is the "like dissolves like" rule. Water typically dissolves inorganic salts (such as lithium chloride) and other ionized species, while solvents (ethyl acetate, methylene chloride, diethyl ether, etc.) dissolve neutral organic molecules. However, some compounds (e.g., alcohols) exhibit solubility in both media. Therefore, it is important to remember that this method of separation relies on **partitioning**—that is, the preferential dissolution of a species into one solvent over another. For example, 2-pentanol is somewhat soluble in water (i.e., 17 g/100 mL H_2O), but infinitely soluble in diethyl ether. Thus 2-pentanol can be preferentially partitioned into ether.

One of the most common uses of **extraction** is during aqueous workup, as a way to remove inorganic materials from the desired organic product. On a practical note, workup is usually carried out using two immiscible solvents—that is, in a biphasic system. If a reaction has been carried out in tetrahydrofuran, dioxane, or methanol, then it is generally desirable to remove those solvents by evaporation before workup because they have high solubilities in both aqueous and organic phases, and can set up single-phase systems (i.e., nothing to separate) or emulsions. Typical extraction solvents include ethyl acetate, hexane, chloroform, methylene chloride, and diethyl ether. All of these form crisp delineations between phases.

The two layers are commonly referred to as the **aqueous phase** and the **organic phase**. It is important to keep track of the phases, as their positions are solvent dependent. For example, diethyl ether is lighter than water, so the organic phase will rest on top in the separatory funnel, whereas methylene chloride is heavier than water and so will sink to the bottom (see Figure 8-1).

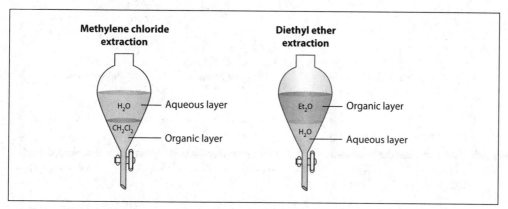

FIGURE 8-1 Two manifestations of an organic/aqueous extraction.

By way of vocabulary, actually two operations are encountered in the separatory funnel. When components are removed from an organic layer by shaking with an aqueous solution, the organic phase is said to be **washed** (e.g., "The combined ether extracts were washed with aqueous sodium bicarbonate solution"). On the other hand, when components are removed from water by treatment with an organic solvent, the aqueous phase is said to be **extracted** (e.g., "The aqueous layer was extracted with three portions of ethyl acetate"). Thus aqueous layers are extracted, and organic layers are washed—although these two terms are sometimes (erroneously) used interchangeably.

Aqueous workup can involve more than just separation. For example, reactions that produce anions (e.g., Grignard reactions) are usually "quenched" with a mildly acidic aqueous solution (e.g., saturated ammonium chloride) at the end of the reaction to neutralize any residual base. The same holds true for very acidic reactions. Thus aromatic nitration reactions (HNO_3/H_2SO_4) are usually quenched by being poured onto a large quantity of ice, which dilutes the acidic environment.

While extractions are usually carried out with a neutral aqueous phase, sometimes pH modulation can be used to advantage. For example, a mixture of naphthalenesulfonic acid and naphthalene can be separated by washing with bicarbonate, in which case the sulfonic acid is deprotonated and partitioned into the aqueous phase. Similarly, a mixture of naphthalene and quinoline can be separated by an acid wash (see Figure 8-2), taking advantage of the basic nature of the heterocyclic nitrogen (pK_a 9.5). If it is necessary to isolate the quinoline, it is neutralized with bicarbonate and extracted back into an organic solvent.

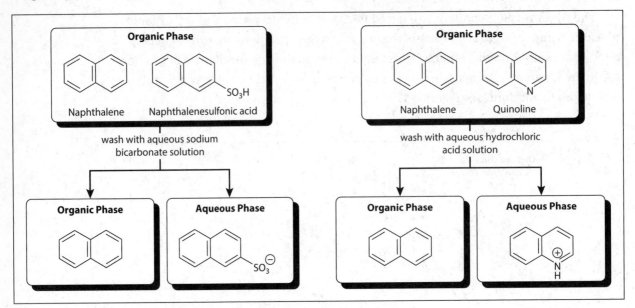

FIGURE 8-2 Two pH-controlled extractions.

Organic solvents are used for workup because they are easily removed by evaporation, leaving behind the organic compound of interest. A common problem encountered at this point is residual water from the aqueous washes. Ethyl acetate and diethyl ether both dissolve large quantities of water (3.3% and 1.2%, respectively). Therefore, it is advantageous to wash these organic layers with brine (saturated NaCl solution) at the end of the extraction sequence—the brine draws out the dissolved water through an osmotic-like effect. For methylene chloride and chloroform, a brine wash is unnecessary, since the solubility of water in these solvents is quite low. Once freed from the bulk of residual water, the organic layer is dried over a desiccant, such as sodium sulfate, calcium chloride, or magnesium sulfate, and then decanted or filtered before evaporation.

Distillation

If chromatography is the most versatile separation method in the laboratory, it might be argued that **distillation** is the most common. This technique is used very frequently for purifying solvents and reagents before use.

SIMPLE AND FRACTIONAL DISTILLATION

When volatile components are being removed from nonvolatile impurities, the method of **simple distillation** is employed (see Figure 8-3). In this familiar protocol, a liquid is heated to the boil, forcing vapor into a water-cooled condenser, where it is converted

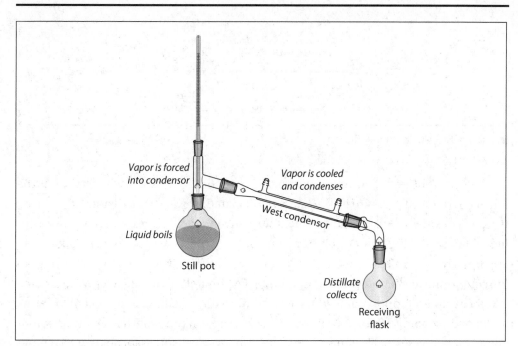

FIGURE 8-3 Simple distillation.

back to liquid and is conveyed by gravity to a receiving flask. When volumes are small (1–10 mL) a special apparatus known as a short-path distillation head is used. This piece of equipment is designed to minimize dead volume in the assembly and maximize recovery of the distillate. Otherwise, the principle is the same.

When separating two liquids with similar boiling points—or substances that tend to form azeotropes, **fractional distillation** is used. In this method, a connector with large surface area (such as a Vigreux column) is inserted between the still pot and the distillation head. The purpose of this intervening portion is to provide greater surface area upon which the vapor can condense and revolatilize, leading to greater efficiency of separation. In a more sophisticated apparatus, the Vigreux column and condensor are separated by an automated valve that opens intermittently, thus precisely controlling the rate of distillation.

DISTILLING HIGH-BOILING COMPOUNDS

For compounds with limited volatility, the technique of **bulb-to-bulb distillation** (see Figure 8-4) is sometimes successful. In this distillation, the liquid never truly boils—that is to say, the vapor pressure of the compound does not reach the local pressure of the environment. Instead, the sample is placed in a flask (or bulb) and subjected to high vacuum and heat, which sets up a vapor pressure adequate to equilibrate through a passage to another bulb, which is cooled with air, water, or dry ice. The temperature differential drives the vapor equilibrium into the cooler bulb, where the compound condenses. This is the same principle behind the Kugelrohr (from German, "bulb and tube") distillation.

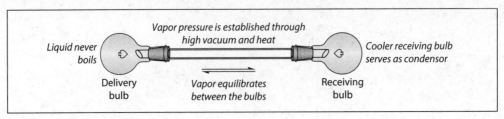

FIGURE 8-4 Bulb-to-bulb distillation.

The effect of temperature on the volatility of compounds is well-known, but the impact of reduced pressure is much less appreciated. However, distillation at reduced pressure, or **vacuum distillation**, brings many advantages. For example, consider a liquid that has a boiling point of 180°C at atmospheric pressure (760 Torr). If you were to attempt that distillation, you would not be surprised to observe charring of the compound at such elevated temperature. Fortunately, reducing the pressure using a water aspirator (approximately 20 Torr total pressure) results in a significant lowering of the boiling point. Figure 8-5 shows this effect using a pressure-temperature nomograph. First, the normal boiling point at atmospheric pressure is located on the center scale; then a straightedge is used to span that point and the distillation pressure on the rightmost scale; tracing the straightedge back to the leftmost scale will provide an estimate of the boiling point at that pressure. Thus a compound with a boiling point of 180°C at 760 Torr will boil at about 80°C under a vacuum of 20 Torr. At 1 Torr (easily attainable with a vacuum pump), the boiling point is well below room temperature! For the purposes of purification, however, you are better off with the aspirator, because at 1 Torr you could not recover the compound using a water-cooled (approximately 20°C) condensor.

Another way to distill sparingly volatile compounds is by **steam distillation**. In a true steam distillation, live steam is introduced into the still pot by means of a metal tube, or dipleg. The steam heats up the pot and carries any vaporized material from the head space to the condensor, where it collects and drains into the receiving flask with the condensed water. In a common modification, water is simply added to the still pot and the mixture is heated in the same fashion as a simple distillation—the steam is thus produced *in situ*. The underlying principle of steam distillation is that an azeotrope forms with water, which has a lower boiling point than the pure compound itself. For example, naphthalene has a boiling point of 218°C, but in the presence of steam an azeotrope is formed, which contains 16% naphthalene and boils at 99°C. In addition, the continual physical displacement of the head space by water vapor also aids in the collection of slightly volatile components.

ROTARY EVAPORATION

There are many occasions when you simply need to remove solvent (e.g., after working up a reaction). In such cases, the volatile compound is the undesired component, so recovering it quantitatively is not of great concern. For this application, the technique of **rotary evaporation** has been developed (see Figure 8-6). A solution of the desired product in some common solvent (ether, methylene chloride, etc.) is placed in a round-bottom flask and placed under an aspirator vacuum while being mechanically rotated. The rotation maintains a fresh film of solution on the flask walls, which maximizes the solvent vapor pressure in a manner reminiscent of a Kugelrohr distillation. The vapor rises to a water-cooled glass coil, where it condenses and collects into a receiving flask. The delivery flask is kept in an ambient temperature bath to counteract the evaporative cooling effect. In this way, 50 mL of methylene chloride can be removed in about 5 minutes. However, if the desired product is somewhat volatile ($bp_{760} < 250°C$), care must be taken to prevent inadvertent loss on the rotary evaporator.

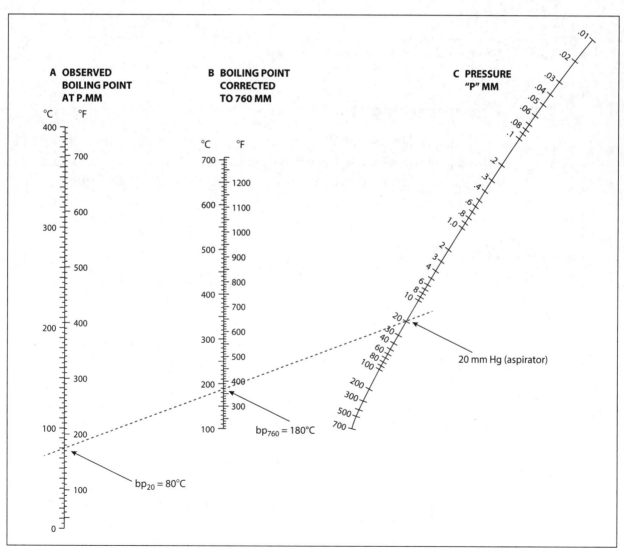

FIGURE 8-5 A pressure-temperature nomograph.

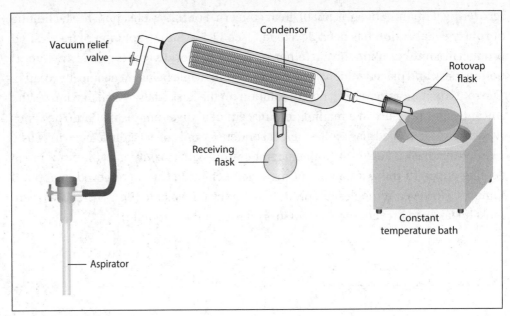

FIGURE 8-6 Components of a rotary evaporator.

Chromatography

Chromatography represents the most versatile separation technique readily available to the organic chemist. Even though it suffers from limitations of cost and scalability, it has found broad application in the purification and analysis of complex chemical systems.

BACKGROUND

Conceptually, the technique of chromatography is very simple—there are only two components: a **stationary phase** (usually silica or cellulose) and a **mobile phase** (usually a solvent system). Any two compounds usually have different partitioning characteristics between the stationary and mobile phases. Since the mobile phase is moving (thus the name), then the more time a compound spends in that phase, the farther it will travel.

Chromatographic techniques fall into one of two categories: analytical and preparative. **Analytical techniques** are used to follow the course of reactions and determine purity of products. These methods include gas chromatography (GC), high-performance liquid chromatography (HPLC), and thin-layer chromatography (TLC). Sample sizes for these procedures are usually quite small, from microgram to milligram quantities. In some cases, the chromatograph is coupled to another analytical instrument, such as a mass spectrometer or nuclear magnetic resonance (NMR) spectrometer, so the components that elute can be easily identified.

Preparative techniques are used to purify and isolate compounds for characterization or further use. The most common techniques in this category are preparative HPLC, preparative TLC, and column chromatography. One popular modification of column chromatography is the flash column, which operates at medium pressures (about 10 psi) and provides very rapid separation (approximately 5 minutes elution times). Column chromatography is suitable for sample sizes ranging from a few milligrams to several grams.

PARAMETERS

For gas chromatography (GC), the mobile phase is an inert carrier gas, such as helium or argon. Therefore, for the components to move, they must be volatile under the analytical conditions. Toward this end, GC columns are usually heated during analysis. The retention time (t_R) can be controlled by the oven temperature—the higher the temperature, the more quickly the sample elutes (see Figure 8-7).

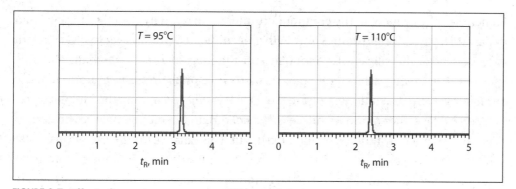

FIGURE 8-7 Effect of oven temperature on GC retention time.

The other methods fall under the category of LC (liquid chromatography), where the mobile phase is a solvent system, which can be used instead of temperature to leverage retention. Occasionally, this is a single solvent, but more often it is a binary mixture of solvents with different polarities. The advantage of the latter is that the bulk polarity can be modulated by varying the ratio of the two solvents.

For example, consider a typical TLC plate (see Figure 8-8) developed in a 1:1 mixture of ethyl acetate and hexane, which exhibits two well-separated components. The spots can be characterized by their R_f **value**, which is defined as the distance traveled from the origin divided by the distance traveled by the mobile phase. Generally speaking, the slower moving component (R_f 0.29) is either larger, more polar, or both. If you wanted a larger R_f value, you could boost the solvent polarity by increasing the proportion of ethyl acetate in the mobile phase. Conversely, more hexane would result in lower-running spots.

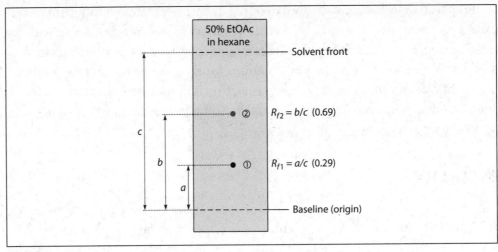

FIGURE 8-8 A typical TLC plate.

NORMAL AND REVERSE-PHASE SYSTEMS

Sometimes one or more of the components interact so strongly with the silica gel that departure from the origin comes only with great difficulty. One answer to this problem is to derivatize the silica with nonpolar substituents, such as long-chain aliphatic residues. This creates a situation known as a **reverse phase system**. In normal phase chromatography, the stationary phase (i.e., silica) is *more polar* than the mobile phase; in reverse phase, the stationary phase is *less polar* than the mobile phase. The derivatized silica is not only much less polar itself, but it also allows for the use of very polar solvents, such as water and methanol. The reversed phase results in some counterintuitive outcomes. For example, more polar components actually elute *faster*, and a more polar solvent system results in an *increased* retention time (i.e., lower R_f value). These parameters are summarized in the following table.

TABLE 8-2 Comparison of Normal and Reverse-Phase Chromatography

Parameter	Normal Phase	Reverse Phase
typical stationary phase	underivatized silica gel	C_8-hydrocarbon derivatized silica
representative mobile phase	ethyl acetate/hexane mixture	acetonitrile/water mixture
more polar components	have lower R_f values	have higher R_f values
increasing solvent polarity	increases R_f values	decreases R_f values

Generally speaking, most analytical methods employ reverse phase systems, whereas the majority of preparative techniques are based on normal silica gel (an outcome largely driven by cost, as the derivatized silica is quite expensive). Among

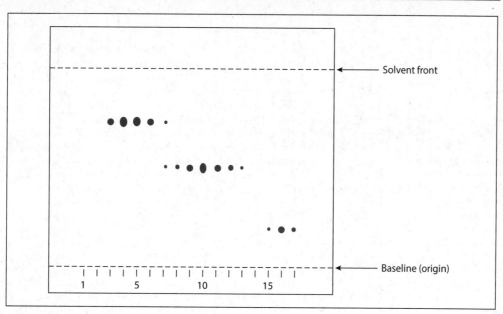

FIGURE 8-9 A typical flash column separation.

preparative techniques, flash columns are the most prevalent. Typical columns range from 0.5–5.0 cm in diameter, with a silica column height of about 15 cm. A sample is loaded to the top of the column and then rapidly eluted by forcing solvent through under medium pressure. A series of fractions are collected, the volume of which is determined by the size of the column—for a 2-cm column, one usually collects 10 mL fractions.

Once collected, the fractions are spotted on a long TLC plate and developed in the same solvent system used for eluting the flash column. Figure 8-9 shows an ideal scenario, in which three components have been successfully isolated in separate fractions. The next step is to combine like fractions into "cuts"—for example, the first cut might contain fractions 3–6; the second cut, fractions 8–13; and the third cut, fractions 15–17. The solvent is then removed by evaporation.

SPECIAL APPLICATIONS FOR BIOMOLECULES

In addition to the standard techniques discussed above, there are two special methods of particular interest to the purification and analysis of molecules of biological interest.

Electrophoresis

One important methodology for the separation and characterization of amino acids and oligopeptides is **electrophoresis**. In this analytical technique, a mixture of amino acids (or oligopeptides) is spotted onto the center of a conductive gel, across which

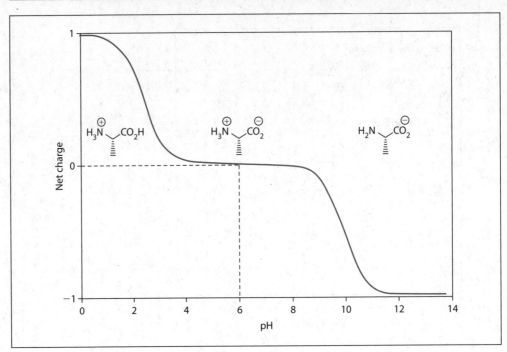

FIGURE 8-10 Net charge of alanine as a function of pH.

is applied an electrical potential. The amino acids then migrate toward the anode or cathode, depending upon the net charge on each molecule (positively-charged species move to the cathode and negatively-charged species move to the anode). The mobility of each ion depends upon its net charge and its mass.

Since amino acids are polyfunctional ionizable molecules, their net charge is a function of pH. In the case of alanine, for example, at very low pH the net charge is +1 (both the carboxylic acid and amine functionalities are protonated)—thus at pH = 2, alanine would move toward the cathode (see Figure 8-10). Conversely, at very high pH the net charge is −1 (both the carboxylic acid and amine functionalities are deprotonated)—thus at pH = 10, alanine would move toward the anode. At pH = 6, there is no net charge on the alanine molecule (positive and negative charges exactly cancel each other)—therefore, alanine would not migrate on an electrophoresis gel at pH = 6. This is known as the **isoelectric point** (pI).

The isoelectric point varies with the identity of the amino acid (or oligopeptide), as shown in the following table. For example, glutamic acid has two carboxylic acid groups and one amine group, which means its isoelectric point is in the acidic range. This makes sense if you consider that for a net charge of zero, each of the carboxylic acid moieties must be half-protonated, which requires a lower pH. As a complementary example, lysine has two amine groups and one carboxylic acid group, which results in an isoelectric point in the basic range. In this case, half of the amines must be deprotonated to achieve a net charge of zero for the molecule.

TABLE 8-3 Isoelectric Points of the Amino Acids

Amino Acid	pI	Amino Acid	pI
Alanine	6.00	Arginine	10.76
Asparagine	5.41	Aspartic acid	2.77
Cysteine	5.07	Glutamic acid	3.22
Glutamine	5.65	Glycine	5.97
Histidine	7.59	Isoleucine	6.02
Leucine	5.98	Lysine	9.74
Methionine	5.74	Phenylalanine	5.48
Proline	6.30	Serine	5.68
Threonine	5.60	Tryptophan	5.89
Tyrosine	5.66	Valine	5.96

This background provides a theoretical framework for understanding the electrophoresis gel shown in Figure 8-11, in which glutamic acid, alanine, and lysine are separated at pH = 6. Because alanine is *at* its isoelectric point, it does not migrate. Glutamic acid, however, is *above* its isoelectric point (3.22), so it bears a net negative charge and will move toward the anode. Conversely, lysine is *below* its isoelectric point (9.74), so it bears a net positive charge and will move toward the cathode.

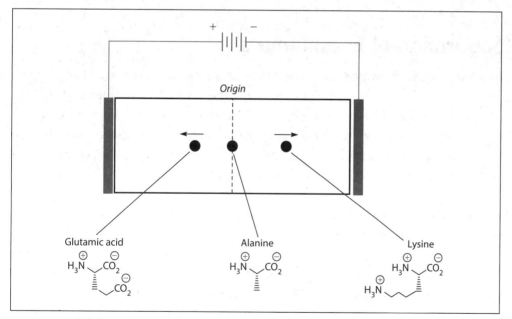

FIGURE 8-11 Gel electrophoresis of three amino acids at pH 6.0.

A common contemporary method for electrophoretic analysis is known as **capillary electrophoresis** or CE (see Figure 8-12). The separatory medium in this technique is not a gel, but rather a capillary with either end immersed in a buffer solution. Application of an electrical potential across the capillary induces a flow of buffer

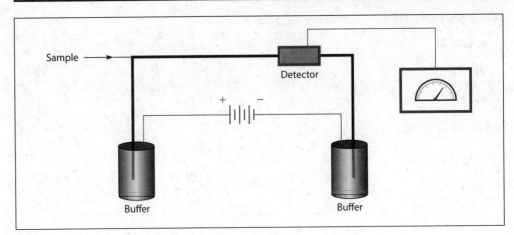

FIGURE 8-12 Schematic of a capillary electrophoresis apparatus.

toward the cathode, a phenomenon known as **electroosmotic flow** (EOF). The sample is introduced either by temporarily replacing the anode-side buffer with a solution of the sample or via a more sophisticated in-line injection system. While the finer details regarding the mode of separation are different for CE versus gel electrophoresis, the general principle of separation based on charge still holds.

Separation of Enantiomers

It is often desirable to prepare compounds as a single enantiomer. There are two general approaches to this problem: (1) by designing a synthesis that results only in a single enantiomer (chiral synthesis), or (2) by synthesizing the product in racemic form and then separating the enantiomers from one another (chiral resolution). The first approach is beyond the scope of this text. The second approach can be accomplished using one of two methods: (1) by preferential crystallization and (2) by chiral HPLC.

In **preferential crystallization**, a racemic mixture is treated with an optically pure compound that can coordinate very tightly with the racemate. Very often this is done with salt formation. For example, consider the chiral resolution of racemic tartaric acid shown in Figure 8-13. When the racemic acid is treated with enantiomerically pure $(3R, 4R)$-quinotoxine, a crystalline salt is formed with the (R, R)-tartrate only. The (S, S)-enantiomer remains in solution. The crystalline salt can be isolated by filtration and then acidified to reform the carboxylic acid as the enantiomerically pure (R, R)-enantiomer.

Two fundamental concepts are important to recognize with this example. First, there is no particular reason the (R, R)-base preferentially formed a precipitate with the (R, R)-acid; it was merely coincidence that these two isomers formed the insoluble salt. Second, the acid exists as a mixture of enantiomers. Recall that enantiomers have

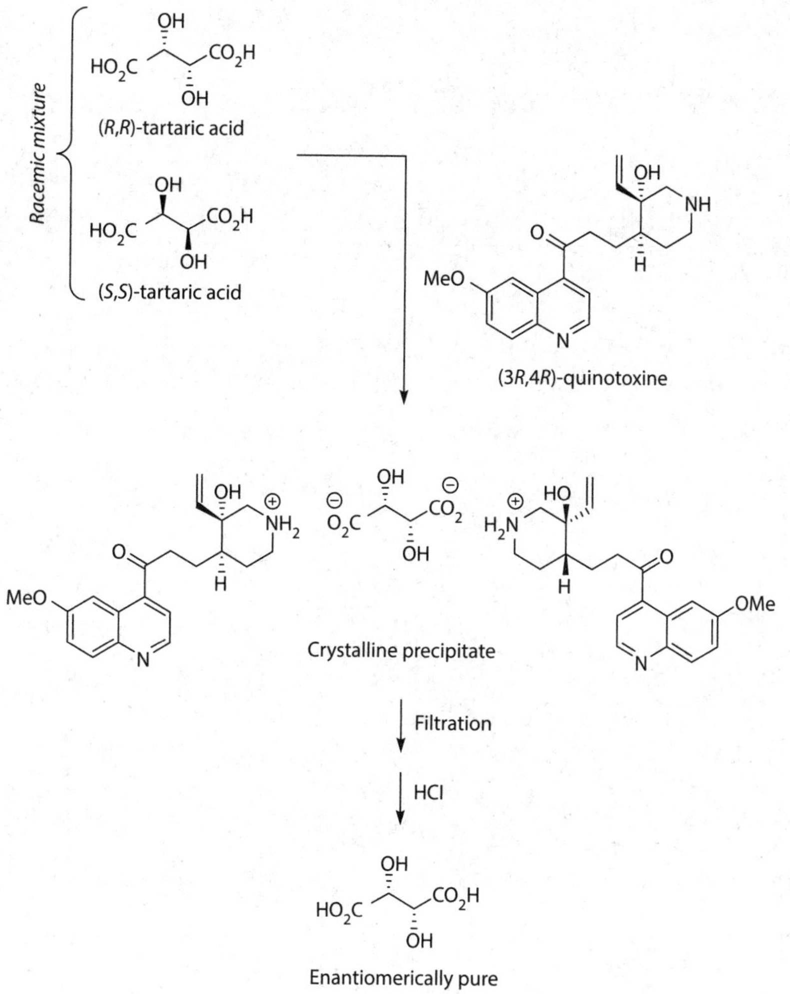

FIGURE 8-13 Chiral resolution of racemic tartaric acid using quinotoxine.

identical physical properties (solubility, melting point, etc.), so it would be impossible to separate enantiomers based on solubility differences. However, with the addition of a chiral amine (quinotoxine), a set of *diasteromeric* salts are formed (*R*, *R*-acid + *R*, *R*-base, and *S*, *S*-acid + *R*, *R*-base). Unlike enantiomers, diastereomers can have radically different physical properties. In this case, the (*R*, *R*-acid + *R*, *R*-base) diastereomer is insoluble, but the (*S*, *S*-acid + *R*, *R*-base) diastereomer remains in solution.

The second general approach to chiral resolution is through HPLC with the use of a **chiral stationary phase**. In this technique, silica gel is derivatized with an enantiomerically pure chiral species (such as the quinine-based stationary phase shown in Figure 8-14). When a mixture of enantiomers travels through such a column, one enantiomer tends to interact more strongly with the chiral stationary phase (another diastereomeric relationship), thereby slowing down its progress through the column.

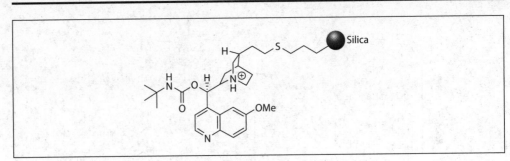

FIGURE 8-14 Example of a chiral HPLC stationary phase.

As with the standard techniques discussed earlier, chromatographic separation is a more expensive approach to chiral separation, but generally a more versatile option.

Structure, Function, and Reactivity of Biologically Relevant Molecules

Read This Chapter to Learn About

➤ Nomenclature of Organic Compounds
➤ Fundamental Reaction Mechanisms
➤ Chemistry of Biologically Important Compound Classes

NOMENCLATURE OF ORGANIC COMPOUNDS

If organic chemistry is a language, then organic compounds constitute its basic vocabulary. Thus, the mastery of basic nomenclature is essential for understanding and communicating organic phenomena.

IUPAC Nomenclature

The entrée into organic nomenclature is typically the class of compounds known as the **simple alkanes**, straight-chain hydrocarbons that are named according to the number of carbons in the chain (see the following table). The first four alkanes bear nonintuitive, historically-derived names; however, from pentane onward they are constructed from the Latin roots. If used as a substituent, the names are modified by changing the suffix -*ane* to -*yl*; thus a two-carbon alkane is ethane, but a two carbon substituent is ethyl.

TABLE 9-1 Simple Alkanes

Name	Number of Carbons	Formula
methane	1	CH_4
ethane	2	CH_3CH_3
propane	3	$CH_3CH_2CH_3$
butane	4	$CH_3(CH_2)_2CH_3$
pentane	5	$CH_3(CH_2)_3CH_3$
hexane	6	$CH_3(CH_2)_4CH_3$
heptane	7	$CH_3(CH_2)_5CH_3$
octane	8	$CH_3(CH_2)_6CH_3$
nonane	9	$CH_3(CH_2)_7CH_3$
decane	10	$CH_3(CH_2)_8CH_3$
undecane	11	$CH_3(CH_2)_9CH_3$
dodecane	12	$CH_3(CH_2)_{10}CH_3$

In the case of **branched alkanes**, **International Union of Pure and Applied Chemistry (IUPAC)** rules dictate that the longest possible chain be used as the main chain, and all remaining carbons constitute substituents. If two different chains of equal length can be identified, then the one giving the fewest number of substituents should be chosen. For example, in Figure 9-1 two 7-membered chains are possible (highlighted in blue). However, the left-hand choice is preferred, since it gives two substituents—as opposed to the right-hand option, which gives only one substituent. This rule may seem arbitrary, but more substituents means less complex substituents, so naming is easier.

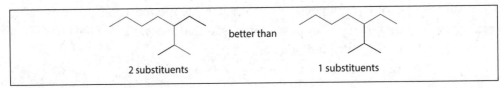

FIGURE 9-1 Maximizing substituents.

The key to understanding IUPAC nomenclature is realizing that it follows syntactical rules just like any other language. A basic premise of this syntax is that there can be only one main chain in a compound, which is grammatically analogous to a noun. Once identified, this main chain may be appended with as many substituents as necessary, but they are always auxiliaries, much like adjectives and adverbs. The following table illustrates this concept with the use of sentence diagrams. Thus in the name, "5-propyldecane," *propyl* is an adjective and *decane* is the noun it modifies.

265

CHAPTER 9:
Structure, Function,
and Reactivity
of Biologically
Relevant Molecules

TABLE 9-2 The Syntax of Nomenclature

Expression	Diagram
embellishment	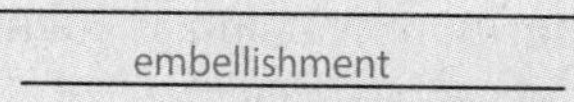 embellishment
embellished **woodwork**	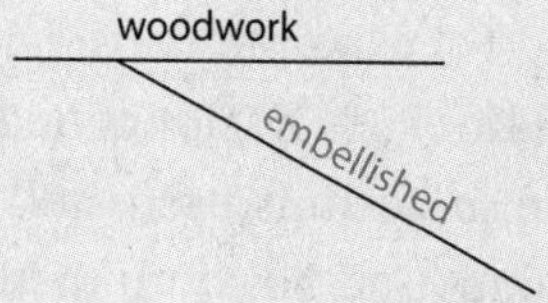 woodwork / embellished
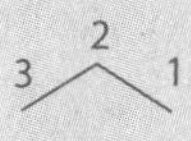 propane	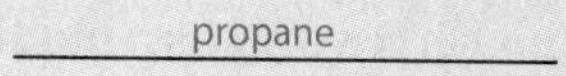 propane
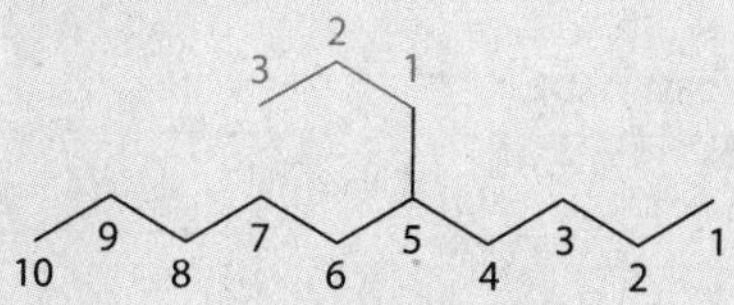 5-propyl**decane**	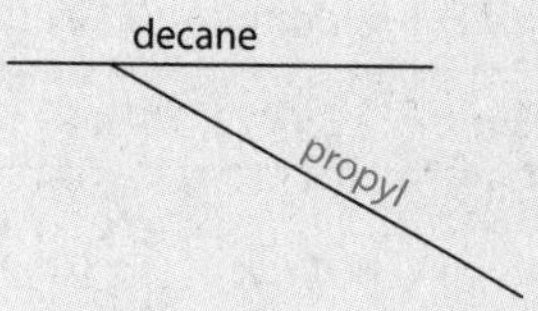 decane / propyl

Generally, compounds contain **functional groups**, which are atomic assemblies associated with certain properties or reactivities, such as the hydroxy group ($-OH$) or the carbonyl group ($R_2C = O$). For the purposes of nomenclature, IUPAC has assigned priorities to these functional groups, as illustrated in the following table.

TABLE 9-3 IUPAC Priorities of the Functional Groups

Functional Group	Formula	As a Parent Compound	As a Modifier
carboxylic ester	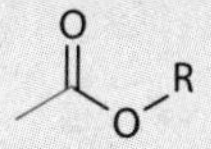	alkyl -oate	—
carboxylic acid	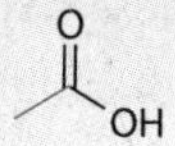	-oic acid	carboxy-
acyl halide	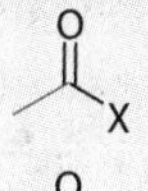 X = Br, Cl, F	-oyl halide	—
carboxamide	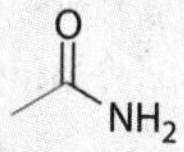	-amide	—
nitrile	$-CN$	-nitrile	cyano-
aldehyde	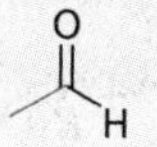	-al	oxo-
ketone	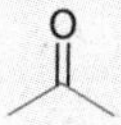	-one	oxo-
alcohol	$-OH$	-ol	hydroxy-
amine	$-NH_2$	-amine	amino-
ether	$-OR$	(only as modifier)	alkoxy-
nitro	$-NO_2$	(only as modifier)	nitro-
halide	$-X$ X = F, Cl, Br, I	(only as modifier)	halo- (e.g., chloro-)

When molecules contain functional groups, then the **parent chain** is defined as the longest possible carbon chain *that contains the highest order functional group*. Once that parent chain is identified, then all other functionalities become **substituents** (modifiers).

For example, consider the two compounds in the following table. Both contain the hydroxy (—OH) functional group, but in the top it defines the parent chain. Therefore, the *-ol* form is used, and the compound is named *propan-2-ol*. However, the lower compound has both the hydroxy and the carbonyl functional groups. Since the carbonyl has the higher IUPAC priority, it defines the parent chain; the hydroxy group thus serves only as a modifier, and the *-ol* suffix is not used.

TABLE 9-4 Functional Groups in the Main Chain and as Substituent

Name	Diagram
propan-2-ol	propan-2-ol
5-(2-hydroxypropyl)decan-3,6-dione	decan-3,6-dione propyl hydroxy

Double bonds add an interesting wrinkle in the process. While they do not carry much priority alone, the parent chain should contain the highest order functional group and as many double bonds as possible, even if this means that a shorter parent chain will be obtained or if other functionality will be excluded. For example, the compound in Figure 9-2 contains four functional groups: the carboxylic acid, carbonyl, hydroxy, and alkenyl functionalities. Of these, the carboxylic acid has highest priority, so the parent chain must include it. It is tempting to also include the carbonyl group to make a 13-carbon chain; however, IUPAC dictates that both double bonds be included (as highlighted), even though this results in a shorter 9-carbon chain that does not encompass the carbonyl functionality.

As the previous examples illustrate, a parent chain may contain multiple functional groups of the same type, or a functional group with one or more double bonds. Using the grammatical analogy, this is like having a compound noun (e.g., *boxcar*). In the former case, appropriate prefixes are used (i.e., *di-*, *tri-*, etc.); in the latter, the *en-* prefix is used, as shown in the following table. However, aside from the alkene, two different

267

CHAPTER 9:
Structure, Function,
and Reactivity
of Biologically
Relevant Molecules

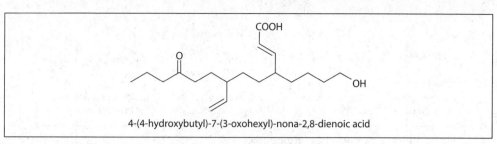

4-(4-hydroxybutyl)-7-(3-oxohexyl)-nona-2,8-dienoic acid

FIGURE 9-2 Naming a multifunctional acyclic compound.

functional groups may not be included in the same parent chain. For example, if an alcohol and a ketone are present in the same molecule, it must be named as a ketone with a hydroxy substituent.

TABLE 9-5 Examples of Multiple Functionalities in the Parent Chain

Multiple Functionalities in the Parent Chain That Are Consistent with IUPAC	Multiple Functionalities in the Parent Chain That Are Not Consistent with IUPAC
Propanedioic acid · · · Propan-1,3-diol	IUPAC: 4-hydroxypentan-2-one (NOT pent-2-on-4-ol)
But-3-en-1-ol · · · Pent-4-en-2-one	IUPAC: 3-oxobutanoic acid (NOT butan-4-on-1-oic acid)

In summary, the parent chain should be established using the following guidelines (in order of priority):

1. Include the highest order functional group.
2. Include as many double bonds as possible.
3. Select the longest carbon chain (with the maximum number of substituents).

Compounds containing cyclic arrays of carbon atoms are known as **carbocycles**. The presence of a ring does not change any of the considerations discussed so far; however, it does force a choice. Either the ring becomes the parent chain or it is part of some substituent. Being cyclic does not confer any special consideration—if it happens to represent the longest chain with the highest-order functional group, then it is the parent chain; otherwise, it is a substituent. Figure 9-3 shows two examples of compounds in which the ring is the parent and two in which the ring is a substituent.

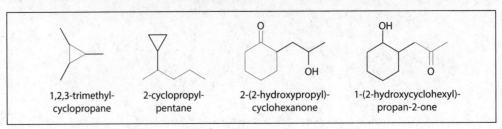

1,2,3-trimethyl-
cyclopropane

2-cyclopropyl-
pentane

2-(2-hydroxypropyl)-
cyclohexanone

1-(2-hydroxycyclohexyl)-
propan-2-one

FIGURE 9-3 Examples of carbocyclic compounds.

Common Nomenclature

With a pretty good understanding of nomenclature rules in hand, consider some miscellaneous vocabulary used by organic chemists to describe carbon centers (Figure 9-4). One set of terms arises from considering how many other carbons are attached to a given center. If a carbon has only one other carbon attached to it, then it is designated a primary (1°) center; if two other carbons are attached, it is a secondary center, and so on. This terminology is also used for substituents, so if a chloro substituent is attached to a carbon that is attached to two other carbons, it is said to be a secondary chloride.

The other way to describe carbon centers is by examining how many hydrogens are attached. Carbons with three hydrogens are called methyl groups; those with two are methylene groups; and those with only one are known as methines. Obviously, these are closely-related terminologies, but they have subtle differences and are used for slightly different purposes.

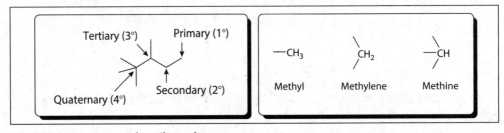

FIGURE 9-4 Two ways to describe carbon centers.

After having touched on common nomenclature, it would also be useful to come to terms with the subject and become conversant with names still found in everyday usage. First consider the pentane molecule on the left side of the following table. When all five carbon atoms are lined up in a row, it is called normal pentane, or *n*-pentane. However, imagine an isomer of pentane in which a methyl group is shifted to the next carbon. Since this isomer has five carbons, old nomenclature still considers it a pentane, but it is clearly a different molecule. Therefore, it is designated isopentane. Finally, a third isomer is possible by connecting all four methyl groups to a common atom. Again, a different molecule is formed, but the name *isopentane* is already taken; with a focus on its newness, it is called *neopentane*.

269

CHAPTER 9:
Structure, Function,
and Reactivity
of Biologically
Relevant Molecules

These three pentane structures can also be used as substituents, as shown (blue line showing point of attachment). Notice that the isopentyl group ends with a bifurcated carbon chain, or a fork. Likewise, the neopentyl group terminates with a three-pronged carbon array. However, all three of these substituents (*n*-pentyl, isopentyl, and neopentyl) are considered primary, since the point of attachment is connected to only one other carbon.

To illustrate secondary and tertiary substituents, consider the three isomeric butanols (see the following table). Normal butanol (*n*-butanol) is a straight-chain primary alcohol. If the hydroxy group is attached to an internal carbon, then it becomes a secondary alcohol, so old nomenclature designates this *sec*-butanol (IUPAC: butan-2-ol). You can also imagine four-carbon alcohol in which the hydroxy group is attached to a tertiary site—this is known as *tert*-butanol, or *t*-butanol (IUPAC: 1,1-dimethylethanol). There is one notable exception to these patterns, namely isopropanol—strictly speaking, it should be called *sec*-propanol, but convention has settled on the former.

TABLE 9-6 Common Substituent Names

Parent	Substituent	Parent	Substituent
n-pentane	*n*-pentyl	*n*-butanol	*n*-butyl
isopentane	isopentyl	*sec*-butanol	*sec*-butyl
neopentane	neopentyl	*tert*-butanol	*tert*-butyl

In addition to substituent oddities, old nomenclature also has different ways of naming parent compounds, some of which are illustrated in Figure 9-5. Sometimes the roots are different, as in formic acid and formaldehyde (vs. methanoic acid and methanal). Other cases seem to be fairly arbitrary, as in acetone and benzophenone. However, there is a logic that underlies some of the common nomenclature. For example, ketones and ethers were named as if the carbonyl or oxygen were a bridge—so any ketone would be named by the two substituents plugged into the carbonyl (e.g., methyl ethyl ketone; ethyl isopropyl ether). Similarly, amines were named by the three substituents plugged into the nitrogen.

From a depictional standpoint, structures in this text and other sources will often be simplified using abbreviations. The following table provides a sampling of some of the more common abbreviations, along with their names and corresponding structures. The bottom three entries are used for generic substituents, so that one structure can represent many possibilities.

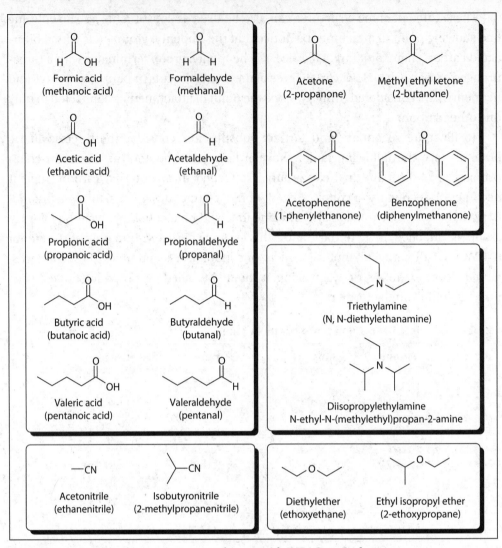

FIGURE 9-5 Examples of common nomenclature (with IUPAC equivalents).

TABLE 9-7 Common Substituent Abbreviations

Abbreviation	Substituent	Structure
Me	methyl	$-\xi\ CH_3$
Et	ethyl	
Pr	propyl	
i-Pr	isopropyl	
Bu	butyl	
t-Bu	*tert*-butyl	

271

CHAPTER 9:
Structure, Function,
and Reactivity
of Biologically
Relevant Molecules

TABLE 9-7 Common Substituent Abbreviations (cont.)

Abbreviation	Substituent	Structure
Ph	phenyl	
Bn	benzyl	
Bz	benzoyl	
Ts	tosyl	
Ms	mesyl	
R	alkyl	any aliphatic group
Ar	aryl	any aromatic group
Ac	acyl	

Naming Stereoisomers

In addition to specifying connectivity, it is often necessary to communicate unequivocally as to how substituents are oriented in space, which enters into the realm of stereochemistry. As far as nomenclature is concerned, there are two types of stereochemistry: absolute and relative.

Absolute stereochemistry deals with the geometry about a chiral center. Thus the relevant nomenclature deals with how to name a given enantiomer. Since any chiral carbon is surrounded by four different things, the first order of business is to prioritize the substituents according to the IUPAC convention known as the **Cahn-Ingold-Prelog (CIP) rules**. The algorithm for CIP prioritization is as follows:

1. Examine each atom connected directly to the chiral center (called the "field atoms"); rank according to atomic number (high atomic number has priority).
2. In the event of a field atom tie, examine the substituents connected to the field atoms.
   (a) Field atoms with higher-atomic-number substituents win.
   (b) If substituent atomic number is tied, then field atoms with more substituents have priority.

For the purposes of prioritization, double and triple bonds are expanded—that is, a double bond to oxygen is assumed to be two oxygen substituents. If two or more field atoms remain in a tie, then the contest continues on the next atom out for each center, following the path of highest priority.

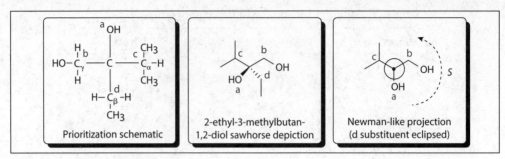

FIGURE 9-6 R/S Designation using CIP rules.

To illustrate the application of the CIP rules, consider the assignment of an enantiomer of 2-ethyl-3-methylbutan-1,2-diol shown in Figure 9-6. The sawhorse depiction in the center shows the three-dimensional arrangement of the atoms. To assign CIP priorities, it is useful to think of the structure with all atoms written out explicitly, as shown on the left. Here the field atoms are an oxygen and three carbons, labeled C_α, C_β, and C_γ. Of the four atoms, the oxygen wins and therefore bears highest priority (a). The next step is to examine the substituents on the remaining field carbons: C_α is connected to two carbons and a hydrogen, C_β is connected to a carbon and two hydrogens, and C_γ is connected to an oxygen and two hydrogens. So assign C_γ as second priority (b), since it is connected to the highest atomic number substituent (oxygen); C_α then assumes third priority (c), since it is connected to two carbons rather than one.

The next step is to orient the molecule so that the lowest-priority field atom (d) is going directly away from you, as is shown on the right side of Figure 9-6. Viewing this projection, observe whether the progression of a → b → c occurs in a clockwise or counterclockwise sense. If clockwise, the enantiomer is labeled *R*; if counterclockwise, *S*. Note that this is simply a nomenclature convention, and it has no relationship to physical reality. Enantiomers are called **dextrorotatory** (*d*) if they rotate plane-polarized light to the right, and **levorotatory** (*l*) if they rotate light to the left. There is no correlation between *R/S* nomenclature and *d/l* behavior.

To add the enantiomeric designation to a chemical name, simply append the information to the far left side and include it in parentheses. The position of the chiral center is also included. Thus 2-ethyl-3-methylbutan-1,2-diol becomes (2*S*)-2-ethyl-3-methylbutan-1,2-diol. If the molecule contains multiple chiral centers, then the designations are simply arranged by number in the same set of parentheses.

As the descriptor suggests, **relative stereochemistry** describes the relationship of two substituents with respect to each other. For example, in cycloalkanes two groups may be situated on the same face (*cis*) or on opposite faces (*trans*), as illustrated in Figure 9-7. The same nomenclature applies to disubstituted alkenes, where the two substituents can be directed toward the same side (*cis*) or opposite sides (*trans*) of the double bond. Unlike enantiomers, these stereoisomers often have markedly different physical properties (boiling points, etc.).

273

CHAPTER 9:
Structure, Function,
and Reactivity
of Biologically
Relevant Molecules

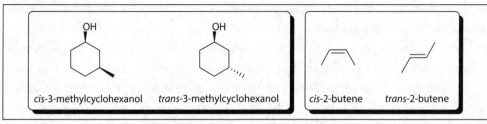

FIGURE 9-7 Relative stereochemistry in cycloalkanes and alkenes.

A more general method for specifying the stereochemistry of alkenes has been adopted by IUPAC. In this protocol, each double bond is virtually rent in two and the substituents on each side are prioritized according to the CIP rules described previously (see Figure 9-8, inset). If the two high priority substituents (a) are pointing in the same direction, the double bond is specified as Z (from the German, *zusammen*, or together); if they point in opposite directions, the double bond is designated E (*entgegen*, or across from). Adding this stereochemical information to the chemical name proceeds exactly as described for R/S designation.

FIGURE 9-8 Stereochemistry of alkenes using CIP (E/Z).

FUNDAMENTAL REACTION MECHANISMS

Even though organic reactions can proceed through seemingly complex mechanisms, there are really just a few basic mechanistic steps that make up the majority of pathways. The most common of these are presented here.

Proton Transfer (p.t.)[1]

Perhaps the most fundamental (but also sorely misapprehended) polar reaction step is the **proton transfer**. Often obscured by the rubric of "acid–base" chemistry, confusion

---

[1]The nomenclature of the fundamental reaction mechanisms is taken from Scudder, P. H. *Electron Flow in Organic Chemistry: A Decision-Based Guide to Organic Mechanisms.* Hoboken, New Jersey: Wiley, 2013.

about the proton transfer begins with neglect of the physical reality behind the process. A **proton** is simply that: a single atomic particle adorned only with its positive charge, like a lacrosse ball being shuttled back and forth between so many tiny electronic nets. A proton transfer is like a hydrogen bond gone to the extreme, and transferable protons are typically those that would be part of hydrogen bond donors; in fact, the transition state for a proton transfer is best described as a hydrogen bond. With this backdrop, it is time to come to terms with the terminology of acids and bases.

There are three general paradigms of acid–base chemistry, as shown in following table. **Arrhenius** developed one of the earliest theories, which led to a broad understanding of acids as proton donors (e.g., HCl) and bases as hydroxide donors (e.g., NaOH). However, in time there were species recognized to exhibit basic behavior that harbored no apparent hydroxide moiety (e.g., ammonia). The **Brønsted theory** reconciled this difference by redefining bases as proton acceptors: ammonia accepts a proton from water and in so doing generates hydroxide. Thus the Brønsted theory did not really affect the roster of recognized acids, but it expanded the understanding of bases considerably.

TABLE 9-8 Three Acid–Base Paradigms

Paradigm	Definition of Acid (example)	Definition of Base (example)
Arrhenius	proton donor (HCl)	hydroxide donor (NaOH)
Brønsted	proton donor (HCl)	proton acceptor (NaOH, **NH$_3$**)
Lewis	electron density acceptor (HCl, **Fe^{3+}**, **BF$_3$**)	electron density donor (NaOH, NH$_3$)

Lewis did for acids what Brønsted did for bases. Brønsted's focus was on the proton and how it is liberated and sequestered by chemical entities. Lewis looked at this situation from the other angle—that is, in terms of what is accepting the proton. If a proton transfer is indeed the extreme form of hydrogen bonding, and if a hydrogen bond donor is potentially anything with a lone pair, then the act of accepting a proton could also be viewed as a donation of electron density. Thus Lewis defined bases as electron density donors and acids as electron density acceptors. This definition really did not expand the realm of bases—in other words, ammonia was still a base whether it was seen as accepting the proton or donating a lone pair for the proton's capture. However, it revolutionized the view of acids. Arrhenius acids were still Brønsted acids, and Brønsted acids were still Lewis acids, but their acidity was based on the activity of a proton—and while the proton is undoubtedly an acceptor of electron density, it is only one of a wide array of electron density acceptors. For example, the iron(III) cation is known to lower the pH of aqueous solutions, but it clearly has no source of protons. However, under the Lewis acid definition, you can see how it functions as an acid in terms of accepting electron density from the six water molecules that form an octahedral arrangement in solution. Ultimately, this complex also provides Brønsted acidity by liberation of a proton (see Figure 9-9).

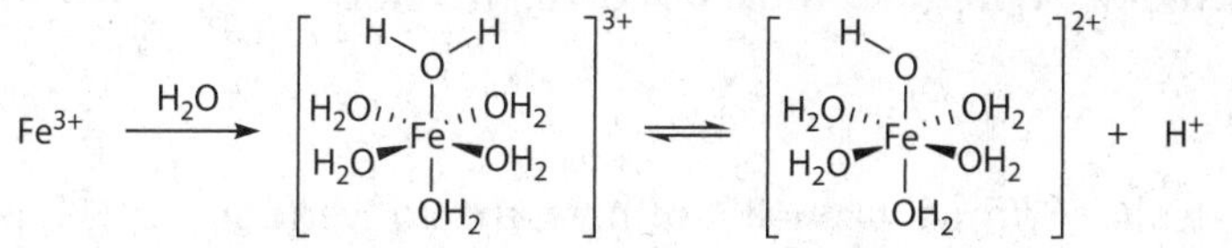

275

CHAPTER 9:
Structure, Function,
and Reactivity
of Biologically
Relevant Molecules

FIGURE 9-9 The aqueous acidity of iron(III) cation.

However, the Lewis definition also extends both acidic and basic behavior into non-aqueous environments, which has obvious significance for organic chemistry. For example, boron trifluoride is a stereotypical Lewis acid, since it only has 6 electrons about boron and therefore is eager to accept an extra electron pair. So Lewis acidic is BF_3 that when dissolved in diethyl ether, it forms a very strong complex with the solvent (see Figure 9-10) in which the ether oxygen bears a formal positive charge and the boron bears a formal negative charge—a species known as a **Lewis acid–Lewis base complex**.

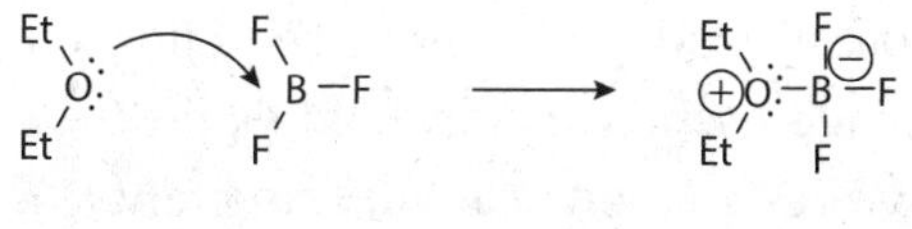

FIGURE 9-10 Formation of a Lewis acid–Lewis base complex.

The Lewis acid–base concept is a workhorse for understanding much of the mechanistic underpinnings of polar chemistry. However, proton transfer can be treated using the Brønsted classification of acids and bases.

Here it is useful to pause and review some basic principles related to Brønsted acidity, beginning with the most familiar proton donor and carrier: water. Pure water provides very low background levels of hydroxide and proton through an equilibrium process known as **autoionization** (see Figure 9-11).

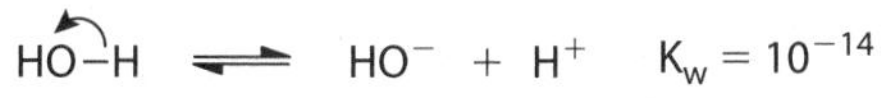

FIGURE 9-11 The autoionization of water

This process is governed by an **equilibrium constant** (given the special designation of K_w) on the order of 10^{-14}. If the equilibrium constant is written in terms of chemical species, you have:

$$K_w = \frac{[H^+][HO^-]}{[H_2O]} = [H^+][HO^-] \qquad (1)$$

where the denominator term drops out of the expression because the concentration of water does not change in the system. Assuming that the only source of proton (or more accurately, hydronium) and hydroxide in pure water is the autoionization process, then the two quantities must be equal; therefore:

$$[H^+] = [HO^-] = \sqrt{10^{-14}} = 10^{-7} \tag{2}$$

To avoid dealing with very small numbers, the convention of pH has been established to express these concentration values, such that:

$$pH = -\log_{10}[H^+] \tag{3}$$

Therefore, if the proton concentration is 10^{-7}, then the pH is 7. An analogous scale, pOH, is used for the hydroxide concentration. In pure water then, the pH and pOH are both 7. When acids or bases are added to the water, the proton or hydroxide levels are increased, respectively. However, in aqueous systems Equation 1 must still be satisfied. Thus as hydroxide levels increase, proton levels must decrease, and vice versa. This constraint can be expressed in terms of pH and pOH as follows:

$$pH + pOH = 14 \tag{4}$$

Similar conventions have been constructed around the expression of acid and base strength. For example, the experimentally derived equilibrium constant for the ionization of acetic acid can be represented as shown in Figure 9-12, where the equilibrium constant bears the special designation of **acidity constant** (K_a).

$$AcO-H \rightleftharpoons AcO^- + H^+ \quad K_a = 2.0 \times 10^{-5}$$

FIGURE 9-12 The ionization of acetic acid

You can also express the acidity constant in terms of chemical species, which has the generic form:

$$K_a = \frac{[H^+][A^-]}{[HA]} = \frac{[H^+][AcO^-]}{[HOAc]} \tag{5}$$

In addition, an analogous scale of pK_a can be used to express the numerical values of the acidity constant according to the relationship:

$$pK_a = -\log_{10}(K_a) \tag{6}$$

Therefore, acetic acid is associated with a pK_a value of 4.7.

There are a few general trends that can be gleaned from the inspection of pK_a values. First, if you understand a strong acid to be one that ionizes to a large extent (i.e., the ionization is a right-handed equilibrium), then you would expect the acidity constant to be greater than unity and consequently the pK_a to be less than zero. By the same token, a weak acid does not completely ionize, so the equilibrium would lie to the left, the acidity constant would be less than unity, and the pK_a value would be greater than zero. However, the more important general trend for the organic chemist is *the lower the pK_a, the stronger the acid.*

277

CHAPTER 9:
Structure, Function,
and Reactivity
of Biologically
Relevant Molecules

A similar construct is used for the strength of bases, which involves pK_b values, and for any conjugate acid–conjugate base pair:

$$pK_a = 14 - pK_b \tag{7}$$

Because of this relationship, organic chemists often take the shortcut of only dealing with pK_a values, whether regarding acids or bases. In other words, ammonia is associated with a pK_b of 4.7, but also with a pK_a of 9.3. Not surprisingly, when values are associated to species in this backward way, the trend is also reversed—that is, *the stronger the base, the higher the corresponding pK_a.*

It is best to think of the pK_a as belonging not to a particular species, but to an equilibrium system involving a conjugate pair. For example, the ammonia/ammonium equilibrium can be expressed as shown in Figure 9-13. Thus ammonium *acting as an acid* (i.e., giving up a proton) has a pK_a of 9.3 and ammonia *acting as a base* (i.e., accepting a proton) is associated with the same pK_a of 9.3. This way, the same data can be used to predict behavior for two different species. In other words, ammonium would be expected to behave as a weak acid and ammonia expected to behave as a weak base.

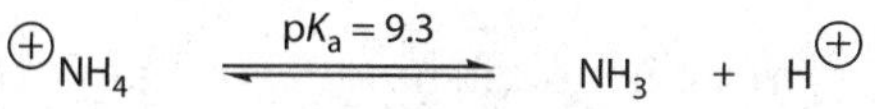

$$^{\oplus}NH_4 \quad \underset{}{\overset{pK_a=9.3}{\rightleftharpoons}} \quad NH_3 \quad + \quad H^{\oplus}$$

FIGURE 9-13 The ammonia/ammonium conjugate pair.

However, ammonia is **amphoteric**—that is, it can also function as an acid, giving up a proton to form the amide anion (see Figure 9-14). This equilibrium is associated with a much higher pK_a of 36. According to the acidity and basicity trends discussed earlier, the conclusion has to be that ammonia is an extremely weak acid and amide is an extremely strong base.

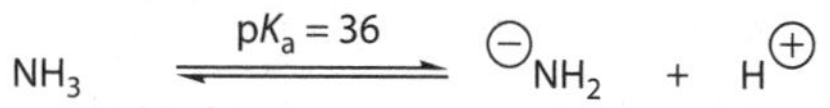

$$NH_3 \quad \underset{}{\overset{pK_a=36}{\rightleftharpoons}} \quad ^{\ominus}NH_2 \quad + \quad H^{\oplus}$$

FIGURE 9-14 The ammonia/amide conjugate pair.

Water is also an amphoteric species—it can act as an acid and lose a proton to form hydroxide, a process with a pK_a of 15.7, or it can function as a base, accepting a proton to become hydronium, which is associated with a pK_a of –1.7. With these two data points, you can draw the following conclusions:

1. Water is a very weak acid.
2. Water is a very weak base.
3. Hydronium is a strong acid.
4. Hydroxide is a strong base.

The following table summarizes benchmark pK_a ranges for some commonly encountered species. Internalizing these benchmarks will help for making sense of other pK_a values discussed in subsequent sections.

TABLE 9-9 Some Useful pK_a Benchmarks

Protonated Form	Deprotonated Form	pK_a
Example of amines acting as acids		
NH_3	NH_2^-	38.0
$(i\text{-}Pr)_2NH$	$(i\text{-}Pr)_2N^-$	36.0
Example of water/alcohols acting as acids		
MeOH	MeO^-	15.7
H_2O	HO^-	15.7
Example of amines acting as bases		
Et_3NH^+	Et_3N	11.0
NH_4^+	NH_3	9.3
HCN	CN^-	9.2
AcOH	AcO^-	4.7
Example of water/alcohols acting as bases		
$MeOH_2^+$	MeOH	−1.7
H_3O^+	H_2O	−1.7
HCl	Cl^-	−7.0
HBr	Br^-	−9.0

Two principles are important in understanding trends in acidity and basicity. First, the strength of an acid and its conjugate base are inversely proportional. In other words, the stronger the acid, the weaker its conjugate base—for example, hydrochloric acid is a very strong acid, whereas chloride is all but nonbasic. Second, it is easiest to understand acid strength in terms of the stability of the anion produced—that is, as the consequent anion becomes more stable, the more likely an acid is to donate a proton to generate that anion. Thus the ability to predict the stability of an anion is helpful in judging the strength of its conjugate acid.

One trend in anion stability can be related to **electronegativity**. For example, examining the simple anions in the latter region of the second row on the periodic table reveals a left-to-right periodic trend (see Figure 9-15). Thus from the methyl anion (pK_a 49) to the fluoride anion (pK_a 3.2) there is a steady increase in anion stability going from left to right, which corresponds to an increasing electronegativity of

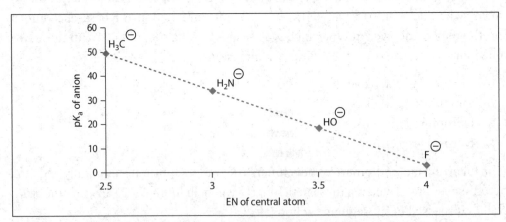

FIGURE 9-15 Anion stability as a function of electronegativity (EN).

279

CHAPTER 9:
Structure, Function,
and Reactivity
of Biologically
Relevant Molecules

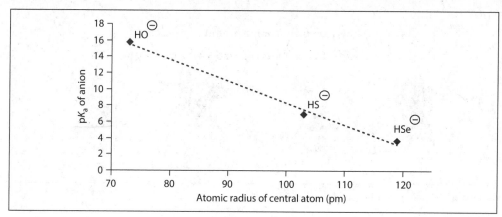

FIGURE 9-16 Anion stability as a function of atomic radius.

the central atom (C → N → O → F). If electronegativity relates to the tendency of an atom to hold onto electron density, then the tighter the electron density is held, the less likely it is to engage in reactivity (such as capture of a proton). Therefore, the more electronegative species tend to be weaker bases.

A similar trend is observed in a vertical cross-section of the periodic table (see Figure 9-16). For example, comparing the simple anions of Group 16, steadily decreasing pK_a values can be observed going from top to bottom. This trend can be rationalized on the basis of **atomic radius**—that is, the larger the volume that the negative charge has to occupy, the more stable the species. Another way to understand this is that larger molecules can minimize electron-electron repulsions more effectively. In summary, anion stability (and thus conjugate acid strength) increases from left to right on the periodic table, and from top to bottom. Making diagonal comparisons becomes more difficult and nonintuitive. For example, silane (SiH_4) is just as acidic as ammonia (NH_3), but arsine (AsH_3)—all the way down in the fourth period—is still 7 pK_a units (i.e., 10 million times) less acidic than water (H_2O).

In more complex molecules, acidity and basicity can be modulated through inductive and resonance effects, as well. For example, compared to acetate's pK_a of 4.7, trifluoroacetate (see Figure 9-17, left) has a pK_a of –0.3, an observation that can be rationalized based on the electron-withdrawing nature of the three fluorine atoms, which stabilize the adjacent negative charge. This would be classified as an **inductive effect**, since the communication is essentially through the σ bond framework. Alternatively,

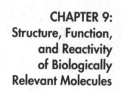

FIGURE 9-17 Inductive and resonance effects on anion stability.

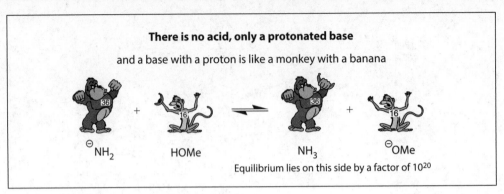

There is no acid, only a protonated base

and a base with a proton is like a monkey with a banana

Equilibrium lies on this side by a factor of 10^{20}

FIGURE 9-18 The simiamorphic proton transfer.

anions can be stabilized through **resonance effects**, as seen in the phenolate anion (Figure 9-17, right), which is almost a million times less basic than methoxide. This difference can be explained by the resonance delocalization of the negative charge throughout the aromatic system.

With this thorough grounding in acid and base strength, you are now prepared to deal with the question of proton transfer *per se*. In other words, how do you use these concepts to predict whether a proton transfer is likely or not? First of all, consider any proton transfer to be an equilibrium at the first approximation. Next, the equilibrium should be cast as a competition between two bases for the same proton—only one base can have the proton at a given time. Consider the behavior of amide (H_2N^-) in methanol (HOMe). Figure 9-18 paints a somewhat unconventional picture of this battle in the form of a chimp and a gorilla fighting for a single banana—assuming pure brawn wins the day, the gorilla will walk away with the prize. To put this in more chemical terms, the two bases vying for the proton are amide (pK_a 36) and methoxide (pK_a 16). Clearly, the amide is the stronger base; therefore the equilibrium will lie to the right, since this is the side that shows the stronger base claiming the proton. Moreover, the magnitude of the equilibrium constant can be estimated by raising 10 to the power of the difference in pK_a values. In this case, $K =$ ca. 10^{20}.

In summary, to estimate the position and magnitude of proton-transfer equilibria, consider the following sequence:

1. Identify the two bases competing for the proton.
2. Assign pK_a values to the bases (not their conjugate acids).
3. Decide which is the stronger base (the higher pK_a).
4. Equilibrium lies on the side that shows the stronger base winning.
5. Equilibrium constant (K) is approximately $= 10^{\Delta pK_a}$.

From a mechanistic standpoint, the proton transfer is quite simple: a lone pair from the basic species attacks the proton and forces it (the proton) to leave its shared electron density behind on the other atom. The proton transfer is also among the fastest reactions known—almost every molecular collision results in effective reaction; thus the rate tends to be controlled by diffusion of the molecules.

281

CHAPTER 9:
Structure, Function,
and Reactivity
of Biologically
Relevant Molecules

Ionization (D$_N$)

Acidity can be described as an ionization event (i.e., an acid loses a proton to become an anion. Another form of ionization is also frequently encountered in organic chemistry—in a sense, it can be thought of as the reverse of a Lewis acid–Lewis base interaction shown in Figure 9-10. In this process, known simply as **ionization**, a sigma bond is cleaved heterolytically to form an **anion** and a **carbocation** (carbon-centered cation). For this reaction to be kinetically relevant, the **leaving group (LG)** must provide a very stable anion, and the carbocation must be secondary, tertiary, or otherwise stabilized (e.g., allylic or benzylic).

It is easy enough to determine whether a substrate will provide a secondary or tertiary carbocation, but the leaving group provides a somewhat more subtle challenge. Fortunately, there is a convenient way to evaluate so-called leaving group ability. In the section on proton transfer, it was concluded that strong acids ionize because they form particularly stable anions. Similarly, an ionization step requires a stable ion to be formed. Thus it follows that the conjugate bases of strong acids make good leaving groups. To state this in the form of a trend, *the stronger the conjugate acid, the better the leaving group.* For example, hydroxide is not a very active leaving group (see Figure 9-19), and if you consider the conjugate acid of hydroxide (namely, water), you would agree that it is a very weak acid (pK_a = 15.7). On the other hand, chloride is a great leaving group; by the same token its conjugate acid (HCl) is without question a very strong acid (p$K_a \ll 0$). Simply by examining a table of pK_a values, you can fairly accurately assess the likelihood of a species to function as a leaving group for ionization reactions.

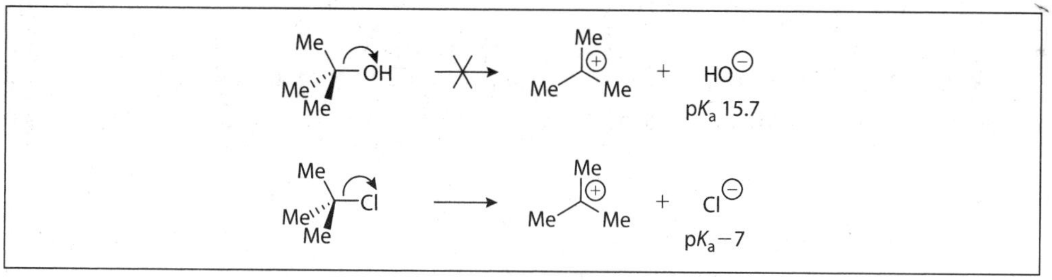

FIGURE 9-19 Impact of leaving group on ionization.

Nucleophilic Capture (A$_N$)

Once a carbocation has been formed, it can suffer subsequent capture by a nucleophile to form a new neutral species. In principle, any species that would be classified as a Lewis base is a potential **nucleophile**, since a nucleophile is also a source of electron density. Even though generic depictions often represent the nucleophile with a negative charge, this is largely stylistic: there are also neutral nucleophilic species. For example, the *t*-butyl carbocation can be captured by methanol (see Figure 9-20) to form an initial adduct that undergoes subsequent proton loss to provide methyl *t*-butyl ether.

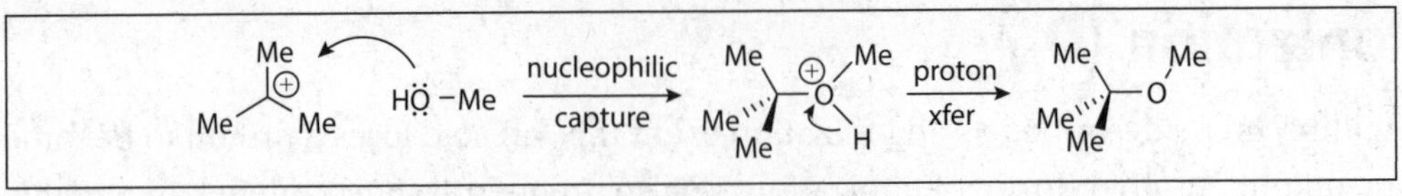

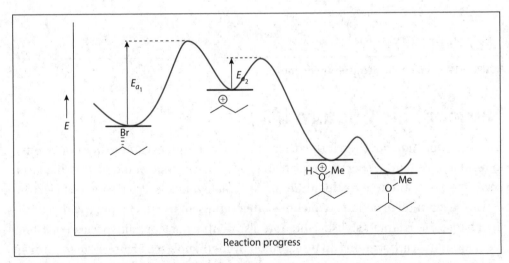

FIGURE 9-20 Nucleophilic capture of *t*-butyl cation by methanol.

When ionization is followed by nucleophilic capture, an overall process known as **unimolecular substitution (S$_N$1)** occurs. An illustrative example is the **solvolysis reaction**, in which solvent molecules act as the nucleophilic species. When 2-bromobutane is dissolved in methanol, ionization ensues to form a secondary carbocation, which is captured by solvent to give (after proton loss) 2-methoxybutane (see Figure 9-21). Note that even though optically pure (*S*)-2-bromobutane is used, the product is obtained as a racemic mixture. The chirality is destroyed in the first step of the mechanism, and the planar carbocation has an equal probability of being attacked from either side by the nucleophile. Indeed, the generation of racemic products from optically pure starting materials is a hallmark of the S$_N$1 reaction.

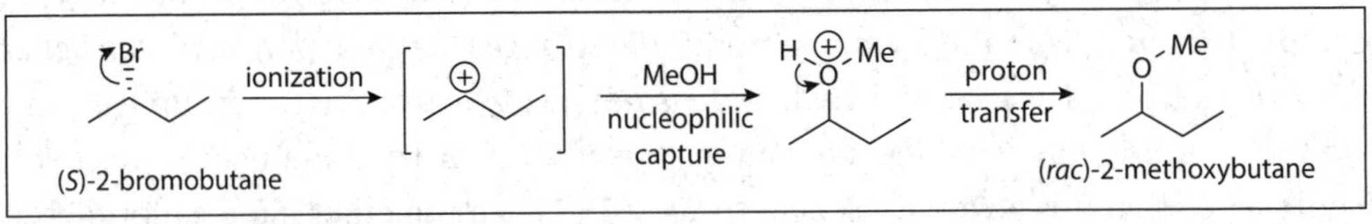

FIGURE 9-21 Solvolysis of 2-bromobutane in methanol.

Another characteristic of this mechanism—as the name implies—is the unimolecular nature of its kinetics. In other words, the rate of the reaction is dependent only upon the concentration of the substrate, according to the rate law:

$$\text{rate} = k[2\text{—bromobutane}] \tag{8}$$

Inspection of the reaction profile (see Figure 9-22) reveals why this is so. Even though there are three discrete steps in the overall mechanism, ionization exhibits the

FIGURE 9-22 The reaction profile of the S$_N$1 mechanism.

283

CHAPTER 9:
Structure, Function,
and Reactivity
of Biologically
Relevant Molecules

highest activation energy. According to the Arrhenius equation, this step is consequently the slowest, or the rate-determining step. Generally speaking, the kinetics of the rate-determining step determine the kinetics of the entire reaction—and since only the 2-bromobutane is involved in the first step, it is the only species that appears in the overall rate law.

Bimolecular Nucleophilic Displacement (S$_N$2)

When the nucleophile is strong enough, substitution can take place directly, without the need for prior ionization. For example, treatment of 2-bromobutane with sodium cyanide leads to direct displacement in one step (see Figure 9-23).

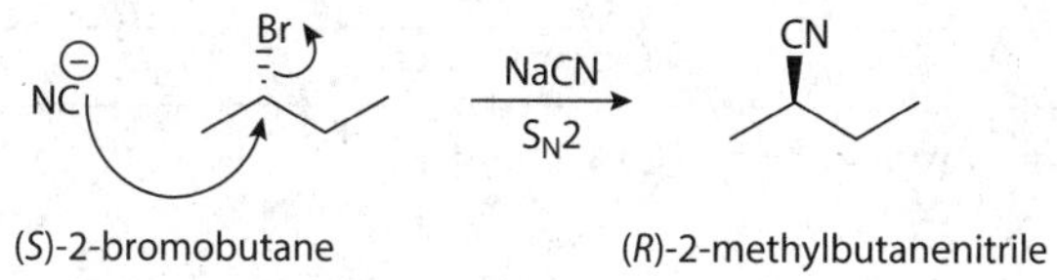

(S)-2-bromobutane   (R)-2-methylbutanenitrile

FIGURE 9-23 S$_N$2 reaction of cyanide with 2-bromobutane.

One significant outcome of the S$_N$2 mechanism is that stereochemical information is preserved. In other words, if the electrophilic center is chiral and the substrate is optically pure, then the product will be optically active, not a racemic mixture. Furthermore, the stereochemistry is inverted about the electrophilic carbon center. This is due to the so-called backside attack of the nucleophile, which approaches the electrophile from the side opposite the leaving group, leading to a trigonal bipyramidal transition state, which is itself a chiral entity (see Figure 9-24). As the reaction proceeds, the three substituents fold back to the other side, much like an umbrella inverting in a gust of wind.

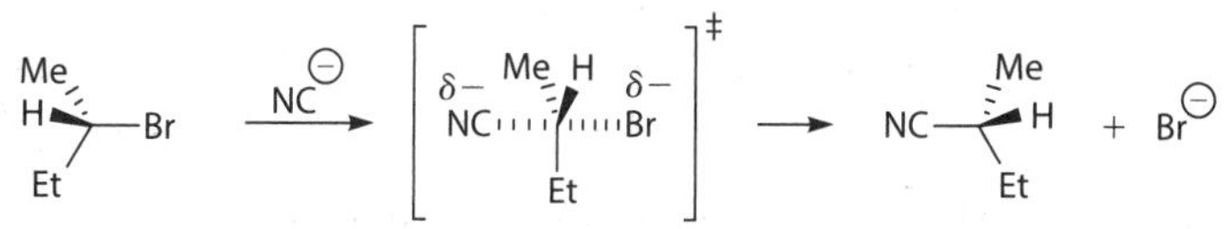

FIGURE 9-24 Inversion of stereochemistry in S$_N$2.

The S$_N$2 reaction proceeds by a concerted mechanism, unlike the stepwise S$_N$1 sequence. A single activation energy governs the kinetics of the process (see Figure 9-25). Since the transition state involves both the substrate and the nucleophile, the rate law must also include terms for both species, as follows:

$$\text{rate} = k[\text{2—bromobutane}][\text{NaCN}] \tag{9}$$

For this reason, S$_N$2 reactions are particularly sensitive to concentration effects—a twofold dilution results in a fourfold decrease in rate.

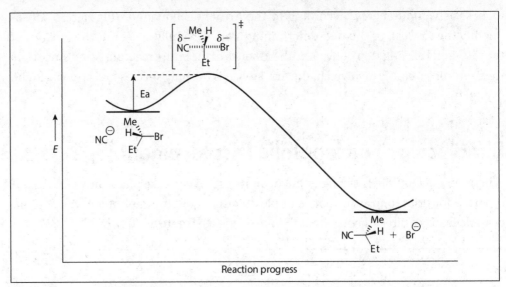

FIGURE 9-25 The reaction profile of the S_N2 mechanism.

Aside from concentration, the rate of the S_N2 reaction also depends upon the nature of the two species involved. Since the backside attack is sterically demanding, S_N2 reactivity drops off as substitution about the electrophilic center increases. Figure 9-26 summarizes the effect of substrate structure on the rate of nucleophilic displacement.

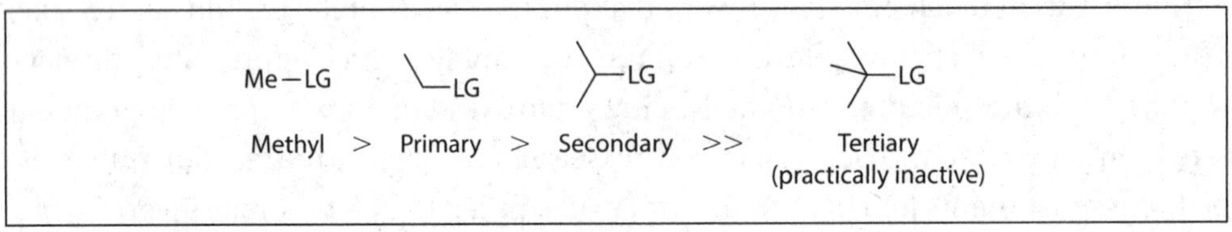

Methyl > Primary > Secondary >> Tertiary (practically inactive)

FIGURE 9-26 Substrate reactivity series for S_N2.

In addition, the strength of the nucleophile has a significant impact on the rate of reaction—the stronger the nucleophile, the faster the S_N2. The following table shows a sampling of some frequently encountered nucleophiles, along with their nucleophilic constants (n_{MeI}). These values are derived experimentally from observing the rate at which the nucleophile engages methyl iodide (an extremely effective electrophile) in S_N2 displacement. As the value of n_{MeI} increases, so does the activity of the nucleophile. Note that these values are logarithmic in nature, much like pH, so that iodide ($n_{MeI} = 7.4$) is roughly 10 times more nucleophilic than hydroxide ($n_{MeI} = 6.5$), which is already quite a competent S_N2 nucleophile.

The tabular data is useful for comparing the strengths of various nucleophiles, but perhaps more important is understanding the periodic trends behind the data. Unlike leaving groups, for which you could apply a simple rule of thumb, predicting nucleophilic behavior is a bit more subtle. However, two general trends are helpful guides. First, there is a left-to-right trend, which can be explored by comparing

285

CHAPTER 9:
Structure, Function,
and Reactivity
of Biologically
Relevant Molecules

TABLE 9-10 Nucleophilic Constants

Species	n_{MeI}	pK_a
MeOH	0.0	−1.7
F^-	2.7	3.5
AcO^-	4.3	4.8
Cl^-	4.4	−5.7
Me_2S	5.3	
NH_3	5.5	9.3
N_3^-	5.8	4.8
PhO^-	5.8	9.9
HO^-	6.5	15.7
Et_3N	6.7	10.7
CN^-	6.7	9.3
Et_3As	7.1	
I^-	7.4	−11.0
Et_3P	8.7	8.7
PhS^-	9.9	6.5
$PhSe^-$	10.7	

Data taken from Pearson, R. G., Songstad, J., *Journal of the Amer-
ican Chemical Society* 1967, 89, 1827; Pearson, R. G., Sobel, H.,
Songstad, J., *Journal of the American Chemical Society* 1968,
90, 319; Bock, P. L., Whitesides, G. M., *Journal of the American
Chemical Society* 1974, 96, 2826. As tabulated in Carey, A., and
Sundberg, R. J. *Advanced Organic Chemistry*. New York, NY:
Springer, 2007.

ammonia ($n_{MeI} = 5.5$) to methanol ($n_{MeI} = 0.0$) and hydroxide ($n_{MeI} = 6.5$) to fluoride ($n_{MeI} = 2.7$). In going *from left to right in a row, nucleophilicity decreases*, a phenomenon that can best be understood in terms of electronegativity: the more tightly
an atom holds onto its electron density, the less likely that electron density is to engage
in other activity, like nucleophilic displacement.

Next there is an up-to-down trend, which is evident in the series of fluoride ($n_{MeI} =$
2.7), chloride ($n_{MeI} = 4.4$), and iodide ($n_{MeI} = 7.4$). Here *nucleophilicity increases
going down a column*. Unlike the first trend, this cannot be explained adequately on
the basis of electronegativity; for example, sulfur and selenium have the same electronegativity (EN = 2.6), yet phenylselenide (n = 10.7) is almost 10 times more effective than phenylsulfide (n = 9.9). The conventional rationale for this effect is that the
attacking centers become larger and more polarizable, which allows the electron density to interact with the electrophilic center at larger intermolecular distances.

The third and most tenuous trend is that *for nucleophiles with the same attacking atom, nucleophilicity tends to track basicity*. Thus the series acetate (AcO^-),
phenoxide (PhO^-), and hydroxide (HO^-) describes successively stronger bases ($pK_a =$
4.8, 9.9, and 15.7, respectively), which are also increasingly more active nucleophiles
($n_{MeI} = 4.3, 5.8,$ and 6.5, respectively). As Figure 9-27 demonstrates, this is a nonlinear
relationship. Keep in mind that when the attacking atoms are different, all bets are off.
For example, iodide ($pK_a = −11$) is a far weaker base than fluoride ($pK_a = 3.5$), but a
far more effective nucleophile.

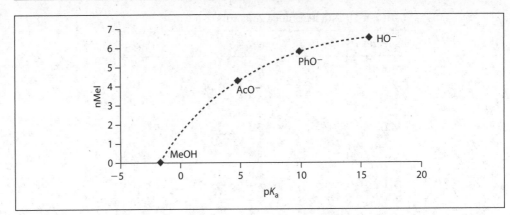

FIGURE 9-27 Correlation of pK_a and n_{MeI} for same attacking atom.

Moreover, structural features can impact the nucleophilicity of certain species. For example, potassium t-butoxide (t-BuOK) is a relatively strong base ($pK_a = 19$), but a poor nucleophile because of steric hindrance about the anionic center. Similarly, lithium diisopropylamide (LDA) is frequently employed as a very strong, non-nucleophilic base, since the anionic nitrogen is imbedded within an almost inaccessible steric pocket. Hexamethyldisilazide (HMDS) is even more sterically encumbered—to function as a nucleophile is a hopeless aspiration (see Figure 9-28).

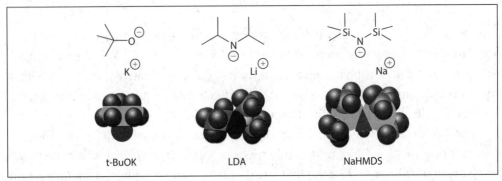

FIGURE 9-28 Sterically hindered anions.

Loss of a Proton to Form a Double Bond (D_E)

When a carbocation has adjacent protons (β-protons), the positive charge on the carbon can be quenched by loss of a proton to form a double bond. The combination of ionization (D_N) and loss of a proton to form a double bond (D_E) is known as **unimolecular elimination (E1)**. Like the S_N1 mechanism, it is stepwise and it is encountered only when a relatively stable carbocation can be formed. This process is exemplified by the dehydration of cyclohexanol in the presence of concentrated sulfuric acid (see Figure 9-29). The mechanism consists of an initial proton transfer, followed by loss of the good leaving group water (ionization), and then loss of a proton to form the alkene.

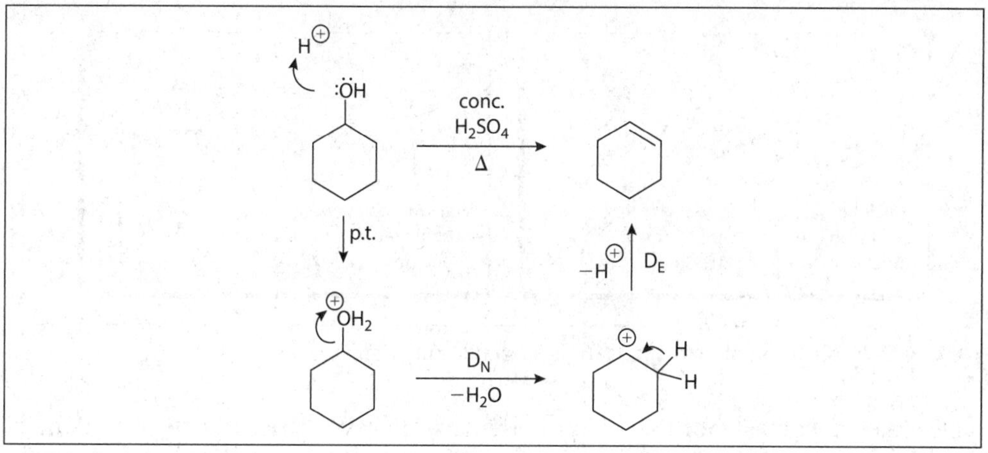

287

CHAPTER 9:
Structure, Function,
and Reactivity
of Biologically
Relevant Molecules

FIGURE 9-29 Dehydration of cyclohexanol via E1 elimination.

Another similarity with S_N1 is the unimolecular nature of its kinetics. In the previous example, the rate of the reaction is dependent only upon the concentration of the cyclohexanol, according to the rate law:

$$\text{rate} = k[\text{cyclohexanol}] \tag{10}$$

Bimolecular Elimination (E2)

With stronger bases, another eliminative pathway becomes feasible, namely **bimolecular elimination (E2)**. This is a concerted process in which the base removes a β-proton as the leaving group leaves. Like the S_N2 reaction, the E2 has a single transition state involving both the base and the substrate; therefore, the observed kinetics are second order and the rate is dependent upon the concentration of both species. Note that as the reaction progresses, two molecules give rise to three molecules, an entropically very favorable result. Therefore, like the E1 mechanism, bimolecular elimination is made much more spontaneous with increasing temperature. A further implication is that, although the **principle of microscopic reversibility** states that the reverse pathway exists, it becomes improbable that the three requisite species will encounter each other in exactly the right geometry to take advantage of that pathway. Thus E2 eliminations tend to be practically irreversible.

It turns out that the β-proton is most susceptible to removal when it is antiperiplanar with respect to the leaving group. The reason for this orientational requirement has to do with orbital overlap between the C—H σ bond and the C—Br σ^* orbital, which is diametrically opposed to the C—Br bond itself. Considering the S_N2 mechanism, for example, the requirement for backside attack also can be rationalized by the σ^* orbital: electron density from the nucleophile lone pair begins to push into the empty antibonding orbital, weakening the corresponding leaving group σ bond and leading to substitution (see Figure 9-30). Similarly, if you think of a base not so much as "pulling off a proton" as "pushing off electron density," then the leaving group σ^* would seem

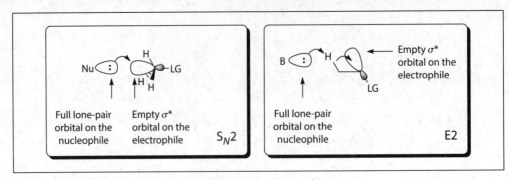

FIGURE 9-30 Implication of σ^* orbitals in bimolecular mechanisms.

to be a likely receptacle for that electron density. However, since the electron density in this case is not coming directly from the base, but rather from the C—H bond being attacked, the C—H bond and the σ^* orbital must be able to communicate—and this is at a maximum when the leaving group is antiperiplanar to the α-proton.

The net result of this constraint is that stereochemical information often transmits from reactant to product. For example, (1S, 2S)-(1-bromo-1-phenyl-2-methylethyl) benzene (see Figure 9-31, top left) undergoes E2 elimination to provide Z-methylstilbene as the sole stereoisomer. To understand this selectivity, it is easiest to depict the substrate as a Newman projection (see Figure 9-31, bottom). Rotating the entire molecule counterclockwise to bring the bromine into the six o'clock position, then rotating the back carbon about the C1—C2 bond to bring the β-proton into the twelve o'clock position, achieves the proper antiperiplanar alignment. Subsequent E2 elimination collapses the molecule to planarity, and becomes clear that the two phenyl groups are indeed on the same side.

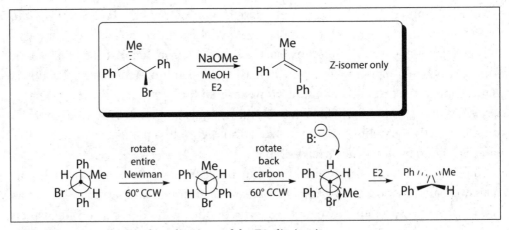

FIGURE 9-31 Stereochemical implications of the E2 elimination.

There are also regiochemical considerations in this reaction, some of which are under our control. For example, consider the E2 elimination of 1-bromo-1-methylcyclohexane under two different sets of conditions (see Figure 9-32). If sodium methoxide is used, the major elimination product is the internal alkene A; however,

289

CHAPTER 9:
Structure, Function,
and Reactivity
of Biologically
Relevant Molecules

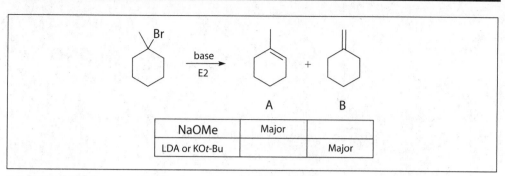

FIGURE 9-32 E2 Elimination of 1-bromo-1-methylcyclohexane.

lithium diisopropylamide (LDA), as well as potassium *t*-butoxide, deliver the product bearing the exo double bond (B) as the predominant isomer.

How can these results be rationalized? First, the outcome with sodium methoxide must be fully understood. Generally speaking, double bonds become thermodynamically more stable as the number of substituents increases. The conventional rationale for this observation is that substituents communicate with *p* orbitals in the π bond through hyperconjugation, in much the same way as you have seen them communicate with (and stabilize) *p* orbitals on radical and carbocationic centers. Using this argument, product A is expected to be thermodynamically more stable by virtue of its more substituted double bond (trisubstituted vs. disubstituted for B). If this stability translates back to the transition state level, then product A is expected to form *faster* and thus accumulate in larger quantities.

Apparently something different is happening with LDA and *t*-butoxide. Keep in mind that these are very bulky bases—as they approach the β-proton, they are very sensitive to the steric environment surrounding it. To produce the more stable product, the base must remove a relatively hindered ring proton—on the other hand, the methyl proton leading to product B is fairly accessible. In other words, changing to a more bulky base alters the relative positioning of the transition states, since steric interactions are worse for the pathway to A versus B. Product A is still thermodynamically more stable, but since the E2 reaction is virtually irreversible, you have trapped the system in a less stable outcome by modifying the activation energies (see Figure 9-33). This is described as using kinetic control to obtain the thermodynamically least stable product.

Nucleophilic Attack of a Double Bond (Ad$_N$)

So far only **nucleophilic attack** at an sp^3-hybridized electrophilic center bearing a leaving group has been discussed. If polar mechanisms involve a flow of electron density from source to sink, then the nucleophile is the electron source and the leaving group is the electron sink. However, another form of electron sink can be imagined—which, after all, is just another way to describe a stabilized negative charge. Figure 9-34 shows two such possibilities. In the first, a nucleophile adds to an electron-deficient

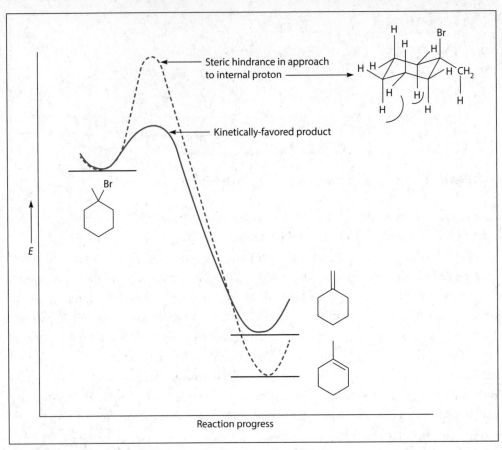

FIGURE 9-33 Kinetic control in the E2 elimination using LDA.

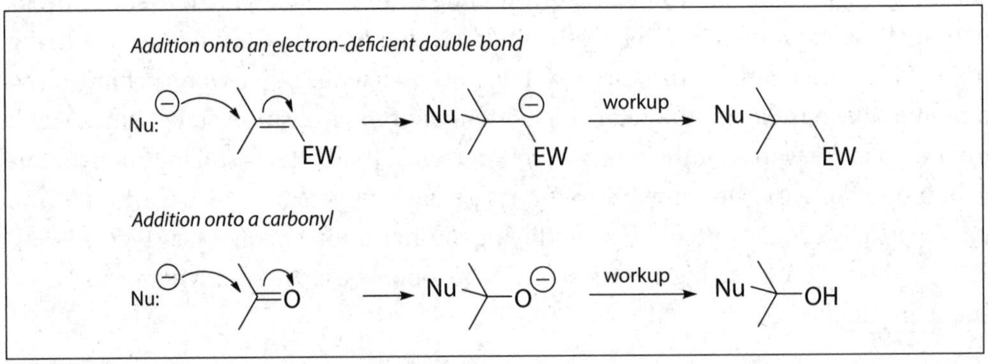

Addition onto an electron-deficient double bond

Addition onto a carbonyl

FIGURE 9-34 Nucleophilic attack at an sp^2 carbon.

double bond in such a way as to place the anionic center adjacent to the stabilizing electron-withdrawing group. This type of reaction is often called conjugate addition, since the stabilizing group is usually a π system in conjugation with the double bond.

The other common mode of addition onto an sp^2 center is by nucleophilic attack onto a carbonyl carbon (see Figure 9-34, bottom). This provides, after aqueous workup, an alcohol—and various modes of carbonyl addition are frequently used for the synthesis of complex alcohols.

291

CHAPTER 9:
Structure, Function,
and Reactivity
of Biologically
Relevant Molecules

Electrophilic Capture of a Double Bond (A_E)

The previous example considers the attack of a nucleophile onto an electron-deficient alkene. However, the large majority of alkenes are actually somewhat nucleophilic. This makes sense if you consider the electronic characteristics of the π bond (see Chapter 7). The π electron cloud is relatively far removed from the coulombic tether of the nuclei. It seems reasonable to assume that the π bond might be polarized toward electropositive species, and in some cases undergo **electrophilic capture**, as illustrated in Figure 9-35.

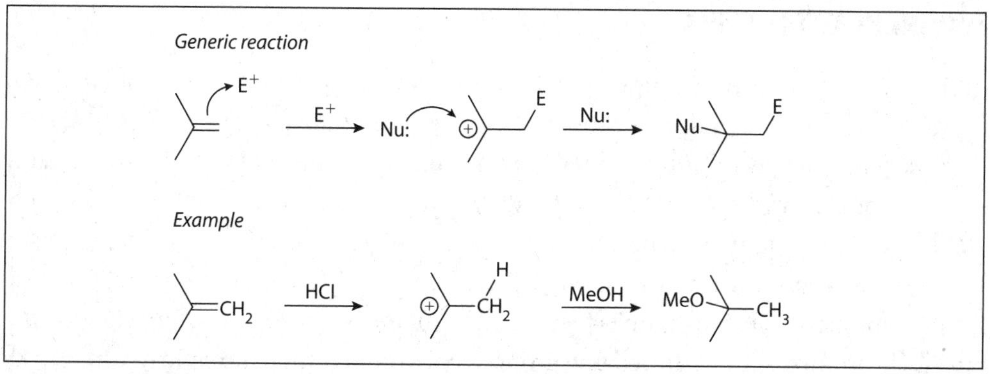

FIGURE 9-35 Electrophilic attack of an alkene.

The carbocation generated by the electrophilic attack is usually trapped by some weak nucleophile (e.g., solvent), much like the second step of an S_N1 reaction. If the alkene is unsymmetrical (i.e., differently substituted on either side of the double bond), then the electrophilic attack will occur in such a way as to give the more substituted (hence, more stable) carbocation. Thus the pendant nucleophile is generally found at the more substituted position. This regiochemical outcome is known as the **Markovnikov effect**, and the more substituted product is dubbed the "Markovnikov" product.

Influences on Reaction Mechanism

The organic chemistry student is often confronted with having to predict whether a given system will react via the S_N1, S_N2, E1, or E2 mechanism. Unfortunately, there is no simple algorithm that generates pat answers; however, a systematic method can be used for assessing each situation and making supportable predictions about reactivity by examining each of several reaction parameters.

SUBSTRATE EFFECTS

First, all four of the reaction mechanisms require a good **leaving group**—without that prerequisite, no system will progress very far. Moreover, the better the leaving group, the faster the reaction. Next, the **electrophilic center** should be characterized—is it

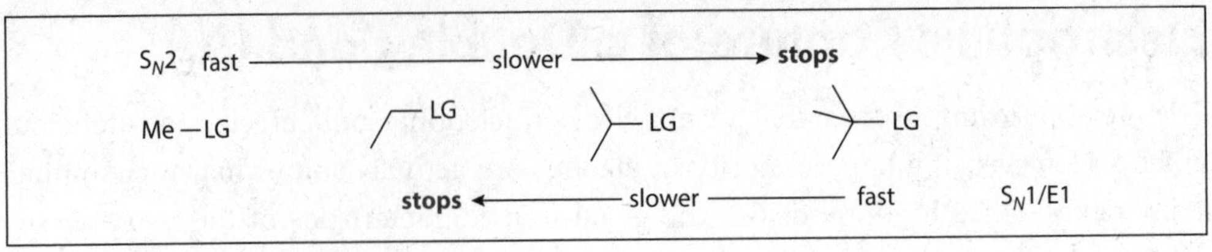

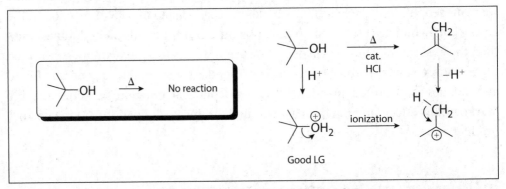

FIGURE 9-36 Substrate trends for S_N2 and $S_N1/E1$.

primary, secondary, or tertiary? If primary, S_N1 and E1 can be ruled out; if tertiary, S_N2 can be excluded. Figure 9-36 summarizes these opposing reactivity trends.

ENVIRONMENT EFFECTS

Another important piece of data is whether the medium is *acidic, neutral,* or *basic.* For example, very basic conditions can favor elimination pathways, since the key step in those mechanisms is proton abstraction. Alternatively, acidic conditions can actually convert poor leaving groups into good ones in situ. To illustrate, *t*-butanol is thermally stable toward E1 elimination because hydroxide (pK_a 15.7) is a poor leaving group (see Figure 9-37, inset). However, in an acidic medium elimination does occur, liberating 2-methylpropene. This reaction is facilitated by an initial proton transfer, whereby the alcohol is protonated and the leaving group is converted from hydroxide to water (pK_a −1.7). Note that the last step liberates a proton, thus completing a catalytic cycle—only a small amount of strong acid needs to be present to promote this reactivity.

FIGURE 9-37 Reactivity of *t*-butanol under neutral and acidic conditions.

NUCLEOPHILE/BASE EFFECTS

Every nucleophile should be suspected of having basic properties and vice versa. Sometimes, the behavior is straightforward—for example, iodide is an excellent nucleophile, but not at all basic; on the other hand, LDA is extremely basic but non-nucleophilic, because of its steric baggage. Very often, however, both basic (i.e., proclivity toward proton abstraction) and nucleophilic (i.e., tendency toward attacking electrophilic carbon) behaviors can be exhibited. Methoxide is a handy example—it is a competent base as well as a nucleophile. Figure 9-38 provides a useful framework for thinking

293

CHAPTER 9:
Structure, Function,
and Reactivity
of Biologically
Relevant Molecules

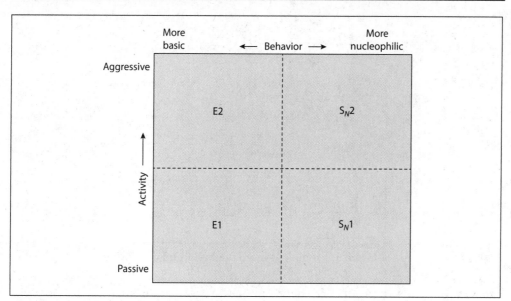

FIGURE 9-38 Cartesian space of the nucleophile or base.

about these properties, that is, in terms of behavior and activity. Since many species can act as either a base or a nucleophile, the **behavior axis** is a way to visualize the idea of a nucleophilicity-to-basicity ratio. For example, phenylsulfide (PhS^-) would have a high Nu/B ratio—because it is more nucleophilic than basic—and t-butoxide would have a low Nu/B ratio, in this case because its nucleophilicity is reduced by sterics. The activity axis is simply a way to think about the magnitude of the nucleophilic or basic property. To illustrate, sodium methoxide would represent a fairly aggressive reagent, which would fall within the upper half of the reactivity space where bimolecular reactions are favored, whereas methanol would be a relatively passive medium, conducive to unimolecular processes in which the leaving group simply leaves without outside influence.

Combined with knowledge of the substrate, this framework can be used to predict the subtle interplay among the reaction mechanisms. Figure 9-39 outlines the various outcomes possible from the interaction of ethyl and t-butyl bromide with methanol and methoxide. In the first example (ethyl bromide with methoxide), the conditions would be characterized as aggressive (i.e., in the upper two quadrants), so the top mechanistic suspects would be S_N2 and E2. Since the electrophile is sterically unencumbered, it is reasonable to expect S_N2 to predominate, although E2 is certainly a contender at high temperatures. In the second example (t-butyl bromide with methoxide), the conditions are still aggressive, but S_N2 can be ruled out altogether because of the steric inhibition of the tertiary center. Thus E2 is the only reasonable choice.

Things get more subtle when only methoxide is absent (second and third examples). Now the conditions are passive, so the lower two quadrants (S_N1 and E1) become most plausible. With the tertiary bromide, both unimolecular mechanisms must be considered, since they are almost always in competition with each other. The

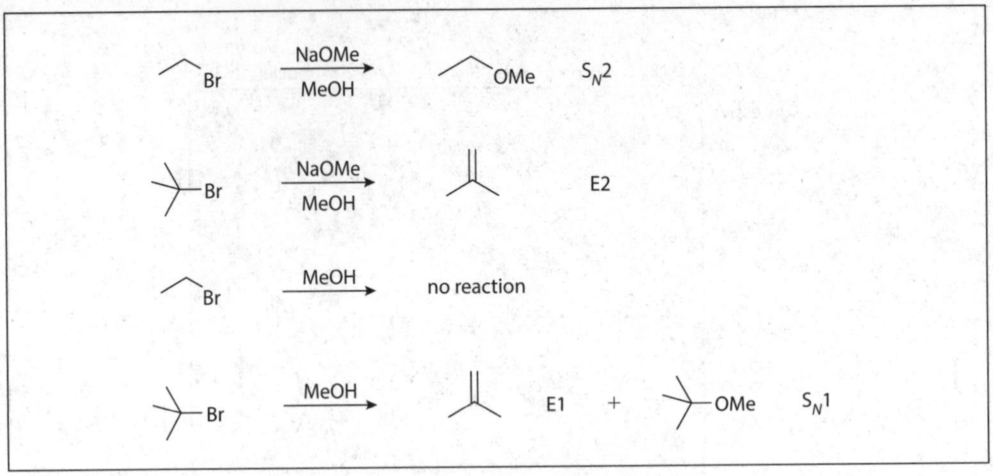

FIGURE 9-39 Behavior of 1° and 3° bromides toward methanol and methoxide.

exact ratio of the two products depends upon the exact conditions, particularly with respect to temperature. However, when a primary halide is used, it would be expected to observe no appreciable reaction. Why? There is no aggressive nucleophile or base (pK_a of methanol is –1.7), nor is it possible for the leaving group to simply leave, because in so doing an unstable primary carbocation would be formed. So the thermodynamically most sensible course to take is to do nothing.

SOLVENT EFFECTS

The rate of S_N1 and S_N2 reactions can be impacted significantly by the choice of solvent. If the transition states for both mechanisms are considered, very different behaviors are encountered as the system approaches the transition state. For example, in a typical S_N2 scenario, a negatively charged nucleophile attacks an electrophilic center. At the transition state, this negative charge is in the act of being transferred to the leaving group—thus the charge is distributed throughout the transition state structure. On the other hand, in the rate-determining ionization step of the S_N1 reaction, a neutral molecule is converted into two charged species; at the transition state, this charge separation is already beginning to occur (see Figure 9-40). Therefore, the stabilization of charges will affect the two mechanisms in very different ways.

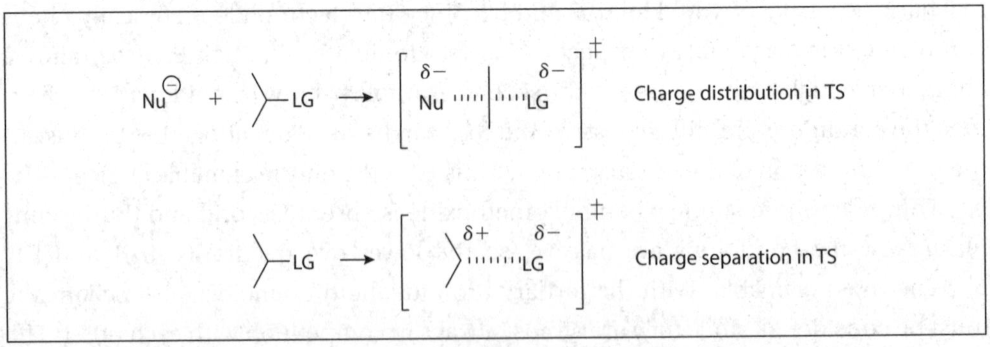

FIGURE 9-40 Differences in S_N1 and S_N2 transition states.

295

CHAPTER 9:
Structure, Function,
and Reactivity
of Biologically
Relevant Molecules

A wide array of solvents are used in organic chemistry; a small sampling is shown in Figure 9-41. The choice of solvent is driven by many practical factors, such as expense, ease of removal, toxicity, flammability, and environmental impact—but there are also mechanistic drivers for running a reaction in a given solvent, particularly in light of the transition state differences discussed previously.

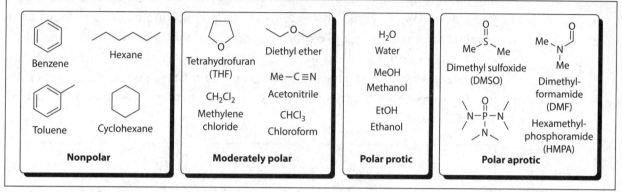

FIGURE 9-41 Some common organic solvents.

For example, **polar aprotic solvents** (DMSO, DMF, HMPA, etc.) are not particularly pleasant or convenient solvents to work with (due to high boiling points and toxicity)—however, they have some peculiar and useful properties, one of which is the differential solvation of ions. The term **aprotic** refers to the fact that these molecules have no protons on heteroatoms (in contrast to water and the alcohols); therefore, they cannot serve as hydrogen bond donors. However, they can stabilize ions by virtue of their polarity. As an illustration, consider a solution of sodium cyanide in DMSO (see Figure 9-42). The sodium cation is very well-stabilized by an organized solvent shell, in which the electronegative oxygen atoms are aligned toward it. However, the cyanide ion is poorly solvated, since the electropositive region of the solvent polar bond is sterically shielded by two methyl groups. The sodium cyanide is drawn into solution because of the overwhelming thermodynamic advantage provided by sodium solvation—but even though the anion is in solution, it is only weakly solvated and very unstable. This is known as the **naked anion effect**, and it results in highly reactive anion species.

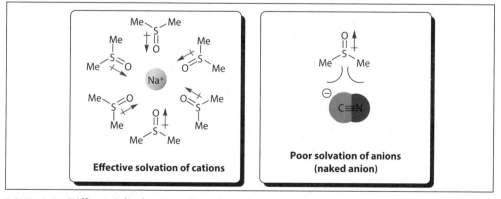

FIGURE 9-42 Differential solvation of ions by polar aprotic solvents.

The naked anion effect can be used to advantage in accelerating the S_N2 reaction. Figure 9-43 shows a hypothetical displacement reaction in two different solvents. In ethanol (left), the anionic nucleophile is stabilized by hydrogen bonding with the protic solvent. In DMSO (right), the nucleophile is poorly solvated and destabilized, and the starting material energy level is consequently increased. The transition state is also affected by this change, but to a much lesser extent—even though it is anionic, the charge is distributed across three atoms. A charge concentrated in a small area (as in cyanide) organizes solvent to a much greater extent than a multicentered array with diffuse charge, so it stands to reason that removal of this stabilization impacts the starting materials more so than the transition state. The end result is that the activation energy is lowered, since the effective energy difference between reactants and transition state is decreased.

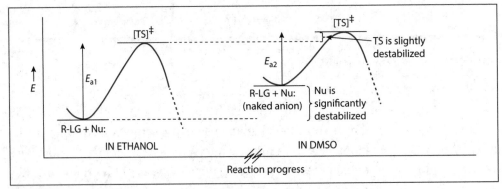

FIGURE 9-43 Acceleration of S_N2 using polar aprotic solvent.

The same principle can be used to rationalize the rate enhancement of S_N1 substitution in **protic solvents** (see Figure 9-44). Compared to an aprotic solvent like THF (tetrahydrofuran), ethanol has the ability to stabilize the nascent charges in the transition state, thereby lowering the activation energy. Generally speaking, the starting material is also slightly stabilized by the more effective solvent, but this is small in comparison to the benefit enjoyed by the transition state. Therefore, the net result is a decrease in the activation energy and an acceleration of the reaction.

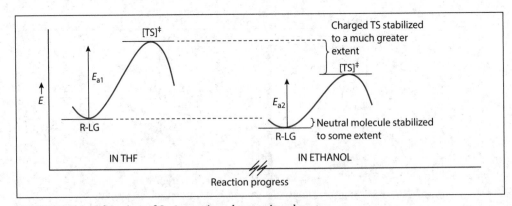

FIGURE 9-44 Acceleration of S_N1 reactions by protic solvents.

297

CHAPTER 9:
Structure, Function,
and Reactivity
of Biologically
Relevant Molecules

In short, the two substitution mechanisms do appear to construct a dichotomy. The following table compares several of the hallmarks for the two mechanisms. For example, the S_N2 reaction results in clean inversion of the electrophilic center, so that any stereochemical information is preserved, whereas the S_N1 pathway leads to scrambling of the stereochemistry at the reactive site. As another example of divergent outcomes, substrates with a primary electrophilic center proceed only through the S_N2 pathway, with S_N1 being unlikely. Conversely, tertiary substrates tend to exhibit only S_N1 behavior, since the steric environment forbids bimolecular displacement. However, secondary electrophilic centers can, in theory, support both types of reactivity—this is where the plot thickens.

TABLE 9-11 Comparison of S_N1 and S_N2 Mechanisms

Behavior	S_N1	S_N2
Overall kinetics	first-order	second-order
Chiral electrophilic centers are	racemized	inverted
Stereochemical information is	destroyed	preserved
Typical nucleophiles	weak	strong
Typical electrophiles	2° or 3°	1° or 2°
Accelerated by	protic solvents	polar aprotic solvents

TEMPERATURE EFFECTS

Just as unimolecular and bimolecular (e.g., S_N1 and S_N2) processes can be in competition with each other, so too can substitution and elimination products arise from the same substrate. One illustration of this phenomenon can be found in the methanolysis of *t*-butyl bromide (see Figure 9-45), in which the initially formed carbocation can either lose a proton to form an alkene or suffer nucleophilic capture by methanol to form (after loss of a proton) methyl *t*-butyl ether.

The most significant point of leverage in controlling this competition is found in the **reaction temperature**. Ultimately, this arises from the fact that **nucleophilic capture** brings two species together to form a single molecule, whereas **elimination** involves a proton transfer from a carbocation to a solvent molecule, thus maintaining

FIGURE 9-45 Competition between E1 and S_N1 mechanisms.

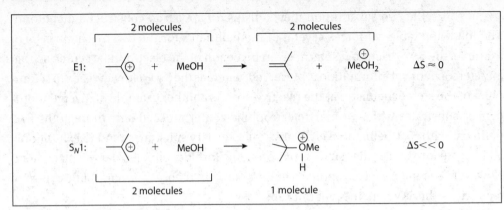

FIGURE 9-46 Entropic differences between E1 and S_N1 mechanisms.

parity between the left and right sides of the chemical equation (see Figure 9-46). As a consequence, the **entropic term** for nucleophilic capture is large and negative (i.e., produces a more ordered system) as opposed to elimination, which is associated with near-zero and sometimes positive entropies of reaction.

The **enthalpic term** is also different: in the previous example, elimination provides a $C-C \pi$ bond worth about 65 kcal/mol, while nucleophilic capture results in a much stronger $C-O \sigma$ bond worth about 90 kcal/mol. Thus were it not for the entropic term, nucleophilic capture would always be the thermodynamically most favorable route. Remember, however, that free energy (and thus spontaneity) is governed by the relationship:

$$\Delta G = \Delta H - T\Delta S \tag{11}$$

Thus as temperature increases, so does the impact of the entropic term. If temperature is kept low, then the enthalpic term dominates and S_N1 is preferred. At higher reaction temperatures, entropic biases begin to emerge until eliminative pathways start to take precedence. The important take-home message is that *as temperature increases, so does the incidence of elimination.*

CHEMISTRY OF BIOLOGICALLY IMPORTANT COMPOUND CLASSES

The incredible molecular diversity in living systems is composed of a remarkably small number of compound classes, the most important of which are discussed here.

Alcohols

The hydroxyl group, the defining characteristic of alcohols, is found in amino acids, such as serine and threonine, as well as the wide landscape of carbohydrates. The following section discusses the preparation and reaction of alcohols.

299

CHAPTER 9:
Structure, Function,
and Reactivity
of Biologically
Relevant Molecules

PREPARATION OF ALCOHOLS

Alkenes are susceptible to acid-catalyzed hydration (Reaction 1) to form the more substituted **alcohol**—the so-called **Markovnikov product**. Under these conditions, p-toluenesulfonic acid (p TsOH) is used as a convenient, organic-soluble source of protons, similar in acidity to sulfuric acid. The **regioselectivity** (that is, *where* the hydroxyl group is installed) is driven by the formation of the more stable carbocation, which is captured by water. A drawback of the methodology is that the carbocations can undergo rearrangement. One way to avoid this unwanted chemistry is to hydrate the double bond in the presence of mercury(II) cation (which acts as a surrogate proton) and then reduce the resulting organomercury intermediate with sodium borohydride, a protocol known as **oxymercuriation/demercuriation** (Reaction 2). The advantage here is that the initially formed mercurinium species never fully opens to a carbocation; therefore, rearrangement is suppressed.

(R1)

(R2)

Alkenes may also be hydrated in an anti-Markovnikov fashion by first being converted to an organoborane intermediate through **hydroboration** (Reaction 3). This species is then subjected to basic oxidative conditions to provide the less substituted alcohol and sodium borate as a by-product. The regioselectivity here is driven not by carbocation stability, but by sterics—the boron (which attaches to what will be the alcohol center) is delivered to the less substituted position.

(R3)

Many synthetically important methods for alcohol synthesis involve **ketones**. For example, ketones and aldehydes can be reduced to the corresponding alcohols by hydride sources, such as lithium aluminum hydride (LAH) and sodium borohydride (Reaction 4). Carbon-based nucleophiles also add to carbonyls. For example, alkyl-magnesium halides serve as sources of carbanions, which add to carbonyls in a protocol known as the **Grignard reaction** (Reaction 5). The nice aspect of this strategy from the synthetic standpoint is that a new carbon-carbon bond is formed in the process, and more complex molecules can be accessed. [Note: as a general convention, this chapter will assume aqueous workup (H_3O^+/H_2O) for all reactions.]

(R4)

(R5)

Reductive strategies can also launch from other carbonyl compounds, such as **esters**. For example, the use of a strong hydride source (such as LAH) leads to the complete reduction of esters to the corresponding alcohols (Reaction 6). Notice that the alcohols produced are necessarily primary.

$$\text{(R6)}$$

Alcohols can be synthesized through the S_N2 displacement reaction using hydroxide as a nucleophile (Reaction 7). Suitable substrates incorporate unhindered electrophilic centers with good leaving groups, such as alkyl halides, tosylates, and mesylates. Since competing elimination is sometimes problematic, primary substrates are preferred.

$$\text{(R7)}$$

X = Br, Cl, I, OTs, OMS

Finally, epoxides suffer ring opening in the presence of a variety of nucleophiles, including hydroxide, alkoxides, amines, and carbanions, to give the corresonding ethanol derivatives (Reaction 8).

$$\text{(R8)}$$

REACTIONS OF ALCOHOLS

Secondary alcohols are oxidized to the corresponding ketones (Reaction 9) in the presence of the **Jones reagent** (potassium dichromate in aqueous sulfuric acid). These conditions are simply a way to produce chromic acid in situ (that is, directly in the reaction vessel), which in turn provides equilibrium quantities of chromium trioxide, the active oxidizing agent. Primary alcohols are oxidized all the way to the carboxylic acid (Reaction 10), since the initially formed aldehyde undergoes hydration to the *gem*-diol (in which two hydroxy groups are on the same carbon) under the conditions—an equally competent substrate for oxidation (see Figure 9-47). The reaction can be stopped at the aldehyde stage (Reaction 11), however, by using pyridinium chlorochromate (PCC). This reagent also provides chromium trioxide, but in a way which does not liberate water (see Figure 9-48). Without water, the aldehyde cannot form the *gem*-diol and is thus trapped.

$$\text{(R9)}$$

$$\text{(R10)}$$

$$\text{(R11)}$$

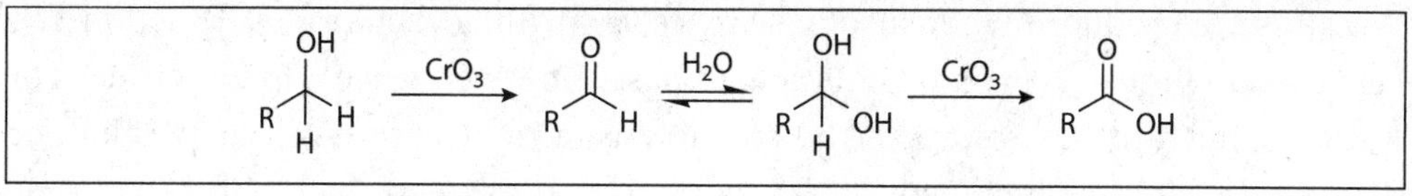

301

**CHAPTER 9:
Structure, Function,
and Reactivity
of Biologically
Relevant Molecules**

FIGURE 9-47 The role of water in the Jones oxidation of primary alcohols.

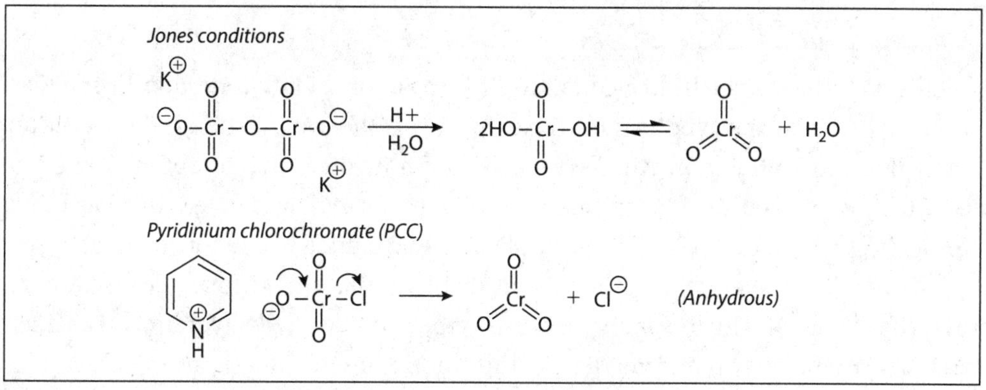

FIGURE 9-48 Two sources for chromium trioxide for oxidation of alcohols.

Often it is useful to convert the hydroxy functionality of alcohols into some other moiety that will serve as a good leaving group. For example, alcohols can be treated with phosphorous tribromide (PBr_3) to give the corresponding alkyl bromide (Reaction 12), or thionyl chloride ($SOCl_2$) to obtain the alkyl halide (Reaction 13). Other good leaving groups include the tosylate (Reaction 14) and the mesylate (Reaction 15) groups. The resulting substrate can then be subjected to nucleophilic substitution of base-catalyzed elimination.

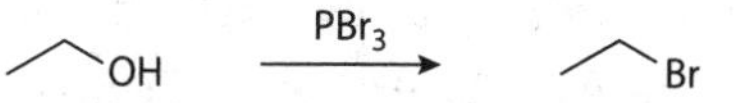

$$(R12)$$

$$(R13)$$

$$(R14)$$

$$(R15)$$

Alcohols are dehydrated in the presence of acid and heat through an S_N1 process (Reaction 16). Two things can be problematic with this protocol. First, regiochemistry can be very hard to control in unsymmetrical alcohols. Second, rearrangements of the intermediate carbocations can lead to product mixtures. A synthetically more relevant method might be to convert the alcohol to a tosylate and then subject it to a base-promoted E2 elimination.

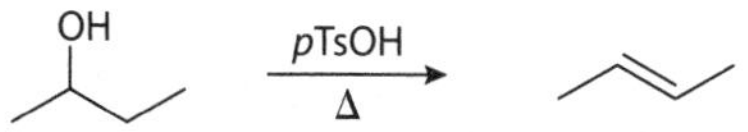

$$(R16)$$

Esters are produced when alcohols are treated with acyl chlorides (Reaction 17). This reaction proceeds even without added base. However, since a full equivalent of HCl is liberated in the course of the alcoholysis, a mild base (such as pyridine or triethylamine) is often included.

$$R-OH \xrightarrow{\quad} \quad (R17)$$

Ethers can be formed from alcohols in either basic or acidic conditions. In practice, however, the base-catalyzed variant (Reaction 18) is the more general. This reaction is known as the **Williamson ether synthesis**, and it involves the deprotonation of an alcohol to form the corresponding alkoxide, which then engages in S_N2 displacement to provide an ether. There is, however, at least one instance where the acid-catalyzed variant provides an avenue not otherwise available, namely in the formation of tertiary ethers (Reaction 19). The mechanism is akin to the acid-catalyzed hydration of alkenes (Reaction 1), whereby an intermediate carbocation is intercepted by the alcohol.

$$R-OH \xrightarrow{\text{base}} \xrightarrow{\quad R' \quad LG \quad} \quad (R18)$$

$$R-OH \xrightarrow[p\text{TsOH}]{\quad} R-O \quad (R19)$$

Aldehydes and Ketones

The chemistry of carbonyl compounds is usually divided into two categories, based on oxidation state: (a) ketones and aldehydes, and (b) carboxylic acid derivatives. The following section discusses the preparation and reaction of aldehydes and ketones.

PREPARATION OF KETONES AND ALDEHYDES

Carbonyl compounds are available from the corresponding alcohols through oxidation. Many reagents can be used for this protocol, but two common examples are the oxidation of secondary alcohols to ketones using Jones conditions (Reaction 9) and the selective oxidation of primary alcohols to aldehydes using PCC (Reaction 11). Of course, PCC (pyridinium chlorochromate) is effective with secondary substrates, as well; in fact, it is the reagent of choice for acid-sensitive alcohols.

$$\xrightarrow[\substack{\text{H}_2\text{SO}_4 \\ \text{H}_2\text{O}}]{\text{K}_2\text{Cr}_2\text{O}_7} \quad (R9)$$

$$\xrightarrow[\text{CH}_2\text{Cl}_2]{\text{PCC}} \quad (R11)$$

303

CHAPTER 9:
Structure, Function,
and Reactivity
of Biologically
Relevant Molecules

When the alcohol is allylic or benzylic, a particularly mild method is available, namely treatment with manganese dioxide in a solvent like methylene chloride (Reaction 20). There are very few other functionalities that are affected by MnO_2, including other alcohols. Thus, allylic and benzylic alcohols can be selectively oxidized in the presence of other alcohol functionality.

$$\text{(R20)}$$

Ketones and aldehydes are also available from the ozonolysis of olefins, or alkenes (Reaction 21). Here two carbonyl compounds are liberated from a single alkene—usually, only one of the products is the desired target. A similar strategy launches from 1,2-diols (aka *vic*-diols), which oxidatively cleave when treated with periodic acid (Reaction 22). Since 1,2-diols can be derived from alkenes by dihydroxylation, this represents an alternative to ozonolysis, which requires very specific (and not universally available) equipment.

$$\text{(R21)}$$

$$\text{(R22)}$$

Aldehydes are also available through a few reductive protocols, including the hydride reduction of acyl chlorides using lithium tri-*t*-butoxyaluminum hydride (Reaction 23), and the selective reduction of esters and nitriles using DIBAL (Reactions 24 and 25, respectively). In the latter case, the initial product is an imine, which is liberated during workup and undergoes acid-catalyzed hydrolysis to the aldehyde under those conditions (see Figure 9-49). In the reduction of both esters and nitriles, the selectivity derives from the nature of the initial adduct, in which the isobutyl groups on the aluminum sterically hinder the addition of another equivalent of hydride.

$$\text{(R23)}$$

$$\text{(R24)}$$

$$\text{(R25)}$$

Terminal alkynes are hydrated in predictable ways to give ketones and aldehydes. For example, the mercury(II)-catalyzed Markovnikov hydration of a terminal alkyne provides the corresponding methyl ketone (Reaction 26). The initially formed product is a so-called enol, which is rapidly isomerized to the carbonyl through a process known as the keto-enol tautomerization (see Figure 9-50). This is really an equilibrium

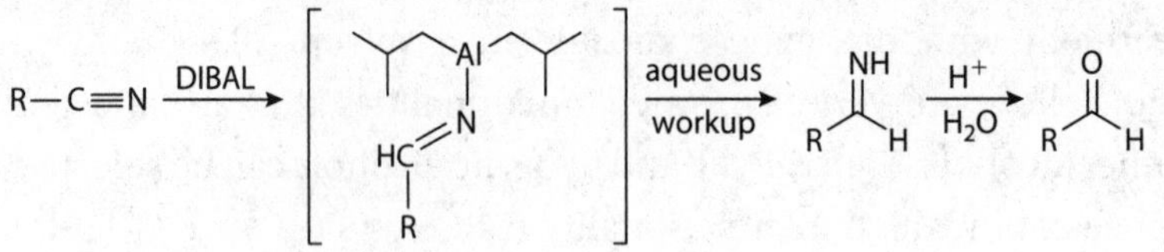

FIGURE 9-49 DIBAL reduction of nitriles.

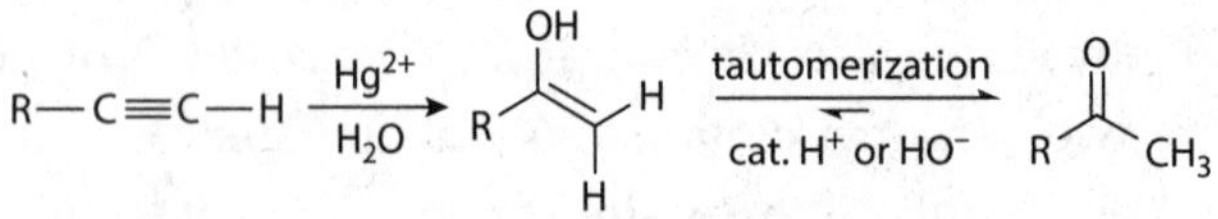

FIGURE 9-50 Keto-enol tautomerization after hydration of an alkyne.

process mediated by either acid or base—in almost all cases, the position of equilibrium lies strongly in favor of the keto form. Anti-Markovnikov hydration of alkynes is also possible using bulky dialkylboranes, such as dicyclohexylborane or disiamylborane (Sia$_2$BH), followed by oxidative workup (Reaction 27). The role of the bulky alkyl groups is to provide greater steric bias in the addition.

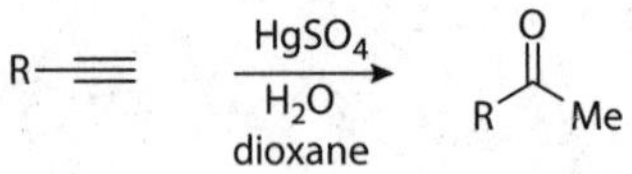

$$\text{(R26)}$$

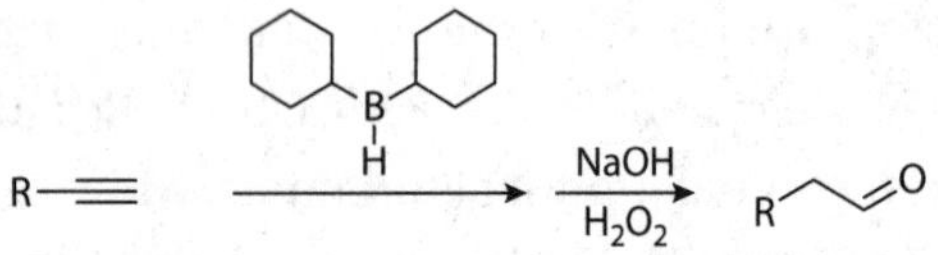

$$\text{(R27)}$$

REACTIONS OF KETONES AND ALDEHYDES

Almost all reactions involving the carbonyl group can be understood in terms of three zones of reactivity (see Figure 9-51). The most familiar of these is the electrophilic carbonyl carbon, made electron-deficient by polarization of both the σ and the π bonds. As a consequence, this center is susceptible to nucleophilic attack. Second, the oxygen's lone pairs can serve as a locus of weak Lewis basicity, which can coordinate to Lewis acids (including protonation). Finally, anions α to the carbonyl are stabilized

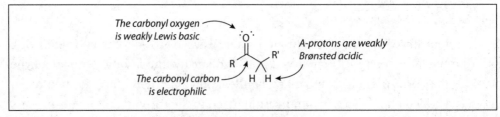

FIGURE 9-51 Three zones of reactivity for the carbonyl group.

305

CHAPTER 9:
Structure, Function,
and Reactivity
of Biologically
Relevant Molecules

by a resonance form that places the negative charge on oxygen; therefore, carbonyl compounds can be deprotonated at the α-position in strong base.

Starting with reactions that involve the carbonyl carbon, ketones and aldehydes can be reduced to the corresponding alcohols using sodium borohydride or LAH—ketones give secondary alcohols, while aldehydes provide primary alcohols (Reaction 4). Carbonyls are also attacked by carbon-based nucleophiles, such as organolithiums and organomagnesium compounds (**Grignard reagents**). The products of these reactions are alcohols in which a carbon-carbon bond has been formed (Reaction 5).

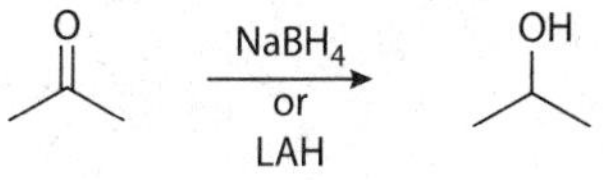

$$\text{(R4)}$$

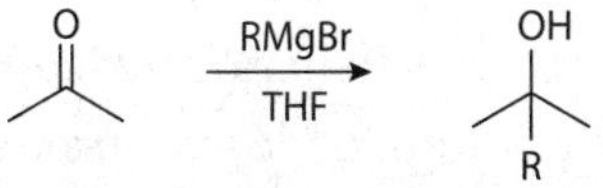

$$\text{(R5)}$$

Ketones and aldehydes are converted to alkenes by the action of phosphonium ylides in a protocol known as the **Wittig reaction** (Reaction 28), which proceeds through initial nucleophilic attack on the carbonyl carbon. The key intermediate in this reaction is the four-membered heterocyclic ring, the oxaphosphetane, which thermally fragments (retro [2 + 2] cycloaddition) to provide the alkene and triphenylphosphine oxide as a by-product.

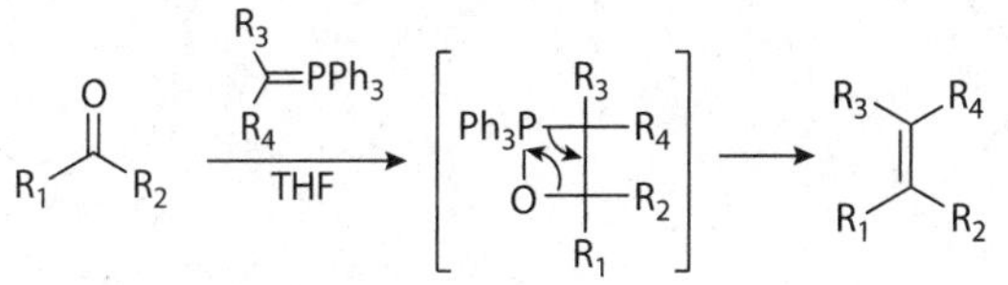

$$\text{(R28)}$$

As a marginal note, although the Wittig reagents look like arcane species, in fact they are quite straightforward to synthesize using triphenylphosphine, a powerful nucleophile that reacts with a broad array of alkyl halides to give alkylated phosphonium salts (see Figure 9-52). These phosphonium salts are acidic by virtue of the strong electron-withdrawing character of the positively-charged phosphorus center—deprotonation with n-butyllithium provides the corresponding ylide.

Carbonyl compounds are converted to acetals by treating with an excess of alcohol in the presence of catalytic quantities of a strong acid, such as p-toluenesulfonic acid (Reaction 29). This is an equilibrium system, which has a favorable enthalpic term (trading a C—O π bond for a C—O σ bond) but an unfavorable entropic term (three molecules going to two molecules). The latter issue is often addressed by using

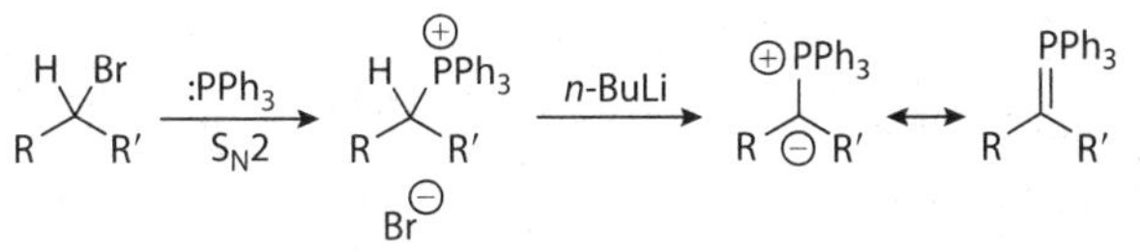

FIGURE 9-52 Preparation of a Wittig reagent.

ethylene glycol (1,2-ethanediol) as the alcohol component, so both hydroxy groups are carried by a single molecule. However, even in the best of circumstances you are often presented with an equilibrium mixture. The classical approach to solving this problem is to use a large excess of alcohol (usually employed as the solvent) to drive the equilibrium forward through Le Châtelier's Principle. If the alcohol happens to be precious and/or the limiting reagent, then an alternative is to sequester the water on the right side with a desiccant, thereby "pulling" the reaction forward. Conversely, to hydrolyze the acetal, the strategy is to add plenteous quantities of water and heat.

$$\underset{R_1 \quad R_2}{\overset{O}{\|}} + 2\,MeOH \underset{}{\overset{\text{cat.}\ p\text{TsOH}}{\rightleftharpoons}} \underset{R_1 \quad R_2}{\overset{MeO \quad OMe}{}} + H_2O \tag{R29}$$

Primary amines add to carbonyls to give **imines** through a sequence of nucleophilic addition, followed by loss of water. The initially formed iminium ion loses a proton to give the observed product (Reaction 30). In the case of a secondary amine, the iminium ion cannot be quenched by loss of a proton on nitrogen, so a proton is lost from the adjacent carbon, yielding an **enamine** (Reaction 31). These reactions are also reversible, so that exposure of imines and enamines to slightly acidic aqueous medium generally yields the starting ketones.

$$\underset{R_1 \quad R_2}{\overset{O}{\|}} \xrightarrow[\text{MeOH}]{R_3-NH_2} \underset{R_1 \quad R_2}{\overset{N^{\,R_3}}{\|}} \tag{R30}$$

$$\underset{R_1 \quad R_2}{\overset{O}{\|}} \xrightarrow[\text{MeOH}]{} \underset{R_1 \quad R_2}{} \tag{R31}$$

Imines can also be intercepted with hydride in situ (i.e., in the same pot) to provide a new amine (Reaction 32). The hydride addition step is a nitrogen analog of carbonyl reduction (Reaction 4); in this case, cyanoborohydride is used as the hydride source, primarily because it is stable toward the reaction conditions. Overall, this process, known as **reductive amination**, converts a carbonyl compound to an amine in one pot.

$$\underset{R_1 \quad R_2}{\overset{O}{\|}} \xrightarrow[\substack{NaBH_3CN \\ MeOH}]{R_3\diagdown\underset{H}{N}\diagup R_4} \underset{R_1 \quad R_2}{\overset{R_3\diagdown N\diagup R_4}{}} \tag{R32}$$

Next turn your attention to reactivity at the α-carbon. Due to the electron-withdrawing character of the carbonyl group, aldehydes and ketones can be deprotonated to form α-carbanions. You have encountered carbanion chemistry before with organomagnesium (Grignard-type) compounds, but those are relatively basic species. The so-called enolate anions derived from carbonyls, however, are less basic and—to some extent—more versatile in their chemistry. One frequently encountered reactivity involves subsequent alkylation with typical electrophiles (Reaction 33).

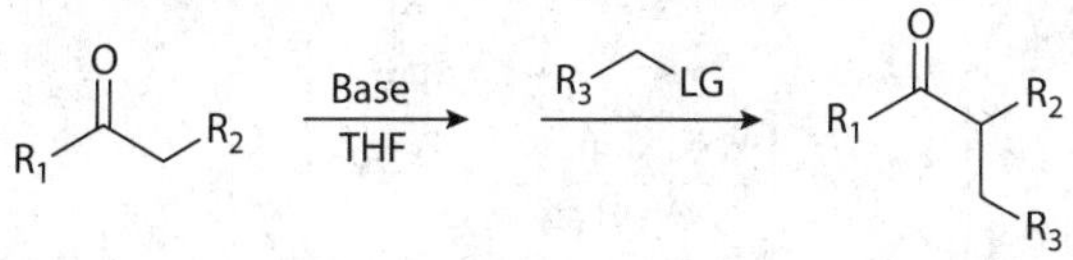

307

CHAPTER 9:
Structure, Function,
and Reactivity
of Biologically
Relevant Molecules

$$(R33)$$

The ease of **deprotonation** varies widely, depending upon the substitution pattern of the carbonyl (Figure 9-53). For example, aldehydes (pK_a = ca. 16) are acidic enough to be completely deprotonated by potassium t-butoxide (pK_a = ca. 19); however, ketones (pK_a = ca. 20) are only partially deprotonated under those conditions. Esters are even less acidic (pK_a = ca. 26), and amides (pK_a = ca. 35) require LDA for full deprotonation. Bearing in mind that the pK_a scale is logarithmic, this knowledge has significant predictive value—furthermore, you can leverage this differential for selectivity and control. For example, a molecule containing both an aldehyde and an ester functionality could, in principle, be selectively deprotonated at the aldehyde.

Aside from the issue of chemoselectivity (targeting one functional group over another), there is also the issue of regioselectivity. Most ketones have α-protons on either side of the carbonyl group. In some cases you can modify conditions to prefer one particular mode of deprotonation. For example, when 2-methylcyclohexanone (see Figure 9-54) is deprotonated with t-butoxide under protic conditions at relatively

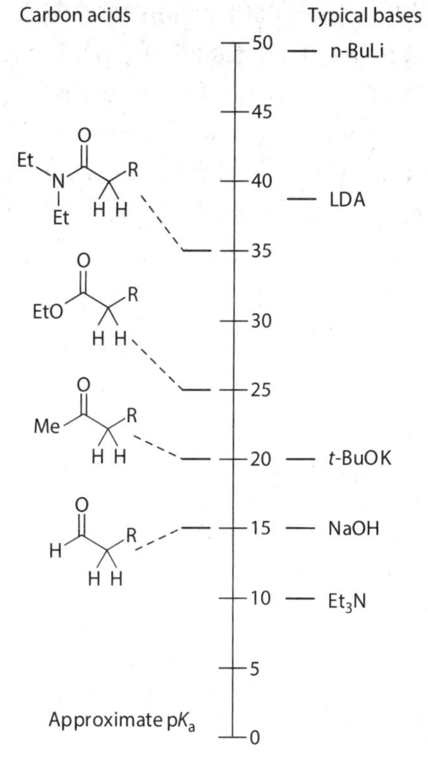

FIGURE 9-53 pK_a values of carbon acids relative to typical bases.

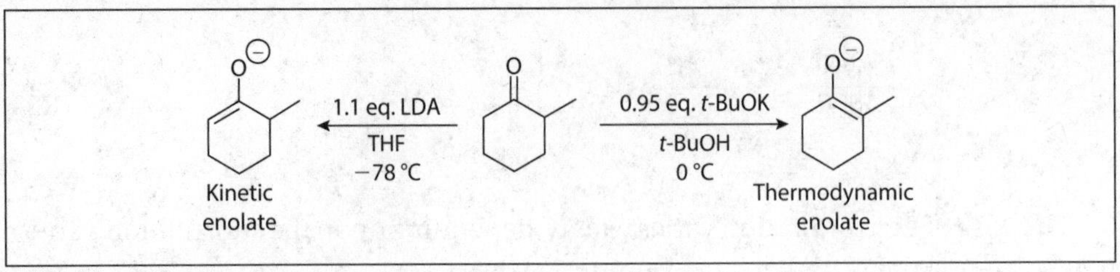

FIGURE 9-54 Kinetic and thermodynamic enolate formation.

high temperature, the thermodynamically more stable enolate (i.e., more substituted double bond) is formed. This is because the *t*-butoxide is not strong enough to completely deprotonate the substrate; therefore, a proton-transfer equilibrium will be set up in which the product distribution is governed by ΔG considerations.

However, when an excess of very strong, hindered base is used (e.g., LDA), the less-substituted enolate is formed. To understand this, you must remember that removal of the methine α-proton is sterically hindered; thus it is kinetically favorable to remove one of the methylene α-protons, even though the product is not the most stable. An excess of base is used to prevent the enolate from equilibrating by way of residual excess ketone, which would serve as a proton source. Low temperature is advantageous, since it allows the reaction to better discriminate between the two activation barriers.

Once formed, these carbanions can interact with many different electrophiles, including another carbonyl compound (Reaction 34). This is analogous to a Grignard addition in some ways, except that the nucleophile is not an organomagnesium species, but an enolate. This process, known as the **aldol reaction**, can take place between two carbonyl compounds of the same type (the so-called homo-aldol condensation) or between two different species (the "mixed," or "crossed," aldol). The latter version works best if one substrate is a ketone and the other an aldehyde, since the aldehyde will tend to function exclusively as the electrophilic species. Alternatively, one could use a carbonyl with no α-protons, for which it would be impossible to generate an enolate anion; therefore, it is relegated to electrophile status.

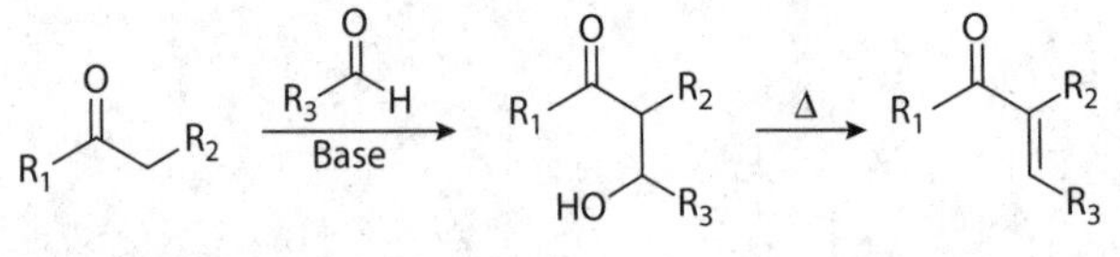

(R34)

Experimental conditions for the aldol condensation can be controlled such that the initially-formed adduct is isolated. However, with extended reaction times or higher temperature, an elimination ensues to provide that α, β-unsaturated carbonyl compound, which is also very synthetically useful.

Electron-deficient double bonds can also serve as competent electrophiles toward enolates (Reaction 35) through a process known as **conjugate addition** (also referred to as the **Michael addition** in some cases). Here only catalytic amounts of base are needed.

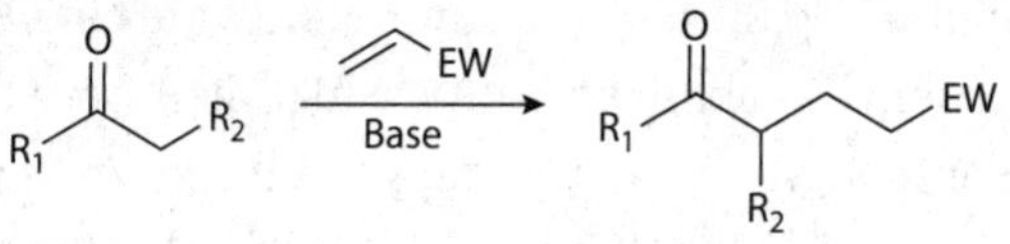

309

CHAPTER 9:
Structure, Function,
and Reactivity
of Biologically
Relevant Molecules

(R35)

A clever combination of the Michael addition and the aldol condensation are revealed in the base-catalyzed reaction of a ketone with the reagent methyl vinyl ketone (MVK), a protocol known as the **Robinson annulation** (Reaction 36). This methodology has the distinction of forming a ring from two acyclic species.

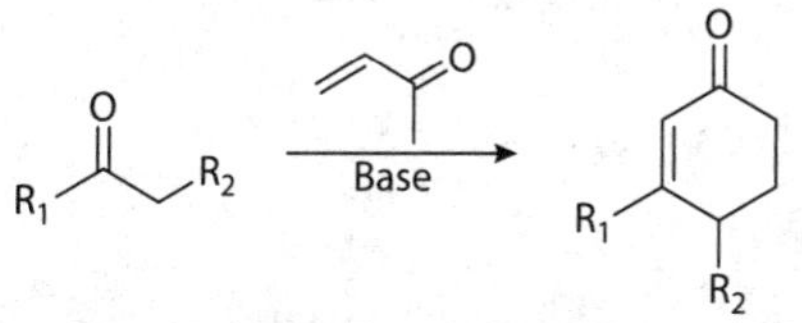

(R36)

The Robinson annulation is an example of a one-pot tandem reaction—that is, two reactions are occurring in sequence without an intervening workup step. The mechanism (see Figure 9-55) starts with deprotonation of the substrate to form an α-carbanion. Michael addition onto MVK provides an initial anionic adduct in which the enolate anion is internal (i.e., more substituted). This species is in equilibrium with the external (less substituted) enolate through a proton transfer reaction. Even though this is an unfavorable equilibrium (i.e., lies to the left), the small equilibrium concentration of the external enolate is much more reactive toward intramolecular aldol condensation; therefore, the equilibrium is driven to the right. The initially-formed aldol alkoxide undergoes proton transfer to provide an enolate, which subsequently eliminates hydroxide to give the cyclic enone product observed.

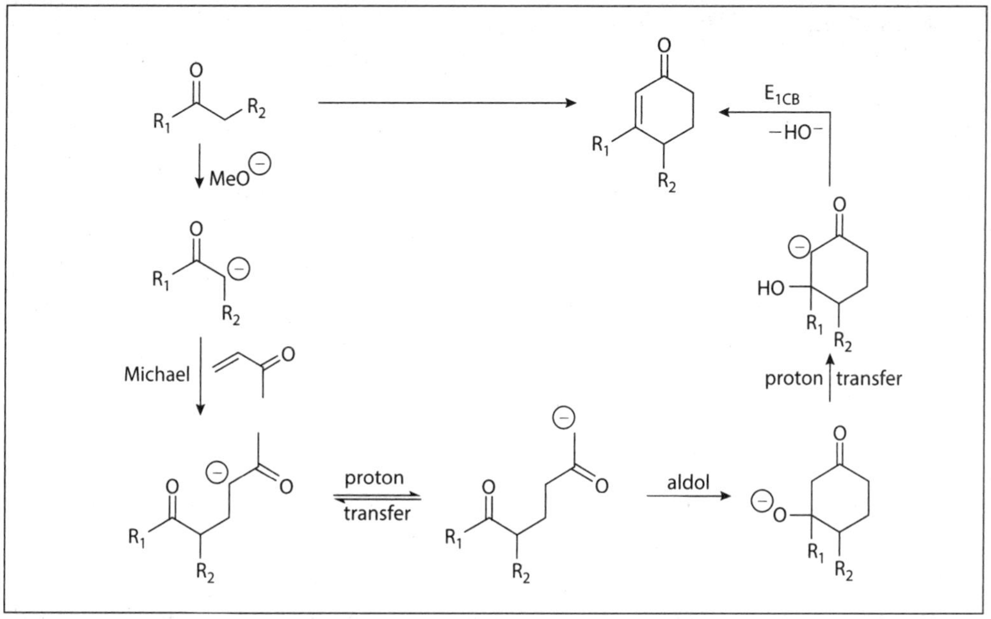

FIGURE 9-55 Mechanistic intermediates in the Robinson annulation.

Finally, under the rubric of functional group transformation, ketones are converted to esters by the action of *m*-chloroperbenzoic acid (*m*CPBA), which can be viewed as an oxygen-transfer reagent, in a protocol known as the **Baeyer-Villiger oxidation** (Reaction 37). In principle, either alkyl group could migrate to the oxygen center—as a general rule, the center that can best support a positive charge has the higher migratory aptitude.

$$\underset{R_1 \quad R_2}{\overset{O}{\|}} \quad \xrightarrow[\text{CH}_2\text{Cl}_2]{m\text{CPBA}} \quad \underset{R_1 \quad O^{\sim R_2}}{\overset{O}{\|}} \tag{R37}$$

Carboxylic Acid Derivatives

The various carboxylic acid derivatives (acids, acid chlorides, esters, amides, and nitriles) exhibit vastly differing properties, yet they share many synthetic pathways. When examining the interconversion of these derivatives, it will be helpful to understand the conceptual framework known as the electrophilicity series of carboxylic acid derivatives. If you bear in mind that the electrophilicity of the carbonyl carbon is rationalized on the basis of a charge-separated resonance structure (see Figure 9-56, inset), then modifications to the structure that destabilize that form should increase reactivity. Thus for acyl chlorides (X = Cl), the inductive effect of the chlorine makes the carbonyl carbon even more electron deficient; therefore, the center is expected to be much more electrophilic. Indeed, most acyl chlorides must be stored over a desiccant to prevent hydrolysis from adventitious water vapor. On the other hand, amides (X = NR_2) are expected to be less reactive by virtue of the fact that the nitrogen lone pair can provide resonance stabilization to the carbonyl carbon. This prediction is supported by the behavior of amides, which tend to be fairly nonreactive.

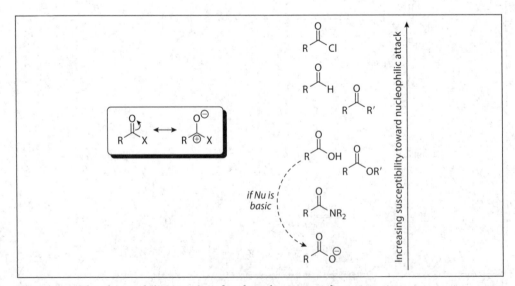

FIGURE 9-56 The electrophilicity series of carbonyl compounds.

311

CHAPTER 9:
Structure, Function,
and Reactivity
of Biologically
Relevant Molecules

This series is also a useful framework for thinking about interconversion among functional groups. In other words, it is difficult to move uphill through the series (e.g., amide → ester) but relatively easy to cascade down from the top (e.g., chloride → acid). Thus many methods for lateral or uphill functional group conversions take advantage of auxiliary high-energy species to drive the chemistry. For example, transforming an acid into an acid chloride (Reaction 42) is an inherently unfavorable uphill event, but you take advantage of the extremely high energy of thionyl chloride to drive the reaction.

PREPARATION OF CARBOXYLIC ACIDS

Carboxylic acids are prepared by the oxidation of primary alcohols under Jones conditions (Reaction 10); the method can also launch from the aldehyde stage (Reaction 38). Generally speaking, secondary alcohols and ketones make less suitable substrates.

$$\text{(R10)}$$

$$\text{(R38)}$$

Carboxylic acids can also be obtained through hydrolytic approaches. For example, exposing an ester to high concentrations of potassium hydroxide at elevated temperatures leads to the production of the corresponding carboxylate salt, a process known as **saponification** (Reaction 39). The reaction proceeds via initial nucleophilic attack of hydroxide to give and anionic tetrahedral intermediate, which collapses to eject either hydroxide or alkoxide. In principle, these two species are similar leaving groups, but when alkoxide is ejected, the carboxylic acid just formed is immediately and irreversibly deprotonated, thus driving the equilibrium to the right. The carboxylate is protonated during workup to give the carboxylic acid. Nitriles are hydrolyzed to carboxylic acids as well (Reaction 40), although this is usually carried out under acidic conditions.

$$\text{(R39)}$$

$$\text{(R40)}$$

A very clever and versatile Grignard methodology allows for the effective functional group transformation from alkyl bromide to alkanoic acid with one extra carbon (Reaction 41). Thus the alkyl halide is treated with magnesium metal to give the corresponding alkylmagnesium halide, which is quenched with carbon dioxide to yield the acid through Grignard addition.

$$R-Br \xrightarrow[\text{THF}]{Mg^0} R-MgBr \xrightarrow{CO_2} R\overset{O}{\underset{OH}{\bigotimes}} \tag{R41}$$

REACTIONS OF CARBOXYLIC ACIDS

Carboxylic acids are converted to the corresponding acyl chlorides by treatment with thionyl chloride or by using oxalyl chloride in the presence of catalytic DMF (Reaction 42). The driving force in the former set of conditions is the liberation of SO_2 gas, while the oxalyl chloride methodology ends up releasing carbon dioxide and carbon monoxide. The latter conditions are advantageous from the practical standpoint of materials handling—thionyl chloride is very corrosive to human tissue and scientific equipment.

$$(R42)$$

Carboxylic acids are usually sluggish toward reduction, since most hydride sources first remove the acid proton. The resulting carboxylate anion is then relatively resistant to nucleophilic attack. However, the use of very active hydride sources (such as LAH, Lithium aluminium hydride) results in reduction to the primary alcohol (Reaction 43).

$$(R43)$$

PREPARATION OF CARBOXYLIC ESTERS

Esters are conveniently prepared by the treatment of an acyl chloride with an alcohol (Reaction 44). Inasmuch as a stoichiometric amount of HCl is liberated as the reaction proceeds, sometimes a buffering tertiary amine is added, such as triethylamine or pyridine.

$$(R44)$$

If the alcohol is in plentiful supply, then the classic approach of mixing acid and alcohol in the presence of strong acid would be appropriate (Reaction 45). This is essentially an equilibrium reaction, so taking measures to drive the equilibrium is sometimes necessary (e.g., adding desiccant to sequester water).

$$(R45)$$

313

CHAPTER 9:
Structure, Function,
and Reactivity
of Biologically
Relevant Molecules

An extremely useful methodology for preparing methyl esters involves treatment of the acid with diazomethane (Reaction 46). The mechanism involves an initial proton transfer from the acid to diazomethane; the subsequently-formed carboxylate anion then displaces nitrogen gas from the protonated diazomethane. The reagent is very selective for carboxylic acids, the conditions are practically neutral, and the only by-product is an inert gas.

$$
\underset{R}{\overset{O}{\underset{\parallel}{C}}}\!\!-OH \xrightarrow[\text{Et}_2\text{O}]{\text{CH}_2\text{N}_2} \underset{R}{\overset{O}{\underset{\parallel}{C}}}\!\!-O\!-\text{Me} \tag{R46}
$$

REACTIONS OF CARBOXYLIC ESTERS

Esters are saponified to the corresponding acids by treatment with potassium hydroxide at high temperatures (Reaction 39). Similarly, esters can engage in a process known as **transesterification** (Reaction 47), whereby the alcohol portion of the ester is exchanged for another species. This is another equilibrium reaction, which can be catalyzed by acid or base.

$$
\underset{R}{\overset{O}{\parallel}}\!\!-OR' \xrightarrow[\text{H}_2\text{O}]{\text{KOH}} \underset{R}{\overset{O}{\parallel}}\!\!-OK \xrightarrow[\text{work-up}]{\text{acidic}} \underset{R}{\overset{O}{\parallel}}\!\!-OH \tag{R39}
$$

$$
\underset{R}{\overset{O}{\parallel}}\!\!-OR' \xrightarrow[\substack{\text{cat. } p\text{TsOH} \\ \text{or NaOR''}}]{\text{R''OH}} \underset{R}{\overset{O}{\parallel}}\!\!-OR'' \tag{R47}
$$

The reduction of esters can provide alcohols upon the treatment with strong hydride sources like LAH (Reaction 6), or aldehydes when the selective reagent DIBAL (Diisobutylaluminium hydride) is employed (Reaction 24). Since acids can be difficult to manipulate, esters are sometimes used as an intermediate from acid to aldehyde via esterification.

$$
\underset{\text{OR'}}{\overset{O}{\parallel}} \xrightarrow[\text{THF}]{\text{LAH}} \diagup\!\!\!\diagdown\!\!\text{OH} \tag{R6}
$$

$$
\underset{R}{\overset{O}{\parallel}}\!\!-OR' \xrightarrow[\text{THF}]{\text{DIBAL}} \underset{R}{\overset{O}{\parallel}}\!\!-H \tag{R24}
$$

PREPARATION OF AMIDES

Analogous to esters, amides are conveniently prepared by the treatment of amines with acyl chlorides (Reaction 48). Primary and secondary amides can be deprotonated at nitrogen and treated wth alkyl halides or tosylates to give the *N*-alkylated derivates (Reaction 49).

$$
\underset{R}{\overset{O}{\parallel}}\!\!-Cl \quad \xrightarrow{\underset{R'}{\overset{H}{\underset{}{N}}}\!\!R''} \quad \underset{R}{\overset{O}{\parallel}}\!\!-\underset{\underset{R''}{|}}{N}\!\!-R' \tag{R48}
$$

$$\text{(R49)}$$

Oximes (derived from ketones and hydroxylamine) are *N*-chlorinated by thionyl chloride (or PCl$_5$) to give an activated species that undergoes **Beckmann rearrangement**, ultimately providing an amide (Reaction 50). In the rearrangement, generally speaking the R-group opposite the oxime hydroxy group migrates.

$$\text{(R50)}$$

REACTIONS OF AMIDES

For the most part, amides are notoriously sluggish in saponification reactions. However, there is a selective method for the rapid and selective hydrolysis of primary amides that relies on nitrous acid (HONO) generated in situ from sodium nitrite and HCl (Reaction 51). The mechanism proceeds via the diazotization of the amide nitrogen, creating a phenomenal leaving group easily displaced by water.

$$\text{(R51)}$$

Amides are reduced to amines when treated with strong hydride sources such as LAH (Reaction 52), but DIBAL selectively provides an imine, which is hydrolyzed during workup to yield ultimately an aldehyde (Reaction 53).

$$\text{(R52)}$$

$$\text{(R53)}$$

Finally, an interesting and very useful functional group transformation is represented by the **Hofmann rearrangement** (Reaction 54), in which an amide is converted to an amine with one less carbon. The mechanism proceeds via initial *N*-chlorination of the amide, which is subsequently deprotonated. The *N*-chloroamide anion suffers loss of chloride to provide an acyl nitrene intermediate, which rearranges to an isocyanate. Aqueous acidic workup releases the amine through hydrolysis.

$$\text{(R54)}$$

315

CHAPTER 9:
Structure, Function,
and Reactivity
of Biologically
Relevant Molecules

Phenols, Hydroquinones, and Quinones

Phenols are characterized by a hydroxyl group directly connected to a phenyl ring, and this array is found in the amino acid tyrosine, as well as the wood polymer lignin. The following section discusses the preparation and reaction of phenols.

PREPARATION OF PHENOLS

Phenols can be prepared from other aromatic compounds by converting the existing functional group to a hydroxy substituent. One of the oldest (but still relevant) such conversions is the **fusion reaction** (Reaction 55), in which benzenesulfonic acid derivatives are cooked up in molten sodium hydroxide to provide the corresponding phenol. The yields for this reaction can be remarkably high, and it represents a very straightforward synthetic path to phenols from benzene.

(R55)

Another route to phenol proceeds via the aniline derivative. Treatment with nitrous acid (formed in situ from sodium nitrite and HCl) promotes diazotization to the diazonium salt, which is then heated in the presence of water to give phenol as the product of hydrolysis (Reaction 56).

(R56)

When electron-withdrawing substituents (nitro, carbonyl, etc.) and potential leaving groups (OTs, Cl, etc.) are situated in a 1,2- or 1,4-relationship, the opportunity arises to engage in a reaction known as **nucleophilic aromatic substitution**. For example, *p*-chloronitrobenzene suffers attack by hydroxide in an addition-elimination sequence to give the corresponding phenol with the ejection of chloride (Reaction 57). Other nucleophiles can also be employed in this protocol.

(R57)

REACTIONS OF PHENOLS

Phenols are relatively acidic (pK_a ca. 9), and so they are easily deprotonated; the resulting phenoxide anion can then serve as a nucleophilic species in the Williamson ether synthesis to provide phenyl alkyl ethers (Reaction 58).

(R58)

Phenols also engage in important condensation reactions with carbonyls. For example, the treatment of phenol with acetone in the presence of strong acid provides the condensation product Bisphenol A, an important monomer for polycarbonates (Reaction 59). Reaction with formaldehyde results in polymerization to form phenol-formaldehyde (PF) resins such as Novolac (Reaction 60), a photoresist used in electronics applications.

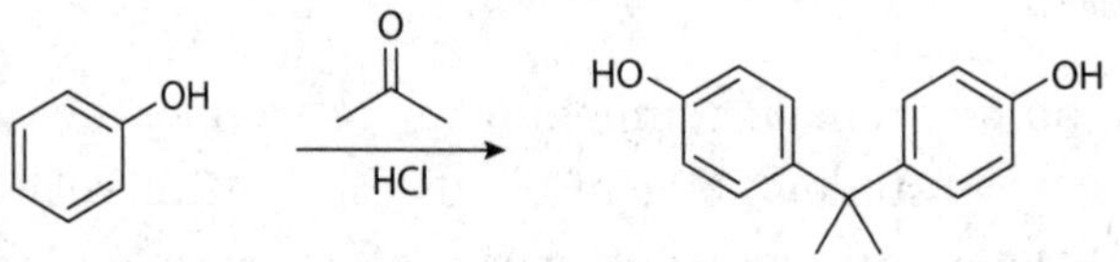

(R59)

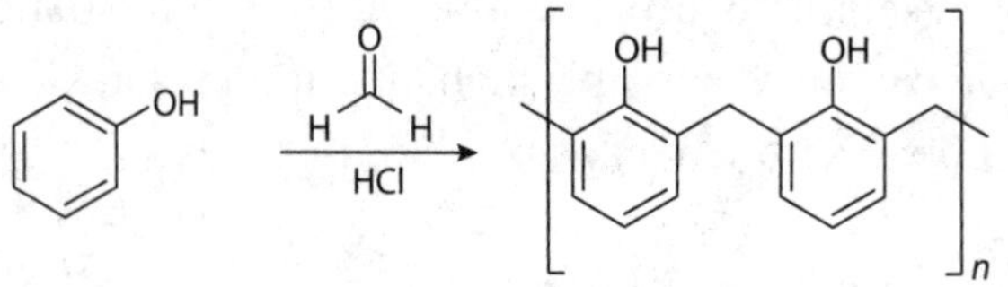

(R60)

PREPARATION OF HYDROQUINONES

Hydroquinones can be prepared from phenols via one of three common protocols: the **Eastman process**, which involves the aerobic oxidation of diisopropylbenzene to the corresponding bisperoxide, followed by acid-catalyzed rearrangement and hydrolysis (Reaction 61); the oxidation of aniline to quinone using manganese dioxide and sulfuric acid, followed by reduction of the quinone with iron (Reaction 62); and the hydroxylation of phenol in the presence of hydrogen peroxide and an iron catalyst (Reaction 63). The last method has a parallel in biological systems inasmuch as cytochrome P-450 is known to oxidize phenols to hydroquinones in vivo through a similar mechanism.

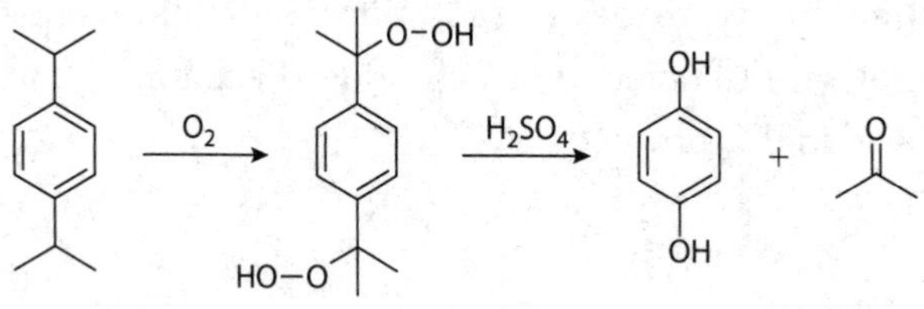

(R61)

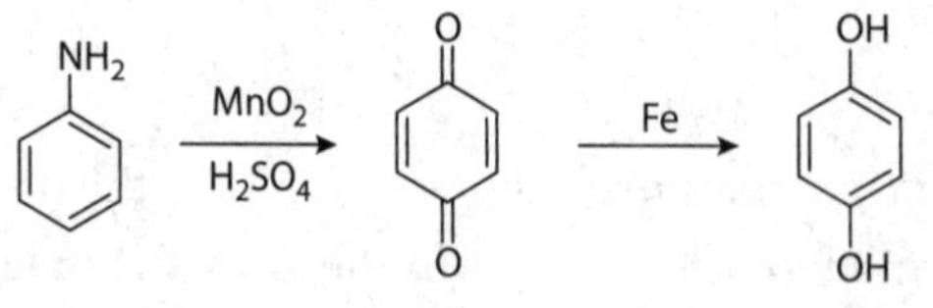

(R62)

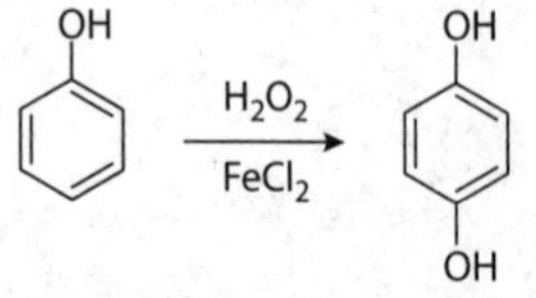

(R63)

317

CHAPTER 9:
Structure, Function,
and Reactivity
of Biologically
Relevant Molecules

REACTIONS OF HYDROQUINONES AND QUINONES

Hydroquinones and quinones (aka benzoquinones) are important synthetically and biologically due to the ease of their interconversion via redox chemistry (see Figure 9-57). The conversion of hydroquinone to quinone proceeds through a 2-electron oxidation and formal loss of H_2. From a redox perspective, hydroquinones are mild $2e^-$ reductants and quinones are mild $2e^-$ oxidants.

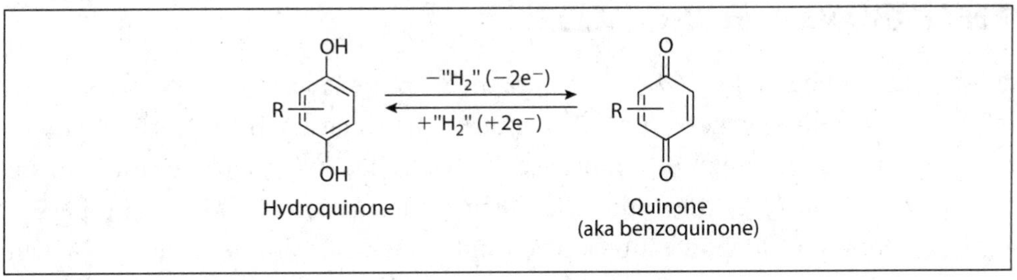

FIGURE 9-57 Facile redox between hydroquinones and quinones.

One common quinone oxidizing agent is 2,3-dichloro-5,6-dicyano-1,4-benzoquinone (or DDQ), which is used frequently for aromatization reactions. For example, DDQ facilitates the conversion of dihydropyridine to pyridine, its oxidized aromatic counterpart (see Figure 9-58). The mechanism involves an initial *hydride* transfer from dihydropyridine to DDQ (the actual redox event), followed by a *proton* transfer from the pyridinium species to the deprotonated quinone. Thus while the oxidation involves the formal transfer of H_2, it is really a sequential transfer of hydride and proton.

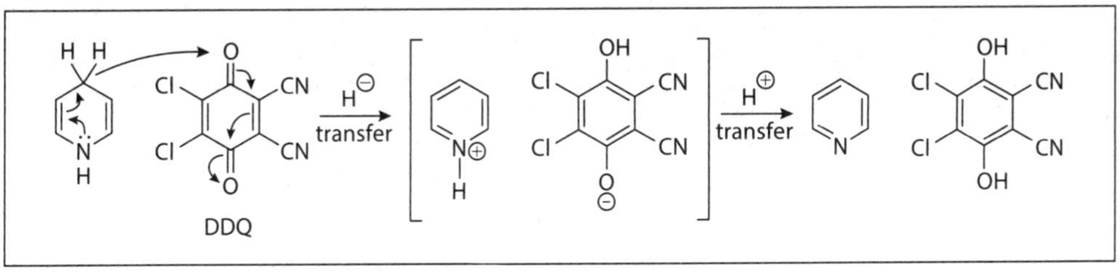

FIGURE 9-58 Mechanism of DDQ oxidation.

These redox events are particularly relevant to biological systems. For example, Coenzyme Q_{10}, or ubiquinone (see Figure 9-59), is a lipophilic benzoquinone derivative that plays a central role in the electron transport chain, and its hydroquinone form ($CoQH_2$) is an important antioxidant that protects against lipid peroxidation.

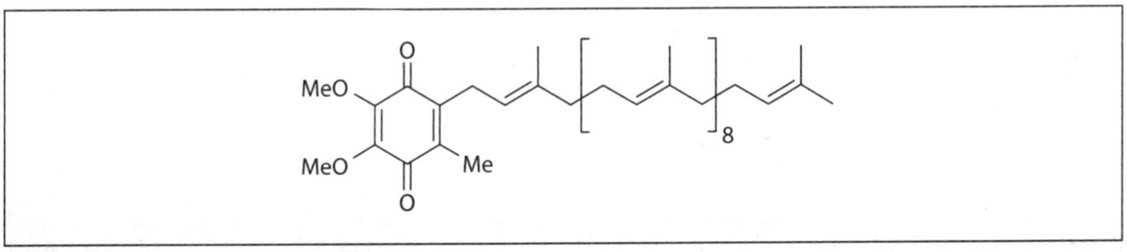

FIGURE 9-59 Coenzyme Q_{10} (ubiquinone).

Amino Acids and Peptides

While there are many types of amino acids, the most important type for biological systems are the **α-amino acids**, which serve as monomers for the construction of **polypeptides**, or **proteins**. The following section discusses the preparation and reaction of amino acids and peptides.

PREPARATION OF AMINO ACIDS

Amino acids can be prepared by several methods in the laboratory. One of the most well-known is the **Strecker synthesis** (Reaction 64), in which aldehydes are treated with sodium cyanide and ammonium chloride, followed by heating in acid. The mechanism (see Figure 9-60) involves the initial acid-catalyzed formation of an iminium species, which undergoes nucleophilic attack by cyanide to form an aminonitrile, which can be isolated. Heating this product in the presence of sulfuric acid leads to the acid-catalyzed hydrolysis of the nitrile moiety for a carboxylic acid functionality, as seen in Reaction 40.

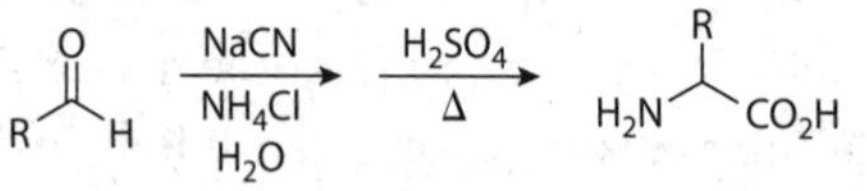

(R64)

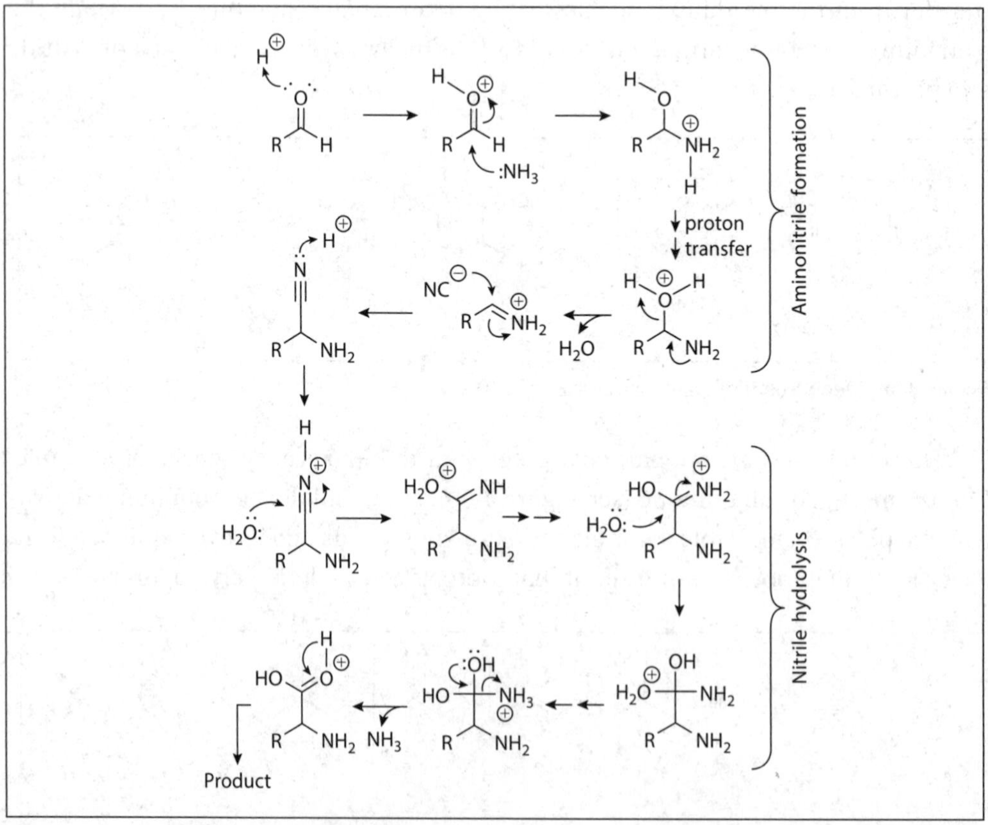

FIGURE 9-60 Mechanism of the Strecker synthesis.

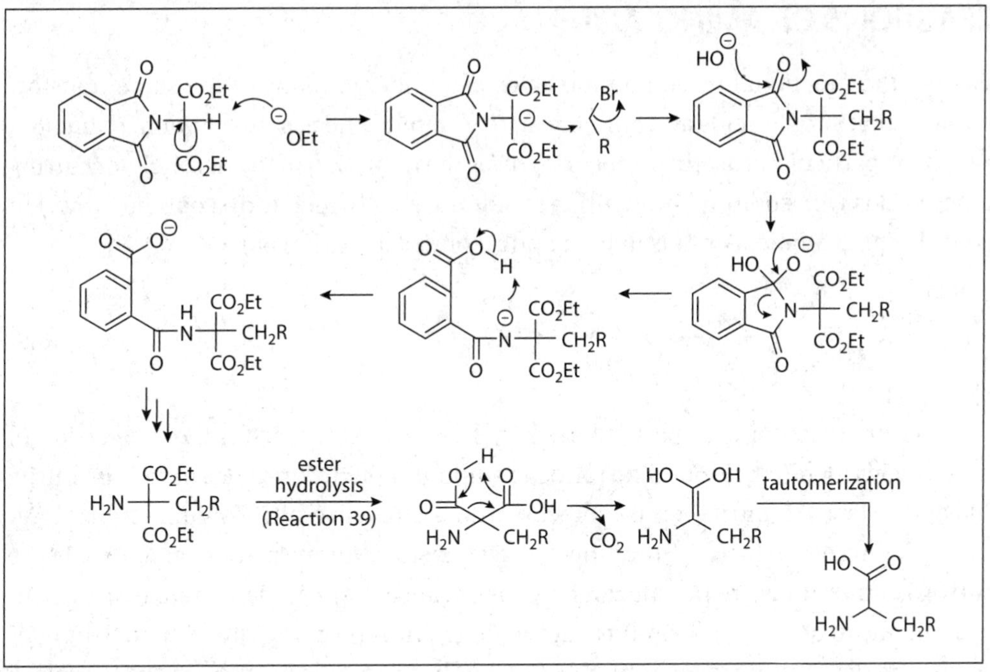

319

CHAPTER 9:
Structure, Function,
and Reactivity
of Biologically
Relevant Molecules

FIGURE 9-61 Mechanism of the Gabriel malonate synthesis.

Another common method is the **Gabriel malonate synthesis** (Reaction 65). In this procedure, the imidomalonate starting material is deprotonated by ethoxide (see Figure 9-61) and the resultant carbanion engages in S_N2 attack of an alkyl halide. Heating in sodium hydroxide leads to hydrolysis of the imide to free the amino group, followed by saponification (Reaction 39) of the aminodiester. The dicarboxylic acid thus formed is thermally unstable, undergoing rapid loss of carbon dioxide to form the amino acid after tautomerization.

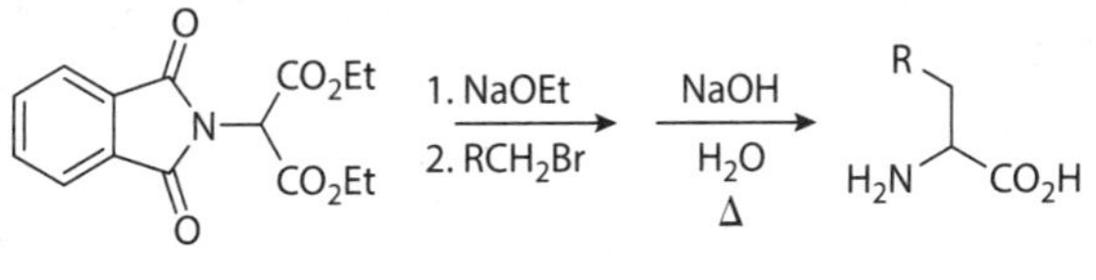

(R65)

Two other synthetic routes deserve mention, although they are less frequently encountered. The first (Reaction 66) involves the bromination of a carboxylic acid under the **Hell–Vollhard–Zelinsky conditions** (bromine and phosphorus tribromide), followed by treatment with ammonia to engage in S_N2 displacement of the bromide. The second is a reductive amination protocol (Reaction 67), in which an α-ketoacid is treated with ammonia in the presence of a reducing agent, such as hydrogen on palladium or sodium cyanoborohydride (Reaction 32).

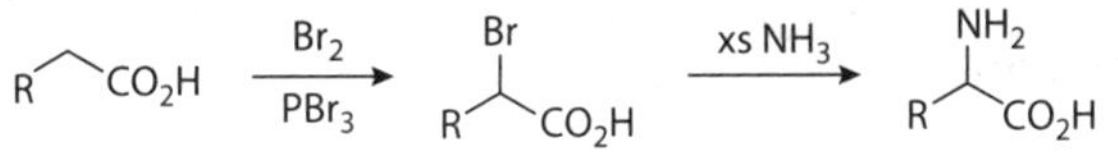

(R66)

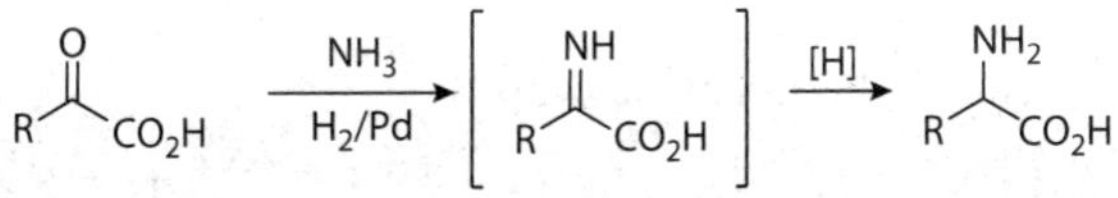

(R67)

REACTIONS OF AMINO ACIDS

Each of the functionalities on amino acids can undergo many of the same transformations that simple acids and amines can (e.g., amide and ester formation, reduction, etc.). One particularly useful protocol involves the reduction of the naturally-occurring amino acids with sodium borohydride in sulfuric acid (which forms borane in situ) to provide chiral amino alcohols in high optical purity (Reaction 68).

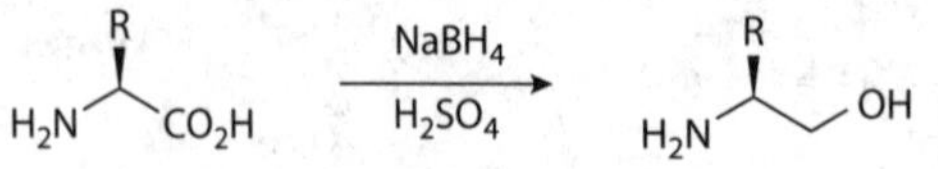

(R68)

Another reaction with particularly high biological relevance is the conversion of amino acids to the corresponding nitroso compounds in the presence of sodium nitrite in acid. At low pH, nitrite ion is a precursor to the reactive nitrosonium ion (see Figure 9-62, inset), which is the species responsible for nitroso formation. These **nitroso compounds** are potent carcinogens because they can dehydrate in acidic environments to become diazonium salts, which in turn react rapidly with nucleophiles to liberate diatomic nitrogen. This reaction has been studied extensively in an effort to understand the health effects of dietary nitrites.

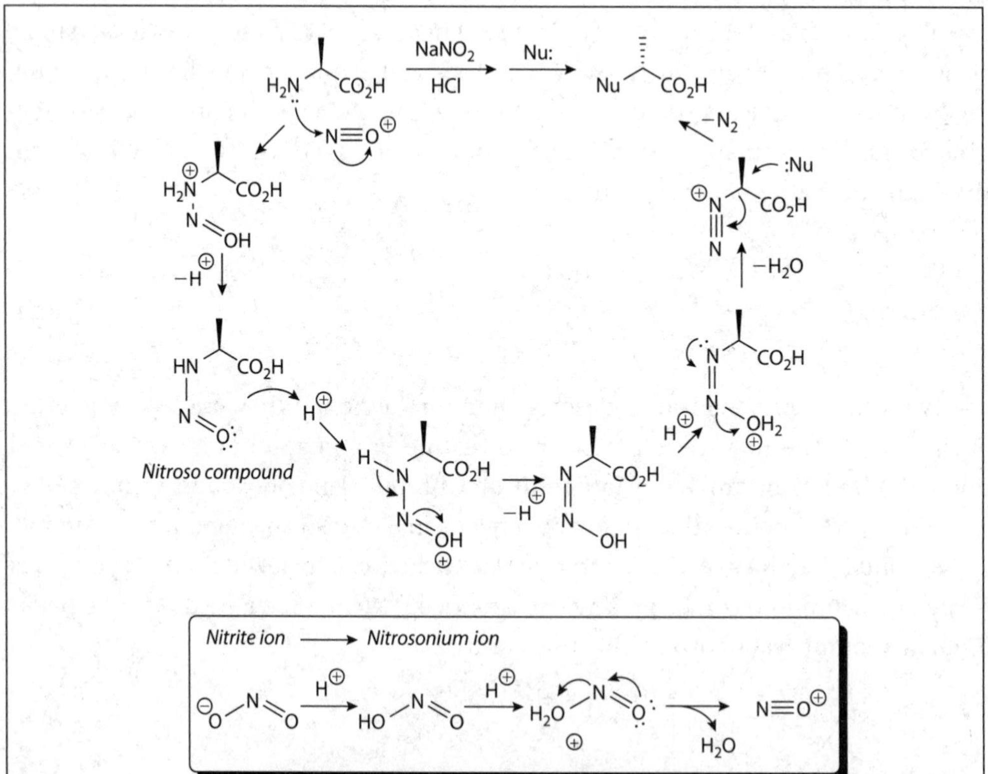

FIGURE 9-62 Conversion of alanine into an alkylating agent via nitroso.

321

CHAPTER 9:
Structure, Function,
and Reactivity
of Biologically
Relevant Molecules

PREPARATION OF PEPTIDES

For the past 50 years, the standard laboratory method to prepare oligo- and polypeptides is the **Merrifield synthesis**. In this procedure, the C-terminal amino acid is first attached to a polymeric solid support to make it insoluble (see Figure 9-63). The growing peptide chain is retained on the resin (which has the physical form of very small beads), and by-products and impurities can be washed off. The N-terminus is initially protected with a *t*-butylcarbonyl (Boc) group to prevent any unwanted nucleophilic behavior by the amine. After the first amino acid is attached, the protecting group is removed by treatment with trifluoroacetic acid. Protonation of the nitrogen sets the stage for subsequent loss of a proton from the *t*-butyl group, resulting in a cascade of electron flow that releases isobutylene and carbon dioxide (both gases), which provides a tremendous entropic driver for this step.

At this point the peptide is extended (see Figure 9-64) by connecting the newly deprotected N-terminus of the chain with another Boc-protected amino acid in the presence of dicyclohexyldiimide (DCC), a coupling reagent. In this series of steps, the

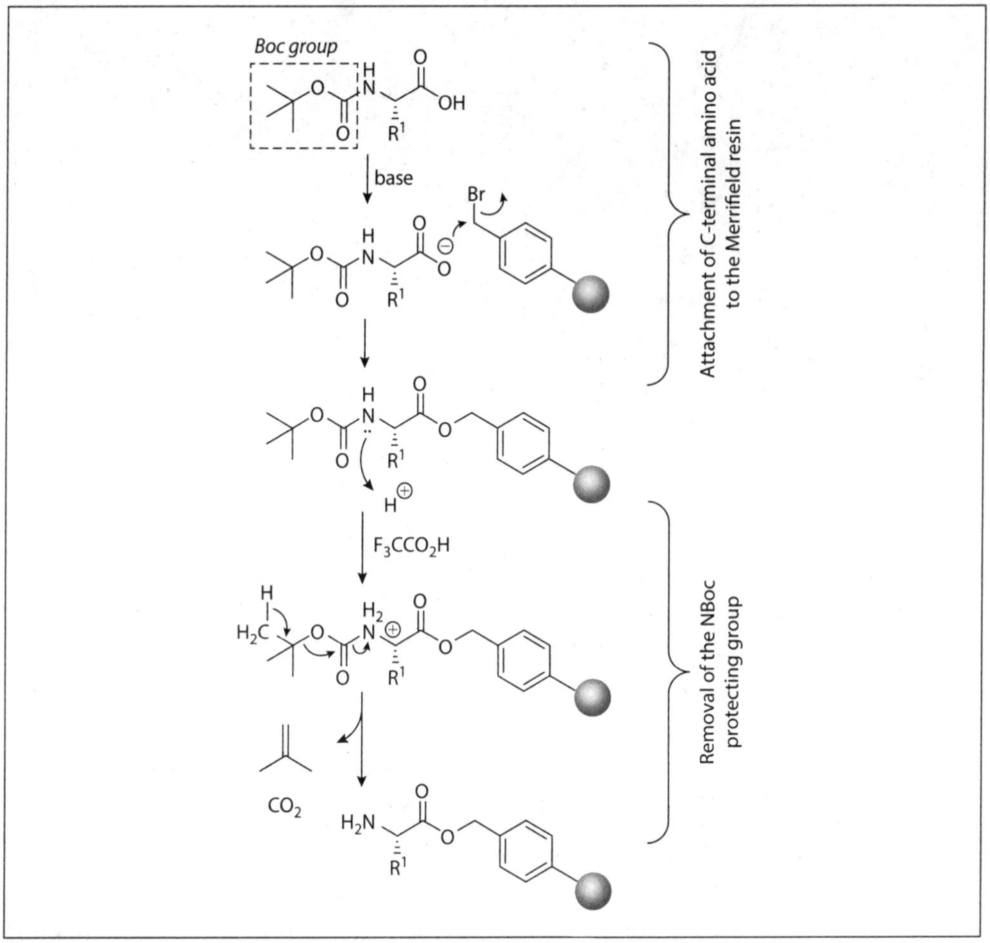

FIGURE 9-63 First steps in solid-phase peptide synthesis (SPPS).

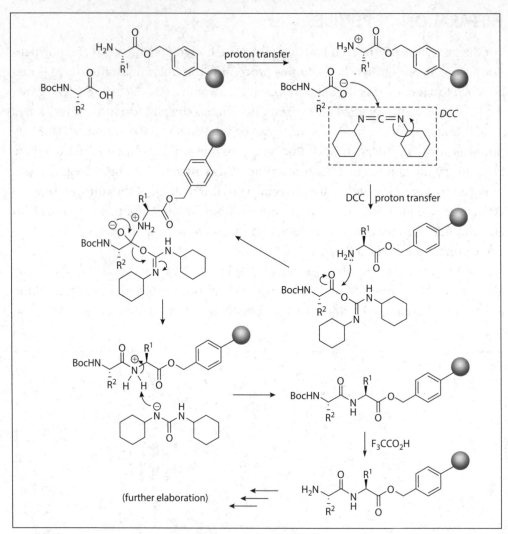

FIGURE 9-64 Extension of the peptide in SPPS by DCC coupling.

carboxylate group of the new amino acid adds to the DCC to provide an activated carboxylic acid derivative (much like an acyl chloride or anhydride). Next, the free amine adds to the electrophilic carbonyl group to give an anionic tetrahedral intermediate, which collapses to eject the dicyclohexylurea anion and provide the new amide bond. Treatment with trifluoroacetic acid then deprotects the N-terminus through the same mechanism shown in Figure 9-63. This process is repeated for each additional amino acid residue.

When the peptide is of the desired length, it is released from the Merrifield resin by treatment with anhydrous hydrofluoric acid (see Figure 9-65). Note that these conditions are selective for ester hydrolysis, leaving the more robust amide bonds intact.

The Merrifield synthesis has been updated in various ways since its introduction. For example, considerable innovation has centered around the optimization of coupling agents and protecting groups so that SPPS can be automated. One modification in this regard is the use of the 9-fluorenylmethyloxycarbonyl (Fmoc) protecting group

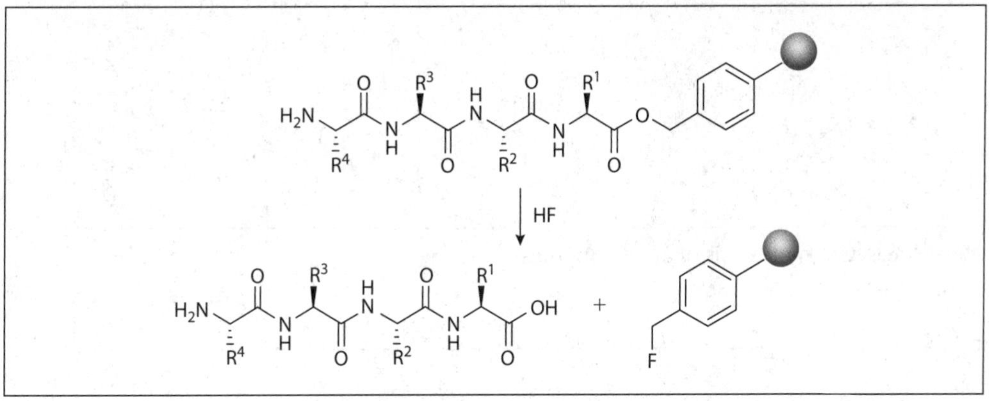

323

CHAPTER 9:
Structure, Function,
and Reactivity
of Biologically
Relevant Molecules

FIGURE 9-65 Release of the completed peptide from the Merrifield resin.

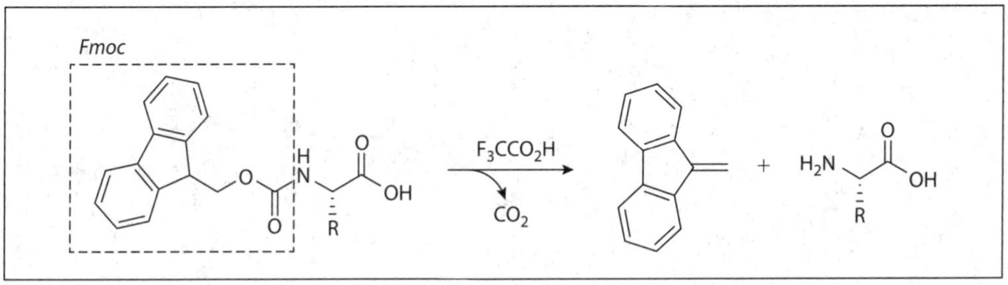

FIGURE 9-66 Deprotection of Fmoc-protected amino acids.

instead of the Boc group (see Figure 9-66). The Fmoc moiety is a very strong chromophore, so the progress of the coupling and deprotection can be monitored spectrophotometrically, which is of obvious advantage for automated protocols. The cleavage of the Fmoc group is exactly analogous to that of the Boc group, with 9-methylenefluorene being liberated instead of isobutylene.

REACTIONS OF PEPTIDES

Because peptides are polyamides, their backbone is resistant to many degradation pathways such as hydrolysis. The digestion of proteins in vivo is carried out with the assistance of enzymes, but in the absence of such catalysis, forcing conditions are required. Thus oligopeptides can be hydrolyzed into their component monomeric amino acids by heating in 6N hydrochloric acid at 110°C for 24 hours (see Figure 9-67).

A more controlled and sequential cleavage of peptides can be carried out by treatment with phenyl isothiocyanate in a protocol known as the **Edman degradation** (Reaction 69). In this procedure the *N*-terminal amino acid is converted into a phenylthiohydantoin (PTH) containing the characteristic side chain (R) of the amino acid. Each PTH can be analyzed against known standards using HPLC techniques. Since the *N*-terminal amino acids can be clipped off and analyzed one at a time, this provides for the unambiguous determination of the primary structure of the peptide.

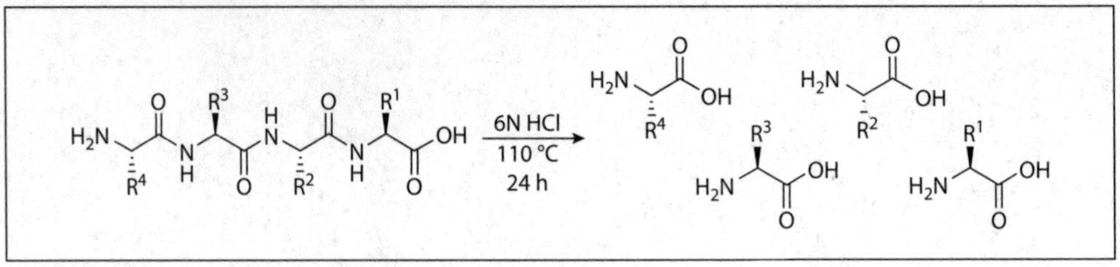

FIGURE 9-67 Acid hydrolysis of an oligopeptide.

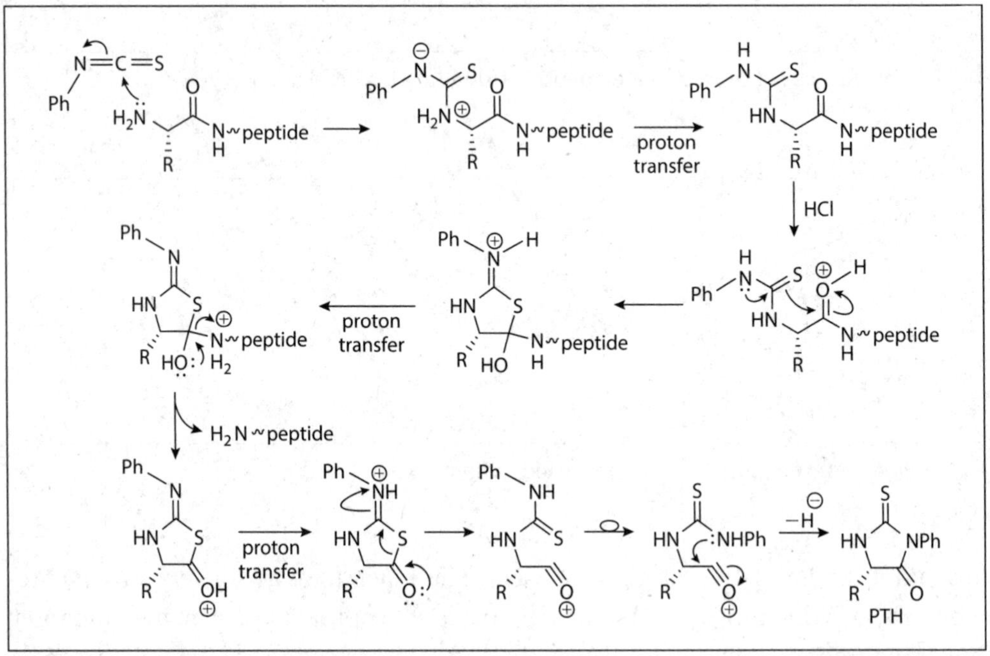

FIGURE 9-68 The mechanism of the Edman degradation.

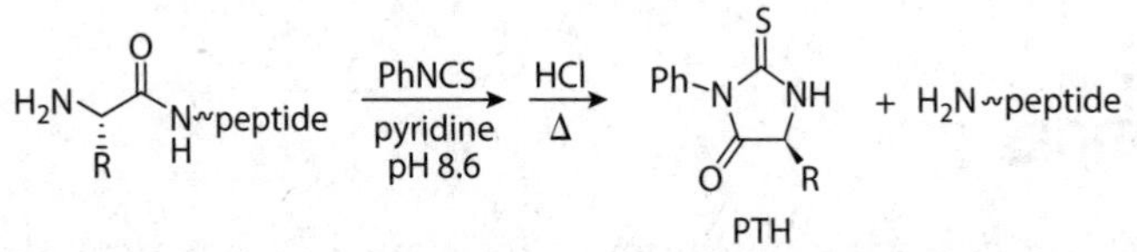

(R69)

The mechanism of the Edman degradation (see Figure 9-68) involves the initial reaction of the *N*-terminus with phenyl isothiocyanate to produce a thiourea. Upon treatment with HCl, the thiourea cyclizes and liberates the remainder of the peptide chain, ultimately forming (after rearrangement) the phenylthiohydantoin.

For the sequencing to be effective, however, all the disulfide (cystine) bridges must be cleaved. Under normal physiological conditions, the disulfide bond is broken by enzymatic reduction; however, it is easily reversible. In the laboratory, a mild reducing agent (like sodium borohydride) can reduce disulfides to the corresponding thiols, and even exposure to atmospheric oxygen is sufficient in many cases to re-create the disulfide bond (see Figure 9-69).

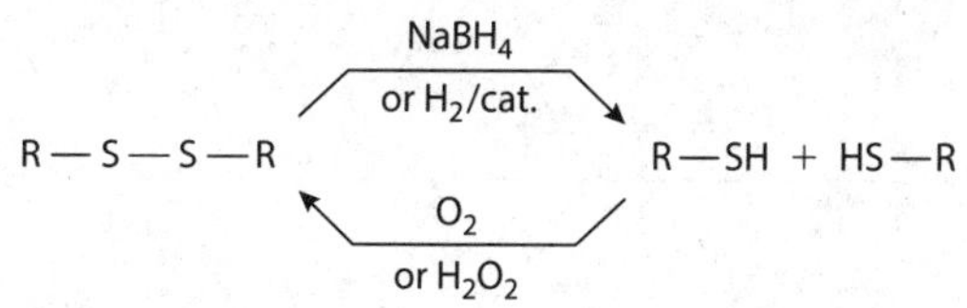

325

CHAPTER 9:
Structure, Function,
and Reactivity
of Biologically
Relevant Molecules

FIGURE 9-69 The interconversion of disulfides and thiols.

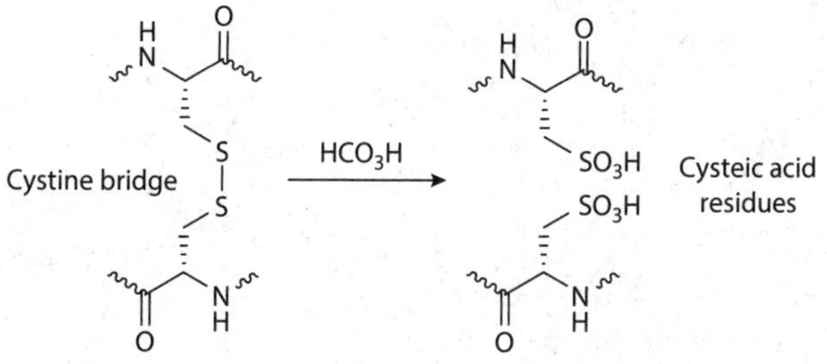

FIGURE 9-70 Irreversible cleavage of cystine bridges using performic acid.

A different outcome is observed if disulfides are treated with strong oxidizing agents instead of mild reducing conditions. For example, the disulfide moiety in a cystine bridge is converted irreversibly to the corresponding sulfonic acid derivative (i.e., cysteic acid) by the action of performic acid (see Figure 9-70).

Carbohydrates

Etymologically "hydrates of carbon," carbohydrates are rich in hydroxyl groups, but also feature the carbonyl functionality as well. The following section discusses the preparation and reaction of carbohydrates.

PREPARATION OF CARBOHYDRATES

The methodology for solid-supported oligosaccharide synthesis has co-evolved with that of solid-supported peptide synthesis (SSPS) discussed earlier. While the strategies are similar, the specific chemistry involved is quite different. Unlike peptide synthesis, which proceeds by forming exactly the same type of amide bond repeatedly, carbohydrate linkages can be made with any of the hydroxy groups on any given sugar, and the stereochemistry at the anomeric carbon adds yet another layer of complexity. Figure 9-71 is thus only one of many approaches to an automated solid-supported oligosaccharide synthesis.

First, the Merrifield resin is modified with 4-octene-1,8-diol, which is deprotonated with potassium hydride and then engages in S_N2 attack at the benzylic position to provide a hydroxyether (see Figure 9-71). This modified resin is allowed to react with an

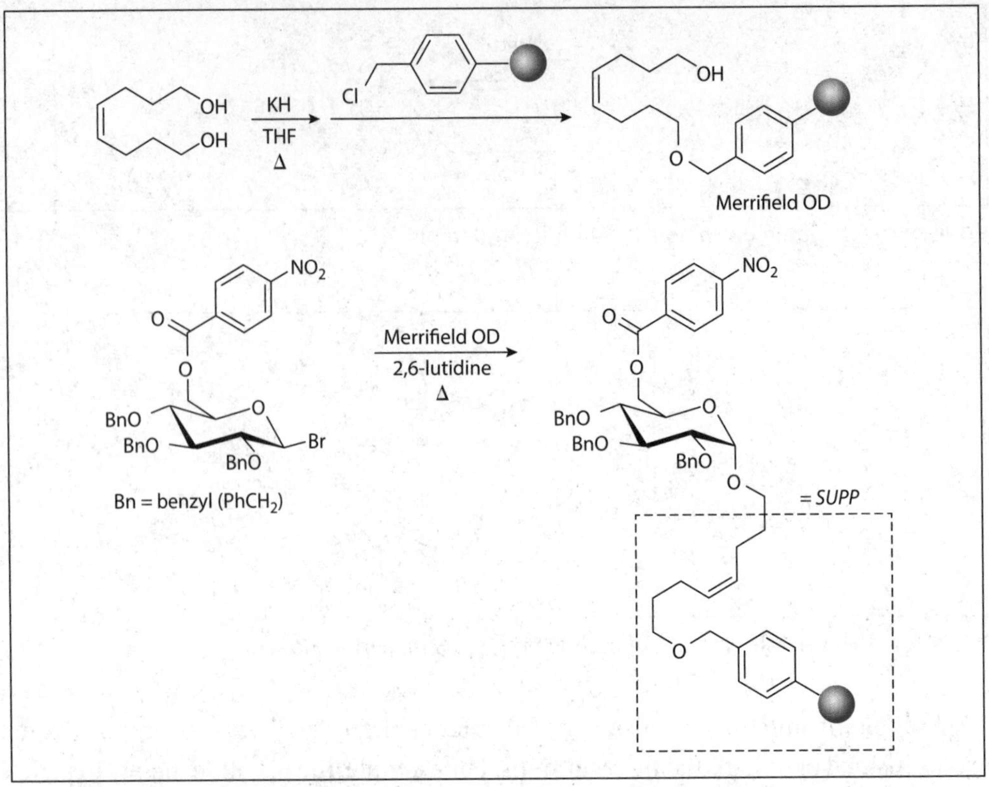

FIGURE 9-71 Preparation of immobilized O-protected glucose derivative.

activated sugar to form a glycoside bond. In this case, the sugar is activated by replacing the C-1 hydroxy with a bromine. Also note that all the remaining hydroxy groups must be protected to avoid competing glycoside formation. Here there are two types of protecting groups: the hydroxy functionalities at C-2, C-3, and C-4 are protected as benzyl ethers, while the hydroxy at C-6 is protected as a 4-nitrobenzoate ester. The latter is conveniently removed by transesterification (Reaction 47) using sodium methoxide in methanol (see Figure 9-72). The free C-6 hydroxy can now be used to form a subsequent glycosidic linkage.

Once it has reached the desired length, the oligosaccharide can be released from the support in one of two ways. The original methodology involved **ozonolysis**, which cleaves the double bond in the tether to form two aldehydes (see Figure 9-73). Another more recent innovation is the use of **olefin metathesis**, which converts the double bond into two terminal alkenes.

REACTIONS OF CARBOHYDRATES

The most biologically relevant reaction of complex carbohydrates is their hydrolysis via cleavage of the glycosidic bonds. In the absence of a catalyst (either an enzyme or mineral acid), polysaccharides are among the most stable biopolymers. The acid-catalyzed hydrolysis of carbohydrates has been studied for well over 100 years, and

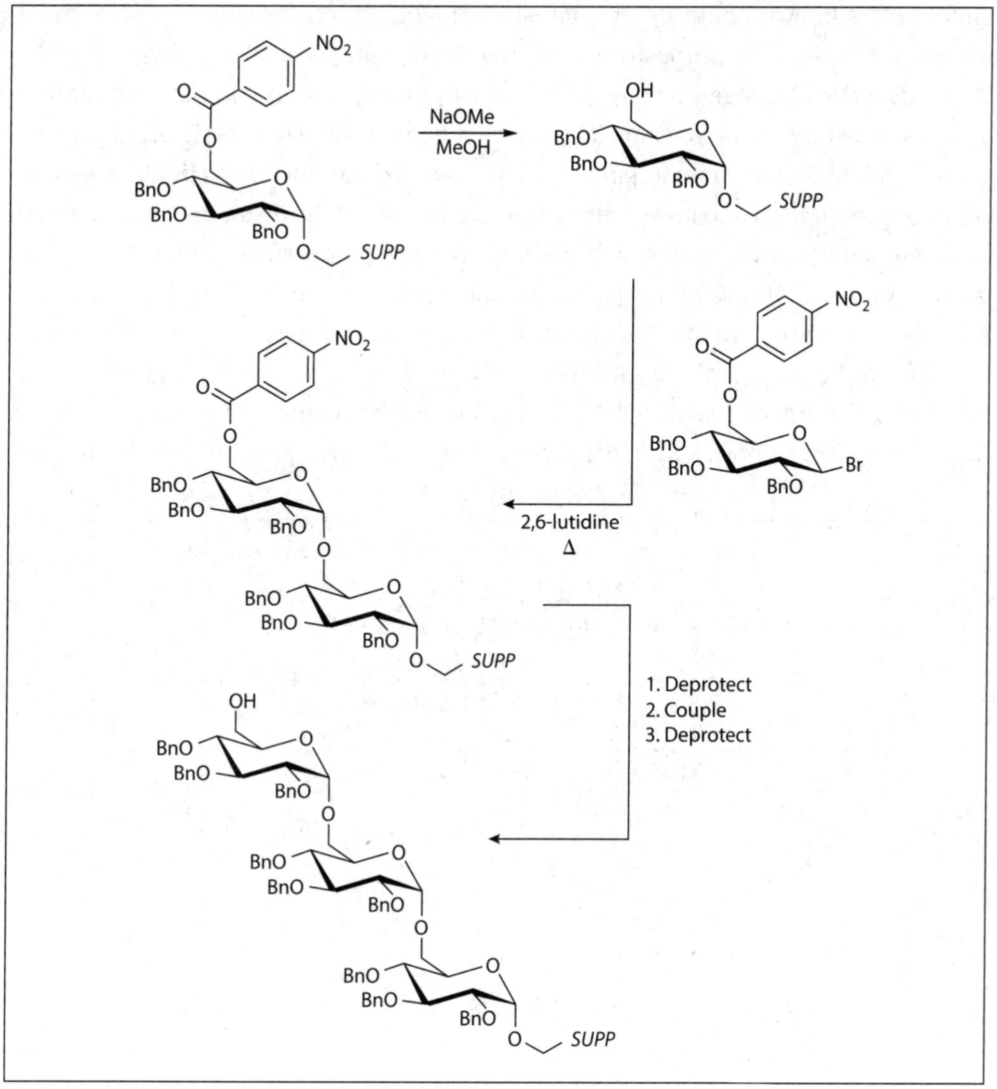

327

CHAPTER 9:
Structure, Function,
and Reactivity
of Biologically
Relevant Molecules

FIGURE 9-72 Elaboration of the oligosaccharide.

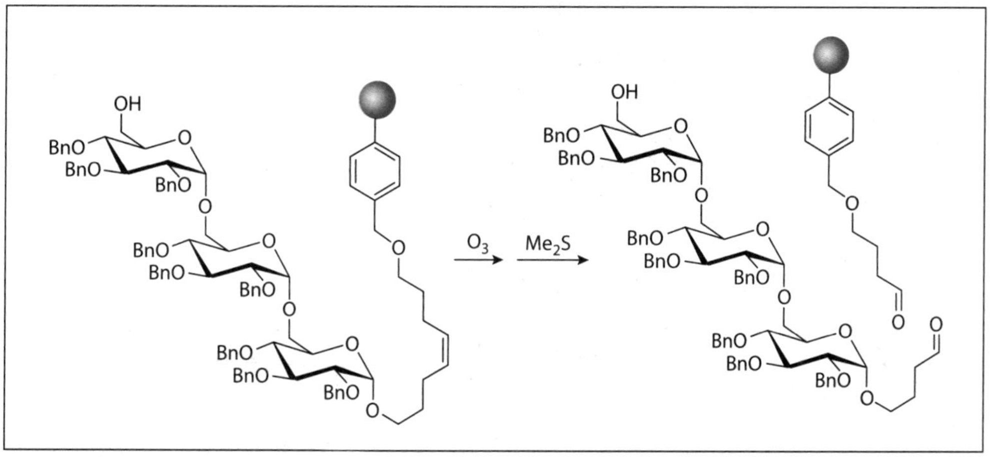

FIGURE 9-73 Release of the oligosaccharide from the support.

quite a bit is known about its mechanism. Generally speaking, there are two major routes of hydrolytic decomposition of glycosides in aqueous acid (see Figure 9-74).

Endocyclic cleavage involves an initial ring-opening step (similar to mutarotation), followed by attack of water to provide a hemiacetal. Hydrolysis of this species gives an aldehyde, which undergoes subsequent recyclization. **Exocyclic cleavage** proceeds by protonation and loss of the C-1 oxygen. Attack of the resultant carbocation by water gives the hydrolyzed product. Furanosides can follow either endocyclic or exocyclic routes, and this depends largely on the particular substrate; however, pyranosides are hydrolyzed predominantly via the exocyclic pathway.

The configuration of the anomeric carbon has an enormous impact on the hydrolytic stability of glycosides, with an α-linkage being much more susceptible to degradation. This is borne out quite dramatically in the divergent behavior of amylose

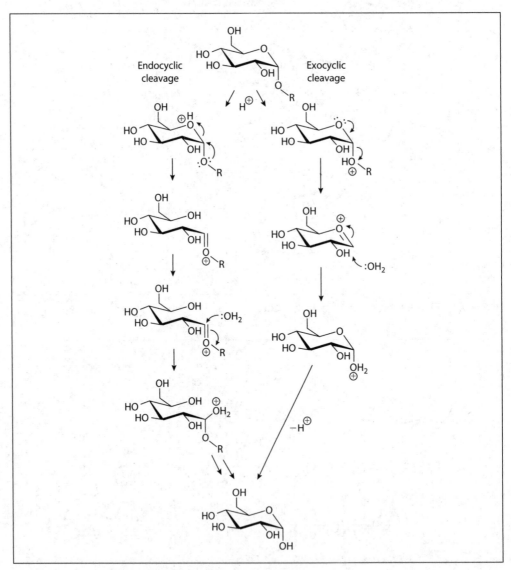

FIGURE 9-74 Two routes of hydrolysis.

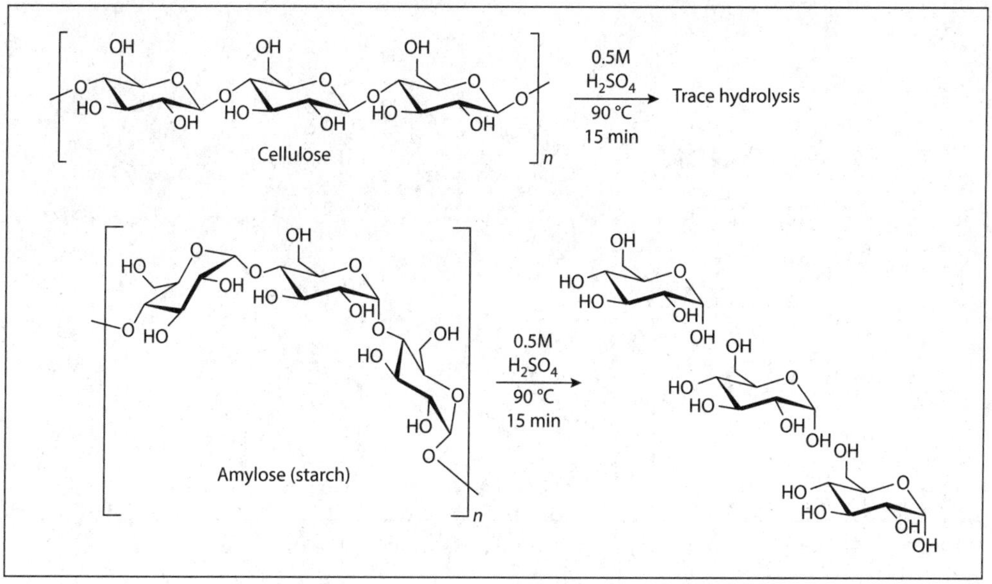

329

CHAPTER 9:
Structure, Function,
and Reactivity
of Biologically
Relevant Molecules

FIGURE 9-75 Differential stability of amylose and cellulose.

(starch) and cellulose in hot dilute sulfuric acid (see Figure 9-75). Under these conditions, amylose is hydrolyzed by more than 97 percent to provide free glucose, whereas cellulose exhibits only trace amounts of hydrolysis.

Lipids

The class of lipids includes fats, waxes, and oils. While there is some diversity in structure among these compounds, the ester functional group is an almost universal feature. The following section discusses the preparation and reactions of triacylglycerols, which include three ester linkages.

PREPARATION OF TRIACYLGLYCEROLS

Triacylglycerols (aka **triglycerides**) can be synthesized using enzyme catalysis or with coupling reagents. When all the fatty acid residues are identical, the enzymatic route is almost exclusively encountered. For triglycerides with multiple acyl components, the coupling strategy is usually advantageous. The two methods can also be used in concert, as shown in Figure 9-76. First, vinyl laurate is esterified under the catalysis of *Candida antarctica* lipase to provide the symmetrical 1,3-dilaureoyl glycerol, which is then coupled to a chlorinated fatty acid 1-ethyl-3-(3-dimethylaminopropyl)-carbodiimide (EDCI) to provide the triglyceride shown. This triacylglycerol was used as an analytical standard for the determination of chlorinated lipids of marine origin.

The mechanism for the last reaction is analogous to the DCC-mediated amide formation shown earlier in Figure 9-64. In essence, EDCI is DCC with a built-in tertiary

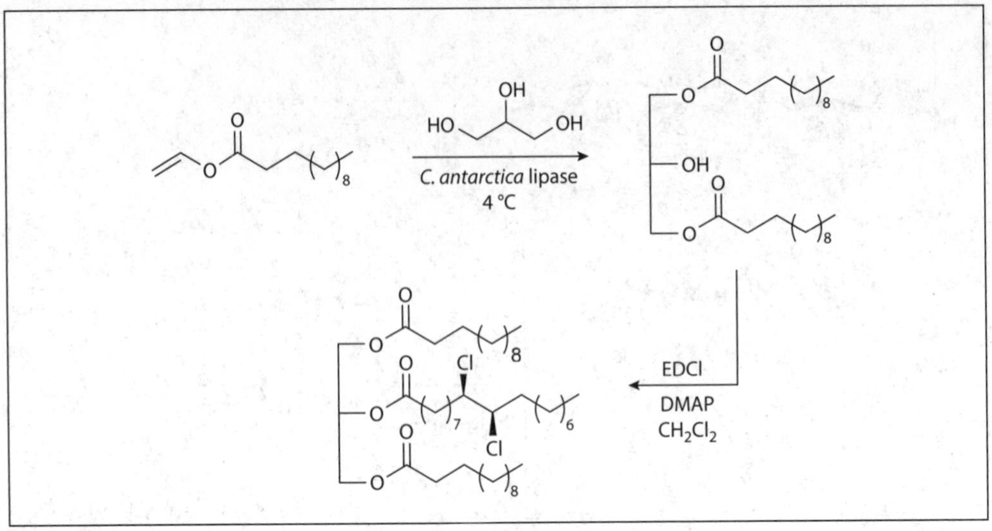

FIGURE 9-76 Enzyme-assisted chemical synthesis of a triacylglycerol.

amine base (see Figure 9-77). Thus the reaction proceeds through initial deprotonation of the acid to provide a carboxylate ion, which adds to the central carbon of the diimide. After a proton is transferred, the free amine coordinates to the alcohol proton, activating it toward an Ad_N attack onto the activated acyl group. Collapse of the anionic tetrahedral intermediate so formed provides the desired ester.

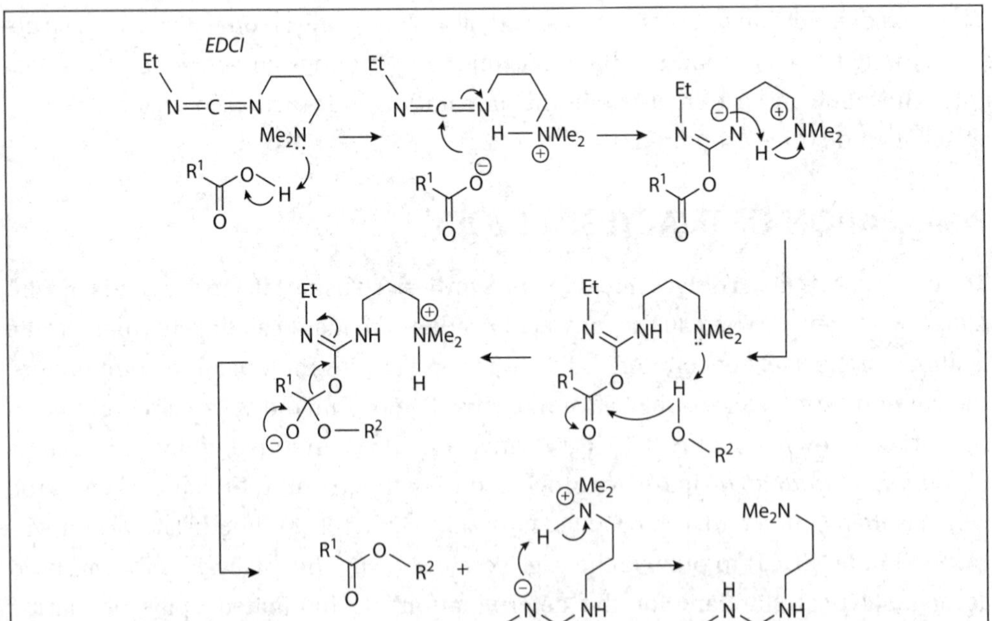

FIGURE 9-77 Mechanism of the EDCI reaction.

331

CHAPTER 9:
Structure, Function,
and Reactivity
of Biologically
Relevant Molecules

REACTIONS OF TRIACYLGLYCEROLS

One of the more common reactions of triglycerides is their base-catalyzed hydrolysis, or saponification (Reaction 39). To provide a historical example, the complete saponification of tallow (see Figure 9-78) provides glycerol and three equivalents of potassium stearate, which was a component of the earliest soaps.

Another particularly important chemical transformation of triglycerides involves their transesterification (see Reaction 47). For example, 1-palmitoyl-2-oleoyl-3-linoleoyl-glycerol, a component of soybean oil, undergoes reaction in refluxing sodium methoxide in ethanol to provide the methyl esters of the three component acid moieties in the original fat (see Figure 9-79). This reaction is relevant to alternative energy sources, as it is used to create biodiesel from renewable feedstocks.

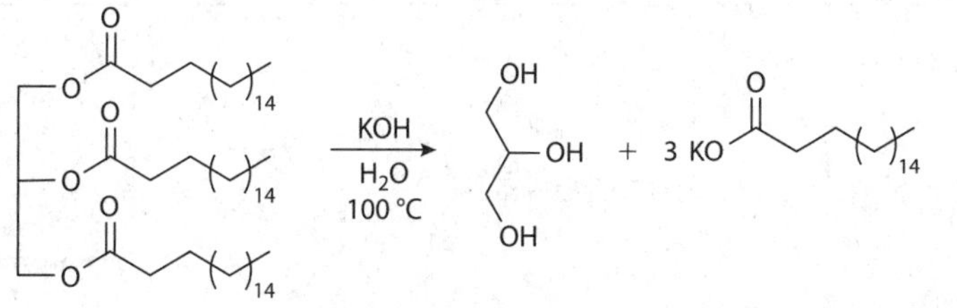

FIGURE 9-78 Saponification of tristearoyl glycerol (tallow).

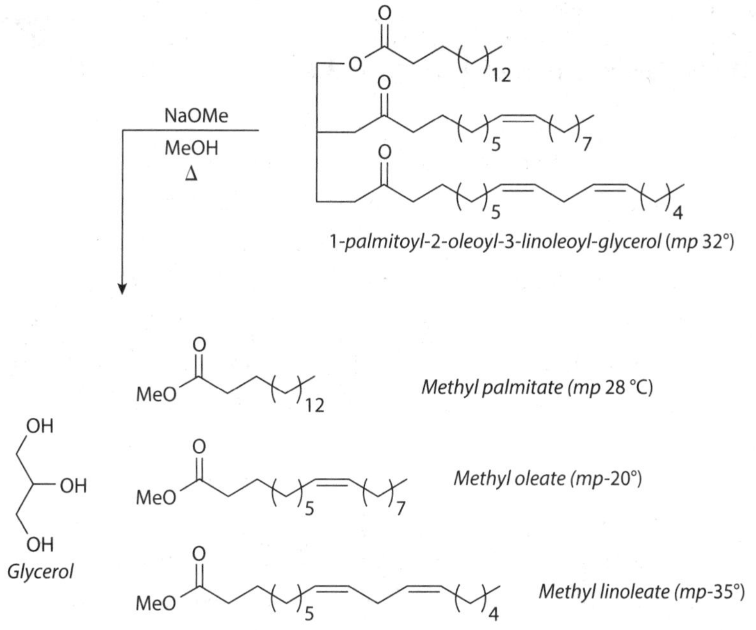

FIGURE 9-79 Transesterification of 1-palmitoyl-2-oleoyl-3-linoleoyl-glycerol.

Nucleotides and Nucleic Acids

Probably the most iconic biomolecule, DNA is a polymeric structure derived from monomeric nucleotides. The following section discusses the preparation and reaction of oligonucleotides.

PREPARATION OF OLIGONUCLEOTIDES

Polynucleotides DNA (deoxyribonucleic acid) and **RNA (ribonucleic acid)** are built up from five heterocyclic bases (see Figure 9-80). Two of these—adenine and guanine—share the purine architecture, an aromatic heterobicyclic system containing four nitrogen atoms. The other three—uracil, thymine, and cytosine—are based on the simpler pyrimidine system, a nitrogenous aromatic system akin to pyridine.

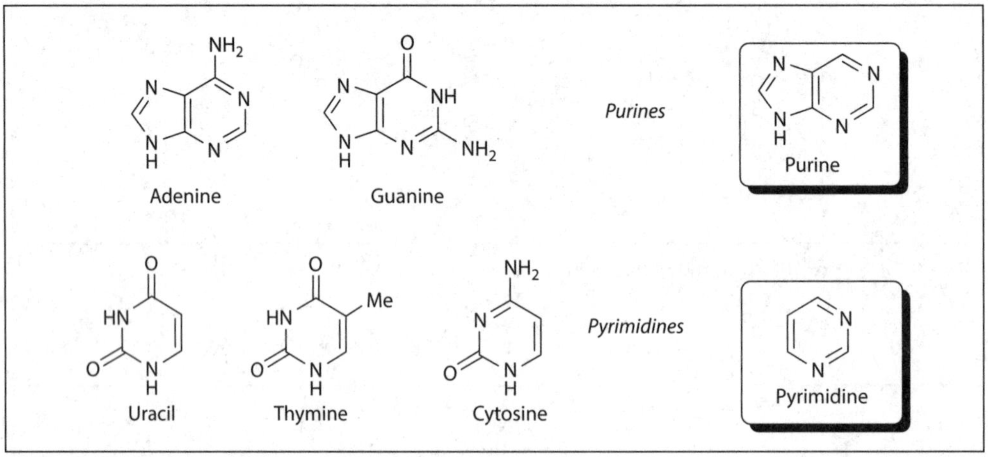

FIGURE 9-80 The five heterocyclic bases in DNA and RNA.

When the bases are connected covalently to a ribose residue, they become known as nucleosides. Thus adenine + ribose = adenosine, and so forth (see Figure 9-81). The nucleosides can be further elaborated by phosphorylation at the C-5 hydroxy, as exemplified by adenosine monophosphate (AMP) and adenosine triphosphate (ATP), which are classified as nucleotides. The monophosphonucleotides can be assembled into oligonucleotides by bridging the C-3 and C-5 hydroxy groups via the phosphate group.

Note that the three types of nucleotides shown in Figure 9-81 exhibit three distinct phosphate linkages. Adenosine monophosphate (AMP) features a phosphate ester, which is formed between an alcohol (the C-5 hydroxy in this case) and phosphoric acid. The essential connectivity here is P-O-C array. Adenosine triphosphate (ATP) also has an ester linkage, but it also features a phosphate anhydride functionality, which is created by the condensation of two phosphoric acid moieties. These

333

CHAPTER 9:
Structure, Function,
and Reactivity
of Biologically
Relevant Molecules

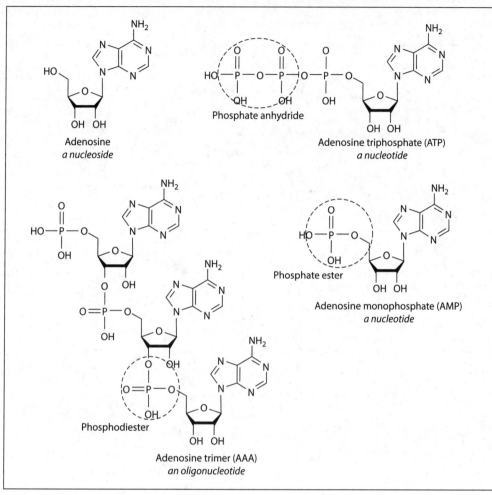

FIGURE 9-81 Nucleosides, nucleotides, and oligonucleotides.

linkages can be recognized by the P-O-P sequence. Finally, one of the essential chemical characteristics of oligo- and polynucleotides is the so-called **phosphate backbone**, which is a series of phosphodiester functional groups. These are formed through the combination of phosphoric acid and two alcohols—therefore, they contain a C-O-P-O-C array.

Very large nucleotide polymers (like DNA) are usually prepared through biochemical (enzymatic) means. However, there exists the need to synthesize smaller, very well-defined oligomers to study specific features of DNA behavior. One answer to this need is found in the solid-supported **Caruthers synthesis** of oligonucleotides (see Figure 9-82). This methodology (also called the **phosphoramidite synthesis**) starts with a nucleoside that is bound to a solid support via the C-3 hydroxy and that has the C-5 hydroxy protected with the 4,4-dimethoxytrityl group, which can be removed under acidic conditions (see Figure 9-83).

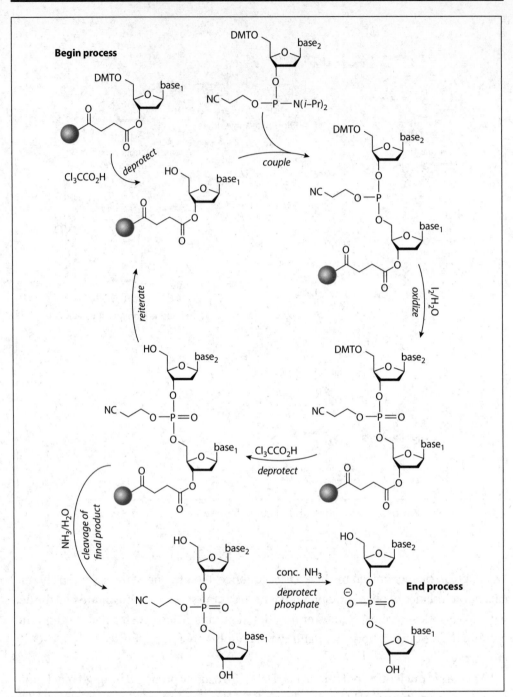

FIGURE 9-82 Solid-supported oligonucleotide synthesis.

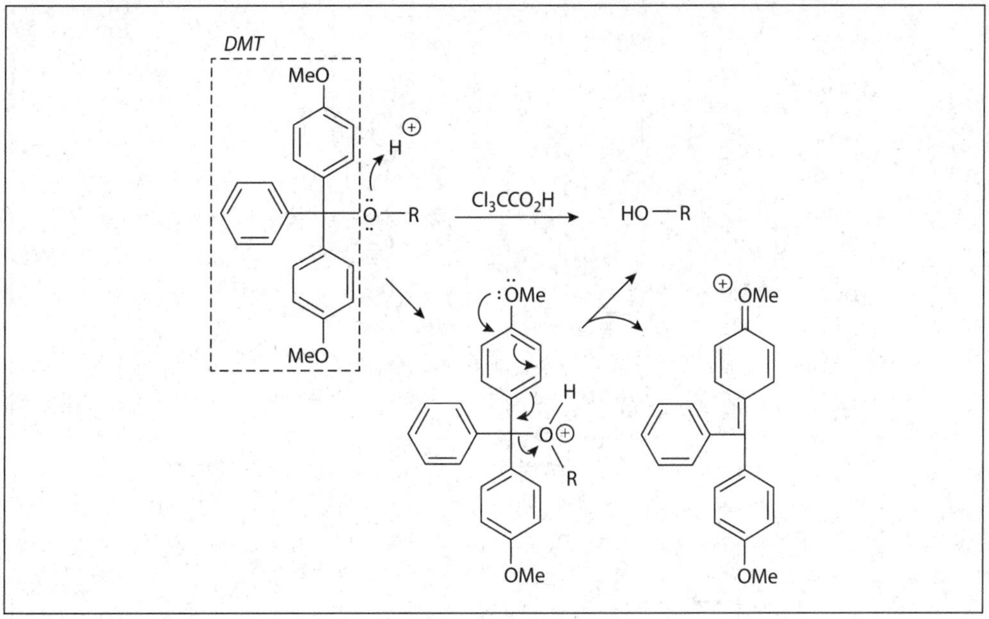

335

CHAPTER 9:
Structure, Function,
and Reactivity
of Biologically
Relevant Molecules

FIGURE 9-83 Deprotection of a DMT-protected alcohol.

Deprotection of the resin-bound base reveals the free C-5 hydroxy group, which can then be coupled to a second nucleoside bearing a phosphoramidite group. Reaction of the C-5 hydroxy of the first nucleoside with the phosphoramidite group of the second leads to a new phosphite ester, which is oxidized to a phosphotriester using iodine in a water-pyridine-THF medium. The C-5 hydroxy group of the newly appended nucleoside is now deprotected, so the attachment of the third nucleoside can be carried out in the same way. When the oligonucleotide has reached the desired length, it is freed from the solid support through ester hydrolysis (aqueous ammonia). Finally, all the phosphodiester groups are deprotected by heating in concentrated ammonia.

REACTIONS OF OLIGONUCLEOTIDES

Perhaps the most important nonenzymatic reaction of oligonucleotides is their base-catalyzed hydrolysis. In the case of RNA (see Figure 9-84), the hydrolysis is especially rapid because of assistance from the C-2 hydroxy group. Consequently, DNA is more stable toward hydrolysis because it is based on 2-deoxyribose, which lacks the C-2 hydroxy group.

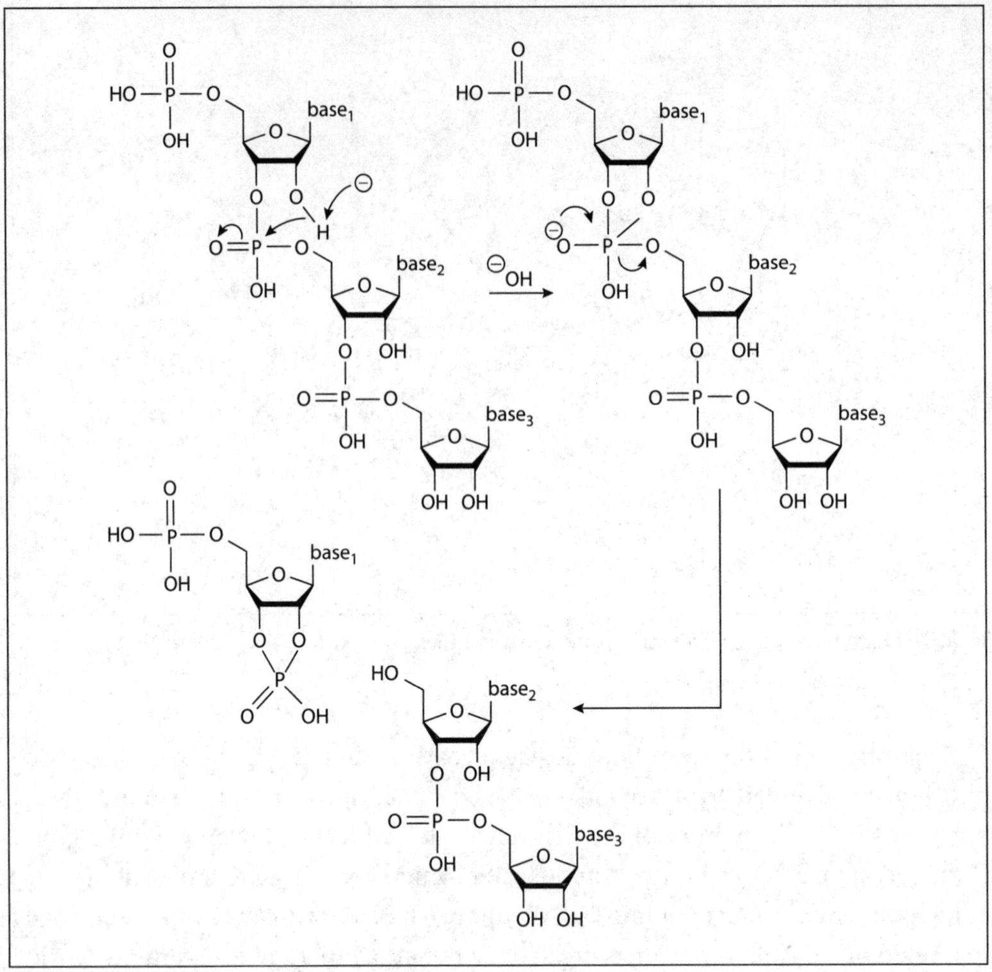

FIGURE 9-84 Hydrolysis of RNA.

Principles of Chemical Thermodynamics and Kinetics

Read This Chapter to Learn About

➤ Enzymes

➤ Principles of Bioenergetics

➤ Thermodynamics: Energy Changes in Chemical Reactions

➤ Kinetics and Equilibrium: Rate Processes in Chemical Reactions

---

ENZYMES

The **cell**, the basic unit of life, acts as a biochemical factory, using food to produce energy for all the functions of life, including growth, repair, and reproduction. This work of the cell involves many complex chemical processes, including respiration and energy transfer, in which specific enzymes are used to facilitate the reactions.

Classification of Enzymes

Enzymes are a special category of proteins that serve as biological **catalysts**, speeding up chemical reactions. The enzymes, with names often ending in the suffix *–ase*, are essential to the maintenance of **homeostasis**, or a stable internal environment, within a cell. The maintenance of a stable cellular environment and the functioning of the cell are essential to life.

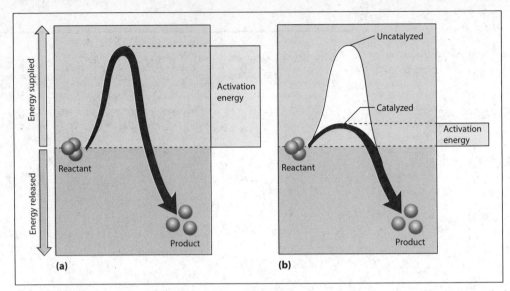

FIGURE 10-1 Lowering activation energy. (*a*) Activation energy is the amount of energy needed to destabilize chemical bonds. (*b*) Enzymes serve as catalysts to lower the amount of activation needed to initiate a chemical reaction. *Source:* From George B. Johnson, *The Living World*, 3rd ed., McGraw-Hill, 2003; reproduced with permission of The McGraw-Hill Companies.

Enzymes function by lowering the **activation energy** (see Figure 10-1) required to initiate a chemical reaction, thereby increasing the rate at which the reaction occurs. Enzymes are involved in **catabolic reactions** that break down molecules, as well as in **anabolic reactions** that are involved in biosynthesis. Most enzymatic reactions are reversible. Enzymes are unchanged during a reaction and are recycled and reused.

Enzyme Structure

As stated earlier, enzymes are proteins and, like all proteins, are made up of **amino acids**. Interactions between the component amino acids determine the overall shape of an enzyme, and it is this shape that is critical to an enzyme's ability to catalyze a reaction.

The area on an enzyme where it interacts with another substance, called a **substrate**, is the enzyme's **active site**. Based on its shape, a single enzyme typically only interacts with a single substrate (or single class of substrates); this is known as the enzyme's **specificity**. Any changes to the shape of the active site render the enzyme unable to function. Enzyme kinetics or the rate of biochemical reactions is described by the **Michaelis–Menten mechanism:**

$$[\text{enzyme}] + [\text{substrate}] \underset{k_{-1}}{\overset{k_1}{\rightleftharpoons}} [\text{enzyme} - \text{substrate complex}] \overset{k_2}{\Rightarrow} \text{enzyme} + \text{products}$$

where k_1, k_{-1}, and k_2 are reaction rate constants.

339

CHAPTER 10:
Principles of
Chemical
Thermodynamics
and Kinetics

Enzyme Function

The **induced fit model** is used to explain the mechanism of action for enzyme function seen in Figure 10-2. Once a substrate binds loosely to the active site of an enzyme, a conformational change in shape occurs to cause tight binding between the enzyme and the substrate. This tight binding allows the enzyme to facilitate the reaction. A substrate with the wrong shape cannot initiate the conformational change in the enzyme necessary to catalyze the reaction.

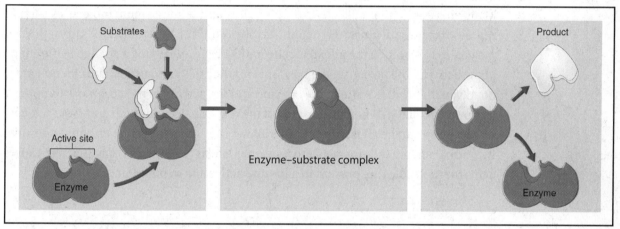

FIGURE 10-2 The induced fit model. Enzymes interact with their substrates to form an enzyme–substrate complex. This complex allows the chemical reaction to occur. *Source:* From George B. Johnson, *The Living World,* 3rd ed., McGraw-Hill, 2003; reproduced with permission of The McGraw-Hill Companies.

Some enzymes require assistance from other substances to work properly. If assistance is needed, the enzyme has binding sites for cofactors or coenzymes. **Cofactors** are various types of ions such as iron and zinc (Fe^{2+} and Zn^{2+}). **Coenzymes** are organic molecules usually derived from vitamins obtained in the diet. For this reason, mineral and vitamin deficiencies can have serious consequences on enzymatic functions.

Factors That Affect Enzyme Function

There are several factors that can influence the activity of a particular enzyme. The first is the **concentration of the substrate** and the **concentration of the enzyme**. Reaction rates stay low when the concentration of the substrate is low, whereas the rates increase when the concentration of the substrate increases. **Temperature** is also a factor that can alter enzyme activity. Each enzyme has an optimal temperature for functioning. In humans, this is typically body temperature (37 °C). At lower temperatures, the enzyme is less efficient. Increasing the temperature beyond the optimal point can lead to enzyme **denaturation**, which renders the enzyme useless. Enzymes also have an **optimal pH** in which they function best, typically around 7 in humans, although there are exceptions. Extreme changes in pH can also lead to enzyme denaturation. The denaturation of an enzyme is not always reversible.

Control of Enzyme Activity

It is critical to be able to regulate the activity of enzymes in cells to maintain efficiency. This regulation can be carried out in several ways. Feedback, or **allosteric inhibition**, illustrated in Figure 10-3, acts somewhat like a thermostat to regulate enzyme activity. Many enzymes contain allosteric binding sites and require **signal molecules** such as **repressors** and **activators** to function. As the product of a reaction builds up, repressor molecules can bind to the **allosteric site** of the enzyme, causing a change in the shape of the active site. The consequence of this binding is that the substrate can no longer interact with the active site of the enzyme and the activity of the enzyme is temporarily slowed or halted. When the product of the reaction declines, the repressor molecule dissociates from the allosteric site. This allows the active site of the enzyme to resume its normal shape and normal activity. Some allosteric enzymes stay inactive unless activator molecules are present to allow the active site to function.

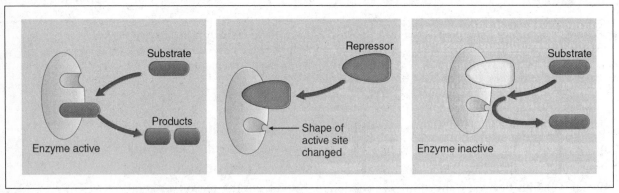

FIGURE 10-3 Allosteric inhibition of an enzyme. Repressors can be used to regulate the activity of an enzyme. *Source:* From George B. Johnson, *The Living World*, 3rd ed., McGraw-Hill, 2003; reproduced with permission of The McGraw-Hill Companies.

Inhibitor molecules also regulate enzyme action. A **competitive inhibitor** is a molecule that resembles the substrate in shape so much that it binds to the active site of the enzyme, thus preventing the substrate from binding. This halts the activity of the enzyme until the competitive inhibitor is removed or is outcompeted by an increasing amount of substrate. **Noncompetitive inhibitors** bind to allosteric sites and change the shape of the active site, thereby decreasing the functioning of the enzyme. Increasing levels of substrate have no effect on noncompetitive inhibitors, but the activity of the enzyme can be restored when the noncompetitive inhibitor is removed.

341

CHAPTER 10:
Principles of
Chemical
Thermodynamics
and Kinetics

PRINCIPLES OF BIOENERGETICS

Overview of Metabolism

Living organisms maintain their systems in a dynamic steady state by taking in food. Energy is extracted from food to build complex molecules from simpler ones, and for storage. Collectively, these processes are called **metabolism**, the enzyme-catalyzed transformation of energy and matter.

The metabolic pathways are a sequence of enzymatic reactions that serves to transform energy and matter. In these sequences, the product of one reaction is the substrate for the next. Intermediates are called **metabolites**. There are two aspects of metabolism: catabolism and anabolism. **Catabolism** involves the breakdown of complex molecules into simpler ones. Food molecules are broken down to building block molecules and energy. Some of this energy is stored as **ATP** (adenosine triphosphate). **Anabolism** involves the biosynthesis of complex molecules from the building blocks. The energy needed for this comes from stored ATP, from high-energy hydrogen in the form of **NADPH** (nicotinamide adenine dinucleotide phosphate).

Bioenergetics/Thermodynamics

Metabolism is quantified using principles of thermodynamics: enthalpy, entropy, and free energy. It is the ΔH, ΔS, and ΔG that is considered. **Enthalpy** is the heat content. The ΔH of a reaction can be determined from the sum of the ΔH_f of the products minus the ΔH_f of the reactants. The **entropy** of a system is the degree of randomness. The more random the system, the higher the S. S cannot be measured, but can be obtained from $\Delta G = \Delta H - T\Delta S$ where ΔG, ΔH, and T can be measured. The **free energy** is the amount of useful work that can be obtained from a system at constant temperature, pressure, and volume. The change in free energy $\Delta G°$ can be derived from the equilibrium constant K of a reaction, where $\Delta G° = -RT \ln K$. R is the gas constant 8.314 J/mol K and T is temperature in Kelvin. ΔG is a measure of the spontaneity of a reaction. If it is a negative value, the reaction is spontaneous (exothermic), and if it is a positive value, the reaction is endothermic.

Phosphorylation/ATP

An unfavorable reaction $(+\Delta G)$ can be driven forward by coupling it to a favorable one, so that the net ΔG is negative. For instance, the formation of glucose-6-phosphate from glucose and phosphate (P_i) is unfavorable, with a ΔG of $+3.3$ kcal. If this reaction is coupled to the hydrolysis of ATP to ADP and P_i, which has a $\Delta G = -7.3$ kcal, then glucose can be phosphorylated with a net $\Delta G = -4.0$ kcal.

Phosphorylation Reaction	ΔG
$ATP + H_2O \longrightarrow ADP + P_i$	-7.3 kcal
$Glucose + P_i \longrightarrow Glucose\text{-}6\text{-}phosphate$	$+3.3$ kcal
$Glucose + ATP + H_2O \longrightarrow Glucose\text{-}6\text{-}phosphate + ADP$	-4.0 kcal

ATP is a high-energy phosphate compound. As such, it has a highly negative ΔG for the hydrolysis of phosphate. All high-energy phosphate compounds have excellent phosphate group transfer potential. ATP transfers phosphate to many sugars and glycerol. The enzymes that catalyze this process are called **hexokinases** and **glycerol kinases**. Kinases are **transfer enzymes**. All high-energy phosphate compounds pass P_i to lower energy acceptors via ATP. The ΔG of ATP hydrolysis, at -7.3 kcal, is intermediate between compounds of high phosphate transfer potential and those with lower phosphate transfer potential. ATP functions as the carrier of phosphate between the catabolic pathways and the anabolic pathways.

Sometimes two terminal phosphates of ATP are removed as pyrophosphate, PP_i, leaving AMP. Energy is obtained by the hydrolysis of pyrophosphate to two phosphates by the enzyme pyrophosphatase as shown:

$$PP_i + H_2O \longrightarrow 2P_i \qquad \Delta G = -7.2 \text{ kcal}$$

The AMP reacts with an ATP to form two ADPs by the enzyme adenylate kinase in the reaction:

$$AMP + ATP \longrightarrow 2ADP$$

Other nucleoside triphosphates are used as well. GTP is used in protein synthesis, CTP is used in lipid synthesis, and UTP is used in polysaccharide synthesis. The NDP or NMP formed is re-phosphorylated by ATP in the reaction:

$$UDP + ATP \longrightarrow UTP + ADP$$

High-energy phosphate compounds act as storage forms of energy. The turnover of ATP is very high. One's body weight in ATP is formed and broken down every 24 hours. Therefore, ATP is not the greatest for energy storage. Creatine phosphate is the storage form of phosphate in humans. During rest, creatine is re-phosphorylated by ATP.

Oxidation–Reduction in Biological Systems

Redox reactions are electron-transfer reactions. **Oxidation** is the loss of electrons while **reduction** is the gain of electrons. The compounds NAD and NADPH are the common reducing agents in metabolic pathways.

$$NADH \longrightarrow NAD^+ + H^+ + 2e^-$$
$$NADPH \longrightarrow NADP^+ + H^+ + 2e^-$$

343

CHAPTER 10:
Principles of
Chemical
Thermodynamics
and Kinetics

The electrons given off are ultimately used to reduce oxygen to water. The ultimate acceptor of electrons derived from food molecules is oxygen. Food molecules transfer electrons to electron carriers such as NAD^+ or FAD. The electrons from the carriers reach oxygen via the electron transport system. Both NAD^+ and FAD are the cofactors for the dehydrogenase enzymes involved in oxidation of food molecules. The breakdown pathways are oxidative, while the anabolic pathways are reductive and use NADPH as the electron donor.

THERMODYNAMICS: ENERGY CHANGES IN CHEMICAL REACTIONS

Thermodynamics is the study of the relationships of enthalpy, entropy (disorder of a system), and free energy. The laws of thermodynamics and certain formulas explain the relationships between free energy, entropy, work, temperature, and equilibrium.

Thermodynamic System and State Functions

A **state function** is a property of a system that depends upon its current condition only. It will not matter how one arrives at that condition. These functions could include ΔE (energy change), ΔU (internal energy change), ΔH (enthalpy change), ΔS (entropy change), or ΔG (Gibbs free energy change). Examples that are not state functions are work (W) and heat (Q).

Zeroth Law of Thermodynamics

The **zeroth law of thermodynamics** explains what happens when three systems are in thermal equilibrium with each other. To summarize, should two systems be separate from each other but both be in thermal equilibrium with a third, then the first two are also in thermal equilibrium with each other. For example, if in a closed system you have three solid metal cubes all at different temperatures and in contact with each other, the heat will flow from the high temperatures to the low temperatures until a thermal equilibrium is reached.

First Law of Thermodynamics

The first law of thermodynamics states that the change in the internal energy of a system is given by $\Delta U = Q + W$, where Q = heat and W = work. U is the sum of the kinetic and potential energies. It is a state function; that is, it depends only on the initial and final states, and not on the path between. The **heat Q** is the energy into or out of a system because of a temperature difference between the system and its surroundings. **Work** W is the energy that results when a force moves an object some distance, d.

The enthalpy H is equal to the quantity $U + PV$, where H is also a state function. ΔH is the difference between the initial and final states; at atmospheric pressure, $\Delta H = Q$.

Second Law of Thermodynamics

The **second law of thermodynamics** states that the **total entropy** of a system and its surroundings always increases for a spontaneous process. This law relates spontaneity to entropy. The effect on the surroundings must be taken into account.

For a spontaneous process, ΔS must be $> Q/T$, and at equilibrium, $\Delta S = Q/T = \Delta H/T$.

ENTROPY: A MEASURE OF SYSTEM DISORDER

Entropy, represented by the symbol S, is a measure of the **disorder of a system**. S is also a state function, and ΔS is the difference between the initial and final states.

If ΔS is positive, the process results in more disorder. If ΔS is negative, the process results in more order.

If disorder is increasing, ΔS_{rxn} is positive. Some examples of processes with increasing disorder include more gas produced than used up; a solid converted to a liquid; and a solid dissolved in a solvent.

If order is increasing, ΔS_{rxn} is negative. Some examples of processes that have increasing order include less gas produced than used up; a liquid converted to a solid; and a solid precipitated from a solution.

RELATIVE ENTROPY FOR GAS, LIQUID, AND SOLID STATES

Different phases of matter will have different degrees of freedom and randomness. The more disorder present in a system, the more entropy that system will have. The letter symbol for entropy is S, and because it is a state function, you look at only the final and initial entropy of a system, ΔS.

Because gas molecules are spread out and have a continuous random, straight-line motion with (ideally) no forces of attraction between them, the entropy of gases is far greater than that of liquids. Liquids and solids both have their molecules touching, but the molecules in liquids have more freedom than those of solids. To summarize ΔS for the phases: gas $>>$ liquid $>$ solid.

Examples of processes in which ΔS is negative might be raking up leaves and placing them in a bag or condensing steam into a liquid. Examples of processes in which ΔS is positive might be the wind blowing those same leaves all over or you spilling a glass of water. One important concept to keep in mind is that the entropy of the universe

345

CHAPTER 10:
Principles of
Chemical
Thermodynamics
and Kinetics

is positive. All of the matter in the universe is believed to have been together at one time until the Big Bang occurred. Since then, the universe has been expanding, which explains why processes in the universe favor a positive value for ΔS. Think about the last time you dropped an egg by accident. When was the last time you saw the egg white, yolk, and shell come back together on its own to re-form the egg?

Calorimetry

HEAT

Heat is closely associated with temperature, but they are very different quantities. **Heat**, or **thermal energy**, is a form of energy that depends on a change of temperature and can be converted to work and other forms of energy. The quantity of heat Q gained or lost by a body is related to the temperature difference ΔT by the following equation:

$$Q = mc\Delta T$$

where m is the mass of the body and c is a proportionality constant termed the specific heat capacity. **Specific heat capacity** is the heat needed to raise the temperature of 1 g of a substance by 1°C. It has the symbol c and the units J/g °C. Thus, $Q = mc\Delta T$, where ΔT is the difference in the initial and final temperatures. The following table lists the specific heats of some common substances.

TABLE 10-1 The Specific Heat of Some Common Substances

Substance	Specific Heat in J/g °C
Al	0.900
Au	0.129
C (diamond)	0.502
Cu	0.385
Fe	0.444
Hg	0.139
H_2O	4.184

EXAMPLE: Calculate the heat needed to raise the temperature of 85.3 g of iron from 35.0 °C to 275.0 °C.

SOLUTION:

➤ The ΔT is 275.0 °C − 35.0 °C = 240.0 °C.
➤ The c for iron is 0.444 J/g °C, given from the table.
➤ Plug the values into the equation and solve for Q:

$$Q = mc\Delta T = (0.444 \text{ J/g °C}) (85.3 \text{ g}) (240.0 \text{ °C}) = 9.09 \times 10^3 \text{ J}$$

Calorimetry involves the use of an insulated container at room pressure to measure the heat changes that occur during a physical or chemical process. Because the calorimeter is insulated, no heat can leave or enter the system, and all of the heat changes that occur within the calorimeter are zero. In other words, the heat that is given off equals the heat that is gained.

Heat released = heat absorbed

and ΔT = higher temperature – lower temperature

The calorimeter itself is ignored in the following calculations.

EXAMPLE: Calculate the final temperature of the system when an 18.4-g sample of aluminum at 215 °C is added to a calorimeter that contains 120.0 g water at 24.5 °C.

SOLUTION:

➤ The c for water is 4.184 J/g °C.

➤ The c for aluminum is 0.900 J/g °C, given from the table.

➤ The ΔT for the water is $x - 24.5$ °C, where x is the final temperature. For water, x is the higher temperature.

➤ The ΔT for the aluminum is 215 °C $- x$, where x is the final temperature. For the aluminum, 215 °C is the higher temperature.

➤ Plugging into the equation $(mc\Delta T)_{H_2O} = (mc\Delta T)_{Al}$ and solving for x:

$$(120.0 \text{ g})(4.184 \text{ J/g} °C)(x - 24.5 °C) = (18.4 \text{ g}) (0.900 \text{ J/g} °C)(215 °C - x)$$

$$x = 30.6 °C$$

Heat of transformation is similar to the specific heat capacity, but it accounts for changes in the phase of the body. The specific heat of a body assumes that no change in phase occurs during a temperature change. In order for a substance to change states of matter—that is, from solid to liquid or from liquid to gas—heat energy must be added to or removed from the substance. The amount of heat required to change the phase of 1 kg of a substance is the heat of transformation L. Thus, the total amount of heat Q gained or lost by a substance of mass m during a change between phases is:

$$Q = mL$$

where L is the heat of transformation unique to the substance. The heat of transformation exists in two forms, according to the particular phase transformation:

➤ **Heat of fusion.** L_f is the amount of heat energy required to change 1 kg of solid matter to liquid or the amount of energy released when changing 1 kg of liquid matter to solid.

➤ **Heat of vaporization.** L_v is the amount of heat energy required to change 1 kg of liquid matter to gas or the amount of energy released when changing 1 kg of gas matter to liquid.

347

CHAPTER 10:
Principles of
Chemical
Thermodynamics
and Kinetics

Heat Transfer

There are three mechanisms of heat transfer: conduction, convection, and radiation, each dependent on the state of matter of the object.

Conduction is the method of heat energy transfer that occurs in solids—for example, the warming of a spoon when cream is stirred in coffee. In conduction, heat energy is transferred by collisions between the rapidly moving molecules of the hot region and the slower-moving molecules of the cooler region. A portion of the kinetic energy from the rapidly moving molecules is transferred to the slower-moving molecules, causing an increase in heat energy at the cooler end and a subsequent increase in the flow of heat.

Convection is the method of heat energy transfer that occurs in liquids and gases—for example, the cooling of coffee after cream is poured into it. Convection represents the transfer of heat energy due to the physical motion or flow of the heated substance, carrying heat energy with it to cooler regions of the substance. In contrast to conduction, convection is the primary mechanism of heat transfer in fluids.

Radiation is the method of heat energy transfer that occurs in space, for example, Earth's surface being warmed by the sun. Radiation represents the transfer of heat energy by electromagnetic waves that are emitted by rapidly vibrating, electrically-charged particles. The electromagnetic waves propagate from the heated body or source at the speed of light.

Endothermic and Exothermic Reactions

Heat is an energy that flows into or out of a system due to a difference between the temperature of the system and its surroundings when they are in thermal contact. Heat flows from hotter to cooler areas and has the symbol Q. If heat is added to a system, Q is positive. If heat is removed from a system, Q is negative. The units of heat are joules (J) or calories. One calorie equals 4.184 J.

A reaction from which heat is given off and has a negative Q is called an **exothermic reaction**. A reaction that requires heat to be added and has a positive Q is called an **endothermic reaction**.

ENTHALPY AND STANDARD HEATS OF REACTION AND FORMATION

Enthalpy is a state function and it is used to denote heat changes in a chemical reaction. It is given the symbol H. Because it depends only on the initial and final states of the system, the difference between these states is ΔH. At standard pressure (1 atm), $Q = \Delta H$.

ΔH_f° is called the **enthalpy of formation** of a substance. It denotes the heat that is absorbed or given off when a substance is produced from its elements at standard temperature (25 °C) and pressure (1 atm).

ΔH°_{rxn} is called the **enthalpy of reaction**. It denotes the amount of heat that is given off $(-\Delta H)$ or absorbed $(+\Delta H)$ by a reaction at standard temperature and pressure. The ΔH°_{rxn} can be calculated from ΔH°_f values. For the reaction

$$aA + bB \rightarrow cC + dD,$$

the ΔH°_{rxn} is

$$\Delta H^\circ_{rxn} = \left[\sum c(\Delta H_f(C)) + d(\Delta H_f(D))\right] - \left[\sum a(\Delta H_f(A)) + b(\Delta H_f(B))\right]$$

HESS'S LAW OF HEAT SUMMATION

Some reactions are the sum of individual reaction steps. To sum reactions, any compound that shows up on the left side of one equation and on the right side of another equation cancels out. **Hess's law** states that the sum of the ΔHs for each individual equation sum to the ΔH_{rxn} for the net equation.

$2C + 2O_2$	$\rightarrow$	$2CO_2$	ΔH_1
$2CO_2$	$\rightarrow$	$2CO + O_2$	ΔH_2
sum $2C + O_2$	$\rightarrow$	$2CO$	$\Delta H_{sum} = \Delta H_1 + \Delta H_2$

EXAMPLE: Determine the ΔH of the following reaction:

$$2S + 3O_2 \rightarrow 2SO_3$$

given these reactions and their ΔHs

$$SO_2 \rightarrow S + O_2 \qquad \Delta H_1 = 297 \text{ kJ}$$
$$2SO_3 \rightarrow 2SO_2 + O_2 \qquad \Delta H_2 = 198 \text{ kJ}$$

SOLUTION:

➤ First, reverse the first equation and reverse the sign of ΔH_1.
➤ Next, double the first equation and double the ΔH_1.
➤ Then, reverse the second equation and reverse the sign of ΔH_2.

$2S + 2O_2$	$\rightarrow$	$2SO_2$	$\Delta H_1 = -594 \text{ kJ}$
$2SO_2 + O_2$	$\rightarrow$	$2SO_3$	$\Delta H_2 = -198 \text{ kJ}$
sum $2S + 3O_2$	$\rightarrow$	$2SO_3$	$\Delta H_{sum} = -792 \text{ kJ}$

Bond Dissociation Energy

If the equation is doubled, then the ΔH°_{rxn} doubles as well.

349

CHAPTER 10:
Principles of
Chemical
Thermodynamics
and Kinetics

The ΔH_f° of a compound can be calculated using bond dissociation energies, found in the following table. The formula is:

$$\Delta H_f^\circ = \sum \text{BE of bonds broken} - \sum \text{BE of bonds formed}$$

where BE is the bond energy per mole of bonds.

TABLE 10-2 Dissociation Energies of Selected Single Bonds in kJ/mole

	H	C	N	O	S	F	Cl	Br	I
H	432								
C	411	346							
N	386	305	167						
O	459	358	201	142					
S	363	272			226				
F	565	485	283	190	284	155			
Cl	428	327	313	218	255	249	240		
Br	362	285		201	217	249	216	190	
I	295	213		201		278	208	175	149

Data from Huheey, J. E., Keiter, E. A., and Keiter, R. L., *Inorganic Chemistry*, 4th ed. New York: Harper Collins, 1993; pp. A21–A34.

EXAMPLE: Determine the ΔH_f° of HF using bond dissociation energies.

SOLUTION:

➤ First write the equation for the formation of HF from its elements:

$$H_2\ (g) + F_2\ (g) \rightarrow 2HF\ (g)$$

➤ For H_2, the BE = 432 kJ/mole.
➤ For F_2, the BE = 155 kJ/mole.
➤ For HF, the BE = 565 kJ/mole.
➤ Substitute the values into the equation and solve for ΔH_f°:

$$\Delta H_f^\circ = [(1 \text{ mole } H_2)(432 \text{ kJ/mole}) + (1 \text{ mole } F_2)(155 \text{ kJ/mole})]$$
$$- [(2 \text{ mole HF}) (565 \text{ kJ/mole})] = -544 \text{ kJ}$$

Free Energy

Free energy has the symbol G and is defined as $H - TS$. One can predict the spontaneity of a process from the sign of ΔG_{rxn}°. Free energy is useful because it eliminates the need to worry about the surroundings.

SPONTANEOUS ENERGY

The equation used is $\Delta G^\circ = \Delta H^\circ - T\Delta S^\circ$. When ΔG° is negative, the reaction is spontaneous as written. When ΔG° is positive, the reaction is spontaneous in the opposite direction.

The maximum work for a spontaneous reaction is equivalent to ΔG. The free energy change is the maximum energy available to do useful work.

THE RELATIONSHIP BETWEEN THE EQUILIBRIUM CONSTANT K AND ΔG

When not at equilibrium, $\Delta G = \Delta G° + RT \ln Q$, where Q is the reaction quotient. Therefore, because $\Delta G = 0$ at equilibrium, $\Delta G° = -RT \ln K$.

EXAMPLE: Calculate K for a reaction for which $\Delta G° = -13.6$ kilojoules (kJ)

SOLUTION:

$$\ln K = \frac{-13,600 \text{ J}}{(-8.314 \text{ J/mol K})(298.2 \text{ K})} = 5.49$$

$$K = e^{5.49} = 242 \quad \text{large } K, \text{ spontaneous reaction}$$

ΔG AND TEMPERATURE

Because $\Delta H° - T\Delta S° = \Delta G°$, the signs of each variable determine the sign of $\Delta G°$. If both $\Delta H°$ and $\Delta S°$ are positive, $\Delta G°$ is negative at high temperatures. If both $\Delta H°$ and $\Delta S°$ are negative, $\Delta G°$ is negative at low temperatures. If $\Delta H°$ is negative and $\Delta S°$ is positive, $\Delta G°$ is always negative. The last case is if $\Delta H°$ is positive and $\Delta S°$ is negative; in this case, $\Delta G°$ is always positive.

EXAMPLE: Estimate the temperature above which a certain reaction becomes spontaneous, if $\Delta H = 178.3$ kJ and $\Delta S = 159$ J/K.

SOLUTION:

➤ At the point between spontaneity and nonspontaneity, at equilibrium, $\Delta G° = 0$
➤ Plug in the values into $T = \Delta H° / \Delta S°$.

$$T = 178,300 \text{ J}/159 \text{ J/K} = 1121 \text{ K}$$

Thermal Expansion

Thermal expansion is a physical phenomenon in which increases in temperature can cause substances in the solid, liquid, and gaseous states to expand.

LINEAR EXPANSION OF SOLIDS

A solid subjected to an increase in temperature ΔT experiences an increase in length ΔL that is proportional to the original length L_0 of the solid. The relation for the linear expansion of solids is:

$$\Delta L = \alpha L_0 \Delta T$$

351

CHAPTER 10:
Principles of
Chemical
Thermodynamics
and Kinetics

where the proportionality constant α is the coefficient of linear expansion and is expressed in units of inverse temperature.

EXAMPLE: A metal cylindrical rod of length $L = 4.0$ meters (m) is heated from $25\,°C$ to $225\,°C$. Given a coefficient of linear expansion of $11 \times 10^{-6}\,°C^{-1}$, determine the change in length following expansion.

SOLUTION: The equation needed to solve this problem is:

$$\Delta L = \alpha L_o \Delta T = \left(11 \times 10^{-6}\,°C^{-1}\right)(4.0\text{ m})\left(225\,°C - 25\,°C\right) = 8.8\text{ mm}$$

VOLUMETRIC EXPANSION OF LIQUIDS

A liquid subjected to an increase in temperature ΔT experiences an increase in volume ΔV that is proportional to the original volume V_o of the liquid. The relation for the volumetric expansion of liquids is:

$$\Delta V = \beta V_o \Delta T$$

where the proportionality constant β is the coefficient of volumetric expansion and is equal to 3α. As is the case for α, the units of β are inverse temperature.

VOLUMETRIC EXPANSION OF GASES

The volumetric expansion of gases can be summarized by two important gas laws: Charles's law and Boyle's law, which can be combined in the ideal gas law.

Charles's law states that at constant pressure P, the volume V occupied by a given mass of gas is directly proportional to the absolute temperature T by:

$$V = kT \quad \text{or} \quad \frac{V_1}{T_1} = \frac{V_2}{T_2}$$

$P = $ constant and k is a proportionality constant.

Boyle's law states that at constant temperature, the volume V occupied by a given mass of gas is inversely proportional to the pressure P exerted on it:

$$PV = k \quad \text{or} \quad P_1 V_1 = P_2 V_2$$

$T = $ constant and k is a proportionality constant.

The **ideal gas law** combines the relations from Charles's law and Boyle's law to yield:

$$PV = nRT \quad \text{or} \quad \frac{P_1 V_1}{T_1} = \frac{P_2 V_2}{T_2}$$

where R is the universal gas constant ($R = 0.082$ L atm/mol K) and n is the number of moles.

Heats of Vaporization and Fusion

The equation for heat given previously cannot be used for a phase change, because there is no temperature difference during a phase change. The temperature remains the same during the freezing/melting process or during the boiling/condensation process. So for an equation that denotes a phase change, such as:

$$H_2O\ (s) \rightarrow H_2O\ (l) \qquad \Delta H_{fus} = 6.01\ kJ/mole,$$

the heat change is the heat needed to convert 1 mole of solid water to 1 mole of liquid water at 0 °C, and is called the **heat of fusion**, ΔH_{fus}.

For the boiling process,

$$H_2O\ (l) \rightarrow H_2O\ (g) \qquad \Delta H_{vap} = 44.6\ kJ/mole$$

The heat change is the heat needed to convert 1 mole of liquid water to 1 mole of water vapor at 100.0°C, and is called the **heat of vaporization**, ΔH_{vap}.

The preceding can be summarized in the following table:

TABLE 10-3 Summary of Phase Transformations

Phase Transformation	Descriptive Term	Temperature Point	Heat of Transformation
Solid state → Liquid state	Melting	Melting point	Heat of fusion
Liquid state → Solid state	Freezing	Melting point	Heat of fusion
Liquid state → Gas state	Boiling	Boiling point	Heat of vaporization
Gas state → Liquid state	Condensation	Boiling point	Heat of vaporization

Phase Diagrams

Phase changes occur due to a change in temperature, pressure, or both. The most common phases are solid, liquid, and gas. The names of the phase changes are as follows:

TABLE 10-4 Summary of Phase-to-Phase Changes

Solid to liquid	Melting
Solid to gas	Sublimation
Liquid to solid	Freezing
Liquid to gas	Evaporation
Gas to liquid	Condensation
Gas to solid	Deposition

A **phase diagram** shows the different phases that a substance is in over a range of temperatures and pressures. A simple phase diagram is shown in Figure 10-4.

The lines in Figure 10-4 represent the boundaries between the phases. Each point on a line represents a certain temperature and pressure for that phase transition. The solid–liquid boundary line extends indefinitely, but the liquid–gas boundary ends at the point C, which is called the **critical point**, and it represents the beginning of the supercritical fluid phase. At all temperatures and pressures beyond those at point C, the substance is in a phase that is in between liquid and gas called **supercritical fluid**.

Point *T* is called the **triple point**. At this pressure and temperature, all three phases coexist in an equilibrium mixture. This means that the actual number of molecules

353

CHAPTER 10:
Principles of
Chemical
Thermodynamics
and Kinetics

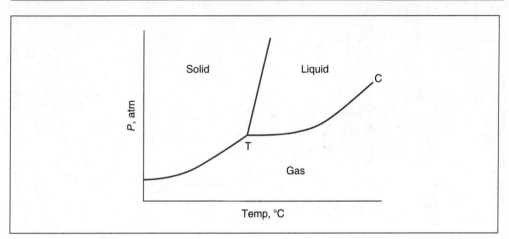

FIGURE 10-4 A typical pressure–temperature diagram.

in each phase remains the same, but the individual molecules are changing their phase.

The boiling and freezing points at 1 atmosphere (atm) pressure are called the **normal boiling point** and the **normal freezing point**. To determine these values, find the temperature that corresponds to 1 atm pressure on the liquid–gas boundary and on the solid–liquid boundary.

The **density** of a substance increases with pressure. Therefore, the relative densities of the phases can be determined by following the phases as the pressure is increased. The phase that exists at the highest pressures is the densest phase. For water, the densest phase is the liquid phase. For most other substances, the solid phase is the densest phase.

KINETICS AND EQUILIBRIUM: RATE PROCESSES IN CHEMICAL REACTIONS

Kinetics is the study of how fast reactions occur; this is called the **reaction rate**. Reaction rates are dependent on the temperature at which the reaction is taking place, on the concentrations of the reactants, and on whether a catalyst is present.

Reaction Rates

Reaction rates are measured experimentally. If the reactant is colored, its absorbance can be followed. At the beginning of the reaction, the absorbance is at a maximum, and it decreases as the reactant disappears (turns into product; see Figure 10-5).

The rate equals the change in concentration with time. The rate is fastest at the beginning of the reaction. An **instantaneous rate** is the change in the concentration of the reactant divided by the change in time, or:

$$\Delta[\text{reactant}] / \Delta t$$

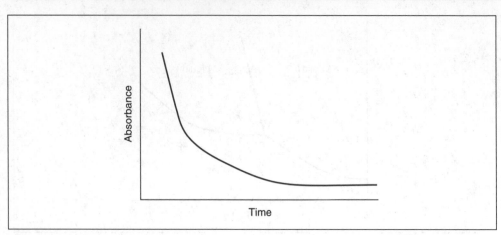

FIGURE 10-5 Reaction rate.

when the change in time, or Δt, is a very small increment of time. This is seen as the tangent to the curve, at any point. The tangent has the steepest slope at the beginning of the reaction (fastest rate), and the flattest slope at the end of the reaction (slowest rate). So the reaction slows with time.

FACTORS THAT INFLUENCE REACTION RATE

The rate at which reactants become products can be manipulated via a number of methods. By no means should you confuse these methods for obtaining more products with the methods for shifting an equilibrium to obtain more product. Two conditions that are needed for a reaction to occur are (1) the reactants' molecules need to collide, and (2) they must do so effectively.

Concentration of Reactants. In order to make more products, reactants need to be in contact with each other. Increasing the concentration of the reactants increases the frequency and likelihood that this process will occur. Consider the following situation. When less A and B are present, their likelihood of collision is low:

A ⟶ B

But if you double the number of A and B, you see that there are more possibilities:

Temperature. An increase in temperature will increase the average kinetic energy of the molecules. With more kinetic energy, the molecules will have a greater velocity according to the equation $KE = \frac{1}{2}mv^2$. If the molecules collide with more kinetic energy, their collisions will be more effective. Therefore, with an increase in kinetic energy, the rate of reaction increases as well.

Activation Energy. Energy, no matter its quantity or its form, is needed to start a reaction. The energy barrier that reactants need to overcome to react is called the

355

CHAPTER 10:
Principles of
Chemical
Thermodynamics
and Kinetics

activation energy, E_a. For an exothermic reaction, the activation energy will be small compared to the activation energy for the reverse reaction. A good example is a stick of dynamite. It takes only a little bit of fire (activation energy) from a match to light the fuse, but the amount of energy released will be enormous in comparison. For an endothermic reaction, the activation energy will be far greater than the activation energy for the reverse reaction.

Physical State. The physical state of the reactants can greatly determine how long it will take for a reaction to take place. Consider the reaction between aqueous silver nitrate and aqueous sodium chloride. When the two reactants are mixed, the following reaction occurs:

$$AgNO_3\ (aq) + NaCl\ (aq) \rightarrow NaNO_3\ (aq) + AgCl\ (s)$$

The mixing of the two clear aqueous solutions immediately produces a white precipitate, silver chloride. The aqueous ionic solutions have their ions ready to react upon contact.

In contrast, consider a reaction between two covalently bonded compounds such as an alcohol and a carboxylic acid. Even though the reaction is typically catalyzed by sulfuric acid, it needs to be refluxed for multiple hours to ensure a high yield of the ester. In order to get the reactants to form an activated complex and start forming products, covalent bonds need to be broken with a sufficient amount of energy. This is a much slower process when compared to aqueous ions.

CATALYSTS

Catalysts speed a reaction rate by lowering the **activation energy** of the reaction. The catalyst may be involved in the formation of the activated complex, the high-energy compound that is partly starting material and partly product, but it is regenerated at the end of the reaction.

Catalysts can be in the same phase as the reactants (homogeneous) or in a different phase (heterogeneous). They can be inorganic or organic. Biological catalysts are called **enzymes**, and they catalyze every biochemical reaction in the body. Enzymes are very specific for their starting material, which is called its **substrate**. They often interact with the substrate like a key fitting into a lock. A three-dimensional site on the substrate acts as the lock, and the enzyme fits into the site, called the **active site**, like a key. Enzymes work optimally within a very narrow range of temperature and pH.

RATE LAW AND RATE CONSTANT

Kinetics studies how the reaction rate changes when the concentrations of the reactants change. This rate data is used to determine the rate law for the reaction. The **rate law** expresses how the rate is affected by the concentrations and by the rate constant.

For a reaction

$$A + 2B \rightarrow products,$$

the rate law is written

$$Rate = k[A]^x [B]^y$$

where [A] is the molarity of A, [B] is the molarity of B, x is the order with respect to A, and y is the order with respect to B.

The rate constant can be used to determine the concentration of the reactant at any point. For a first-order reaction (overall), the equation is:

$$\ln[A]_t = \ln[A]_0 - kt$$

where ln means natural log, $[A]_0$ is the concentration of A at the beginning of the reaction ($t = 0$), and $[A]_t$ is the concentration of A at time t; k is the rate constant, and t is the time.

EXAMPLE: For a first-order reaction

$$A \rightarrow product,$$

the rate constant is $3.02 \times 10^{-3} \ s^{-1}$. The concentration of A initially is 0.025 M.

SOLUTION:

1. Calculate the [A] after 172 s.
2. Calculate the time for the [A] to reach 1.13×10^{-3} M.
3. Calculate the time needed for 98% of the [A] to react.

   ➤ Plug in $[A]_0 = 0.0250$ M, $t = 172$ s, $k = 3.02 \times 10^{-3} \ s^{-1}$

$$\ln[A]_t = \ln 0.0250 - (3.02 \times 10^{-3} \ s^{-1})(172 \ s)$$

$$= -3.69 - 0.519$$

$$= -4.21$$

$$[A]_t = e^{-4.21} = 0.015 \ M$$

➤
$$\frac{\ln[A]_t}{\ln[A]_0} = -kt$$

$$\ln \frac{0.015}{0.0250} = -(3.02 \times 10^{-3} \ s^{-1}) \cdot t$$

$$-0.511 = -3.02 \times 10^{-3} \ s^{-1} \cdot t$$

$$t = \frac{0.511}{3.02 \times 10^{-3} \ s^{-1}} = 169 \ s$$

357

CHAPTER 10:
Principles of
Chemical
Thermodynamics
and Kinetics

$$\frac{\ln[A]_t}{\ln[A]_0} = -kt$$

$$\ln \frac{2\%}{100\%} = -(3.02 \times 10^{-3}\,s^{-1}) \cdot t$$

$$t = 1294\,s$$

REACTION ORDER

Rates usually relate to the concentration of a reactant in one of three ways: by not changing, by changing proportionately to the change in concentration, or by changing as the square of the change of the concentration.

➤ As the concentration of A is changed, the rate does not change (see Figure 10-6a). The rate is unaffected; the order with respect to A is 0.

➤ As the concentration of A is changed, the rate changes proportionally (see Figure 10-6b). If [A] is doubled, the rate doubles, and so on. The order with respect to A is 1.

➤ As the concentration of A is changed, the rate changes as the square of the change in the concentration (see Figure 10-6c). If [A] is doubled, the rate quadruples, for instance. The order with respect to A is 2.

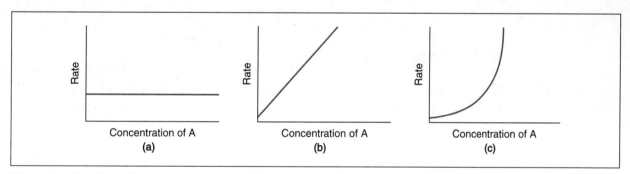

FIGURE 10-6 Relation of rate to concentration of reactant.

The orders of each reactant are thus determined by observing how the rate is affected by the change in the concentration of each reactant. Only one order can be determined at a time. All other concentrations must remain constant; only the concentration of the reactant being studied is changed. The rates are shown under various conditions; these are used to determine the rate law and the rate constant, k, is then calculated.

EXAMPLE: For the reaction

$A + B + C \rightarrow$ products,

determine the rate law and calculate the rate constant using the following data:

Run	[A] (M)	[B] (M)	[C] (M)	Rate (M/s)
1	0.003	0.001	1.0	1.8×10^4
2	0.003	0.002	1.0	3.6×10^4
3	0.006	0.002	1.0	7.2×10^4
4	0.003	0.001	2.0	7.2×10^4

SOLUTION:

➤ From run 1 to 2, the [B] is doubled. The rate doubles, so the order of B is 1. (The rate is directly proportional to the concentration of B.)

➤ From run 2 to 3, the [A] is doubled. The rate doubles, so the order of A is 1. (The rate is directly proportional to the concentration of A.)

➤ From run 1 to 4, the [C] is doubled. The rate quadruples, so the order of C is 2. (The rate is proportional to the square of the concentration of C.)

➤ So the rate law is:

$$\text{rate} = k[\text{A}]\,[\text{B}]\,[\text{C}]^2$$

➤ Using the data from run 1, the rate constant k is calculated:

$$1.8 \times 10^{-4} = k[0.003]\,[0.001]\,[1]^2$$

$$k = 60\ \text{M}^{-3}\text{s}^{-1}$$

Rate-Determining Step

Not all reactions take place in a single step. Instead, many reactions have multiple steps, each with its own activation energy. These individual steps are called elementary steps and, when added together, produce the overall reaction. The step with the greatest energy barrier to overcome will be the slowest step. It is considered to be the **rate-determining step**. For example, when you consider the overall reaction:

$$2\text{NO}\ (g) + \text{Cl}_2\ (g) \rightarrow 2\text{NOCl}\ (g),$$

there are actually two elementary steps:

> Step 1: $\text{NO} + \text{Cl}_2 \rightarrow \text{NOCl}_2$
> Step 2: $\text{NOCl}_2 + \text{NO} \rightarrow 2\text{NOCl}$

To actually know the rate-determining step, you must know the observed rate law. For this particular reaction, the slower step is the second elementary step.

How would you know if the reaction takes place in one step? According to the overall reaction, two molecules of nitric oxide gas, $\text{NO}(g)$, must make contact and react with chlorine gas to form the product. It is highly unlikely that a termolecular reaction will

359

CHAPTER 10:
Principles of
Chemical
Thermodynamics
and Kinetics

take place. Instead, you see that there are bimolecular reactions taking place to form an intermediate, which is consumed in the next step. If one substance were to form a product or intermediate, that type of reaction would be considered to be unimolecular.

Activated Complex or Transition State

Activation energy is needed to provide reactants with enough energy to produce an intermediate between the reactants and products. Once this energy has been achieved, the reaction then reaches a **transition state** in which the reactants start to form the products. This transition state is also called the **activated complex**. The complex formed has its own potential energy called the **potential energy of the activated complex**. This point of a potential energy diagram will be a maximum level, meaning that the complex is less stable and that the next steps of the reaction will be exothermic. This complex is usually a short-lived substance. Once the complex is formed, the products begin to form immediately so as to become a lower-energy, more stable substance.

Interpretation of Energy Profiles

In order to track the energy changes over the course of a reaction, an energy profile (or reaction coordinate diagram) is used. A typical energy profile looks like Figure 10-7.

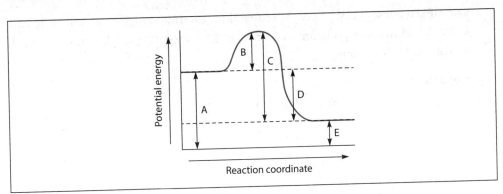

FIGURE 10-7 Typical energy profile.

Figure 10-7 has the following features:

A: The potential energy of the reactants
B: The activation energy of the forward reaction
C: The activation energy of the reverse reaction
D: The heat of reaction, ΔH
E: The potential energy of the products

An example of a multistep energy profile is demonstrated in Figure 10-8. The first energy barrier, requiring more activation energy, would be the rate-determining step for this sample reaction.

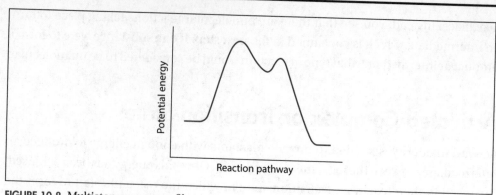

FIGURE 10-8 Multistep energy profile.

ARRHENIUS EQUATION

If the **energy of activation**, E_a, for a reaction is known (this is the minimum energy needed for a reaction to occur), and the rate constant for one temperature is known, the rate constant at any other temperature can be calculated using the **Arrhenius equation**:

$$\ln \frac{k_2}{k_1} = \frac{E_a}{R}(1/T_1 - 1/T_2)$$

where k_1 is the rate constant at temperature T_1, k_2 is the rate constant at temperature T_2, T_1 and T_2 are in Kelvin, $R = 8.314$ joules (J)/mole K, and E_a is the activation energy.

> **EXAMPLE:** For a certain first-order reaction, the rate constant at 190 °C is 2.61×10^{-3} and the rate constant at 250 °C is 3.02×10^{-3}. Calculate the energy of activation of this reaction.
>
> **SOLUTION:**
>
> $$k_1 = 2.61 \times 10^{-3} \quad \text{at } T_1 = 463.2 \text{ K}$$
>
> $$k_2 = 3.02 \times 10^{-3} \quad \text{at } T_2 = 523.2 \text{ K}$$
>
> So
>
> $$\ln \frac{3.02 \times 10^{-3}}{2.61 \times 10^{-3}} = \frac{E_a}{8.314}\left(\frac{1}{463.2} - \frac{1}{523.2}\right)$$
>
> $$\ln 1.16 = \frac{E_a(2.48 \times 10^{-4})}{8.314}$$
>
> $$\frac{0.148(8.314)}{2.48 \times 10^{-4}} = E_a$$
>
> $$5.0 \times 10^3 \text{ J/mole} = E_a$$

Kinetic Control Versus Thermodynamic Control of a Reaction

Sometimes a reaction has competing pathways that can lead to different products, even though the reactants are exactly the same. One pathway may require a lower

361

CHAPTER 10:
Principles of
Chemical
Thermodynamics
and Kinetics

activation energy, or one may form a more stable product than another. The reaction that is governed by a lower activation energy will produce a kinetically-controlled product. A reaction that is favored because it forms a more stable product does so by forming a thermodynamically-favored product. The energy profile shown in Figure 10-9 summarizes these two competing possibilities.

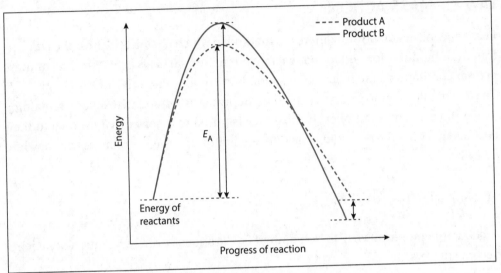

FIGURE 10-9 Kinetic control versus thermodynamic control.

Product A was the kinetically-favored (lower activation energy) product, while Product B was formed via a thermodynamically-favored pathway (more stable product).

Equilibrium in Reversible Chemical Reactions

Equilibrium occurs with reactions that are reversible when the **forward reaction rate** equals the **reverse reaction rate**. Using various formulas, the rate at which a reaction occurs before reaching equilibrium and the concentrations of the products can be determined.

For a reversible reaction, the starting material (on the left) is converted into the product (on the right) at a rate equal to $k[A]^x$:

$$A \rightleftarrows B$$

At a certain point in the progress of the reaction, some of the B that has formed begins to convert to A at a rate equal to $k_{-1}[B]^y$. There comes a point when the forward rate and the reverse rate are equal, and the concentrations of A and B no longer change, although each reaction is still proceeding. This is called the **equilibrium point**. The net numbers of A and B present in the reaction flask remain the same. It appears that the reaction has stopped.

EXAMPLE: If one begins with 100 molecules of A, A begins immediately to turn into B. When enough B's are present, they start to turn back into A. At the equilibrium point, there are, for example, 60 A's and 40 B's. The reactions, both forward and reverse, are still proceeding, but the reaction rates are equal, so there remain at all times 60 A's and 40 B's.

LAW OF MASS ACTION

For a reaction at equilibrium, there is a method in which chemists express the concentration of products formed to the reactants remaining. This is called the **law of mass action**. For example, the following reaction is at equilibrium: $wW + xX \longleftrightarrow yY + zZ$. The law of mass action expresses the ratio of products formed to reactants remaining where the concentration of each substance is raised to a power that is equal to their coefficient. Using the preceding reaction at equilibrium, the law of mass action would look like:

$$K_{eq} = [Y]^y [Z]^z / [W]^w [X]^x$$

A good mnemonic device to remember is, "Products over reactants; coefficients become powers."

The phases of the substances involved in the equilibrium are important to note as well. The law of mass action will include only aqueous substances (*aq*) or gaseous substances (*g*). It will not include solids (*s*) or liquids (*l*). When including an aqueous substance, the concentration should be noted in molarity, M. When gases are involved, the partial pressure of each gas is used. Applying these rules to a purely hypothetical reaction at equilibrium: $2W (aq) + 3X (s) \longleftrightarrow 4Y (l) + 5Z (g)$ the law of mass action would result in:

$$K_{eq} = [Z]^5 / [W]^2$$

EQUILIBRIUM CONSTANT

The **equilibrium constant K** describes the extent to which the forward reaction proceeds before reaching the equilibrium point. Is there a lot of A left over, or just a little? K is a constant value at a constant temperature; it does change with temperature.

If K is large (>1), there is mostly product and very little starting material left at the equilibrium point. This is a **product-favored reaction**.

If K is small (<10^{-4}), there is mostly starting material left over, and very little product formed at the equilibrium point. This is a **reactant-favored reaction**.

With a medium K (between 1 and 10^{-4}), a lot of product is formed, but there are still substantial quantities of starting material left.

363

CHAPTER 10:
Principles of
Chemical
Thermodynamics
and Kinetics

Factors Affecting Equilibrium Constant—Equilibrium Expression. The equilibrium constant K depends on temperature and is related to the amounts of starting material and product in the following manner:

$$aA + bB \rightleftarrows cC \qquad K_c = \frac{[C]^c}{[A]^a[B]^b}$$

where a, b, and c are the molar coefficients and $[\,] =$ mole per liter (mol/L)

EXAMPLE:

$$N_2 + 3H_2 \rightleftarrows 2NH_3$$

SOLUTION:

$$K_p = \frac{(P_{NH_3})^2}{(P_{N_2})(P_{H_2})^3} \text{ in terms of pressure}$$

Only gases (with pressures) and species in solution (with concentrations) affect the equilibrium. Solids and liquids do not appear in the equilibrium expression.

EXAMPLE:

$$C\,(s) + 2Cl_2\,(g) \rightleftarrows CCl_4\,(g)$$

SOLUTION:

$$K_p = \frac{(P_{CCl_4})}{(P_{Cl_2})^2}$$

Given the K and the initial conditions (concentrations or pressures), you can calculate the equilibrium conditions of the products.

If the K is $<10^{-4}$, the reaction does not proceed far before equilibrium. Very little product is formed, and the amount of starting material has changed very little. You can neglect the change in the starting material because it is such a small amount.

EXAMPLE: If you start with 0.240 mole SO_3 in a 3.00-L container, calculate the equilibrium concentrations of SO_2 and O_2 in the reaction:

$$2SO_3 \rightleftarrows 2SO_2 + O_2 \qquad K = 9.6 \times 10^{-8}$$

SOLUTION:

➤ The balanced chemical equation is used to set up an ICE (Initial, Change, Equilibrium) table

TABLE 10-5 ICE Table for a Balanced Chemical Equation

Initial	$2SO_3$ 0.080 M	$\rightleftharpoons$	$2SO_2$ 0	$+$	O_2 0	Initial amounts in M or pressure
Δ	$-2x$		$+2x$		$+x$	For every 2 moles of SO_3 that react, 2 moles of SO_2 and 1 mole of O_2 are formed.
Equilibrium	0.080 M		$2x$		x	Add the values in the column to get the equilibrium value; you can neglect the change to the SO_2; these values go into the K expression.

➤ Write the K expression:

$$K = \frac{[SO_2]^2\,[O_2]}{[SO_3]^2}$$

➤ Plug in the equilibrium values and solve for x:

$$9.6 \times 10^{-8} = \frac{[2x]^2\,[x]}{[0.080]^2}$$

➤ $x = 5.4 \times 10^{-4}$

➤ So the equilibrium concentrations of SO_2 and O_2 are:

$$[SO_2] = 2x = 1.1 \times 10^{-3}\ M$$

$$[O_2] = x = 5.4 \times 10^{-4}\ M$$

You can calculate the K if given the initial conditions (concentrations or pressures) and either the percentage of starting material that reacts or one of the actual equilibrium values.

EXAMPLE: You have 0.40 atm of CH_4 and 0.65 atm of H_2S initially. Calculate the K of the following reaction if 25% of the CH_4 remains at the equilibrium point.

SOLUTION:

Initial	CH_4 (g) 0.40	$+$	$2H_2S$ (g) 0.65	$\rightleftharpoons$	CS_2 (g) 0	$+$	$4H_2$ (g) 0
Δ	$-x$		$-2x$		$+x$		$+4x$
At equilibrium	0.10		0.05		0.30		1.20

➤ The numbers on the bottom line were determined using the information given in the problem. If you start with 0.40 atm of CH_4 and 25% remains at the equilibrium point, then (0.40 atm) (0.25) = 0.10 atm is what remains of the CH_4 at equilibrium.

➤ Then using the equation $0.40 - x = 0.10$, you get $x = 0.30$ atm.

➤ Plugging in this value for x on the change line and adding the columns, the

365

CHAPTER 10:
Principles of
Chemical
Thermodynamics
and Kinetics

other equilibrium values are obtained.

➤ Now you write the K expression.

$$K = \frac{(P_{CS_2}) \, (P_{H_2})^4}{(P_{CH_4}) \, (P_{H_2S})^2}$$

➤ Plug in the bottom line values to calculate K.

$$K = \frac{(0.30) \, (1.20)^4}{(0.10) \, (0.05)^2} = 2.5 \times 10^3$$

LE CHATELIER'S PRINCIPLE

Le Chatelier's principle states that if you subject a system that is at equilibrium, to some change in conditions, the equilibrium shifts so as to counteract the change. For example, note the following reaction:

$$2FeCl_3 \, (s) + 3H_2O \, (g) \rightleftarrows Fe_2O_3 \, (s) + 6HCl \, (g) \quad \text{endothermic}$$

TABLE 10-6 Summary of Changes in Reactions in Equilibrium

Change	Counteraction	Direction of Equilibrium Shift
Add some water vapor	Remove the water vapor	$\rightarrow$
Remove some HCl	Make more HCl	$\rightarrow$
Remove some Fe_2O_3	No counteraction	No change
Add some HCl	Remove some HCl	$\leftarrow$
Increase the volume (decrease the pressure)	Increase the pressure (make more gas molecules)	$\rightarrow$
Decrease the volume (increase the pressure)	Decrease the pressure (remove gas molecules)	$\leftarrow$
Heat the reaction	Remove the heat	$\rightarrow$
Cool the reaction	Increase the heat content	$\leftarrow$

Unit II Minitest

31 Questions

This minitest is designed to assess your mastery of the content in Chapters 6 through 10 of this volume. The questions have been designed to simulate actual MCAT questions in terms of format and degree of difficulty. They are based on the content categories associated with the Foundational Concept that is the theme of this unit. They are also designed to test the scientific inquiry and reasoning skills that the test makers have identified as essential for success in medical school.

In this test, most of the questions are based on short passages that typically describe a laboratory experiment, a research study, or some similar process. There are also some questions that are not based on passages.

Use this test to measure your readiness for the actual MCAT. Try to answer all of the questions within the specified time limit. If you run out of time, you will know that you need to work on improving your pacing.

Complete answer explanations are provided at the end of the minitest. Pay particular attention to the answers for questions you got wrong or skipped. If necessary, go back and review the corresponding chapters or text sections in this unit.

Now turn the page and begin the Unit II Minitest.

Directions: *Choose the best answer to each of the following questions. Questions 1–5 are based on the following passage.*

Passage I

Fritz Haber (1868–1934) was a German chemist who designed a method for making ammonia from nitrogen and hydrogen. This was to Germany's advantage during World War I. The Haber process is an industrial method for making ammonia, NH_3. This process takes N_2 and H_2 gases and combines them at high temperatures (425 °C) and high pressures (200 atm) to force the triple-bonded nitrogen gas to react according to the reversible reaction:

$$N_2 + 3H_2 \leftrightarrow 2NH_3 + heat$$

The higher the pressure, the better the rate of reaction will be. A catalyst is also used in the reaction. Once made, ammonia can be used as a fertilizer, household cleaner, precursor to munitions, and smelling salts.

1. The K_{eq} for the reverse reaction is written as:
   A. $[NH_3]^2/[N_2][H_2]^3$
   B. $[N_2][H_2]^3/[NH_3]^2$
   C. $[NH_3]^2/[N_2] + [H_2]^3$
   D. $[N_2][H_2]/[NH_3]$

2. Which of the following scenarios shifts the reaction to the left?
   A. Not cooling the ammonia once it is formed
   B. Reacting the nitrogen and hydrogen at a higher pressure
   C. Adding more nitrogen gas and hydrogen gas to the reaction
   D. Using a catalyst

3. Addition of a catalyst will change:
   A. the heat of reaction
   B. the potential energy of the reactants
   C. the potential energy of the activated complex
   D. the point of equilibrium

4. The most probable point in the reaction that serves as the rate-determining step is:
   A. the cooling of the ammonia from a gas to a liquid
   B. the breaking of the bond between the hydrogen atoms
   C. nitrogen and hydrogen atoms reacting to form ammonia
   D. the breaking of the bond between the nitrogen atoms

5. The value of K_{eq} for this reaction can change with temperature. Given the temperatures of 300 °C, 400 °C, 500 °C, and 600 °C, which of the following is MOST likely the K_{eq} value when the reaction takes place at 600 °C?

    A. 4.3×10^{-3}

    B. 1.6×10^{-4}

    C. 1.5×10^{-5}

    D. 2.3×10^{-6}

Questions 6 and 7 are not based on a passage.

6. Which of the following BEST demonstrates the Lewis definition of an acid–base reaction?

    A. $HCl + NaOH \rightarrow NaCl + H_2O$

    B. $HCl + NH_3 \rightarrow NH_4^+ + Cl^-$

    C. $BF_3 + NH_3 \rightarrow F_3BNH_3$

    D. $CaO + SiO_2 \rightarrow CaSiO_3$

7. Which of the following are the BEST conditions for carrying out the following transformation shown?

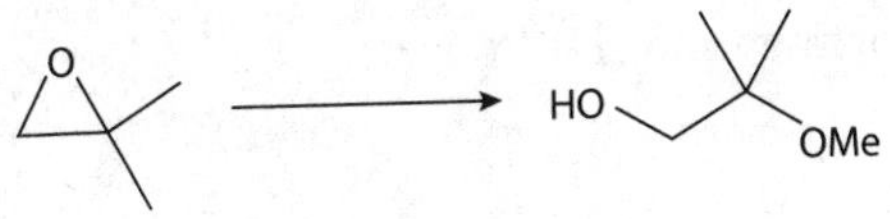

    A. sodium methoxide in methanol

    B. methyl iodide in methanol

    C. *p*-toluenesulfonic acid in methanol

    D. sodium iodide in methanol

Questions 8–11 are based on the following passage.

Passage II

When Compound A (shown) is treated with ozone followed by dimethylsulfide, two new products (B and C) are formed, both of which contain carbonyl groups. On the other hand, treatment of Compound A with pyridinium chlorochromate (PCC) results in a single new product (D).

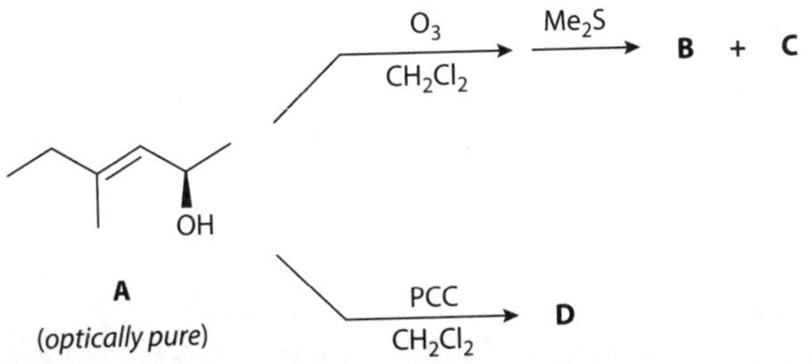

8. What is the best IUPAC name for Compound A?

   A. $(2R, 3Z)$-4-methylhex-3-en-2-ol

   B. $(2R, 3E)$-4-methylhex-3-en-2-ol

   C. $(2S, 3Z)$-4-methylhex-3-en-2-ol

   D. $(2S, 3E)$-4-methylhex-3-en-2-ol

9. The identities of ozonolysis products B and C are BEST described as:

   A. propanal and 2-hydroxypropanal

   B. propanal and 4-hydroxybutanone

   C. 2-butanone and 2-hydroxypropanal

   D. 2-butanone and 4-hydroxybutanone

10. In comparing the physical properties of starting material A and oxidation product D,

    A. the starting material (A) has a lower boiling point and the lower R_f value.

    B. the starting material (A) has a lower boiling point and the higher R_f value.

    C. the starting material (A) has a higher boiling point and the lower R_f value.

    D. the starting material (A) has a higher boiling point and the higher R_f value.

11. The most reasonable pK_a for the starting material (A) is:

    A. -7

    B. 7

    C. 17

    D. 27

Questions 12–16 are not based on a passage.

12. The final result of ATP production after anaerobic respiration is:

    A. the same as the amount of ATP made in aerobic respiration.

    B. equal to the amount of ATP made in glycolysis.

    C. low relative to the amount of ATP made in aerobic respiration.

    D. high relative to the amount of ATP made in aerobic respiration.

13. The drug DNP destroys the H^+ gradient that forms in the electron transport chain. The MOST likely consequence would be:

    A. the cells are forced to perform fermentation.

    B. ATP production increases.

    C. glycolysis stops.

    D. oxygen consumption increases.

14. Which set of conditions shown here will NOT favor an S_N2 reaction?

   A. a strong nucleotide

   B. a leaving group on a primary carbon atom

   C. a lower temperature

   D. a solvent of a higher polarity

15. The approximate pK_a value of an organic compound is 50. This organic compound is MOST likely:

   A. an alcohol

   B. a carboxylic acid

   C. a terminal alkyne

   D. an alkane

16. The carbon dioxide exhaled by animals is produced in:

   A. glycolysis

   B. lactate fermentation

   C. Krebs cycle

   D. electron transport chain

Questions 17–20 are based on the following passage.

Passage III

Reductive amination of Compound A with dimethylamine in the presence of sodium cyanoborohydride at pH 5.5 results in the formation of N, N,2,2-tetramethylpropan-1-amine.

On the other hand, Compound A reacts with methylmagnesium bromide to give another product (Compound B), which contains a hydroxyl group.

17. Which of the following is the most reasonable structure for Compound B?

   A.

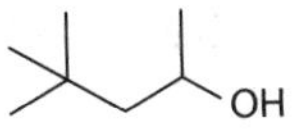

   B.

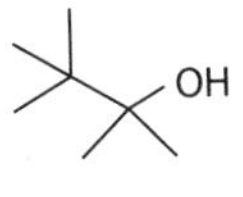

   C.

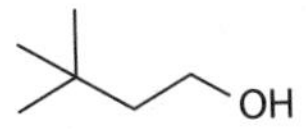

   D.

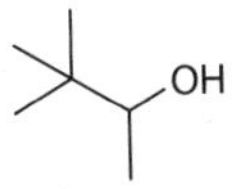

18. Sodium cyanoborohydride is used instead of lithium aluminum hydride (LAH) for the reductive amination because:

    A. sodium cyanoborohydride is a stronger source of hydride than LAH.

    B. sodium cyanoborohydride is a milder source of hydride than LAH.

    C. sodium cyanoborohydride is more sterically hindered than LAH.

    D. sodium cyanoborohydride is less sterically hindered than LAH.

19. The BEST synthesis of methylmagnesium bromide (MeMgBr) is through:

    A. the treatment of methane with magnesium metal and sodium bromide.

    B. the treatment of methane with magnesium bromide.

    C. the treatment of bromomethane with magnesium metal.

    D. the treatment of methylmagnesium with bromine.

20. The functional group present in Compound A is BEST described as a(n):

    A. ketone

    B. ester

    C. alcohol

    D. aldehyde

Questions 21–25 are based on the following passage.

Passage IV

Human tooth enamel is composed of the mineral hydroxyapatite, which has the formula $Ca_5(PO_4)_3OH$. It is insoluble in water, but due to its basicity, it is soluble in acid solution.

Plaque forms on teeth due to a combination of carbohydrates and proteins, called mucin, which produces a film that builds up if not removed by thorough cleaning of the teeth and gums. Plaque traps food particles, which can be fermented by bacteria and produce lactic acid. Saliva does contain buffering agents that can neutralize acid in the mouth, but saliva cannot penetrate solid plaque. Lactic acid levels can drop to as low as pH 4.5 inside the plaque. As the plaque becomes more acidic, hydroxyapatite is converted to calcium hydrogen phosphate, which dissolves in water. The equation is as follows:

$$Ca_5(PO_4)_3OH \ (s) + 4 \ H_3O^+ \ (aq) \rightarrow 3 \ CaHPO_4 \ (aq) + 2 \ Ca^{+2} \ (aq) + 5 \ H_2O \ (1)$$

When the hydroxyapatite reacts, cavities can form. The addition of fluoride to municipal water supplies and to toothpaste has lowered the incidence of cavities in children in the United States. Many children also have fluoride treatments as part of their routine dental care.

Fluoride has the ability to replace the hydroxide ion in hydroxyapatite, forming a compound called fluoroapatite. Fluoroapatite not only has a smaller K_{sp} value than hydroxyapatite, it is less basic as well. Thus it is far less soluble in acid solution. The reaction of fluoride with hydroxyapatite is as follows:

$$Ca_5(PO_4)_3OH\ (s) + F^-\ (aq) \rightleftharpoons Ca_5(PO_4)_3F\ (s) + OH^-\ (aq)$$

The K_{sp} of hydroxyapatite is 7×10^{-37}. The K_{sp} of fluoroapatite is 1×10^{-60}.

21. The dissolution of hydroxyapatite in water is BEST represented by:

    A. $Ca_5(PO_4)_3OH\ (s) \rightleftharpoons 5\ Ca\ (aq) + 3\ PO_4\ (aq) + OH\ (aq)$

    B. $Ca_5(PO_4)_3OH\ (s) \rightleftharpoons Ca_5\ (aq) + (PO_4)_3\ (aq) + OH\ (aq)$

    C. $Ca_5(PO_4)_3OH\ (s) \rightleftharpoons Ca_5\ (PO_4)_3^{+1}\ (aq) + OH^-\ (aq)$

    D. $Ca_5(PO_4)_3OH\ (s) \rightleftharpoons 5\ Ca^{+2}\ (aq) + 3\ PO_4^{-3}\ (aq) + OH^-\ (aq)$

22. Why does the equilibrium of the reaction of hydroxyapatite with fluoride lie to the right?

    A. Fluoride is a weaker base than hydroxide.

    B. Hydroxide can be removed as it is formed by buffers in saliva.

    C. Fluoroapatite is less soluble than the reactant.

    D. The product solidifies onto the surface of the tooth.

23. A larger K_{sp} value means that:

    A. reactants predominate.

    B. products predominate.

    C. there is a lower concentration of ions.

    D. the solid is less soluble.

24. What is the effect on the solubility of hydroxyapatite if calcium ions are added to a saturated solution?

    A. The equilibrium will shift to the right.

    B. The equilibrium will shift to the left.

    C. There will be no effect.

    D. More hydroxyapatite will ionize.

25. The solubility of hydroxyapatite, x, can be found from:

    A. $K_{sp} = x^3$

    B. $K_{sp} = x^5$

    C. $K_{sp} = x^7$

    D. $K_{sp} = x^9$

Questions 26 is not associated with a passage.

26. Which of the following represents the proper Lewis structure for fluoride?

A. $:\ddot{F}\cdot$

B. $:\ddot{F}:$

C. $:\ddot{F}:^+$

D. $:\ddot{F}:^-$

Questions 27–31 are based on the following passage.

Passage V

In a laboratory exercise, a student was given a variety of unknown compounds, all household chemicals, to identify. The student was told that the unknowns included $NaCl$, $NaHCO_3$ (baking soda), sugar ($C_{12}H_{22}O_{11}$), $MgSO_4$ (Epsom salts), $Na_2S_2O_3$ (a photographic fixer), cornstarch, and chalk ($CaCO_3$). The student was asked to identify six of the unknowns using a series of qualitative tests.

The student was also given the following information:

➤ Starch and one of the other compounds are insoluble in water. The rest are soluble in water.

➤ Chalk produces a gas when treated with acid.

➤ Starch turns blue when treated with iodine.

➤ $MgSO_4$ produces a milky precipitate when treated with aqueous ammonia.

➤ $NaHCO_3$ turns pink when treated with phenolphthalein.

➤ $Na_2S_2O_3$ decolorizes iodine solution.

➤ $NaCl$ conducts electricity in solution.

➤ Sugar does not conduct electricity in solution.

The student prepared a flow chart that would aid in doing the experiments in a systematic manner and allow efficient identification of the unknowns.

Experiment

The six unknowns were tested for solubility and conductivity. Each unknown was reacted with the following four reagents: acid, phenolpthalein, ammonia, and iodine. The results of these tests are in the table below. A Y indicates a positive test or reaction, and an N indicates a negative test or no reaction.

Unknown	Solub	Conductivity	Acid	Phenolphthalein	NH_3	I_2
A	Y	Y	N	N	N	N
B	N	N	Y	N	N	N
C	Y	Y	N	N	Y	N
D	N	N	N	N	N	Y$_{BLUE}$
E	Y	Y	Y	Y	N	N
F	Y	Y	N	N	N	Y$_{COLORLESS}$

From these results the student was able to identify all six unknowns.

27. Which of the following unknowns is also insoluble in water?

   A. $NaHCO_3$

   B. $Na_2S_2O_3$

   C. $CaCO_3$

   D. $MgSO_4$

28. Unknown C was determined to be:

   A. $NaHCO_3$

   B. $Na_2S_2O_3$

   C. $CaCO_3$

   D. $MgSO_4$

29. Unknown A was determined to be:

   A. $CaCO_3$

   B. NaCl

   C. $Na_2S_2O_3$

   D. starch

30. The reaction of chalk, $CaCO_3$, produces a gas when treated with acid. This gas is:

   A. oxygen, O_2

   B. carbonic acid, H_2CO_3

   C. carbon dioxide, CO_2

   D. hydrochloric acid, HCl

31. The milky precipitate that is formed when $MgSO_4$ reacts with aqueous ammonia solution is most likely:

   A. $Mg(OH)_2$

   B. $(NH_4)_2SO_4$

   C. $Mg(NH_3)_2$

   D. NH_4OH

This is the end of the Unit II Minitest.

Unit II Minitest Answers and Explanations

1. **The correct answer is B.** When writing the K_{eq} for a reaction, you need to remember "products over reactants, coefficients become powers." Looking at the reaction in reverse, ammonia is the reactant and the nitrogen and hydrogen gases are the products. This is best demonstrated by choice B.

2. **The correct answer is A.** Because the reaction is exothermic, the addition or presence of heat (a product) will cause more products to be present. More products present will mean that the reaction will shift to produce more reactants. This is why it is vital to cool the ammonia once it is formed. The next two choices favor the reaction to proceed to the right. Choice D, the catalyst, has no effect on the point of equilibrium. However, the catalyst will help equilibrium be achieved faster.

3. **The correct answer is C.** The addition of a catalyst will lower the activation energy by producing an alternative pathway for the reaction to proceed. This makes the potential energy of the activated complex lower. Because the potential energy of the reactants and products does not change, the heat of reaction will not change as well.

4. **The correct answer is D.** The rate-determining step is the slowest of the elementary steps of the reaction. The reaction has to overcome the triple-bonded nitrogen to form nitrogen atoms that need to react. This is why the 79 percent of the atmosphere which is nitrogen gas is considered inert (for the most part).

5. **The correct answer is D.** Because the reaction is exothermic, the increase in temperature will drive the equilibrium to the left. This causes more reactants to form. A greater concentration of reactants means a greater value in the denominator of the K_{eq} expression and a lower K_{eq} value.

6. **The correct answer is C.** This question touches on four different definitions of acids and bases. While they do not replace each other, they do enhance each other, depending upon the conditions. Choice A is the classic Arrhenius definition in which H^+ and OH^- neutralize to form water. Choice B shows a proton transfer and demonstrates the Brønsted–Lowry definition. The reaction in choice C shows the ammonia (base) donating a pair of electrons to boron trifluoride (acid), which is indicative of the Lewis definition of an acid–base reaction. The final reaction in choice D shows the less popular Lux–Flood definition in which an O^{2-} ion is transferred from the base (CaO) to the acid (SiO_2).

7. **The correct answer is C.** The product shown is the result of a nucleophilic ring opening of an epoxide. Methyl iodide can be discounted because it does not represent a competent nucleophile. Sodium iodide does provide a good nucleophile (iodide), but it would not provide the product shown. The choice then becomes one of base-catalyzed or acid-catalyzed ring opening in methanol. Here the regiochemistry is the deciding factor. Note that the methoxy group ends up at the more substituted position; yet methoxide (Condition A) would attack at the least hindered (less substituted) position. However, under acidic conditions, the protonated epoxide already starts to open, elongating the bond between the oxygen and the more substituted carbon (i.e., more able to sustain positive character). The lone pair on the methanol is then attracted to the developing positive charge at that site, leading to the product shown.

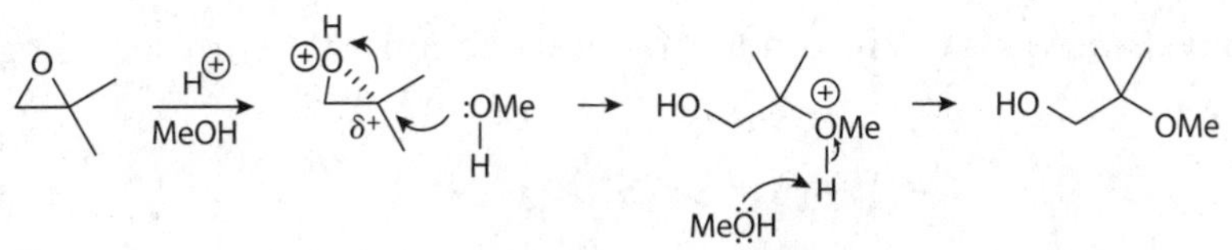

8. **The correct answer is B.** Starting with the chiral center, the priorities can be assigned as follows:

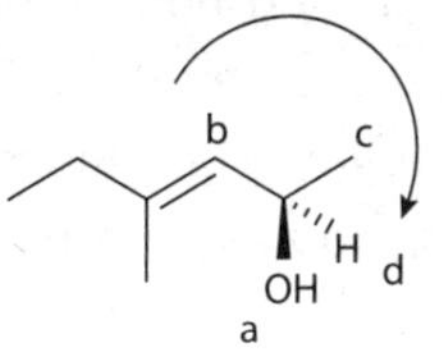

Because the lowest priority is directed away from the observer, and the progression a → b → c describes a clockwise motion, the chiral center is *R*. The double bond is specified using the same priority rules. Assigning priority to the substituents on either side of the double bond, you have:

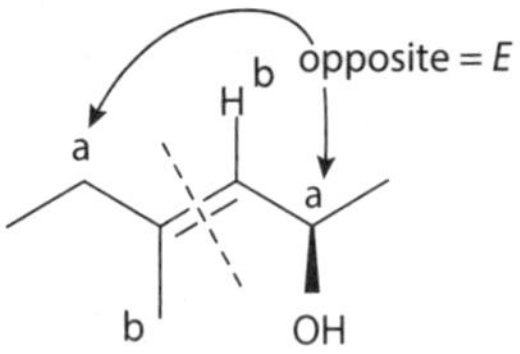

Because the two substituents of the same priority are on opposite sides of the double bond, it is given the *E* (*entgegen*) designation.

9. **The correct answer is C.** Recall that ozonolysis is a type of oxidative cleavage that severs a double bond and, in the case of a reductive workup such as dimethyl sulfide, places a carbonyl at each terminus of the olefin:

2-hydroxypropanal

2-butanone

Because the total carbon count is the same, choices A and D can be excluded (6 carbons and 8 carbons, respectively). The decision between choice B and choice C is governed by regiochemistry (the hydroxyl group remains on the 3-carbon fragment).

10. **The correct answer is C.** The product of the oxidation is the corresponding ketone, as follows:

The molecular weights of the two compounds are virtually identical; therefore, physical properties are governed primarily by differences in functional groups. Compared to ketones, alcohols can serve as both hydrogen bond donors and acceptors, and thus form more extensive H-bond networks, resulting in higher boiling points (e.g., consider the extraordinarily high boiling point of water). For the same reason, an alcohol tends to bind more tightly to the polar silica gel in chromatography, resulting in lower R_f values.

11. **The correct answer is C.** For the purposes of acidity, the starting material is best classified as a secondary alcohol. A suitable familiar model for such a substrate is 2-propanol (isopropanol), which has a pK_a of about 17.

12. **The correct answer is C.** Aerobic respiration produces far more ATP than anaerobic respiration. The process of anaerobic respiration produces 2 ATP (both from glycolysis), whereas aerobic respiration produces about 36 ATP from glycolysis, Krebs cycle, and the electron transport chain. The most accurate answer would be choice C: anaerobic respiration produces far less ATP than aerobic respiration.

13. **The correct answer is A.** If the H^+ (proton) gradient were to be destroyed, the electron transport chain would be affected, as it is the only step of cellular respiration that relies on a concentration gradient. You must look for the choice that relates to how a cell performs cellular respiration without an electron transport chain. The only option is to move to anaerobic respiration, which requires fermentation, as indicated by choice A.

14. **The correct answer is D.** S_N2 reactions take place with stronger nucleophiles, leaving groups on primary carbon atoms and at lower temperatures. A polar solvent favors the formation of ions, a characteristic *not* found in S_N2 reactions.

15. **The correct answer is D.** Ethanol has a pK_a of about 16 and, as expected, acetic acid has a pK_a of about 4.8 as the lower pK_a value. Terminal alkynes can give up their terminal hydrogen atoms in a base so as to react and extend the carbon chain when reacted with the proper alkyl halide. A terminal alkyne has a pK_a value of about 25 for its terminal hydrogen atoms. Alkanes are not very acidic at all and have a very high pK_a value of about 50.

16. **The correct answer is C.** This question relies on direct recollection of the steps of aerobic respiration. During the Krebs cycle, CO_2 is released as citric acid, broken down, and rearranged. There is no release of CO_2 in any other steps of aerobic respiration.

17. **The correct answer is D.** The conditions leading to the formation of $N,N,2,2$-tetramethylpropan-1-amine represent reductive amination, which occurs between amines and carbonyl compounds in the presence of a reducing agent such as sodium cyanoborohydride. Since the amine component is given as dimethylamine, then consideration of the remaining carbon fragment leads to the conclusion that Compound A is the aldehyde. The conditions leading to Compound B are evocative of the Grignard reaction, which proceeds by nucleophilic addition to a carbonyl.

Compound A   **Compound B**

18. **The correct answer is B.** Sodium cyanoborohydride is a much milder source of hydride than LAH, which allows for its use under the acidic conditions necessary for iminium formation. If LAH were placed in an environment of pH 5.5, the following reaction would immediately (and violently) ensue:

$$H^- + H^+ \rightarrow H_2(g)$$

19. **The correct answer is C.** Grignard reagents are prepared by the reduction of haloalkanes with magnesium metal, following the mechanism shown here:

20. **The correct answer is D.** Examination of the amine product reveals a methylene group (i.e., 2 hydrogens) adjacent to the nitrogen. Only one of the hydrogens came from the hydride source (blue); the other (red) was already attached to the carbonyl carbon, meaning the starting material was an aldehyde.

21. **The correct answer is D.** Choice D shows all correct charges and coefficients for the equation. Five moles of calcium ions contribute $+10$. Three moles of phosphate ions contribute -9. One mole of hydroxide ions contributes -1. Adding them together results in a net of zero, signifying that the overall charge of the products is equal to the charge of the reactant.

22. **The correct answer is A.** The direction will lie toward the species that is the stronger base. Because hydroxide is a stronger base than fluoride, the equilibrium will lie to the right.

23. **The correct answer is B.** A larger K_{sp} means that the substance is more soluble and that more ions will be produced. Because the ions are the products, a larger K_{sp} means that the products predominate.

24. **The correct answer is B.** A common ion lowers the solubility of the salt. An increase in calcium ion is an increase in the concentration of a product. The equilibrium will then shift to the left so as to consume this increase and make more reactant.

25. **The correct answer is D.** Choice D shows the correct Lewis structure for fluoride ion. Fluorine atom starts with seven valence electrons. Adding one more electron to complete the octet, produces an ion with a negative 1 charge.

26. **The correct answer is D.** A total of 9 ions are formed when hydroxyapatite dissolves. Because the coefficient of each ion becomes the power of the concentration, you have $[x]^5 \cdot [x]^3 \cdot [x]^1 = [x]^9$.

27. **The correct answer is C.** To determine the unknowns, you begin by summarizing the given information as follows:

Compound	Given information
NaCl	solutions are conductive
$NaHCO_3$	turns pink with phenolphthalein
Sugar	solutions are non-conductive
$MgSO_4$	produces a white precipitate with ammonia
$Na_2S_2O_3$	decolorizes iodine
Cornstarch	insoluble in water and turns blue with iodine
$CaCO_3$	produces a gas with acid
????	one unidentified compound is insoluble

You are given the information that starch and another compound are insoluble. The two insoluble compounds from the results table are B and D. Compound D can be identified as starch because it is the only substance that turns blue with iodine. To identify compound B you must try to find a distinguishing property. The only positive chemical test for compound B is the reaction with acid. Compound E also reacts positively with acid. Compound E can be identified as $NaHCO_3$ because it is the only substance that reacts with phenolphthalein. You are given the information that $CaCO_3$ reacts with acid, so it must be the insoluble compound. This problem could also be solved by recalling the basic solubility rules which include: All sodium salts are soluble (eliminating choices A and B). All sulfates are soluble with a few exceptions such as Pb^{2+}, Ba^{2+}, and Hg_2^{2+} (eliminating choice D). All carbonates with a few exceptions are insoluble (confirming choice C).

28. **The correct answer is D.** The only positive chemical test for C was the reaction with ammonia. You are given the information that $MgSO_4$ produces a milky-white precipitate with ammonia.

29. **The correct answer is B.** Of the seven compounds about which information is given, five have at least one reaction with the chemical reagents: $NaHCO_3$ (phenolphthalein), $MgSO_4$ (ammonia), $Na_2S_2O_3$ (iodine), cornstarch (iodine), and $CaCO_3$ (acid). This leaves only NaCl and sugar. These two are distinguishable based on conductivity. NaCl solutions are conductive as is unknown A, but sugar solutions are non-conductive, so unknown A must be NaCl.

30. **The correct answer is C.** Ionic carbonates and hydrogen carbonates (also called bicarbonates) react with acids to form the unstable compound carbonic acid. Carbonic acid rapidly decomposes to carbon dioxide and water. The gas observed is carbon dioxide.

    The reaction for carbonates is:

    $$CO_3^{2-}(aq) + 2H^+(aq) \rightarrow \text{``}H_2CO_3(aq)\text{''} \rightarrow H_2O(l) + CO_2(g)$$

    The reaction for hydrogen carbonates is:

    $$HCO_3^-(aq) + H^+(aq) \rightarrow \text{``}H_2CO_3(aq)\text{''} \rightarrow H_2O(l) + CO_2(g)$$

31. **The correct answer is A.** Ammonia is a base that produces hydroxide ions in water by abstracting a proton from a water molecule.

    $$NH_3(aq) + H_2O(l) \rightleftharpoons NH_4^+(aq) + OH^-(aq)$$

    The hydroxide ions combine with magnesium ions to form the sparingly soluble compound magnesium hydroxide which appears as a white precipitate.

    $$Mg^{2+}(aq) + 2OH(aq) \rightarrow Mg(OH)_2(s)$$

Cumulative Minitest

30 Questions   30 Minutes

This cumulative minitest is designed to assess your mastery of the content in this volume. The questions have been designed to simulate actual MCAT questions in terms of format and degree of difficulty. They are based on the content categories associated with the Foundational Concepts that are the themes of this volume. They are also designed to test the scientific inquiry and reasoning skills that the test makers have identified as essential for success in medical school.

In this test, most of the questions are based on short passages that typically describe a laboratory experiment, a research study, or some similar process. There are also some questions that are not based on passages.

Use this test to measure your readiness for the actual MCAT. Try to answer all of the questions within the specified time limit. If you run out of time, you will know that you need to work on improving your pacing.

Complete answer explanations are provided at the end of the minitest. Pay particular attention to the answers for questions you got wrong or skipped. If necessary, go back and review the corresponding chapters or text sections.

Now turn the page and begin the Cumulative Minitest.

Directions: *Choose the best answer to each of the following questions. Questions 1–5 are based on the following passage.*

Passage I

Blood pressure, or the force provided by the pumping heart to push the blood through the arteries of the circulatory system, plays an important role in the overall health of an individual and his/her propensity to cardiovascular disease. Blood pressure is typically measured in units of mm Hg. A normal value of systolic blood pressure for a healthy adult at rest is 120 mm Hg. In order to understand and research the influence of blood pressure and the resultant blood flow through a blood vessel, one often uses the mathematical relation known as Poiseuille's law.

Blood flow through a segment of blood vessel can be approximated by the flow of a fluid through a rigid pipe of constant radius using Poiseuille's law. Poiseuille's law describes the volumetric flow rate of a fluid, Q, as:

$$Q = \frac{\Delta P \cdot \pi \cdot R^4}{8 \cdot \eta \cdot L}$$

where ΔP = pressure gradient between two ends of the pipe; η = viscosity of the fluid; R = pipe radius; and L = pipe length.

The fluid's speed through the pipe, v, is related to the volumetric flow of the fluid by:

$$v = \frac{Q}{A}$$

where A is the cross-sectional area of the pipe. A fluid flowing through a pipe of constant radius has a greater speed at the center of the pipe than at the sides of the pipe.

1. Although it is commonly used to explain the dynamics of blood flow through a blood vessel, Poiseuille's law is an approximation. One possible reason that Poiseuille's law serves as an approximation is:
   A. tissue elasticity of the blood vessel.
   B. neutral pH of the blood.
   C. length of the blood vessel.
   D. variation in pressure gradient.

2. By what factor would the flow rate increase in a blood vessel whose radius was increased by 2?
   A. 4
   B. 8
   C. 16
   D. 32

3. A blood vessel of radius 10 mm is partially obstructed to 1/2 of its original radius. If the average blood speed is initially 100 cm/s, what is the average blood speed in the obstructed area?

   A. 50 cm/s

   B. 100 cm/s

   C. 200 cm/s

   D. 400 cm/s

4. The kinetic energy per unit volume of blood passing through a segment of blood vessel at a speed of 0.50 m/s is: (Note: the density of blood, $\rho_b = 1.0 \times 10^3$ kg/m^3)

   A. 100 J/m^3

   B. 115 J/m^3

   C. 120 J/m^3

   D. 125 J/m^3

5. A blood vessel segment with a pressure of 130 mm Hg at one end of the vessel (Point A) and a pressure of 100 mm Hg at the other end (Point B) yields a volumetric blood flow rate of 5000 mL/min. If the pressure at Point A is now elevated to 150 mm Hg and the pressure at Point B elevated to 120 mm Hg, the resultant volumetric blood flow will be:

   A. 5000 ml/min

   B. 10,000 ml/min

   C. 20,000 ml/min

   D. 40,000 ml/min

Questions 6 through 8 are not based on a passage.

6. A solution is prepared with 25 g of NaCl in 500 mL of water. The molarity of the solution is:

   A. 0.37 M

   B. 0.52 M

   C. 0.86 M

   D. 0.98 M

7. The pH of a solution with $[H^+] = 7.5 \times 10^{-5} \dfrac{moles}{L}$ is most closely:

   A. 2

   B. 4

   C. 6

   D. 8

8. Given the chemical equation $Zn + HCl \rightarrow ZnCl_2 + H_2$, the balanced equation is:

   A. $2Zn + 2HCl \rightarrow ZnCl_2 + H_2$

   B. $Zn + 2HCl \rightarrow ZnCl_2 + H_2$

   C. $2Zn + HCl \rightarrow 2ZnCl_2 + H_2$

   D. $Zn + 2HCl \rightarrow ZnCl_2 + 2H_2$

Questions 9–13 are based on the following passage.

Passage II

An important characteristic of the thermal properties of matter is the specific heat capacity. The specific heat capacity, designated by the symbol c, represents the amount of thermal energy (in joules) required to raise the temperature of 1 kg of the substance by 1 °C. The specific heat capacity, c, of an object is related to the thermal energy, Q, by the equation: $Q = mc\Delta T$, where m is the mass of the object (in kilograms) and ΔT is the change in temperature (in degrees Celsius).

An experimental procedure used to determine the specific heat capacity of an object is known as calorimetry. In a typical calorimetry experiment, one places the object of known mass and initial temperature into a container (also referred to as a calorimeter) usually filled with water of known mass, specific heat capacity, and initial temperature. In these types of experiments, the object is usually at a much higher temperature than the water. As the object is placed in the water, the object at the higher temperature loses heat while the water at the lower temperature gains heat. The transfer of heat continues until the system (object and water) reaches the same temperature (thermal equilibrium). Based on the relationship between the transfer of thermal energy in a calorimeter, it is possible to determine the specific heat capacity of an unknown sample, assuming that all other information is known or can be easily obtained.

9. The units of specific heat capacity are:

   A. $\dfrac{J}{kg \cdot {}^\circ C}$

   B. $\dfrac{kg \cdot {}^\circ C}{J}$

   C. $\dfrac{J \cdot {}^\circ C}{kg}$

   D. $\dfrac{J \cdot {}^\circ C}{kg}$

10. In one experiment, a scientist noted that the measured heat of the object in water taken after some time was less than the expected theoretical calculation. A possible reason for the discrepancy was that the theoretical calculation probably did not take into account:

    A. initial temperature of water
    B. loss of heat to the environment
    C. size of the object
    D. amount of water

11. Assuming the calorimeter is a closed system, the correct expression for the exchange of thermal energy in a calorimeter experiment is:

    A. Heat gained by object + Heat gained by container = Heat lost by water
    B. Heat gained by object = Heat lost by water + Heat lost by container
    C. Heat lost by object + Heat lost by container = Heat gained by water
    D. Heat lost by object = Heat gained by water + Heat gained by container

12. The calorimetry experiment and the calculations used to determine the specific heat capacity of the unknown object is based upon:
    A. Zeroth Law of Thermodynamics
    B. First Law of Thermodynamics
    C. Second law of Thermodynamics
    D. Third Law of Thermodynamics

13. Hot coffee at a temperature of 73 °C is poured into a cup of volume 250 mL. Over a certain time, the coffee has cooled to room temperature (22 °C). If the thermal energy released to the environment is 50 kJ, the specific heat capacity of the coffee is: (NOTE: Assume the density of coffee is equal to the density of water ($\rho = 1 \frac{g}{mL}$).)

    A. $2.4 \dfrac{g \cdot °C}{J}$

    B. $2.4 \dfrac{J}{g \cdot °C}$

    C. $4.1 \dfrac{g \cdot °C}{J}$

    D. $4.1 \dfrac{J}{g \cdot °C}$

Questions 14–16 are not based on a passage.

14. A 5-kg stone dropped from a height of 25.0 m reaches a velocity of 22 m/s as it strikes the ground. The final speed of a 10-kg stone dropped from 25.0 m will be:
    A. 10 m/s
    B. 17 m/s
    C. 22 m/s
    D. 44 m/s

15. The electric force that exists between two charged particles $q_1 = +2.0 \ \mu C$ and $q_2 = +3.0 \ \mu C$ is 250 N. The distance of separation between the two charged particles is:
    A. 1.5 cm
    B. 4.6 cm
    C. 7.8 cm
    D. 15.0 cm

16. The force exerted on a 500-g object causing it to accelerate 6 m/s^2 is:
    A. 3 N
    B. 30 N
    C. 300 N
    D. 3000 N

Questions 17–21 are based on the following passage.

Passage III

The space shuttle's reusable solid rocket boosters provide most of the liftoff thrust to propel the rocket into orbit at about 45.7 km above Earth's surface.

The propellant for each of the two solid rocket boosters weighs 5×10^5 kg. The propellant consists of a mixture of powdered aluminum and solid ammonium perchlorate which react upon ignition as follows:

$$10Al\ (s) + 6NH_4ClO_4\ (s) \rightarrow 4Al_2O_3\ (s) + 2AlCl_3\ (s) + 3N_2\ (g) + 12H_2O\ (g)$$

$$\Delta G_{rxn} = -8421\ kJ$$

The aluminum powder is 16% by weight of the propellant, and the ammonium perchlorate is 69.8% by weight. Also added is a catalyst, a binding agent, and an epoxy curing agent which makes the consistency of the propellant much like a rubber eraser.

Ammonium perchlorate decomposes at 240 °C to chlorine, oxygen, nitrogen, and water vapor. It is the oxygen reacting with the aluminum that provides the huge amounts of thrust needed for the orbiter to escape the gravitational pull of the earth. For every gram of aluminum that reacts, 33 kJ of thermal energy is released. The reaction heats the inside of the solid rocket boosters to 5800 °C causing the gaseous products to expand rapidly. It is the expanding gases that lift the rocket booster. All of the fuel is burned in about two minutes.

Aluminum has a ΔH°_{vap} of 294 kJ/mole, and its boiling point is 2792 K.

17. Why is the aluminum used in the solid rocket boosters in powder form?
    A. Powder can be distributed evenly throughout the propellant.
    B. Powder will react faster.
    C. Powder provides more surface area for the reaction to take place.
    D. All of the above

18. The value of ΔS°_{vap} of aluminum is:
    A. 9.5 kJ/mole K
    B. 87 J/mole K
    C. 12 J/mole K
    D. 105 J/mole K

19. What is the approximate total number of moles of aluminum in the solid rocket boosters?
    A. 18 million moles
    B. 6 million moles
    C. 3 million moles
    D. 18 thousand moles

20. What is the approximate percentage of oxygen, by weight, in the solid propellant contributed by the ammonium perchlorate?

   A. 38%

   B. 70%

   C. 47%

   D. 14%

21. What is the average velocity of the space shuttle as it approaches its orbit?

   A. 23 km/min

   B. 858 mi/hr

   C. 382 m/sec

   D. all of the above

Questions 22–25 are not based on a passage.

22. What is the electron configuration of the ion of cobalt that is present in CoC_2O_4?

   A. $1s^2 2s^2 2^6 3s^2 3p^6 4s^2 3d^7$

   B. $1s^2 2s^2 2^6 3s^2 3p^6 3d^7$

   C. $1s^2 2s^2 2^6 3s^2 3p^6 3d^7 4s^2$

   D. $1s^2 2s^2 2^6 3s^2 3p^5 4s^2 3d^5$

23. Which of the following is a proper Lewis structure for the oxalate ion $C_2O_4^{-2}$?

   A.

   B.

   C.

   D.

24. From the top of a 35-m building, two objects identical in size, shape, and mass are released at the same time with one dropped from rest and the other thrown downward with a speed of 15 m/s. After the first second, you can state that:

   A. Both objects will accelerate at the same rate, equal to $-9.8 \, m/s^2$.

   B. Both objects will accelerate at the same rate, equal to $-15 \, m/s^2$.

   C. The thrown object will accelerate faster than the object released from rest.

   D. Both objects will not accelerate.

25. The volume of $4.0\,M\,H_2SO_4$ required to prepare 600 mL of $0.5\,M\,H_2SO_4$ is:
    A. 30 mL
    B. 45 mL
    C. 60 mL
    D. 75 mL

Questions 26–30 are based on the following passage.

Passage IV

Continual exposure to indoor air pollutants in homes or other residential structures poses significant environmental and health concerns. One such pollutant is radon, a radioactive gas found in the soils and rocks of the earth's crust that permeates into homes through gaps in the floor, cracks in walls, or through the water supply. Radon is invisible and odorless, and becomes a concern when elevated concentrations of the gas are allowed to build up inside the home.

The isotope of radon commonly found in homes is Radon-222, a product of the uranium-238 decay chain, formed by the decay of Radium-226 through the emission of an alpha particle. An alpha particle is a type of ionizing radiation involved in the decay process of some unstable atoms. An alpha particle is a helium nucleus with two protons and two neutrons. Alpha particles, however, are heavy in comparison to other particles emitted during decay processes such as electrons and thus only travel on the order of several centimeters before they have depleted their energy.

Radon-222, in turn, decays spontaneously into Polonium-218 by emitting an alpha particle according to:

$$\text{Radium-226} \rightarrow \text{Radon-222} + \alpha$$
$$\downarrow$$
$$\text{Polonium-218} + \alpha$$

Radium-226 has a half-life of 1,600 years and Radon-222 has a half-life of 3.8 days.

26. Assuming an initial concentration of radon gas inside a house, what fraction of the initial concentration will remain in the house after four half-lives?
    A. 0.940
    B. 0.500
    C. 0.125
    D. 0.060

27. In general, isotopes have:
    A. same atomic number, different mass number, same chemical properties, and different physical properties
    B. different atomic number, same mass number, same chemical properties, and different physical properties
    C. same atomic number, different mass number, different chemical properties, and same physical properties
    D. different atomic number, same mass number, different chemical properties, and same physical properties

28. The atomic composition of $^{222}_{86}$Rn is:
    A. 222 protons, 136 neutrons, and 86 electrons
    B. 222 protons, 136 neutrons, and 222 electrons
    C. 86 protons, 222 neutrons, and 86 electrons
    D. 86 protons, 136 neutrons, and 86 electrons

29. Given that 86 is the atomic number of Rn-222, then the number of neutrons of Po-218 is:
    A. 148
    B. 134
    C. 124
    D. 120

30. Rn-222 spontaneously decays to Po-218 by the emission of an alpha particle. The correct balanced expression of this reaction is given by the following:
    A. $^{222}_{86}$Rn $\rightarrow$ $^{218}_{84}$Po $+$ $^{4}_{2}$He
    B. $^{222}_{86}$Rn $\rightarrow$ $^{218}_{85}$Po $+$ $^{2}_{1}$He
    C. $^{222}_{86}$Rn $\rightarrow$ $^{218}_{85}$Po $+$ $^{4}_{2}$He
    D. $^{222}_{86}$Rn $\rightarrow$ $^{218}_{84}$Po $+$ $^{2}_{1}$He

Cumulative Minitest Answers and Explanations

1. **The correct answer is A.** A description of Poiseuille's law stated that it was a relation used to determine the volumetric flow rate of a fluid through a rigid pipe of constant radius. No variable in Poiseuille's law implies a need or knowledge of the pH of the fluid so that is not an issue and choice B is not correct. Blood vessel length and pressure gradient are variables addressed in the equation and found in measurements of a blood vessel. It is the vessel elasticity that is present in normal vessels that is not described by Poiseuille's law. In fact, the inclusion of elasticity effects into a mathematical equation of blood flow through a vessel results in a significantly complicated calculation. Thus the correct answer is choice A.

2. **The correct answer is C.** From Poiseuille's law, flow rate is proportional to $(Radius)^4$. This means that if the radius of the blood vessel is increased by 2 or doubled, then the flow rate increases by $(2 \cdot Radius)^4 = 16 \cdot (Radius)^4$.

3. **The correct answer is D.** From the passage, the average blood speed is given by: $v = \dfrac{Q}{A}$, where A is the cross-sectional area of the pipe. Since the flow rate is constant,

$$Q_{\text{orig}} = Q_{\text{obs}}$$

Or:

$$v_{\text{orig}} \cdot A_{\text{orig}} = v_{\text{obs}} \cdot A_{\text{obs}}$$

In the question, $v_{\text{orig}} = 100$ cm/s, $A_{\text{orig}} = \pi (10\,\text{mm})^2$, and $A_{\text{obs}} = \pi (5\,\text{mm})^2$. Thus,

$$v_{\text{obs}} = v_{\text{orig}} \cdot \left(\frac{A_{\text{orig}}}{A_{\text{obs}}} \right) = \left(100\,\frac{\text{cm}}{\text{s}} \right) \cdot \left(\frac{\pi (10\,\text{mm})^2}{\pi (5\,\text{mm})^2} \right) = \left(100\,\frac{\text{cm}}{\text{s}} \right) \cdot (4) = 400\,\frac{\text{cm}}{\text{s}}$$

4. **The correct answer is D.** The kinetic energy per unit volume of blood is defined by the equation:

$$KE = \frac{1}{2} m v^2 = \frac{1}{2} (\rho \cdot V) v^2$$

where ρ is the density of blood and V is its volume. Substituting given values into the equation yields:

$$KE = \frac{1}{2} \left(1000\,\frac{\text{kg}}{\text{m}^3} \cdot V \right) \cdot \left(0.5\,\frac{\text{m}}{\text{s}} \right)^2 = 500 \cdot 0.25\,\frac{\text{J}}{\text{m}^3} = 125\,\frac{\text{J}}{\text{m}^3}$$

5. **The correct answer is A.** The flow rate, as described by Poiseuille's law, is directly proportional to the change in pressure and not any one specific pressure value. Although the individual pressure values in the second case are both elevated, the difference in the pressure values still remains the same, i.e., 30 mm Hg. Thus the resultant volumetric blood flow will not have changed and is 5000 mL/min and the correct answer is choice A.

6. **The correct answer is C.** First you must calculate the number of moles of NaCl:

$$\text{Number of moles of NaCl} = \frac{\text{Amount of NaCl present in grams}}{\text{Molecular weight of NaCl}}$$

$$= \frac{25\,\text{g}}{58.4\,\frac{\text{g}}{\text{mole}}} = 0.43\,\text{moles}$$

Molarity is defined as the number of moles in 1 liter of solution. There are 0.43 moles in 0.5 L (or 1/2 of a liter) of solution and thus molarity, $M = 2 \times 0.43\,\frac{\text{moles}}{\text{L}} = 0.86\,\text{M}$.

7. **The correct answer is B.** The pH of a solution is defined as:

$$\text{pH} = -\log[7.5 \times 10^{-5}] = -\log[7.5] - \log[10^{-5}]$$

$$= -0.875 - (-5) = -0.875 + 5 = 4.13$$

8. **The correct answer is B.** A chemical equation is balanced when the number of atoms on the left side of the equation is equal to the number of atoms on the right side of the equation.

	LEFT SIDE			RIGHT SIDE		
CHEMICAL EQUATION	Zn	H	Cl	Zn	H	Cl
$2Zn + 2HCl \rightarrow ZnCl_2 + H_2$	2	2	2	1	2	2
$Zn + 2HCl \rightarrow ZnCl_2 + H_2$	1	2	2	1	2	2
$2Zn + HCl \rightarrow 2ZnCl_2 + H_2$	2	1	1	2	2	4
$Zn + 2HCl \rightarrow ZnCl_2 + 2H_2$	1	2	2	1	4	2

The only equation in which both sides are equal in terms of the number of atoms is $Zn + 2HCl \rightarrow ZnCl_2 + H_2$.

9. **The correct answer is A.** Rearranging the equation for thermal energy given in the passage to solve for the specific heat capacity:

$$Q = mc\Delta T \Rightarrow c = \frac{Q}{m\Delta T}$$

Substituting the units for each of the variables represented in the equation for c yields:

$$c = \frac{Q}{m\Delta T}\left[\frac{J}{\text{kg} \cdot {}^\circ\text{C}}\right]$$

10. **The correct answer is B.** A calorimetry experiment is based upon the principle of the conservation of energy, i.e., the heat lost by the object is equal to the heat gained by the water and the container. It is possible that if the calorimeter is not a closed system, heat could also be lost to the environment. Any loss of heat encountered experimentally must be accounted for theoretically if the specific heat of the object to be calculated is to be correct. Thus, the correct answer is choice B.

11. **The correct answer is D.** Thermal energy travels from hot to cold. Thus, the heat exhibited by the unknown object will lose its heat once placed into the calorimeter. The heat lost by the object will be transferred to the water and the container. This is summarized by the conservation of energy. The correct answer is choice D.

12. **The correct answer is B.** This question can be answered by summarizing the definitions for all four Laws of Thermodynamics:

    Zeroth Law of Thermodynamics If two objects A and B are in thermal equilibrium, and objects B and C are also in thermal equilibrium, then objects A and C are also in thermal equilibrium.

    First Law of Thermodynamics This law, a generalized expression of the law of conservation of energy, states that the thermal energy (heat) added to a closed system (ΔQ) is equal to the increased internal energy of the system (ΔU) plus the amount of energy in the form of work done by the system (ΔW) or $\Delta Q = \Delta U + \Delta W$.

    Second Law of Thermodynamics A system subjected to a spontaneous change will respond such that its disorder or entropy will increase or at least will remain the same.

    Third Law of Thermodynamics As the temperature of a system approaches absolute zero, its entropy approaches a minimum value.

    The correct response is choice B.

13. **The correct answer is D.** This problem can be solved by first writing down the equation for thermal energy and then algebraically solving for the specific heat capacity:

    $$Q = mc\Delta T \Rightarrow c = \frac{Q}{m\Delta T}$$

    The heat released to the environment is 50 kJ but because it is removed from the coffee as opposed to being added to the system, the value for Q is negative and thus $Q = -50\,\text{kJ}$. The change in temperature is $\Delta T = T_f - T_i = 22\,°\text{C} - 71\,°\text{C} = -49\,°\text{C}$. The final unknown is the mass of the coffee which is not given in the problem but the volume of coffee can be calculated with the knowledge of the density of the coffee which is equivalent to the density of water. The mass of the coffee can be found from:

    $$\rho = \frac{m}{V} \Rightarrow m = \rho V = \left(1\frac{\text{g}}{\text{mL}}\right)(250\,\text{mL}) = 250\,\text{g}$$

    Substituting into the expression for the specific heat capacity yields:

    $$c = \frac{Q}{m\Delta T} = \frac{-50,000\,J}{(250\,\text{g})(-49\,°\text{C})} = 4.08\frac{J}{\text{g} \cdot °\text{C}}$$

14. **The correct answer is C.** The question involves the effect of mass on the final velocity of an object dropped from rest. The equation used to determine the final velocity of an object dropped from rest is:

$$v_f^2 = v_i^2 + 2a\Delta y$$

where $a = -g$ and $\Delta y = -$height (as measured from the top and moving downward). As one can see, mass is not a factor in the equation and thus doubling the mass will not have an effect on the final velocity of the object as it strikes the ground.

15. **The correct answer is A.** The equation that relates the electric force (F), the electric charge of two charged particles (q_1, q_2) and the distance of separation between the charged particles (r) is given by Coulomb's law:

$$F = k\frac{q_1 q_2}{r^2}$$

Rearranging the equation for the distance of separation yields:

$$r = \sqrt{\frac{kq_1 q_2}{F}}$$

Substituting into the expression for r gives:

$$r = \sqrt{\frac{\left(9 \times 10^9 \ \frac{\text{N} \cdot \text{m}^2}{\text{C}^2}\right)(+2.0 \times 10^{-6} \ \text{C})(+3.0 \times 10^{-6} \ \text{C})}{(250 \ \text{N})}}$$

$$= 1.469 \times 10^{-2} \ \text{m} = 1.47 \ \text{cm}$$

16. **The correct answer is A.** Force can be determined using Newton's Second Law: $\mathbf{F} = m\mathbf{a}$. In this case, m = mass = 500 g and $\mathbf{a}$ = acceleration = 6 m/s². However, before one can substitute these values into the equation, the mass must be expressed in units of kilograms, not grams. Thus, the mass value given above must be divided by 1000, meaning the decimal place is moved to the left by three places. Therefore, m = 0.500 kg, $\mathbf{a}$ = 6 m/s² and

$$\mathbf{F} = (0.500 \ \text{kg})(6 \ \text{m/s}^2) = 3.0 \ \text{N}$$

17. **The correct answer is D.** The kinetic molecular theory states in part that for reactions to occur reactants must come in contact with each other. The speed of a reaction depends on several factors including the concentration of the reactants, and the probability of reactants coming together. A powder can be more evenly distributed than chunks of aluminum which makes the concentration even throughout the booster. In other words there will not be any volumes with low or zero concentration of aluminum. This means that choice A leads to a faster reaction. The greater the surface area of the reactants, the more potential places where the reactants can meet and lead to a successful reaction. This means that choice C leads to a faster reaction. Choice B simply restates that choices A and C lead to a faster reaction. Because choices A, B, and C are all true, choice D (all of the above) is the best answer.

18. **The correct answer is** D. Vaporization at the boiling point is defined as an equilibrium process. For an equilibrium process, ΔG is defined to be zero, meaning there is neither a tendency for the reaction to shift to the right (products) nor to the left (reactants). From the definition of free energy,

$$\Delta G = \Delta H - T\Delta S$$

Because $\Delta G = 0$ at the boiling point, the above equation rearranges to:

$$\frac{\Delta H_{vap}}{T} = \Delta S_{vap} \quad \text{or} \quad \frac{294\,\text{kJ/mol}}{2792\,\text{K}} = 0.105\,\text{kJ/molK} \quad \text{or} \quad 105\,\text{J/molK}$$

19. **The correct answer is** B. This problem is worked in the following steps:

$$\begin{array}{ccccccc}
mass & 1 & mass & 2 & mass & 3 & mass & 4 & mol \\
one\ booster & \rightarrow & two\ boosters & \rightarrow & Al(kg) & \rightarrow & Al(g) & \rightarrow & Al
\end{array}$$

(1) There are two rocket boosters each with a mass of 5×10^5 kg of propellant, so the total mass is 1×10^6 kg.

(2) The propellant is not all aluminum, so you must use the percentage Al to determine how much of the propellant is aluminum. A percentage of 16% means that 16 out of every 100 parts of the total are aluminum.

$$1 \times 10^6 \,\text{kg propellant} \times \frac{16\,\text{kg Al}}{100\,\text{kg propellant}} = 1.6 \times 10^5 \,\text{kg Al}$$

(3) Molar mass are usually given in g/mol so we need to convert kg Al to g Al

$$1.6 \times 10^5 \,\text{kg Al} \times \frac{1000\,\text{g Al}}{1\,\text{kg al}} = 1.6 \times 10^8 \,\text{g Al}$$

(4) Finally, the g of Al are converted to moles using the atomic mass of aluminum.

$$1.6 \times 10^8 \,\text{g Al} \times \frac{1\,\text{mol Al}}{27\,\text{g Al}} = 5.9 \times 10^6 \,\text{mol Al}$$

This answer is closest to 6 million moles. Note that if you do not include both boosters (step 1 omitted), you will get incorrect answer choice C. You will get incorrect answer choice A if only one booster is used and the total mass is used (steps 1 and 2 omitted). You will get incorrect answer choice D if steps 1, 2, and 3 are omitted.

20. **The correct answer is A.** This problem is worked in the following steps.

$$\underset{propellant}{100\,g} \xrightarrow{1} NH_4ClO_4 \xrightarrow{2} \underset{O}{mass} \xrightarrow{3} \underset{O}{\%}$$

(1) Because you have a percentage, it is convenient to pick a 100 g sample of the propellant to start your calculation. You could pick any size, but 100 g makes the calculation simpler. The propellant is 69.8% ammonium perchlorate, so there are 69.8 g of ammonium perchlorate in 100 g of propellant.

(2) To get the mass of oxygen, you must determine how much oxygen is in a sample of ammonium perchlorate. The molar mass of ammonium perchlorate is the sum of the atomic masses of the atoms in one mole: $(14.01) + (4 \times 1.008) + (35.45) + (4 \times 16.00)g = 117.49\ g/mol\ NH_4ClO_4$. In one mole of ammonium perchlorate, there are 64.00 g of oxygen.

$$69.8\,g\,NH_4ClO_4 \times \frac{64\,g\,O}{117.49\,g\,NH_4ClO_4} = 38.02\,g\,O$$

(3) Finally, because 100 g of propellant was used to start the calculation, the percentage of oxygen is (38.02 g O/100.0 g total) × 100% = 38% O.

21. **The correct answer is D.** The average velocity over a time interval is:

$$v_{ave} = \frac{\Delta d}{\Delta t} = \frac{d_f - d_i}{t_f - t_i}.$$

where $d = $ distance, $t = $ time, Δ indicates change, and the subscript f indicates final and the subscript i indicates initial. If you take the surface of Earth as $d_i = 0$ and the time the rocket boosters are lit as $t_i = 0$, then $d_f = 45.7$ km and $t_f = 2.0$ min. This leads to an average velocity of 45.7 km/2.0 min = 22.9 km/min (choice A). You must check if choices B and C are numerically equal to choice A.

For choice B,

$$22.9\,\frac{km}{min} \times \frac{1\,mi}{1.609\,km} \times \frac{60\,min}{1\,hr} = 858\,\frac{mi}{hr}$$

For choice C,

$$22.9\,\frac{km}{min} \times \frac{1000\,m}{1\,km} \times \frac{1\,min}{60\,sec} = 382\,\frac{m}{sec}$$

Choices A, B, and C are equal, so the correct answer is "all of the above."

22. **The correct answer is B.** To work this problem you must recognize the common polyatomic ion oxalate, $C_2O_4^{2-}$. Because the compound CoC_2O_4 is neutral, the charge on the Co must balance the charge on the oxalate. For this to be true, cobalt must be a 2+ ion. Neutral cobalt atoms have 27 electrons and have electron configuration $1s^2 2s^2 2p^6 3s^2 3p^6 4s^2 3d^7$ (Answer choices A and C). It may seem that choice D is the correct answer because it removes the last two electrons that entered the atom. In the ions of transition metals the 4s electrons are lost before the 3d even though the 3d are the last to go into the atom. This means all transition metal cations have the electron configuration $[NG]nd^x$, where [NG] is the noble gas core electron configuration, nd is the appropriate 3, 4, 5, or 6d level, and x is the number of electrons needed to give the correct charge. Because Co must lose 2 electrons to obtain a 2+ charge, it loses its two 4s electrons leaving seven 3d electrons and the electron configuration: $1s^2 2s^2 2p^6 3s^2 3p^6 3d^7$ which is answer choice B.

23. **The correct answer is A.** The total number of valence electrons for oxalate is $(2 \times$ # valence e^- per C$) + (4 \times$ # of valence e^- per O$) + (2$ extra electrons for the 2- charge$) = (2 \times 4) + (4 \times 6) + (2) = 34$ electrons. Structure B is incorrect because the upper two oxygen atoms do not have an octet of electrons. Structure C has 36 or 2 too many electrons, so it is incorrect. Structure D is incorrect because while it has the correct number of electrons, it places a formal change on all atoms including an unlikely positive charge on oxygen. Structure A has 34 electrons and has only two formal charges and the formal charges reside on the electronegative oxygen atoms.

24. **The correct answer is A.** In free-fall motion along the y-axis, whether the object is dropped or thrown, once it leaves the hand of the thrower, the only force acting on the object is gravity, meaning that both objects accelerate at 9.8 m/s^2. The only difference between the two objects is their initial velocity which is 0 m/s for the dropped object and -15 m/s for the thrown object.

25. **The correct answer is D.** This problem can be solved using the relationship:

$$M_1 V_1 = M_2 V_2$$

where: M_1 is the molarity of the original solution ($M_1 = 0.5\ M$)

           V_1 is the volume of the original solution ($V_1 = 0.6$ L)

           M_2 is the molarity of the new solution ($M_2 = 4.0\ M$)

           V_2 is the volume of the new solution ($V_2 =$ unknown)

$$V_2 = \frac{M_1 V_1}{M_2} = \frac{(0.5\ M)(0.6\ \text{L})}{(4\ M)} = 0.075\ \text{L} = 75\ \text{mL}$$

26. **The correct answer is D.** The half-life of a radioactive substance is the time it takes for the number of radioactive nuclei to decrease by one-half. So if [Rn] represents an initial quantity of Rn-222, then:

$$[Rn] \xrightarrow{\text{1 half-life}} \frac{1}{2}[Rn] \xrightarrow{\text{1 half-life}} \frac{1}{4}[Rn] \xrightarrow{\text{1 half-life}} \frac{1}{8}[Rn] \xrightarrow{\text{1 half-life}} \frac{1}{16}[Rn]$$

So, after four half-lives, the number of radioactive nuclei in an original sample of Rn-222 is reduced by $\frac{1}{16}$ or 0.06.

27. **The correct answer is A.** This question can be answered by general knowledge of the chemical composition of elemental substances and isotopes. Isotopes are nuclei with different number of neutrons and the same number of protons. Because the number of protons is described by an element's atomic number (Z), isotopes have the same atomic number but a different mass number that is defined as the total number of nucleons (protons and neutrons). Chemical properties of an element are based on the number and arrangement of electrons while physical properties arise from the nucleus. Because isotopes have the same number of electrons, as indicated by the atomic number (Z), isotopes have the same chemical properties. In addition, isotopes have a different number of neutrons, as indicated by the mass number (A) and thus have different physical properties.

28. **The correct answer is D.** In general, the atomic composition of an element, X, is given by $^A_Z X$ where:

A = mass number = number of nucleons = number of protons and neutrons

Z = atomic number = number of protons = number of electrons

$N = A - Z$ = number of neutrons

Thus, $^{222}_{86}$Rn has 86 protons, $222 - 86 = 136$ neutrons, and 86 electrons.

29. **The correct answer is B.** Radon-222 decays spontaneously into Polonium-218 by emitting an alpha particle which means that the atomic number of Polonium-218 is 84. The number of neutrons in Polonium-218 can be determined by $N = A - Z = 218 - 84 = 134$.

30. **The correct answer is A.** The atomic number of Rn-222 is 86 and the atomic number of Po-218 is 84. An alpha particle is a helium nucleus which has two protons and two neutrons. Thus, for an alpha particle, $A = 4$, $Z = 2$ and $^4_2\alpha$. In order for a reaction to be correct, it must be balanced as far as each side having the same quantities of A and Z. The correct reaction described in the problem is: $^{222}_{86}$Rn $\rightarrow$ $^{218}_{84}$Po $+ ^4_2$He.

Evaluation Chart

Use this Evaluation Chart to analyze your results for the Cumulative Minitest. Check the Answers and Explanations section to see which answers you got correct and which ones you missed. For each question that you missed, find the question number in the left column of the chart below. Look in the right column to see the chapter that covers the content area for that question. If you missed questions in a specific content area, you need to pay particular attention to that area as you study for the MCAT.

Item Number	Content Area
1.	**Chapter 2**: Importance of Fluids for the Circulation of Blood, Gas Movement, and Gas Exchange
2.	**Chapter 2**: Importance of Fluids for the Circulation of Blood, Gas Movement, and Gas Exchange
3.	**Chapter 2**: Importance of Fluids for the Circulation of Blood, Gas Movement, and Gas Exchange
4.	**Chapter 2**: Importance of Fluids for the Circulation of Blood, Gas Movement, and Gas Exchange
5.	**Chapter 2**: Importance of Fluids for the Circulation of Blood, Gas Movement, and Gas Exchange
6.	**Chapter 6**: The Unique Nature of Water and Its Solutions
7.	**Chapter 6**: The Unique Nature of Water and Its Solutions
8.	**Chapter 6**: The Unique Nature of Water and Its Solutions
9.	**Chapter 10**: Principles of Chemical Thermodynamics and Kinetics
10.	**Chapter 10**: Principles of Chemical Thermodynamics and Kinetics
11.	**Chapter 10**: Principles of Chemical Thermodynamics and Kinetics
12.	**Chapter 10**: Principles of Chemical Thermodynamics and Kinetics
13.	**Chapter 10**: Principles of Chemical Thermodynamics and Kinetics
14.	**Chapter 1**: Translational Motion, Forces, Work, Energy, and Equilibrium in Living Systems
15.	**Chapter 3**: Electrochemistry and Electrical Circuits and Their Elements
16.	**Chapter 1**: Translational Motion, Forces, Work, Energy, and Equilibrium in Living Systems
17.	**Chapter 6**: The Unique Nature of Water and Its Solutions
18.	**Chapter 10**: Principles of Chemical Thermodynamics and Kinetics
19.	**Chapter 6**: The Unique Nature of Water and Its Solutions

(Continued)

Item Number	Content Area
20.	**Chapter 6**: The Unique Nature of Water and Its Solutions
21.	**Chapter 1**: Translational Motion, Forces, Work, Energy, and Equilibrium in Living Systems
22.	**Chapter 7**: The Nature of Molecules and Intermolecular Interactions
23.	**Chapter 7**: The Nature of Molecules and Intermolecular Interactions
24.	**Chapter 1**: Translational Motion, Forces, Work, Energy, and Equilibrium in Living Systems
25.	**Chapter 6**: The Unique Nature of Water and Its Solutions
26.	**Chapter 5**: Atoms, Nuclear Decay, Electronic Structure, and Atomic Chemical Behavior
27.	**Chapter 5**: Atoms, Nuclear Decay, Electronic Structure, and Atomic Chemical Behavior
28.	**Chapter 5**: Atoms, Nuclear Decay, Electronic Structure, and Atomic Chemical Behavior
29.	**Chapter 5**: Atoms, Nuclear Decay, Electronic Structure, and Atomic Chemical Behavior
30.	**Chapter 5**: Atoms, Nuclear Decay, Electronic Structure, and Atomic Chemical Behavior

Notes

Notes